THE EMERGENCE OF YOUTH SOCIETIES

Also by David Gottlieb and Jon Reeves

Adolescent Behavior in Urban Areas:
A Bibliographic Review and Discussion of the Literature

The Emergence of Youth Societies

A CROSS-CULTURAL APPROACH

David Gottlieb
Jon Reeves
Warren D. TenHouten

THE FREE PRESS, *New York*
COLLIER-MACMILLAN LIMITED, *London*

A DIVISION OF THE MACMILLAN COMPANY

Printed in the United States of America

Collier-Macmillan Canada, Ltd., Toronto, Ontario

Library of Congress Catalog Card Number: 66-13598

TO R. S. SHRIVER

who has made a significant difference
in the lives of thousands
of adolescents throughout the world.

CONTENTS

INTRODUCTION

There is general agreement among many students of adolescent behavior that the emergence of distinct youth cultures is related to the emergence of industrialization. More specifically it is felt that with the formation of elaborate technological systems there is a need for trained specialists and experts. With the demand for skilled personnel there must be the organization of training institutions which will fill the changing needs of the society. This shift in occupational needs results in a dramatic alteration in where the socialization of the young will take place and in who will be responsible for their socialization. In our own society the demand for skilled professionals as opposed to laborers and unskilled workers has meant that more and more young people are going to school for longer and longer periods of time. The extent to which the family will be involved in the training of the young has changed with the emergence of our industrialized society. Prior to this century and as is still the case with the less-developed nations of the world the family was more directly involved in the socialization of the young. Vocational skills as well as personal values and attitudes could be passed along from one age grade generation to the next with a minimum of influence from outside sources. Within this limited and relatively homogeneous setting a set of traditional mores and customs could be transferred from father to son and mother to daughter. In cases where the socialization of youth was shared by people outside of the immediate family there was general agreement and understanding as to who would do the training and what the nature of this training was to be. This same pattern of mutual consensus in the phenomena of child training existed in our society as well as among people in social systems in other parts of the world. Industrialization stimulated dramatic alterations in the social structure of this nation and in other nations as well and continues to have an impact among those cultures which are currently undergoing changes in their economy and social structure.

One effect of this change in the socialization process has been the development of a situation where young people are placed in a social setting apart from their own families for extended periods of time since the training of the young must take place outside of the home. In addition, the training itself is frequently conducted by "outsiders" who have only limited contact with the family and its traditions. The place for training in our society as well as others becomes the school. Here youths are taught not only basic academic skills and occupational abilities but are also introduced to a variety of ideas that may be in conflict with the ideas and values held by their parents. The learning that takes place in the educational institution is not restricted to what is expressed by teachers but includes in addition the ideas, values, and attitudes of peers. By removing the young from the home setting for long periods of time, and by transferring adolescent interest outward, away from the family as a vital reference point, the school becomes a center where the adolescent comes to focus on his peer group as a vital reference point. Or as James Coleman has noted,

> With his fellows, he (the adolescent) comes to constitute a small society, one that has most of its important interactions within itself, and maintains only a few threads of connection with the outside adult society.[1]

In relating the emergence of youth cultures to the growth of technology, industrialization, and the social division of labor, we are proposing that this sequence is not necessarily a culture-bound phenomenon. In other words it is entirely possible, indeed probable, that if the progression holds true for the United States it would also be reflected in the development of other nations throughout the world. If, in fact, industrialization is a contributing factor in the development of adolescent cultures, one would expect to see evidence of this in other countries. Among those with a high degree of industry and technological development we would expect to find much in the training and behavior of the youth which would indicate the formation of adolescent subcultures. Among those nations which are in the process of industrializing and expanding we would expect the least number of comparable behaviors.

To clarify, let us note that we would not expect a one-to-one comparison in the area of adolescent behavior among cultures (nations). What we would expect is that the behavior of the youth would reflect certain characteristics which would be comparable among nations regardless of the cultural content of those nations. For example, while we would not expect to find clothing and grooming practices and courtship and dating practices which were fully analogous, we would expect to find analogous behaviors in the selection of referents by the adolescent, the

1. James S. Coleman, *The Adolescent Society* (New York: The Free Press, 1961), p. 3.

adolescent's attitudes toward traditional practices in his culture, the training of the adolescent for a productive adult life, the reliance of the youth on the values and attitudes of the peer group as opposed to the parental group, and so forth.

If, in fact, the presence of what has come to be known as "adolescent cultures" is more dependent on the structural characteristics of a society than its particular cultural content, it should be possible to examine the phenomena of adolescent behavior meaningfully among cultures. With the possibilities for such an approach to the study of adolescence we undertook the following:

INITIAL AIMS OF THE RESEARCH

I. The compilation of a cross-cultural bibliography dealing with materials pertaining to the training and behavior of adolescents.
II. The development of a theoretical model which would allow for the study of adolescents in different kinds of social and cultural settings.
III. The application of the proposed theoretical model to a series of empirical studies dealing with adolescents and their socialization in order to gather some insight as to the strengths and weaknesses of the proposed model.

The purpose of the bibliography is to give those who are concerned with the study of adolescent behavior and those who are responsible for the training of the young some indication of the state of knowledge in this field at this time. In addition we hope, by the compilation of this bibliography, to identify certain areas of continuity in the findings and methodology employed by those who have attempted to study the adolescent. It is our firm belief that much is to be gained in both the applied and pure areas by the presentation, review, and discussion of this literature.

The theoretical model presented in this text is the result of a detailed examination of the materials included in the bibliography. It is based on our analysis of the findings of others working independently in a variety of cultural settings. From this analysis we have concluded that there are great similarities in the reported behavior, attitudes, aspirations, and values of youth from different nations and places. Our review of much of these data suggests that there is substantial evidence that there are some striking continuities in the structure and substance of adolescent behavior. There appear to be certain elementary processes that occur in different types of societies and within divergent groupings in the same society.

The model, then, is an attempt at the development of a theory and a method which we believe will allow for an efficient and valid means to be used in the cross-cultural study of adolescents.

The reader will note in our discussion of the model that we have employed "Facet Design" as developed by Louis Guttman. We are indeed indebted to him for the cooperation and intellectual stamina he invested in the development of this model.

A final note on the bibliography: A brief examination of the cross-cultural, available materials made it clear at an early point that it would be advisable to go beyond the professional journals for bibliographic materials. Thus, it was decided to include information from sources other than the publications of various professional groups: sources such as government-sponsored research, the findings of international organizations, magazines and publications available to the general public, and general informational publications of various governments and service organizations. In addition, universities in other countries were contacted in an attempt to establish some degree of cooperation in the finding and listing of the available materials.

In conclusion, the authors wish to express their deep gratitude to the many people in many different places who assisted in the collection of the bibliography and to the International Programs-Ford Foundation at Michigan State University which made funds available for this project.

David Gottlieb
Jon Reeves
Warren D. TenHouten

THE EMERGENCE OF YOUTH SOCIETIES

1. ADOLESCENT BEHAVIOR:

A CROSS-CULTURAL APPROACH

In a preliminary work Gottlieb and Guttman advanced the hypothetical framework that adolescents behave much the same anywhere, in any socio-cultural context, in that they will become oriented to (involved with) referents whom they perceive as having the desire and the ability to help them attain skills, goals, and roles (ends) and that they will not become oriented to referents whom they perceive as having neither the desire nor the ability to help them attain these same ends.[1]

Any research or theoretical analysis necessarily begins with such predilections and orientations for stating the problem to be investigated and for developing certain kinds of hypotheses, assumptions, and postulates.[2] When this orientation reaches a certain level of specificity, it may be described as an explicational model.[3]

Assumptions, by definition, are not directly under investigation; but they are characterized by the possibility that an empirical study using a certain set of assumptions might generate findings that would demand that they be modified or discarded. Our formulation here begins with the following assumptions:

1. David Gottlieb and Louis Guttman, "A Facet Design Approach to the Study of Youth Culture," Mimeographed (November, 1962), pp. 1-3.

2. A group of postulates is a group of statements which purport to define an object of study. Here, the object of study is a system of interaction.

3. An "explicational model" has the primary goal of explicating, or rendering precise, one or more basic concepts: see Joseph Berger *et al.*, *Types of Formalization in Small-Group Research* (Boston: Houghton Mifflin Company, 1962), p. 9.

assumptions

1. The adolescent wishes to attain skills, goals, and roles (ends).

2. The adolescent perceives referents in terms of a certain end.

3. These referents are perceived as having differential power means (ability) and intentions (desire) to help the adolescent attain an end.

4. Adolescent goals may vary from one society to the next and within subgroupings in any particular society.

5. No statement is ever made about the "objectivity" (validity) of the adolescent's perceptions with respect to goals or referents.

6. Perception precedes involvement: Perceptions can be made without involvement, but involvement cannot occur without prior perception.

7. The adolescent is the initiator in his involvement.

The next step is to set up an explicational model for the entire proposition. Such a model must be consistent with these seven assumptions, must exhaust the variables and classes of variables to be used, and must provide a formal procedure for combining and interrelating variables. What is needed is a group of postulates.

An applicable methodological tool for the construction of such a model is found in Guttman's "metatheory of facets," which consists of facet design and facet analysis.[4]

A brief exegesis of facet theory is in order here. The concept of facet comes from the algebra of abstract sets.[5] If V represents a set (a collection of things) defined as the Cartesian product of say, sets A and B, such that $V = A \times B$, then A and B are facets of V. This is *all* that facet means. Now suppose that $a_1, a_2, \ldots, a_n$ are the elements of A and $b_1, b_2, \ldots, b_m$ are the elements of B. Clearly V has n times m elements, where "times" means ordinary arithmetic multiplication. This is the only sense in which the word "product" is used in Cartesian product: It does not imply manipulation, but only the structuring of facets and their elements in (here, sociological) space. There are n ways of choosing an element from A, and m ways of choosing an element from B, so there are n times m possible *profiles* over A taken with B. Any collection of elements, choosing one from each facet, is defined as a profile over V.

---

4. The technical concept to be denoted by "facet" was formally proposed by Guttman in "An Outline of Some New Methodology for Social Research," *Public Opinion Quarterly*, 18 (Winter, 1954-1955), p. 399.

5. A good introduction to abstract systems is found in Daniel T. Finkbeiner, II, *Introduction to Matrices and Linear Transformations* (San Francisco and London: W. H. Freeman and Company, 1960), pp. 1-18 and p. 209.

Hence, the set V can be defined as the set of all possible profiles v over V.[6]

In summary, facet designing, or "facetizing," consists of defining the variables of a given study as the Cartesian products of the elements of more inclusive sets. The novelty, and the usefulness, of this method of procedure is that it formalizes the intuitive processes involved in constructing relevant concepts and variables for a scientific study. This "spelling out" of variables helps decide which belong with which and which should be retained.

Five facets will constitute the observational basis for developing a metatheoretical system, or model, which will be presented next. The terms will be defined following this section to a limited extent. The construction of a model such as the "facet paradigm" presented here is a necessary first step in any research procedure, whether formal or intuitive. It will then be necessary to develop postulates and propositions, with the ultimate goal of constructing a theory of adolescent behavior. Of course, an explicational model is not itself a theory: It is rather the parturiency of theory.

THE FACET PARADIGM: $V = P \times A \times B \times C \times D$

Facets		*Population of Adolescents*		*Adolescent's Behavior*		*Behavioral Properties of Referents*		*Referents*		*Ends: Skills, Goals, Roles*
									to help attain	
V	=	P	×	A	×	B	×	C	×	D
		(p_1)		(perceives) a_1		(desire or intention) b_1		(parents) c_1		(social) d_1
		(p_2)						(peers) c_2		(occupational) d_2
(elements)		• • •								
		(p_n)		(becomes involved with or oriented to) a_2		(power means or ability to provide opportunities) b_2		(society) c_3		(intellectual or academic) d_3
								(siblings) c_4		(financial) d_4
								(spouse) c_5		

6. For a fuller explication of the *vocabulary* of facet theory, see Guttman, "Notes on Terminology for Facet Theory," reprinted from the *Proceedings of the Fifteenth International Congress of Psychology* (Amsterdam: North-Holland Publishing Company, 1959), pp. 130-132.

All propositions constructed from these variables (elements and combinations of elements) [7] involve decisional processes on the part of the adolescent. An adolescent's perceptions, and in particular his information about certain properties of potential or actual referral categories, is an important behavioral property. It is assumed that the adolescent has knowledge about the relevant aspects of referents in his social environment with respect to attaining his goals. This knowledge may or may not be objectively valid, but it *will* be organized in a relatively well-ordered set of preferences. It is also assumed that the adolescent has evaluative (ranking) skills that will enable him to "calculate" alternative choices of referents with which to become involved.

To the extent that the adolescent optimizes referent choosing (on the basis of his perceptions) he is rational. It is not hypothesized that the adolescent is always rational. On the contrary, it will be hypothesized that the adolescent will be more rational under some conditions than under others.

7. The combinations are not restricted to profiles over five facets. Profiles over fewer facets can be considered, as well as subsets of elements from the same facet.

2. THE MODEL:

AN EMPIRICAL APPLICATION

On the basis of the explicational model and the preliminary assumptions presented in the preceding pages it was possible to develop and empirically test some propositions generic to the general orientation.

A paper-and-pencil questionnaire was administered to 447 students in an undergraduate sociology class at a large state university.[1] The students were asked a series of questions about their occupational goals. This was followed by questions dealing with five types of reference groups with which respondents might be involved in an interactive attempt to attain their occupational goals. The referents were parents, siblings, spouse, peers, and teachers. Each student who answered for each kind of referent counts five times in the following data. Hence, the number of cases appearing in hypotheses refers to the number of referents answered for, rather than to the number of students answering. The unit of analysis is not the student *per se*, but the perception of, and interaction with, these five referents.

Six substantive hypotheses are developed, all of which are supported by the data. The first four go together, as do the last two. Two mathematical models will be presented, one for the first four hypotheses, and one for the last two. The following four hypotheses will be considered first:

---

1. The data and hypotheses are adapted from Warren D. Ten Houten, "Methodological Innovations and Models on the Structure of Reference Group Behavior," unpublished M.A. Thesis, Michigan State University, 1963, Chaps. 2-3.

HYPOTHESIS 1 ($\bar{D}$, $\bar{A}$): If a referent is perceived as having no desire and no ability to help the student attain an occupational goal, the student will be involved with that referent at a low level.

HYPOTHESIS 2 (D, A): If a referent is perceived as having both desire and ability to help the student attain an occupational goal, the student will be involved with that referent at a high level.

HYPOTHESIS 3 ($\bar{D}$, A): If a referent is perceived as having ability but not desire to help the student attain an occupational goal, the student will be involved with that referent at an intermediate level.

HYPOTHESIS 4 (D, $\bar{A}$): If a referent is perceived as having desire but not ability to help the student attain an occupational goal, the student will be involved with that referent at an intermediate level.

The basic data used in the testing of these four hypotheses are presented in Table 1.

TABLE 1—Observed Distributions of Involvement with Five Referents in Four States of Perceived Desire and Ability to Help the Student Attain an Occupational Goal

		LEVEL OF INVOLVEMENT					
Perceptual States		*None* 1	*Very Little* 2	*Little* 3	*Moderate* 4	*High* 5	*Total (Number)*
Neither Desire Nor Ability	Per cent	55.4%	34.4%	20.4%	8.0%	1.6%	
	(Number)	(67)	(63)	(51)	(37)	(5)	(223)
Desire But Not Ability	Per cent	35.5%	50.8%	38.0%	21.6%	13.9%	
	(Number)	(43)	(93)	(95)	(100)	(42)	(373)
Ability But Not Desire	Per cent	6.6%	13.1%	8.8%	11.3%	6.6%	
	(Number)	(8)	(24)	(22)	(52)	(20)	(126)
Both Desire And Ability	Per cent	2.5%	1.6%	32.8%	59.1%	77.9%	
	(Number)	(3)	(3)	(82)	(273)	(236)	(597)
	Total Per cent	100.0%	99.9%	100.0%	100.0%	100.0%	(1319)

The data in Table 1 are clearly consistent with Hypotheses 1-4. In Table 2, the correspondence of the data and the hypotheses is shown in a more obvious manner. Level of involvement is dichotomized. The percentage distributions are computed horizontally, over each perceptual state, rather than vertically over each level of involvement, as was done for Table 1.

TABLE 2—Observed Dichotomized Distributions of Involvement with Five Referents in Four States of Perceived Desire and Ability to Help the Student Attain an Occupational Goal

Perceptual States		LEVEL OF INVOLVEMENT: None, Very Little, or Little	Moderate or High	Total (Number) and Per cent
Neither Desire	Per cent	81.2%	18.8%	100.0%
Nor Ability	(Number)	(181)	(42)	(223)
Desire But	Per cent	61.9%	38.1%	100.0%
Not Ability	(Number)	(231)	(142)	(373)
Ability But	Per cent	42.9%	57.1%	100.0%
Not Desire	(Number)	(54)	(72)	(126)
Both Desire	Per cent	14.7%	85.3%	100.0%
And Ability	(Number)	(88)	(509)	(597)

Hypotheses 1-4 can be statistically tested by comparing the average level of involvement in each of the four states, to determine if the differences are significant. The averages are presented in Table 3.

TABLE 3—Average Level of Involvement with Five Referents in Four States of Perceived Desire and Ability to Help the Student Attain an Occupational Goal: 5 = High, 4 = Moderate, 3 = Little, 2 = Very Little, 1 = None

Perceptual State	Mean Involvement	Median Involvement	(N)
Neither Desire nor Ability	2.36	2.22	(223)
Desire Only	3.01	3.13	(373)
Ability Only	3.41	3.64	(126)
Both Desire and Ability	4.01	4.30	(597)

A matrix of chi-square statistics was computed from the data in Table 1 to determine whether the differences between medians are statistically significant with respect to the null hypothesis that each pair of states come from populations with the same medians. The results of these median tests are presented in Table 4. The chosen probability of Type I error is .01. In five of the six cases the direction of the hypothesis can be predicted, as Hypotheses 1-4 represent a partial ordering. From Table 3 it is apparent that the differences are in the predicted direction. The critical value of chi-square of 6.64.

TABLE 4—Chi-Square Tests of Differences in Medians of States of Perceived Desire and Ability to Help the Student Attain an Occupational Goal

Case	Desire Only	Ability Only	Both
Neither	23.2 *	40.7 *	194.1 *
Desire Only	—	10.3 *	264.8 *
Ability Only	—	—	12.0 *

* Medians are significantly different beyond the 99% certainty level.

These results lend support to the hypothesized ordering of involvement. The direction of differences is as predicted, with highest involvement in the "both" case and lowest in the "neither" case. Furthermore, all six differences are statistically significant. It should be pointed out, however, that the samples are not entirely independent.

A method by which the actual distributions of involvement for the four states of desire and ability can be predicted will be developed next to strengthen this analysis. A formalization that represents in a simple manner such a specific type of "observed" social phenomenon can be termed a "representational model." [2]

The following model consists of three cases. A similar analysis leads to a predicted distribution of involvement for the two cases of both desire and ability and neither desire nor ability. From this, the proportion of responses at each involvement level can be deduced for the third case, which consists of the other two perceptual states, desire only and ability only.

According to Hypothesis 1, where referents are perceived as having neither desire nor ability to help, the predicted result of this perceptual state is *low* intensity of involvement. Hence, it can be expected that the proportion of responses for each level of involvement corresponding to this perceptual state will be the greatest at the low involvement categories. It can also be expected that the very highest proportion of involvement will occur at the extreme of "no involvement." It follows that the proportion involved at the next highest level, which is "very little," will be some fraction of the proportion at "no involvement." Also, the proportion at the *next* highest level, which is "little," will be some frac-

2. Berger, et al., op. cit., p. 37.

tion of the proportion at "very little." In general, it can be expected that the proportion involved at *any* level is some fraction of the proportion involved at the next *lowest* level. It would be convenient to assume that the fractional decrease for every increase in involvement level is the same over every level of involvement.

Mathematically, this relationship between the two independent variables, the *state* of perceiving $(\bar{D}, \bar{A})$ and the resultant intensity of involvement I can be expressed as a differential equation. For the sake of simplicity, the perceptual state will be treated as a single variable, so that an *ordinary* differential equation can be used.

$$\frac{dp\ [I|\ (\bar{D}, \bar{A})]}{dI} = -\ mp\ [I|\ (\bar{D}, \bar{A})], \qquad (1)$$

where p = proportion involved, and where I = 1(none), 2, 3, 4, 5 (high).

Verbally, this means that the change in proportion involved (given the perceptual state of neither desire nor ability) with respect to change in the intensity of involvement is a fixed fraction (m) of the proportion involved at the next lowest level.

Since the data in Table 1 necessarily deal with discontinuous jumps in involvement, this equation can be simply reformulated in terms of finite differences.

$$pI_{i+1} = mpI_i, \qquad (2)$$

where i = 1(none), . . . , 5(high).

This model can be tested by finding the constant m that gives the closest fit between the theoretical and the observed proportions (from Table 1). A criteria of minimizing the total squares of the differences will be used to determine goodness of fit. Here, the best fit $m = .57$. The first proportion, 55.4, is the first observed value, which the model predicts, with the consequent loss of one degree of freedom. The observed and predicted proportions are presented in Table 5.

TABLE 5—Observed and Predicted Proportions at Each Level of Involvement for Five Referents Perceived as Having neither Desire nor Ability to Help the Student Attain an Occupational Goal

Perceptual State: No Desire and No Ability	LEVEL OF INVOLVEMENT None 1	Very Little 2	Little 3	Moderate 4	High 5
Observed Proportion	.554	.344	.204	.080	.016
Predicted Proportion	.554	.316	.180	.103	.058

The sum of the squared differences is 36.9

The observed and predicted distributions are presented visually in Figure 1.

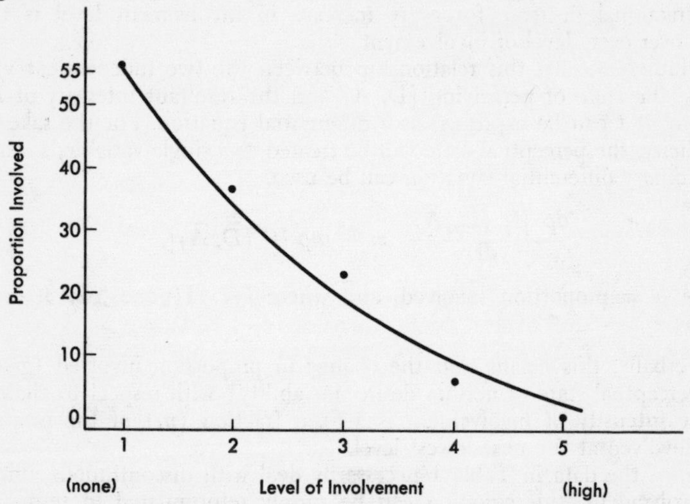

FIGURE 1—Theoretical Curve and Observed Values: Neither Desire nor Ability

It is predicted that there are no inversions. The probability of this happening by chance is $1/5! = 1/120$. No inversions are found, which supports the representation. A perfect rank order pattern is followed both by the observed and predicted values.

According to Hypothesis 2, where referents are perceived as having both desire and ability to help, the predicted result of this perceptual state is *high* involvement. By the same reasoning used in the first case, it can in general be predicted that the proportion involved at *any* level is some fixed fraction of the proportion involved at the next *highest* level. This relationship can be mathematically expressed in the following equation.

$$\frac{dp[I \mid (D, A)]}{dI} = kp[I \mid (D, A)] \qquad (3)$$

where $I = 1, 2, 3, 4, 5$.

In terms of finite differences, the following equation is obtained.

$$pI_{i-1} = kpI_i. \qquad (4)$$

Using the same criterion of goodness of fit, the best fit $k = .59$. The observed and predicted proportions are presented in Table 6.

TABLE 6—Observed and Predicted Proportions at Each Level of Involvement for Five Referents Perceived as Having Both Desire and Ability to Help the Student Attain an Occupational Goal

Perceptual State: No Desire and No Ability	LEVEL OF INVOLVEMENT None 1	Very Little 2	Little 3	Moderate 4	High 5
Observed Proportion	.025	.016	.328	.591	.779
Predicted Proportion	.094	.160	.271	.460	.779

It is predicted that there are no inversions. One inversion occurs, however, at "very little." There is a very small N at this level, only 3. In computing the rank order correlation, the highest proportion is omitted because it is always trivially true. The obtained r_r, where $n = 4$, is .800. The relationship between predicted and observed values is presented in Figure 2.

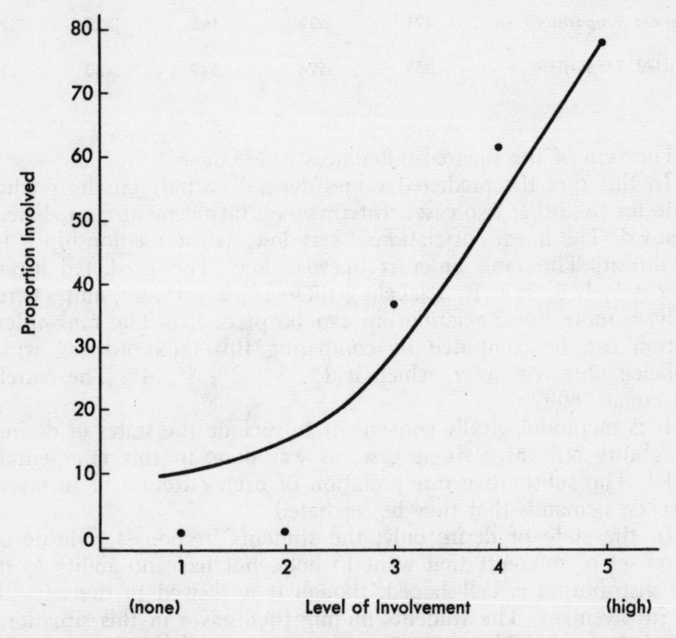

FIGURE 2—Theoretical Curve and Observed Values: Both Desire and Ability

From the sum of the squares of the differences, and the statistical tests, it is apparent that the case of neither fits better than the case of both, though both are acceptable.

Once having predicted the proportions for these two cases at each involvement level, it is simply a matter of subtracting the proportions at neither and both from 1.00 to deduce the predicted distributions in the third case—the additive union of the two states of desire only and ability only. The observed and predicted proportions are presented in Table 7.

TABLE 7—Observed and Predicted Proportions at Each Level of Involvement for Five Referents as Having Either Desire Only or Ability Only to Help the Student Attain an Occupational Goal

Perceptual States: Desire Only or Ability Only	LEVEL OF INVOLVEMENT None 1	Very Little 2	Little 3	Moderate 4	High 5
Observed Proportion	.421	.639	.468	.339	.205
Predicted Proportion	.352	.524	.549	.430	.163

The sum of the squared differences is 345.8.

In this case the predicted values depend *entirely* on the predictions made for the other two cases. Intermediate involvement is predicted and obtained. The linear correlation is very low, as the relationship is highly curvilinear. The rank order is likewise low. The predicted ascending order is 5, 1, 5, 2, 3. By relabeling these 1*, 2*, 3*, 4*, and 5*, respectively, a more linear relationship can be predicted. The rank-order correlation can be computed by comparing this rank ordering with the relabeled observed order, which is 1*, 3*, 2*, 5*, 4*. The correlation (r_r) equals .800.

It is methodologically convenient to include the states of desire only and ability only as a single case, as was done in this representational model. The substantive interpretation of each criterion of involvement, however, demands that they be separated.

In the state of desire only, the students' responses indicate a perceived set of referents that want to help, but have no ability to do so. The distribution is bell-shaped, though it is skewed to the left, toward low involvement. The students finding themselves in this situation take what help is available, as it was not psychologically unpleasant to do so.

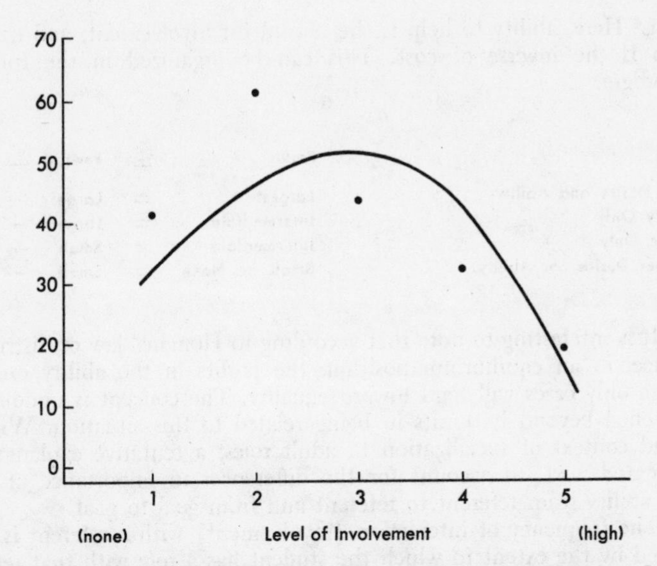

FIGURE 3—Theoretical Curve and Observed Values: Desire Only plus Ability Only

In the case of ability only the distribution is bimodal. It is not skewed in either direction. In this perceptual state, decisions on whether or not to go to a referent were more polarized than for the desire only case. It was more unpleasant to go to these referents, but at the same time the reward for doing so was much greater. It is this case that produces hostility to referents, and a sense of alienation. An example is found in the Southern United States Negro adolescent, who frequently perceives that while Caucasian referents have the ability to help the adolescent attain his goals they lack the desire to do so.[3] Hence, alienation and intergroup hostility. This process is also evident in male initiation ceremonies in primitive and traditional societies, as will be shown in the following section of this report. The diversity of social situations in which these processes are seen to operate demonstrates the point made in the introductory chapter, that there are some striking continuities in the structure of adolescent behavior, both within and among societies.

These observations can be organized in terms of interpersonal exchange. Homans has suggested that, psychologically, Profit = Reward —

3. The situation is similar, though less pronounced, in an integrated Northern high school or college. See David Gottlieb, "The Social Systems of Negro and White Youth," preliminary report, dittoed, 1964.

Cost.[4] Here, ability to help is the reward for involvement, and desire to help is the inverse of cost. This can be organized in the following paradigm.

Case	Profit	=	Reward	—	Cost
Both Desire and Ability	Largest	=	Large	—	Small
Ability Only	Intermediate	=	Large	—	Large
Desire Only	Intermediate	=	Small	—	Small
Neither Desire nor Ability	Small or None	=	Small	—	Large

It is interesting to note that according to Homans' law of distributive justice, in an equilibrium position, the profits in the ability only and desire only cases will tend toward equality. The concept is undoubtedly stretched beyond its limits in being related to this situation. Within a broad context of socialization to adult roles, a tentative explanation is presented next, to account for the differences in importance of desire and ability from referent to referent and from goal to goal.

The frequency of interaction (involvement) with a referent is determined by the extent to which the student has a *role* with that referent. The goal of the student refers to a perceived future state of affairs involving *new* role relationships. New roles are attained through two broadly defined interactional processes; *intentional instruction* and *incidental learning*, which operate conjointly.[5] Intentional instruction refers to formal institutions of role socialization for the performance of prescribed acts. Incidental learning refers to processes of identification with, an emulation of, role models in the imitator's behavioral field.

Different goals will correspond to different socialization processes. An instrumental goal, such as an occupation, will be primarily obtained through intentional instruction. Social goals, on the other hand, are more informally learned.

Given this relationship between learning processes and kinds of goals, it seems reasonable to hypothesize that the relevance of a kind of referent will depend on the goal sought. A teacher provides intentional instruction for attaining an occupational goal; an older sibling provides a role model for learning social skills. Here, for occupational goals of college students, ability was somewhat more predictive of high involvement than was desire.

---

4. The cost of a particular course of action is the equivalent of the forgone value of an alternative, a familiar economic assumption. The formula is presented in George C. Homans, "Social Behavior as Exchange," *American Journal of Sociology*, 63 (1958), 597-606.

5. Theodore R. Sarbin, "Role Theory," in Gardner Lindzey (ed.), *Handbook of Social Psychology: Volume I, Theory and Method* (Reading, Mass.: Addison-Wesley Publishing Company, Inc., 1954), p. 226.

A sociometric experiment by Gilchrist[6] on the factors influencing choice of a partner for a two-person task adds some evidence to this conceptualization of the relation between choice of interaction and the "goodness" of a referent's activities. For "intellectual" activities (instrumental), a partner was most often chosen who had been initially successful; for "social" task (expressive), a partner was most often chosen on the basis of previous interaction.

Tables 3 and 4 indicate that, in this study, ability is more predictive of high involvement than desire. Since the goal is instrumental, this is as expected. A breakdown by referents in these two cases should show that desire is relatively more important for incidental learning referents and that ability is relatively more important for intentional instruction referents. Spouse and siblings are the most "incidental" of the set of referents. Peers are somewhat incidental, but within a university, the structure of peer interactions is certainly relevant to success in college, and hence to success after college. Teachers are clearly in the intentional instruction case. The data are presented in Table 8.

TABLE 8—Average Level of Involvement with Each of Five Referents Perceived as Having Desire Only, and Ability Only, to Help the Student Attain an Occupational Goal: 5 = High, 4 = Moderate, 3 = Little, 2 = Very Little, 1 = None

		AVERAGE INVOLVEMENT			
Type of Role Relationship	Referent	Desire Only	(N)	Ability Only	(N)
Incidental Learning	Spouse	4.00	(7)	2.00	(1)
Incidental Learning	Siblings	2.62	(128)	3.16	(37)
Intermediate	Parents	3.56	(61)	3.12	(24)
Intermediate	Peers	3.28	(127)	3.74	(27)
Intentional Instruction	Teachers	3.34	(50)	3.65	(37)
Total	All Five	3.01	(373)	3.41	(126)

In general, the predicted trend is followed, not only relatively, but absolutely as well. There is one exception: for siblings, ability is more predictive of high involvement than is desire. The questions on siblings, however, did not control for age, with the result that desire only did not produce involvement for a very young sib with absolutely *no* ability to

6. J. D. Gilchrist "The Formation of Social Groups under Conditions of Success and Failure," *Journal of Abnormal and Social Psychology,* 47 (1952), 174-187.

help. The question on parents is also difficult to interpret, as no breakdown was made between father and mother. While both parents socialize incidentally, it is generally accepted that the father is more task-oriented and instrumental than the mother.[7]

The next hypothesis resolves the predictive problems for the two cases of desire only and ability only. The independent variables in the preceding hypothetical system can be generalized and interrelated to obtain a more general proposition. Perceived ability to help can be viewed as the capacity of a referent to provide opportunities for the attainment of an adolescent's goal. An index of social distance can be constructed to order all referents on a continuum of social distance. Hence, it is appropriate to refer to close referral points, and to distant ones.

The key to this proposition is found in Stouffer's demographic law of intervening opportunities.[8] He found that there is no necessary relationship between mobility and distance, as formulated in a classic statement by Ravenstein, that "Most people go a short distance, few people go a long distance."[9] Stouffer introduced the concept of *intervening opportunities*, and formulated and confirmed the following proposition:

> . . . the number of persons going a given distance is directly proportional to the number of opportunities at that distance and inversely proportional to the number of intervening opportunities.[10]

This proposition seems so generic to demographic analysis, that an attempt was made to generalize it to *sociological* analysis. Analogies between demographic migration and sociological orientation (involvement) can be organized in the following paradigm.

Demographic Migration	Sociological Orientation
1. Migration to a physical point; movement over physical space.	1. Orientation to a referral point; movement over social space.
2. Perceived physical distance properties of the point of destination, with accessibility defined in terms of "physical friction of space" and	2. Perceived social distance properties of the referral point of destination, with accessibility defined in terms of "social friction of space"

7. See e.g., Talcott Parsons, et al., *Family Socialization and Interaction Process* (New York: The Free Press, 1953).

8. Samuel A. Stouffer, "Intervening Opportunities: A Theory Relating Mobility and Distance," *American Sociological Review,* 5 (1940), 845-867.

9. E. G. Ravenstein, "The Laws of Migration," *Journal of the Royal Statistical Society,* 48 (1885), 167-235; 52 (1889), 240-305, cited in Stouffer, op. cit., p. 845.

10. Ibid. Subsequent studies have applied the model to other populations with considerable success. For a bibliography, see Stouffer, "Intervening Opportunities and Competing Migrants," *Journal of Regional Science,* 2 (1960), 1-2.

measured by criteria such as time and distance.	and measured by criteria such as cost and distance.
3. Perceived opportunities to attain goals at potential points of destination.	3. Perceived opportunities to attain goals at potential referral points, i.e., the perceived ability to help of referral points.

It is now possible formally to state Hypothesis 5.

Hypothesis 5: The number of students oriented to referral points at a given social distance is directly proportional to the perceived ability to provide opportunities of all referral points at that distance, and inversely proportional to the number of intervening opportunities.

All social distances S are considered a band of width ΔS, so the opportunity at each distance is denoted $\Delta X/\Delta S$. The intervening opportunities

$$X = \sum_{s=1}^{s-1} (\Delta X/\Delta S)$$

The number of students oriented to referents at a given distance is denoted $\Delta P/\Delta S$. Using this notation, the hypothesis can be reformulated as a difference equation:

$$\frac{\overline{\Delta P}}{\Delta S} = \frac{K\,\Delta X}{X\,\Delta S} \tag{5}$$

where K is a constant.

This model represents a third level of formalization. From the facet paradigm, an explicational model, this research progressed to a representional model interrelating the variables in the facet design. A substantive shortcoming of that model, its inability to distinguish between desire only and ability only, led to the development of a more general explanatory statement to account for a variety of observed processes. This may be termed a propositional model.[11]

Opportunity to obtain help from a referral point at a given social distance was measured by finding the mean average abilities of all referents at that distance. Great ability was weighted 3, some 2, little 1, and none not at all. In these data, fewer opportunities were perceived at greater social distances: the rank-order correlation was .567. If an intervening opportunities model is more adequate than a straight opportunities model, then a higher rank-order correlation should be obtained by using Equation (5).

---

11. The formalization is isomorphic to the initial proposition, i.e., it is a model of the proposition denoted Hypothesis 5. A model that is a formalization of an entire theory would be a *theoretical-construct* model: See Berger, et al., op. cit., p. 67.

The index of social distance was based on responses to two questions. The first question measures the direction of distance; it is based on the extent to which a referent is perceived as agreeing, being neutral to, or disagreeing with the student's choice of an occupational goal. The second question measures the intensity of social distance; it is based on the extent to which a referent is perceived as being interested in the student's attaining an occupational goal. Guttman has demonstrated that the direction and the intensity are the first two principal components (axes) in *any* scalable attitude.[12] The Bogardus scale, and other techniques, ordinarily measure these components in a way that they cannot be separated.

If these two questions really do measure the direction and the intensity of social distance, the relationship between them should be U-shaped, as predicted by Guttman.[13] The data follow this pattern. As the direction becomes very positive, intensity is increased; as the direction becomes very negative, intensity is increased.

The social-distance scale necessary for the testing of Hypothesis 5 requires only that ranks can be established. Both components are scaled from 0 (the point of minimum distance) to 3 (the point of maximum distance). There are five measures of agreement. The original four measures of interest are here dichotomized. The scale is presented in Table 9. It should be pointed out that false assumptions are used, as the scale points are treated as equidistant, interval measurement is used, and the components are given equal weight.

There is one tie, at social distance rank (5). The two cases are combined in the analysis. Hence, the scale consists of nine distances.

The number of involvements with referral points at each social distance is independently measured as the number of "highly involved" responses for referents.

The computations used in these predictions are presented in Table 8. At the first distance, the prediction is trivially true, as a correct constant K can always be found. Here $K = .59885$. One degree of freedom is lost in computing r_r. This constant drops out of every *other* predicted value, as it appears in both the numerator and denominator.

The differences in average opportunities at each social distance were not different enough to allow a very satisfactory adjustment of the *values* predicted to the *number* of high involvements found at each

12. Louis Guttman, "The Principal Components of Scalable Attitudes," in Paul F. Lazarsfeld, *Mathematical Thinking in the Social Sciences* (New York: The Free Press, 1954), pp. 219-226.

13. "If (a) scalable attitude has a meaningful zero-point (point of indifference), then as people have rank farther and farther to the right of it, they should become more and more positive, and hence more and more intense. Similarly, as ranks get farther and farther to the left of the zero-point, they should become more and more negative, and hence also indicate more intensity. Intensity accordingly should have a U or J-shaped relation with the underlying rank order," ibid., p. 229.

TABLE 9—Social Distance ($0 \leq S \leq 6$), Social Distance Rank (1 = Least, . . . , 9 = Greatest), and Number of Responses (N) for Five Referral Points

		LEVEL OF AGREEMENT				
Level of Interest	*Distance*	*Strongly Agree 0*	*Agree .75*	*Indifferent 1.50*	*Disagree 2.25*	*Strongly Disagree 3.00*
	•					
	•					
Very	•					
Intense or Some	0	0 (1) N = 668	.75 (2) N = 656	1.50 (3) N = 151	N = 24 2.25 (4)	N = 3 3.00 (5)
Little or None	3	3.00 (5) N = 18	3.75 (6) N = 84	4.50 (7) N = 185	5.25 (8) N = 16	6.00 (9) N = 4

TABLE 10—Computation of Predicted Involvement with Five Referents as Different Social Distances (1 = Least, . . . , 9 = Greatest)

;ocial Dis- ance S	$\frac{\Delta X}{\Delta S}$ (Rank)	$X = \sum_{S=2}^{8} \frac{\Delta X}{\Delta S}$	$\frac{\Delta P}{\Delta S} = \frac{1}{X}\frac{\Delta X}{\Delta S}$ (Rank)	$\left(\frac{\Delta P}{\Delta S}\right)^2$	$K\left(\frac{\Delta P}{\Delta S}\right)^2$ Number
1	2.265 (1)	—	K(2.265) = 1.63941 (1)	2.34612	376
2	1.947 (3)	2.265	.85960 (2)	.73891	119
3	1.694 (6)	4.212	.40218 (3)	.16175	26
4	1.778 (5)	5.906	.30105 (4)	.09063	14
5	1.923 (4)	7.684	.25026 (5)	.06263	10
6	1.466 (8)	9.607	.15260 (7)	.02329	4
7	1.541 (7)	11.073	.13917 (8)	.01937	3
8	2.083 (2)	12.614	.16513 (6)	.02727	4
9	1.000 (9)	14.697	.06804 (9)	.00463	1
;als				2.47550	557

social distance. A closer fit to the numbers is obtained by squaring the $\Delta P/\Delta S$ values obtained, before multiplying through by $C = 161.15$ to obtain computed numbers at distances 2 through 8. (No prediction is made for the first distance, where, by definition, there are *no* intervening opportunities.) This of course preserved the rank order, though the predicted numbers are closer to those observed. The justification for doing this of course is dependent on future testing of the model.

The actual number of high involvements with referents is presented in Table 11. These numbers are compared with the numbers computed in Table 10. Again, it should be reemphasized that these numbers are only tentatively regarded as *predictions*. At this stage of theoretical development, only the rank order is predicted directly from Equation (5). It is these ranks that are compared to observed order.

Since rank 1 is always correctly predicted by choosing the proper K, including it always improves the rank-order correlation. Thus, it is better to omit it from the rank-order correlation, and use $n = 8$. The correlation obtained is .717, which supports Hypothesis 5. It should be recalled that a correlation between distance and opportunities at each distance was only .567. Hence, the intervening model is much more predictive.

The numbers obtained in Table 11 are presented visually in Figure 4.

In terms of statistical goodness of fit, a Kolmogorov-Smirnov one-sample test, with two tails, results in a D of .048. The probability that $D = .048$, under the null hypothesis that the observed scores come from a population having the given theoretical distribution, is between .20 and .15. Thus some nonrandom disagreement is likely, but the result is not significant at the .05 level.

An immediate usage of this mathematical formalization is that by assuming continuity of social distance, it is possible to *deduce* the relationship between P and X, between the number of orientations and perceived ability to help. By assuming continuity, Equation (5) can be restated as $dP/dS = K/X\ (dX/dS)$. Integrating both sides yields

$$P = \ln X + C. \tag{6}$$

Once having established a mathematical relationship between P and S, it is possible to deduce the relationship between P and X. The result of this deduction is the final hypothesis of this section.

> Hypothesis 6: The greater the perceived opportunities to obtain help from a referent, the greater the level of involvement with that referent. For increasing ability on the part of a referent, involvement increases, but at a decreasing rate: involvement varies as the natural logarithm of opportunities.

Since Hypothesis 5 is true, this hypothesis is true by definition where

$$X = \sum_{i=2}^{9} (\Delta X/\Delta S)_i, \quad P = \sum_{i=2}^{9} (\Delta X/\Delta S)_i, \qquad \text{and} \qquad C = 2.361$$

TABLE 11—Observed and Computed Distributions of Number of Student Involvements with Five Referral Points over Different Social Distances

Number of Student Involvements		*(least)* 1	2	3	4	5	6	7	8	9	*Total*
	(Number)	(376)	(147)	(18)	(2)	(4)	(4)	(4)	(3)	(0)	(558)
Observed	Per cent	67.4	26.3	3.2	.7	.4	.7	.7	.5	0	99.9%
	Rank	1	2	3	5	8	5	5	7	9	—
	(Number)	(376)	(119)	(26)	(14)	(10)	(4)	(3)	(4)	(1)	(557)
Computed	Per cent	67.5	21.6	4.7	2.5	1.8	.7	.5	.7	0	100%
	Rank	1	2	3	4	5	7	8	6	9	—

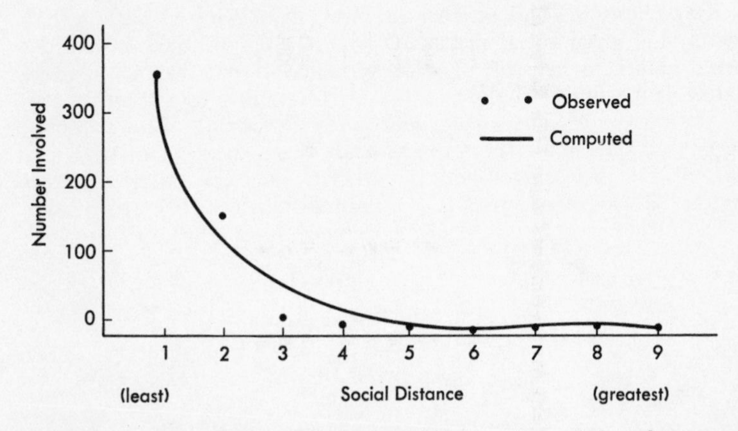

FIGURE 4—Observed and Computed Number of Involvements at Different Social Distances

for these data. The predictions are as accurate as before, except that cumulative sums are used. Since $P = \ln X + C$, $d(\ln X + C)\ /dS = 1/X\ (dX/dS)$. It can be deduced that $S = (\ln X + e^{x} - C)/C$, giving the relationship between S and X.

The six hypotheses developed in this section have all been supported for a sample of students at a large state university, with respect to attaining their occupational goals. It has been suggested that the salience of a criterion for involvement will vary from referent to referent and from goal to goal. At the same time, however, it is also hypothesized that the *process* by which a person becomes oriented to a referent is the same in any concrete social situation. In the pages to follow, these hypotheses will be examined in terms of several kinds of people and a variety of referents. To facilitate this analysis, these hypotheses will be restated here in a manner free of any specified population or referent or goal.

Hypothesis 1: If a referent is perceived as having neither desire nor ability to help a person attain a goal, that person will be involved with that referent at a low level.

Hypothesis 2: If a referent is perceived as having both desire and ability to help a person attain a goal, the person will be involved with that referent at a high level.

Hypothesis 3: If a referent is perceived as having ability but not desire to help a person attain a goal, the person will be involved with that referent at an intermediate level.

Hypothesis 4: If a referent is perceived as having desire but not ability to help a person attain a goal, the person will be involved with that referent at an intermediate level.

Hypothesis 5: The number of individuals involved with referral points at a given social distance is directly proportional to the perceived ability to help of all referral points at that distance, and inversely proportional to the number of intervening opportunities.

Hypothesis 6: The greater the perceived opportunities to obtain help from a referent, the greater the level of involvement with that referent. For increasing ability, involvement increases, but at a decreasing rate; involvement varies as the natural logarithm of opportunities.

3. A GENERAL CONSIDERATION OF ADOLESCENCE: AN APPLICATION OF THE MODEL

Adolescence can be given a sociological definition usable for a comparative, cross-cultural study of adolescence. In every society, the basic and common biological fact of pubescence [1] is marked by a set of cultural definitions which ascribe to each *age grade* [2] its basic characteristics. The similar distinctions between the physical manifestation on the one hand and the socio-cultural and behavioral on the other is described by Stone and Church.[3] An age grade is thus always a broad definition of human potentialities and obligations at a given stage of life. As such, it

1. Cf. David P. Ausubel, *Theory and Problems of Adolescent Development* (New York: Grune & Stratton, Inc., 1954).

2. "Age grade" is formally defined by Radcliffe-Brown as the ". . . recognized division of the life of the individual as he passes from infancy to old age. Thus, each person passes into one grade after another . . . through the whole series." See A. R. Radcliffe-Brown, "Age Organization Terminology," *Man*, 13 (1929), 21.

3. L. Joseph Stone and Joseph Church, *Childhood and Adolescence: A Psychology of the Growing Person* (New York: Random House, Inc., 1962), pp. 4-11.

involves general and basic role dispositions into which specific roles are built.[4]

The hypothetical framework outlined earlier provides a frame of reference within which adolescence can be studied comparatively. Before attempting to do so, however, it is necessary to elaborate some relevant correlates to general types of societies—the standard trichotomy of primitive, traditional, and modern will be employed here.

Caution must be used, however, in order to avoid overgeneralizing similarities and dissimilarities among the three types of social systems. We begin with the following continuities among types:

1. In most societies the attainment of full membership is defined in terms of transition from one age grade to another.

2. "Within all societies there is some definition—whatever the degree of its formalization—of the 'adult man' or full member of the society, and of the point at which the individual may acquire all the paraphernalia of full status and enter the first stages of the adult age span."[5]

3. This entrance usually—and it seems, necessarily—coincides with the transition from the family of orientation to that of procreation, as it is through this transition that the definite change of age roles, from receiver to transmitter of the cultural tradition, from child to parent, is effected. (Eisenstadt, p. 30)

4. "Groupings of children or adolescents are common in every society, no matter what its structure. In all societies the children are drawn together for various reasons . . . and thus learn the various types and rules of cooperative behavior and some universalistic norms which are of secondary importance in these societies." (Eisenstadt, p. 46)[6]

The transmission of the individual from an adolescent to an adult role is emphasized of course in ceremony and ritual: in primitive society, in the various *rites de passage* and other symbolism and ritualism. But the *dramatic* elements of passage are not universal. Traditional societies have an intermediate amount of ritual, especially in the traditional folk festivals of peasant communities (such as rural carnivals) in which youth and marriage are emphasized.[7] In the "modern" type of society, the

---

4. S. N. Eisenstadt, *From Generation to Generation: Age Groups and Social Structure* (New York: The Free Press, 1956), p. 22.

5. Ibid., p. 30. Further references to this book will be embodied in the text, in parentheses as the next sections are heavily dependent on Eisenstadt's analysis.

6. Also see Otto F. Raum, *Chaga Childhood: A Description of Indigenous Education in an East African Tribe* (London: Oxford University Press, 1940).

7. See Andre Varagnac, *Civilisation Traditionelle et Genres de Vie* (Paris: A. Michel, 1948), pp. 132-182; Richard Thurnwald, *Die Mengchlich Gesellschaft in Ihren Ethno-Soziologie Ischen Grundlegen,* B. II (Leipzig, W. de Gruyter & Co., 1931), 281-284: It is emphasized that among peasants marriage and family rites become more important than initiation

boundaries that separate adolescence from adulthood are extremely diffuse and at times quite vague.

It has often been noted that as societies progress from primitive to traditional to modern the boundaries between the age grades of adolescence and adulthood become less formalized and more diffuse. Another related phenomenon is the increasing articulation and common identification within the adolescent age grade (functional age segregation). When this articulation and identification reach a high level, they are commonly defined as an "adolescent subculture." "The adolescent becomes . . . 'cut off' from the rest of society, forced inward toward his own age group, [and] made to carry out his whole social life with others his own age. With his fellows, he comes to constitute a small society, one that has most of its important interaction *within* itself, and maintains only a few threads of connection with the outside adult society." [8] The adolescent becomes oriented to his peers, and seeks goals within his peer subculture even at the risk of social rejection from adult referents.

The problems of age segregation and the emergence of the adolescent subculture in modern society is a crucial problem in the world today. There has been a veritable revolution in world expectations, and an accelerating desire to modernize among "underdeveloped" (primitive and modern) societies. The adolescent may well determine the direction, form, and rate of success of this developmental process of modernization and the concomitant epigenesis of new social and political and economic forms.

In Africa, one-half of the population is under 20 years of age, whereas in a modern industrial society such as the United States, one-third of the population is projected to be over 60 years old within a decade. The implication is clear: in the rapidly changing "emergent" nations, huge proportions of the population *are* adolescents, and it is

---

rites. (At the level of modern society, initiation rites become virtually absent, and if present, informal.) For a full documentation of one society, see L. Low, *Lebansalter in der Judischen Literatur* (Szegedim, 1875), in Eisenstadt, op. cit., p. 236.

8. James S. Coleman, *The Adolescent Society: The Social Life of the Teenager and Its Impact on Education* (New York: The Free Press, 1962), p. 3. Coleman adds, with justification, that ". . . most students of adolescent behavior have agreed upon the existence of an adolescent subculture, a fact which is indisputable at the extreme of gang behavior. See Frederick Thrasher, *The Gang: A Study of 1,313 Gangs in Chicago* (Chicago: University of Chicago Press, 1936); and Albert Cohen, *Delinquent Boys: The Culture of the Gang* (New York: The Free Press, 1955)." For a differing point of view, see Frederick Elkin and William A. Westley, "The Myth of the Adolescent Peer Culture," *American Sociological Review,* 20 (1955), 680-684.

these adolescents who will determine the maintenance of cultural continuity or be the innovators of discontinuity and social change.

It has been shown that an age grade represents a general diffuse pattern of behavior proper to a man at a given stage of life. "It contains certain definite expectations of future activities, and of relationships with other people at the same or at different stages of their life careers." (Eisenstadt, p. 22) The "expectations of future activities," of course, means the fulfilling of adult roles—the attainment of skills, goals, and roles—as perceived ends of the adolescent. The "relationships with other people" at the adolescent stage of the life career refers to the process of interaction with people, and categories of people, which can be classified by broad criteria in an interpersonal effort to attain the desired ends.

In every interaction, there are alternatives for the actor involved: that is, there is choosing. The *process* by which adolescents choose with whom to become involved to attain their ends is the question to which a comparative analysis can be directed. It is our most general metatheoretical orientation that this process is essentially the same in any cultural setting. The following analysis is an attempt at "resetting" materials dealing with adolescents from different societies into our goal-attainment model.

ADOLESCENCE IN PRIMITIVE SOCIETY

Anthropologists have demonstrated that, in primitive societies, *ascribed criteria* are a central means of social stratification; and, as societies evolve to more complex and more modern forms, *achieved criteria* become relatively more salient bases of stratification. An important criterion in primitive society is that of age groups.

A consequence of the relative importance of ascribed criteria in primitive societies and tribes is that the expectations of society for adolescents are explicit, formal, and generally unambiguous. The transition from adolescence to adult status is generally institutionalized. The adolescent is acutely aware of status differentials between age grades, as are the adults.

This situation can be immediately "fit" into our hypothetical framework. This construction is not universal to primitive society, nor to the societies considered, but it is highly characteristic of the *most* primitive societies, particularly of segmentary acephalous tribes and familistic societies.

1. By assumption, the adolescent desires to attain goals, skills, and roles in the adult society.
2. The adult age grade(s) possesses the power means to help the adolescent attain these ends.
3. Helping the adolescent, however, involves loss of power and

status, as it puts the adolescent on equal power basis in the competition for allocation of social rewards, resulting in potential loss of status and power for the older age groups. Helping the adolescent results in his becoming a "full man."

4. Adults do not want to share or lose access to these social rewards, and consequently do not desire to help the adolescent: there is an effort on the part of the adults to maintain a great social distance.

5. The adolescent perceives that the adults have the ability but not the desire to help the adolescent attain his ends.

This situation has been described mathematically and substantiated empirically for a nonprimitive sample of adolescents. Item 5 above represents the "psychologically ambiguous case," or the "unbalanced case." It was hypothesized that this results in *hostility* to adult referents. Since this hostility is reciprocal and embedded in primitive social structure, and since any society must maintain social control of disruptive behavior, an institutionalized method of control can be expected. Male initiation ceremonies served this function, in which hazing and genital operations are indices of adult hostility directed at the adolescent.

In primitive society, the relation of the adolescent to his peers (those in the same age group) is in general quite the opposite.

1. By assumption, the adolescent desires to attain ends. Peers as well as adults are potential sources of help.

2. The peer age grades do not in general have as much power to help the adolescent attain his ends as adult age grades.

3. Helping the adolescent does not involve loss of power and status, but in most cases confers it, though this attaining of ends does not confer *full* adult status, i.e., it does not produce the "full man."

4. Peers frequently change status *en bloc,* as a group, and have equal status, and consequently do want to help the adolescent: there is an effort to minimize social distance.

5. The adolescent perceives that his peers have the desire but not the ability to help him attain his ends.

Here we see a *dilemma.* The level of involvement with a referral category is hypothesized to be directly proportional to the perceived opportunities at a given social distance and inversely proportional to the cumulated ability to help of all closer referents. The adolescent age groups perceive a distant (adult) age set that can help them attain status, and concomitantly perceive closer age peers that cannot help to as great an extent.

The result of this dilemma, the "solution" for the adolescent in primitive society is competitiveness and hostility with superior age sets that can help, even to the point of organized physical combat to try to attain social status, and cooperation and friendliness with age peers, as a means to attain from peers as much gratification as is possible within the social structure. The fact that the *rites de passage* are so formalized indicates a functional response to this perceptual dilemma. Explicit and institutionalized roles, norms, and symbolic ritualism must exist to control the interset hostilities and assure smooth cultural continuity.

This hypothetical model will be tested against Eisenstadt's excellent analysis of types of age groups in primitive tribes and societies. (pp. 56-114)

It should be noted at this point that the following discussion will be limited to a consideration of each tribe or society as a more or less integrated *social system*. The articulation of the tribe or society to larger units, such as tribal federations or nation states, will be considered beyond the immediate scope of this presentation.

A. *Primitive, Segmentary, Acephalous Tribes*

1. *Nuer*[9] (pp. 59-63)

The *Nuer* are a pastoral Nilotic tribe of the southern Sudan. The age-set system stratifies the entire tribe. It covers the entire life span and is rigidly adhered to. But it does not constitute, as with many of this type of tribe, the military organization or a corporate group with common activities. "It is more general social relations, chiefly of a domestic or kinship order . . . [and] when a boy passes into the grade of manhood his domestic duties and privileges are radically altered. From being everybody's servant and an inferior, he becomes an independent adult." (p. 60) This transmission is accompanied by ceremony and initiation rites, which bestow the statuses of adult dating patterns, warrior, herdsman, and husband-father, with the process of initiation consummated by battle, dwelling with peers, cultivation of gardens, and marriage.

The change to adult status is sudden and great. Adult sets are stratified by age (seniority) but all manhood privileges are enjoyed by all adult age sets.

Social distance between adolescent and adult age grades can be characterized as follows: (a) segregation of sets at sacrificial feasts; (b) an injunction against fighting with elders, deference in discussion, deference in etiquette, and so forth.

In general, the age-set system tends to emphasize sharply the difference between boy and adult status, and enrollment in an age set is connected with initiation ceremonies.

The different age statuses are fully institutionalized and formal: there is no deviant behavior or ideology.

---

9. Eisenstadt's description is adapted from E. E. Evans-Pritchard, "The Nuer Age Sets," *Sudan Notes and Records,* XIX (1933-35), pt. II; Evans-Pritchard, "Kinship and the Local Community Among the Nuer," in A. R. Radcliffe-Brown and Daryll Forde (eds.), *African Systems of Kinship and Marriage* (Oxford: International African Institute, 1950).

Interaction between age mates is affective and comradely: adolescents are "brothers" to each other. (The entire *Nuer* stratification system is based on extended kinship relations.) The adolescent peers are on a basis of complete equality.

In this society, adults can help but do not desire to do so; peers cannot help much, but do support each other as much as they are able. As predicted, this dilemma results in interage-grade hostility, and a highly formalized and visible ceremony of initiation into full adult status.

2. *Nandi* [10] (pp. 63-67)

The *Nandi* are a segmentary tribe in Kenya. They have a cyclical age-set system. Every male belongs to one of seven age sets, each of which is divided into four "fires," two junior and two senior. "The sets contained two groups of boys, one of warriors and four of elders. The set of warriors was the ruling set which went to war and enjoyed most privileges." (p. 63) A man born into a set stays in it permanently, with set succession in a recurring 105-year cycle.

All men of one age set are equal *vis-à-vis* one another: sentiments of companionship are common.

The transfer of government from one age set to another is effected at a special ceremony (the *sowet*). "At the ceremony there is usually a symbolic show of force between the retiring and the new warrior age set, the retiring age set being unwilling to relinquish its privileges. (Among some other tribes of the *Nandi* group, and especially among the Kipsigis, there is real animosity between adjacent sets, the set holding power being prepared to hand it over only after some real fights.)" (pp. 64-65)

Here is evidence for the generalized theory of intervening opportunities. The ability of the superior (warrior) set to hand over power and status (ends of the adolescents) is institutionalized in ritual ceremonies. "The age groups are fully conformist and no deviant behavior or ideological tendencies are developed." (p. 66) (As with the *Nuer*.) The function of having the ability to help is explicit, and is perceived by all age sets. But it is true that understanding a function does not obviate its existence.

The warrior clearly does not desire to hand over his status, which means, among other things, a severe restriction of sexual license: this causes overt jealousy between overlapping sets. "Strong feelings of competition and animosity exist between adjacent sets—especially when the time for transmission of government function comes . . ." (p. 66)

The *Nandi* adolescent perceives a dilemma: a distant set of warriors

---

10. See Alfred C. Hollis, *The Nandi, Their Language and Folklore* (1909); George W. B. Huntingford, *The Political Organization of the Nandi*, unpublished B.Sc. Thesis, University of Oxford, 1947; Huntingford, *The Nandi of Kenya: Tribal Control in a Pastoral Society* (London: Routledge & Kegan Paul, 1953).

that can help him attain ends, and closer age peers that cannot help, but would if they could. As predicted, the result is involvement with both superiors and peers, with hostility to the superiors and a lack of hostility between peers.

3. The Plains Indian Age Societies:
Mandan, Arapaho, Gros Ventre, Blackfoot,
and especially the Hidatsa[11] (pp. 67-70)

Full membership—adult status—in these societies is based on ownership through adolescent age peers *purchasing* the rights of manhood (which are largely ceremonial) as a collectivity from the next oldest group. There is a remarkable hierarchy of status based on age. The buyers are termed "sons" and the sellers "fathers." Progression in status group is based entirely on age, though the *direct* basis of membership is purchase.

There is cooperation among alternate classes. For example, when age class 2 attempts to buy membership in class 3, it can rely on help from class 4, and on the other even-numbered classes. A similar bond unites the odd-numbered classes. Between the odds and the evens there is a "class struggle."

Age groups have unified organization throughout the tribe regulating members' behavior *vis-à-vis* one another. There is also corporate organization oriented toward achieving ceremonial status through purchase.

Here we have a more complicated situation between adolescents and their older referents. Our model enables us to make the following predictions, all of which are supported:

1. Adjacent older groups have the ability but not the desire to help the adolescent attain membership. "Relations between adjacent groups are competitive and semiaggressive." (p. 70)

2. Alternate older groups have both the desire and the ability to help the adolescent attain membership. "Relations between . . . alternate ones are more friendly." (p. 70)

---

11. There is an abundant literature on the Plains Indians, but very few full analyses. The fullest details and discussions are found in Robert H. Lowie, ed., "Plains Indian Age Societies—Historical and Comparative Summary," *Anthropological Papers of the American Museum of Natural History*, XI, Part XIII. Among the most important papers in this volume are Clark Wissler, "Blackfoot Societies"; Lowie, "Societies of the Hidatsa and Mandan Indian"; A. Skinner, "Societies of the Iowa Indian." See also Alfred Bowers, *Mandan Social and Ceremonial Organization* (Chicago: University of Chicago Press, 1950); Henry Elkin, "The Northern Arapaho of Wyoming," in Ralph Linton (ed.), *Acculturation among Seven Indian Tribes* (New York: D. Appleton-Century Company, Inc., 1940), pp. 207-259; Lucien Hanks and Jane Richardson, *Tribe Under Trust: A Study of the Blackfoot Reserve of Alberta* (Toronto: University of Toronto Press, 1950), p. 328.

3. Peers have both the desire and the ability to help the adolescent. All mobility is collective. "Age-group activities foster general feelings of solidarity between age mates . . ." (p. 70)

In the Plains Indian societies, the "ideal" typology begins to break down, but the *process* of orientation to referents is as predicted.

B. *Primitive Centralized Chiefdoms and Monarchies*

1. *Nupe*[12] (pp. 79-83)

The *Nupe* are a semifeudal kingdom in Nigeria. They are a highly differentiated society relative to the segmentary, acephalous tribes that have been considered. At this level of societal development, the typology for primitive society is modified again, as age is less central as a criterion of status, and social differentiation is less explicit and *passage* is not as formally institutionalized.[13]

Age sets differ in villages and in the capital. The age-set system is nonuniform, noncentralized, and not uniformly enforced. There are three age grades; children (age 10-15); adolescents, the "society of young men" (age 16-20); and the "society of old ones" (age 21-30, and mostly married).

Membership in an age grade is primarily concerned with the acquisition of titles accompanied by definite rights and obligations. Titles are bestowed *by peers*, and constitute a rigid hierarchy, with corresponding differentiation in duties and privileges, as well as a constant byplay of ambition and rivalry, modeled after the political system of the adults. Age-grade responsibility is regarded by adolescents as planned anticipation of adult responsibilities.

Promotion of an age grade occurs *en bloc*, with a reshuffling of rank occurring: advance is corporate and almost automatic, with no deviant

---

12. This description is based on Siegfried F. Nadel, "The Ganni Ritual of Nupi: A Study of Social Symbiosis," *Africa*, XIX (1949). Also see Nadel, *A Black Byzantium: The Kingdom of the Nupe in Nigeria* (Oxford: Oxford University Press, 1942).

13. Eisenstadt also considers conciliar (acephalous) primitive villages (pp. 70-75), in particular, the *Yako*. This has been left out of this analysis because the information available did not allow an adequate test of the theoretical model. However, it is relevant to note that in these societies the age-group criterion does not dominate the behavior and attitudes of all members of society, and the scope of the members' behavior is not as full as in the *Nuer* and *Nandi*.

The age groups do not form fully autonomous or autocephalous groups, as in most of their activities they are directed by "outsiders" such as village officials.

Entrance into age groups is a basic prerequisite of full social status, but membership in more advanced stages of age groups is not a main indicator of social status.

tendencies. Again, the allocation of status is a private affair of the age grade. Membership in an age group is an important, although not the main, prerequisite for full membership in society.

For the *Nupe* adolescent, mobility and the attaining of ends occur within an age group, as intergroup mobility is automatic. The relation of the adolescent to his peers is one of competitive rivalry: it can be generalized that peers have the ability to help but not the desire. This situation is the opposite of the "usual" situation for adolescents in primitive society. Hostilities are, as predicted by the hypothetical framework, directed at the peers instead of the adults. "A father or older brother will always help a boy to fulfill the various duties of hostility toward his age mates which are expected of him . . ." (p. 81) (Parents are generally retired members of the senior age grade, outside of the age system.)

The society (the highest grade) and those adults participating in political life *can* help the adolescent to the extent that they provide interactive (learning) role models, to which the adolescent orients by emulation. Adults have no lack of desire to help. Hence, as predicted, there is involvement with the adults but not hostility.

2. *Nyakyusa Age Villages* [14] (pp. 83-87 and 253-258)

The criterion of relative age (in the general system of the family) is a basis of membership adhered to with some minor exceptions. Age groups are given strong emphasis during sexual maturation and the transition period to marriage.

An age village consists of a group of age mates with their wives and young children. The village starts at about 10 or 11, on the edge of their fathers' village. Boys are expected to eat and sleep with their peers. A village lasts throughout the life of the boys that establish it. Strong solidarity and attachment among mates constitutes one of the main values of the society.

Parents, and other adults in the father's village, regard fathers and sons as "mixed company." There are explicit ideological bases for the parents not helping the adolescent attain full status, which comes with marriage and full autonomy. Also, a great social distance is maintained.

Age groups are the main territorial units of the tribe. They encompass all of the social life of their members. It is a well-known sociological

---

14. This description is based on M. Wilson, "Nyakyusa Age-Villages," *Journal of the Royal Anthropological Institute,* 79 (1951). Also see G. Wilson, "An Introduction to Nyakyusa Society," *Bantu Studies,* X (1936); G. Wilson, *The Land Rights of Individuals among the Nyakyusa* (Rhodes Livingstone Institute), Paper 1; M. Wilson, *Good Company* (London: Oxford University Press, 1951).

datum that when power has an ecological basis, it is more threatening.[15] This potential power of adolescents is controlled by a formal ceremony of the *ubusoka,* the "coming out," in which each village of young men is established (which means the elders must move, even if land is available for all). This is accompanied by great ceremony. The administrative power and military leadership are handed over to the young generation. This pattern of age group villages is unique in human society.

Adults have the ability to help but not the desire. Peers have both the desire and ability to help one another, by establishing separate residence, coming out, and gaining full status. As predicted, there is great tension and conflict between generations, and strong solidarity and cooperation among peers.

A major thesis in Eisenstadt is that

> . . . Age groups tend to arise when the structure of the family or descent group blocks the younger members' opportunities for attaining social status within the family because . . . the older members block the younger ones' access to the facilities which are prerequisite to full adult status. . . . (p. 248)

This can be restated in the vocabulary of our model. Parents can help the adolescent attain his goals (full status) but they do not do so because, *within the context of the family,* this involves loss of status for the adults. The *Nyakyusa* represent an extreme example of this.

"While *Nyakyusa* community life is based on age, the distribution of wealth is directed into kinship channels. All important wealth . . . is inheritable within the kinship group . . . ," (p. 253) which is *a*territorial, being dispersed among age villages.

Cattle are the main elements of bride price. Since polygamy is the social ideal, there is strong potential conflict generated between older and younger brothers as well as between generations. This sibling conflict is rooted in the possibility of the elders' using their cattle for buying themselves additional (young) wives instead of furnishing the bride price for the younger members of the family (lineage). This also affects

---

15. Solidarity increases when there is a territorial base for a group. For example, region is the major source of political conflict. Aterritorial groups almost never dismantle a society. A territorial group is more threatening by the very nature of political power: The state is a monopoly of power in a given area. "The power organization of every society is ecological. Every group which concentrates in one part of this territory . . . potentially endangers the monopoly by being able to organize an independent political unit. A group which is ecologically dispersed, on the other hand, has no monopoly over any area and is therefore in no position to create a monopoly of power." In Amitai Etzioni, "The Ghetto—a Re-evaluation," *Social Forces,* 37 (1959), 259.

an individual's economic independence, as only a married man gets his own fields to till, until which time he has to work for the father (while living in a different village). (pp. 253-254) Parents *and* siblings, faced with the potential loss of wives and labor, respectively, have a vested interest in withholding full status from the adolescent. As a result of these social structural arrangements, the marriage age of males is relatively high, the younger people having quite a long wait before being provided with the necessary bride price.

". . . We find among the *Nyakyusa* an institutionalization of age homogeneous groups which serves to ease the tension between generations, a tension engendered because of the elders' monopolization of all avenues to marriage and economic independence." (p. 255) Our model has led to the prediction that this tension between parents and adolescents, and between siblings and adolescents, leads to a high level of dependence on peers. This is clearly substantiated: "The tension is eased through the establishment of age villages with their own strong solidarity, and through the device of handing over political power to each successive generation as it attains social maturity." (p. 255)

Another index of intergenerational conflict in *Nyakyusa* society is the ideology of decorum about the sexual activities of adults. The incest theme is strong, with complete avoidance practiced to obviate dangers such as seduction of the father's or older brother's wives by the adolescent. "The sharpening of incest taboos and restrictions on sexual relations within the family unit postpones the young members' attainment of full sexual maturity." (p. 248)

3. *The Murngin* [16] (pp. 249-250)

In this Australian tribe, we find an extreme and complete case of a social institution relating to intergenerational strife in primitive society. *Gerontocracy*, i.e., the preferential allocation of roles to older people, is highly developed. The older people have the most prestige-bearing positions in the ritual, economic, and quasi-political (advisory) fields. Age grading is explicit and formalized.

Murngin totemic myths give ideological and religious expression to the various *rites de passage*.

The threat of the adolescents is handled by having the boys "retreat" to a camp of their own. A rigid system of age grading, connected as it is with sexual dichotomy and family positions, is attended by a strong emphasis on differential authority of the various age grades. With the attainment of full social status (especially sexual) the age-group life of the *Murngin* ceases.

---

16. See W. Lloyd Warner, *A Black Civilization: A Social Study of an Australian Tribe* (New York: Harper & Brothers, 1937); and a short summary in William J. Goode, *Religion among the Primitives* (New York: The Free Press, 1951), pp. 79ff., 128ff., and 174ff.

ADOLESCENCE IN TRADITIONAL SOCIETY

In primitive society we have seen the institutionalization of "delayed" maturity, both in the sexual and socio-economic spheres. In peasant societies, to be considered in this section, economic implications of age grading are more cogent.

A. *Irish Peasants*[17]

In significant social events in Irish peasant society—the *cuuyaird* or visit, the ecological arrangement of the household, the Sunday afternoon gatherings, wakes, weddings, and christenings—age groupings are observed.

It has been postulated that peasant (traditional) societies are intermediate between primitive and modern society with respect to the overall importance of age as a criterion of social status. In these Irish villages, the age criterion is not the sole criterion of the formation of age groups and cliques. The boundaries of age groups and age cliques are less pervasive, and more diffuse. Other factors, such as marital status and family status, become more important. But even these nonage criteria are not very consistent and not very rigidly adhered to. (p. 90) It has also been postulated that an increase in common identification or functional age segregation occurs in the transition from primitive to traditional society. The opportunities presented to adolescents by older age grades are not as clear, nor as real. The result, in Irish villages, is that the groups are organized into cliques ". . . with varying degrees of cohesion and stability, whose main activities are 'social' and recreational." (p. 90)

Age groups are not fully institutionalized. There exist strong elements of antagonism between age groups, especially between youth and the age group of old people. The activities of youth bind the young men together in common interest and provide a scope of action in which they are comparatively free but which keeps them divorced from community-wide status and power.

Irish society is extreme in the deferment of full status to the young. Marriage is long delayed, and *full* status comes only in old age. The most important features of this system are based on property, the family farm unit. The farm is inherited only by one son, and he is helped by the father until he reaches advanced age. "Until then the son (or sons) who may already have grown young children of their own (and sometimes

---

17. See Conrad M. Arensberg and Solon T. Kinball, *Family and Community in Ireland* (Cambridge, Mass.: Harvard University Press, 1948); and Arensberg, *The Irish Countryman: An Anthropological Study* (Gloucester, Mass.: Peter Smith, 1959).

even grandchildren), do not own any property, and are entirely subordinated to their father. This subordination even includes dependence on him for pocket money, let alone food, clothing, etc. It is the father who plans work on the farm, and it is he who participates in the councils of the village and in public affairs. From all these activities the sons—who may be called 'boys' until the age of 50-60—are excluded." (p. 256)

Here is a familistic society defined in terms of kinship and descent with respect to authority and status. The young are precluded from attaining social maturity. It is the exclusion of various grades of "boys" [18] from full status that gives rise to various informal age groups.

As membership is based mostly on status within the family, a younger man who happens to be a full man, i.e., owner of a farm, usually participates in the old men's *cuuyaird*.[19] The fact of property ownership can remove a person from the status of boy to that of full man. The *cuuyaird* is the arbiter of public opinion in the village: it is the scene of community decision making. The propertyless younger men do not enjoy such status and participation. The younger men's participation, even preoccupation, with games, etc., is an index of this exclusion. Within this sphere they maintain a loose solidarity, based on ". . . semiopposition to the elders and their values." (p. 257) Tension between the two generations is continuous—the older generation accusing the younger of lack of reverence and discipline, and extolling the "good old days," while the younger tend (not completely) to accuse the older ones of being autocratic.

Irish intergenerational tension is certainly consistent with our hypotheses. Status is withheld from adolescents, and they cannot attain fully adult roles, and consequently withdraw within their peer groups, from which they *can* attain goals. The goals attained within peer groups are social, rather than occupational and economic. Here we have a functional age segregation, a bifurcation of goals and values between generations, and in-group solidarity. This reemphasizes our earlier reference to Coleman, in which he refers to the adolescent being "cut off" from the rest of society, forced inward toward his own age group, and made to carry out his whole social life with others his own age. Certainly Coleman's study of the American high school shows that this phenomenon is even more developed in modern society. But here, in the intermediate

---

18. In Section II of this Chapter, adolescence was differentiated from pubescence. Here is a case where it is not entirely sociologically unrealistic to refer to 50-year-olds as "adolescents."
Membership in these "age" groups is usually acquired, however, not directly according to the criterion of age, but rather to the authority structure of the family.

19. See Arensberg and Kimball, op. cit., Chapters VI and X.

level of societal development, the "beginnings" of this phenomenon are manifest:

> The young men's cliques constitute an "insulated" sphere of social activities which is only partly institutionalized within the social structure of the village. It provides a psychological outlet for the young person's need for a group in which he is a full member, without being subject to any authority but his own. . . . And yet it must be emphasized that the existence of these "age groups" constitutes a constant force of deviant behavior, albeit one which is insulated and . . . a transitory phase in his development. (p. 258)

In contradistinction to our sample of primitive tribes and societies, we see the development of deviant *ideological* tension between generations.

B. Other Peasant Societies

Eisenstadt very briefly supports the above hypothesis by comparing the authority structure of the Irish peasant society with that of other peasant groups: the Welsh, traditional Chinese, Guatemalan, French-Canadian peasantry, and the historical European peasant societies. (See Eisenstadt, p. 258, for references.)

ADOLESCENCE IN MODERN SOCIETY

On the first page of this chapter, it was proposed that there are some striking continuities in the structure of adolescent behavior. In the societies considered so far, this orientation has in general been supported. It has been shown that there are very similar processes of becoming involved with types of referents to attain types of goals. Bloch and Niederhoffer postulate that:

> The adolescent period in all cultures, visualized as a phase of striving for the attainment of adult status, produces experiences which are much the same for all youth, and certain common dynamisms for expressing reaction to such subjectively held experiences. The intensity of the adolescent experience . . . depends on . . . the degree to which the society tends to facilitate entrance into adulthood by virtue of institutionalized patterns, ceremonies, rites, and rituals, and socially supported emotional and intellectual preparation. When a society does not make adequate preparation . . . equivalent forms of behavior arise spontaneously among adolescents themselves, reinforced by their own group structure.[20]

---

20. Herbert Bloch and Arthur Niederhoffer, *The Gang: A Study in Adolescent Behavior* (New York: Philosophical Library, 1958), p. 17. This view is supported by cross-cultural comparisons, e.g., the *Manus* and the *Comanche*, pp. 134-135.

The discussion to this point has emphasized the processes of transition from adolescence to adulthood. This passage is widely regarded as one of the major status transitions in human society. From a few specimens taken from primitive and traditional societies, we have observed that the attainment of adult status is stressful in a number of different cultural settings.

Cloward and Ohlin concur with a generally acknowledged view that the transition is ". . . especially difficult in Western societies because of the extreme complexity of the occupational structure. . . . Our occupational system is technical and specialized; the successful pursuit of many occupational roles requires years of formal training and preparation. Males ordinarily are denied full status, marriage, and adult roles during this period."[21] By comparison, in less-developed societies, the occupational system is relatively simply and undifferentiated. The problems of cultural transmission of skills can be attained within the family, rather than in formal learning institutions.

We see here, and elsewhere, consensual support (which is not tantamount to proof) for our general orientation. It is natural to ask to what extent the hypothetical framework is anticipated in research literature. A construction similar to the first three hypotheses has been developed, independently, by Miller,[22] in a typology of lower-class American youth based on the gap between aspirations and possibilities of achievement:

1. *"Stable" lower class.* This group consists of youngsters who . . . do not aspire to higher status or who have no realistic possibility of achieving such aspirations.

2. *Aspiring but conflicted lower class.* This group represents those for whom family or other community influences have produced a desire to elevate their status, but who lack the necessary personal attributes or cultural "equipment" to make the grade, or for whom cultural pressures effectively inhibit aspirations.

3. *Successfully aspiring lower class.* This group, popularly assumed to be the most prevalent, includes those who have both the will and the capacity to elevate their status.

This typology can be criticized on several grounds. There is a generally vague vocabulary: adolescents are viewed in terms of (a) "aspiring," "desiring," and "willing" to elevate their status, or being inhibited from such aspirations, and (b) having or not having "realistic possibilities," "personal attributes," and "cultural 'equipment' " to change their status. It is not clear whether the implied self-evaluation is based on

21. Richard A. Cloward and Lloyd E. Ohlin, *Delinquency and Opportunity: A Theory of Delinquent Gangs* (New York: The Free Press, 1963), p. 54.

22. In W. C. Kvaraceus and W. B. Miller, *Delinquent Behavior: Culture and the Individual* (Washington, D. C.: National Education Association, 1959), p. 72. An important criticism is found in Cloward and Ohlin, op. cit., pp. 65-76.

objective conditions, or on perceptions: e.g., "cultural 'equipment' " could refer to either. In our model, (a) is *desire* and (b) is *ability*.

The typology evidently involves both self and others as referents. The "self" is social, for full maturation—the attainment of "selfhood"—comes from full involvement in a social system. The adolescent, who universally wants full status in a social system, will find it in involvement with referents that can confer this status, and desire to do so.

Miller's culture-conflict theorizing leads to a prediction that "discrepancies between aspirations and possibilities of achievement are a major source of pressures toward delinquent behavior." [23] This conclusion conflicts with his hypothesis that delinquency is a consequence of conformity to lower-class values. The prediction that the second case represents adolescents in a state of stress, hostile to society, and dependent peers, is consistent with our hypothetical system.

It would be an outright impossibility to review or systematically examine the imbroglio of literature on adolescent behavior in the next several pages. Instead, a special emphasis will be placed on one study, by Bloch and Flynn.[24] This brief treatment will not *prove* our hypotheses, but it will become apparent that they are supported to a high level of verisimilitude.

The authors attempt to schematize social correlates of three psychological types of delinquents.

The *defective superego delinquent* has a family characterized as follows:

> Broken (separation, desertion, divorce, death); large number of siblings, many delinquents; parental conflict and hostility; lack of conventional moral ideas; ineffective control.

Every entry in this description is correlated in research literature with an inability of parents to provide opportunities for their children to attain goals. In addition, the "parental conflict and hostility" indicate a lack of desire, or intention, to help the adolescent. Hence, we can predict little involvement with parents, and a higher level of involvement with peers. Parents and peers are seen as *competing references*. An empirical hypothesis is implicit in this concept:

---

23. See *Ibid.*, p. 74. The authors take the ". . . view that pressures toward the formation of delinquent subcultures originate in marked discrepancies between culturally induced aspirations among lower-class youth and the possibilities of achieving them by legitimate means." (See p. 78.)

24. Herbert A. Bloch and Frank T. Flynn, *Delinquency: The Juvenile Offender in America Today* (New York: Random House, Inc., 1956). For a succinct summary, see Oliver Moles, Ronald Lippitt, and Stephan Withey, *Selective Review of Research and Theories Concerning the Dynamics of Delinquency* (Ann Arbor, Michigan: Institute for Social Research, 1959), pp. 7-8.

HYPOTHESIS 7: The less the level of involvement with parents, the greater the level of involvement with peers; and vice versa.

This is supported by the findings. The ". . . orientation of the child . . ." is described as "usually member of gang; ready response to peer-age culture." In addition, the adolescent is readily suggestible to *delinquent* peer groups, and delinquent offenses are of a gang character. In this case, the defective superego type, the onset of delinquency is the most rapid: the frequency of delinquency is the greatest under age 12.

The goals of these adolescents are essentially financial and social: the form of delinquency is burglary, and other offenses characteristic of organized delinquent groups. Also, the educational attainment is low, as these adolescents "generally do not complete grade school education; frequently [are] found in elementary schools; [and are] over-age in grade level."

At this point, we can introduce a theoretical consideration of family structure, involving parents and siblings. The presence of older siblings provides role models for the process of learning social and interactional skills. Sibling role models are available primarily to those adolescents that have older sibs. The availability of such models contributes positively to social adjustment and to personality development.[25] Hence, younger sibs will be better adjusted to their social environment. As family size increases, the probability that any randomly chosen child will have older siblings increases, and hence the probability that they will have sibling social role models increases. The result is better social adjustment for younger siblings. A corollary of this result pertains to a special case of generalized role models: viz., *peer* role models. The adolescent with older siblings will be more successfully adjusted to peers, and will be integrated in the peer subculture available to him.

The variable most often related to the study of delinquency is social class, which is usually indexed by one or more crude measures of socioeconomic status. "Juvenile delinquency and the delinquent subculture in particular are overwhelmingly concentrated in the male, working-class sector of the juvenile population" is the conclusion drawn by Cohen in his *Delinquent Boys*.[26] Cohen, and Whyte before him, offer a purport of explanation in terms of lower-class value patterns.[27] The lower-class

25. See Diane TenHouten "Siblings and Socialization," unpublished M.A. Thesis, Michigan State University, 1965. The patterns of learning roles and skills are theoretically related to the personality development of the child. This is supported by an exhaustive review of the major research on sibling structure in a context of the family in Western industrial society.

26. Albert K. Cohen, *Delinquent Boys: The Culture of the Gang* (New York: The Free Press), pp. 37-44 *et passim*.

27. William F. Whyte, *Street Corner Society* (Chicago: University of Chicago Press, 1937).

"corner boy"[28] way of life militates against vertical mobility, and against social, educational, and occupational success in the larger middle-class society. Whyte's core thesis is that lower-class value patterns emphasize the learning of *social* skills: "corner boys" are encultured to these values. Lower-class boys with a "deviant" middle-class value orientation emphasize values and goals and patterns of activity leading toward social mobility: these are the "college boys." Cohen, in general, accepts Whyte's findings, and adds that:

> The working-class child is more often thrown upon his own or the company of an autonomous group of peers. He is freer to explore in many areas forbidden to the middle-class child and to encounter a variety of troubles, scrapes and personally meaningful problems. His learning is likely to be a product of "having fun" or to be motivated by the solution of immediate practical problems. Motivation to work for remote goals attainable only by rational, systematic, self-denying discipline is weak, because the discipline itself is not recognized as a virtue deserving of reward by his parents.[29]

The second type of delinquent described by Bloch and Flynn is the *relatively weak ego* type. Adolescents in this category are described as "insecure; highly aggressive and hostile; marked anxiety; considerable internal conflict." In short, sadly lacking in social skills.

This type of delinquent is described as ". . . frequently oldest child in small families," which meets the hypothesized criterion for inability of siblings to provide opportunities to attain social skills. The families are characteristically unbroken and native-born.

The group character of the offenses displays poor social skills, as they are "incorrigible" and "destructive," i.e., *antisocial.* Offenses were least oriented to peer-age delinquency, and were above all not *gang* delinquencies.[30]

This type comes from the best residential areas, which are settled and have adequate and conventional institutions.

Their scholarship is average to poor, but the best of the three types

---

28. Cohen adds "delinquent boys" to Whyte's classification of "corner boys" and "college boys." Miller's "stable" lower-class boys (type one) is nearly identical to what both Cohen and Whyte refer to as "corner boys": See Kvaraceus and Miller, op. cit., p. 72; and Cloward and Ohlin, op. cit., p. 92.

29. Cohen, op. cit., p. 100.

30. An interesting illustration of this is presented in Ira Henry Freeman's novel, *Out of the Burning: The Story of a Boy Gang Leader* (New York: Crown Publishers, Inc., 1960). The hero is the youngest of five children, and is extremely socially adept. He is the leader of a delinquent fighting gang. His oldest brother, who is also the oldest child, engages in a kind of isolated, nongang delinquency pattern that is extremely antisocial and shows a high level of interpersonal inadequacy, imperceptiveness, and aggressiveness.

of delinquents. They seldom leave school, and are not as apt to be employed while students.

The general orientation is neither to family nor to peers, but to society, to attain educational and long-range occupational ends. Here we see the articulation of higher socio-economic status with middle-class values emphasizing deferred gratification.[31]

Bloch and Flynn's third personality structure is the relatively integrated delinquent. This type is characterized by relatively integrated personality controls, and can be expected to become a mature adult. They are less delinquent than are the other two types. Recidivism is 22.2 per cent as compared with 52.6 and 51.6 per cent for the defective superegos and the weak egos. Also, the average time of first adjudication is 15-16 years old, much older than for the other two personality types.

Both parents and peers are able to provide opportunities: (a) family structure is stable, with good marital relations and conventional moral ideas; there are effective techniques of control over their children; (b) there is close participation in the dominant peer-age culture, and performance in school is longer and better than for the other two types.

It is difficult to discern the causes of delinquency in this type. Nearly all adolescents engage in delinquency (as legally defined) to some extent. Perhaps this type is demonstrating little more than "normal" deviation.[32] Their principal lack is the "unstable and poor community controls" and "less desirable residential areas." Also, the usual pattern is to seek employment upon completion of high school, which is seen as "typical of low-status class and income levels."

Although Bloch and Flynn have found some systematic differences in the kind and quantity of delinquency associated with different personality types, an explanation of these differences is found in different social and cultural environments. In this sense, our orientation is one of "cultural transmission" or "culture conflict" rather than "psychogenic." Delinquency, from this viewpoint, is ". . . not an expression or contrivance of a particular kind of personality; it may be imposed upon any kind of personality if circumstances favor intimate association with delinquent models." [33] Of course Cohen is acutely aware that the phe-

31. For documentation, see Leanna K. Barker's study of 75 "working-class" and 71 "middle-class" boys in an Indiana junior high school, unpublished, but reported in Cohen, op. cit., pp. 105-108.

32. These delinquents are either one-time offenders, or members of organized delinquent groups. Cohen claims that ". . . practically all children, regardless of social class, commit delinquencies, is beyond dispute," op. cit., p. 38.

33. Ibid., pp. 13-14. A classic statement of this "cultural-transmission" theory of juvenile delinquency is contained in Clifford R. Shaw and Henry D. McKay, *Social Factors in Juvenile Delinquency*, Vol. II of National Commission of Law Observance and Enforcement, *Report on the Causes of Crime* (Washington: U. S. Government Printing Office, 1931).

nomena of delinquency are to be explained with both cultural and psychogenic factors: they are complementary. In fact, his point of departure is the psychogenic assumption that all human action—not delinquency alone—is an ongoing series of efforts to solve problems, which involve, until they can be resolved, a certain tension, and a disequilibrium.[34] This is the actor's frame of reference. It is at the concern for the perceived situation, rather than the objective situation itself, that *this* study departed. In this choosing process, the adolescent, to attain satisfactory solutions, must actually change his frame of reference. "The actor may give up pursuit of some goal which seems unattainable, but it is not a 'solution' unless he can first persuade himself that the goal is, after all, not worth pursuing; in short his values must change." [35]

This orientation enables the hypothetical framework developed here to potentially explain such phenomena as the growth and institutionalization of adolescent subcultures. For ". . . the crucial condition for the emergence of new cultural forms is the existence, *in effective interaction with one another, of a number of actors with similar problems of adjustment.*" [36] When there are significant groups in similar circumstances that perceive conceivable solutions to their problems which do not exist as a cultural model, a *new* solution may have more appeal than previously institutionalized responses. If innovators in the new solution (in the social milieu perceived by members of groups of adolescents) are supported and rewarded by other groups, by their referents, the result is mutual exploration and joint elaboration of the new solution.[37] This orientation to social change was employed by Cohen to explain the emergence of institutionalized juvenile delinquency. This conception of

---

34. Cohen, op. cit., p. 51. It is not necessary to assume, as Cohen does, that attainment of goals results in equilibrium. An alternative view—after Emile Durkheim, *Suicide: A Study in Sociology*, trans. by J. A. Spaulding and George Simpson, ed. by Simpson (New York: The Free Press, 1951), esp. Chap. 5—would be to postulate that the attainment of goals leads to the desire to attain *new* goals. Our model can be viewed as a game, where the players, on the basis of their information, play rationally to optimize their reward. But in life, as in the general theory of games, rational behavior is not tantamount to homeostasis: See Norbert Wiener, *Cybernetics: Or Control and Communication in the Animal and the Machine,* second ed. (Cambridge, Mass.: The M.I.T. Press, 1961), esp. p. 159.

35. Cohen, op. cit., p. 53.

36. Ibid., p. 59. Italics in text.

37. Ibid., pp. 59-60. An interesting example of such a collective response is the "mass psychoneurosis" in World War I. In order to avoid an unpleasant situation (combat), a few soldiers would "innovate" symptoms of being gassed. "In a few hours a large percentage of this group would begin to drift into the dressing stations, complaining of indefinite symptoms." Edward A. Strecker, *Beyond the Clinical Frontier* (New York: W. W. Norton & Company, Inc., 1940), pp. 77-78, quoted in Cohen, op. cit., p. 62.

social change is equally extensile to the emergence of nondelinquent adolescent subcultures.

If adolescents systematically perceive new ways to attain goals, from references that have not been a legitimate channel of goal attainment, the fact that even a few innovators act rationally to optimize their goals will enhance the chances that other adolescents in the same situation would engage in this activity.

The literature on the behavior of crowds is yet another source of evidence for this innovation process. Cohen refers to the ". . . ability of a propitious interaction situation to generate, in a short time, collective although necessarily ephemeral and unstable solutions to like problems." [38] For example, mob action is usually always preceded by a period of milling during which common sentiments are elaborated and supported.[39]

At this point, the reader may be thinking about the occupational structure of modern Western society. Reference was made to this at the beginning of this section, but it was left dangling to a certain extent. In a society such as the United States, the child is functionally segregated by age. He is not in the economy. The male child perceives that his father is a specialist in his occupational role and is not equipped to help him attain the generalized preparation for the attainment of occupational goals.

The father is in certain respects not an adequate role model for his son. He performs his occupational roles outside of the home. Often, his *social* interaction with *his* peers is also centered outside of the home. And interaction with female peers in the home is restricted by a plethora of social norms. (The father-mother relationship is slightly different, as a role model.) This family structure contributes to the importance of older siblings as role models, and the extreme interpersonal dependence on peers. Adolescent peer interaction is often centered around learning social skills, and a frantic, largely unsuccessful attempt to develop stable interpersonal relations, to establish meaningful same-sex and cross-sex relations within their age grade.[40]

SUMMARY AND CONCLUSIONS

Our purpose in this section of the discussion was to relate the structure of our theoretical model to a variety of studies dealing with the socialization of youth. For the most part an attempt has been made to reanalyze the conclusions drawn by others within the framework of the

---

38. Cohen, op. cit., p. 63.

39. Cf. Kimball Young, *Social Psychology*, 2nd ed. (New York: F. S. Crofts & Co., 1946), p. 398.

40. See D. Ten Houten, op. cit.

proposed scheme. Through a review of the literature pertaining to different kinds of social systems we have indicated that there are striking similarities in the structure and substance of youth behavior and that it is possible to better understand our observations of youth through the application of this model.

The theoretical and hypothetical system discussed in this text is not of course in any final stage of development nor has it been subject to any rigid empirical cross-cultural validation. On the contrary, research related to the model has consisted of studies dealing with a homogeneous group of college students and comparative studies of Negro and white adolescents in different kinds of school settings. The initial analysis of data from these studies and the application of the model to research done by others in other cultures would, we propose, indicate that the model is viable and worthy of further study and commentary.

4. PRESENTATION AND DISCUSSION OF THE LITERATURE

ASIA AND THE NEAR EAST

The organization of this section differs from other sections of the bibliography in that the geographical areas discussed are separated in the bibliographical listing. The discussion in this section covers the following areas:

1. South Asia
2. East Asia
3. Southeast Asia
4. The Near East

In the bibliographical section following the discussion the entries are listed according to major area and specific country.

References noted in the discussion will include area, country, and reference number to assist in the location of discussed items.

Among the countries of Asia represented in this section and in the bibliography immediately following, it becomes apparent that the work concerning adolescents which is here reported falls into several categories. That is to say that there appear to be several areas of major interest which account for much of the available literature. The reasons for this are not readily apparent, but a few possibilities may be suggested. (The specific countries for which entries have been noted are as follows:)

South Asia	*Southeast Asia*	*East Asia*	*The Near East*
Afghanistan	Burma	China	Algeria
Ceylon	Cambodia	Japan	Egypt
India	Indonesia	Korea	Iran
Pakistan	Laos	Mongolia	Iraq
General	Malaya	Taiwan	Israel
	Philippines	General	Jordan
	Thailand		Lebanon
	Vietnam		Morocco
	General		Saudi Arabia
			Syria
			Turkey
			Yemen
			General

First, the kinds of problems most frequently investigated are those which loom large in many countries: problems of culture change; educational development and reform; the attitudes and values of adolescents; marriage and courtship practices; the growth, nature, and control of juvenile delinquency; and the adolescent in relation to the family, the school, and the teacher. A second possibility is the nature and composition of the academic facilities in the various countries. In many areas, the work has been sponsored and conducted by students from western countries. In other cases the work has been supported by national groups and government agencies.

One of the areas of interest is the role of education and the adjustment of the population in a period of social change. In many cases the institution of education can be seen as a stimulus for unrest among the young. This unrest is manifested in the changing social structure, the attitudes and interests of youth, the activities of youth, and the selection of new leaders in the involved areas.

Speaking of the formation of the new elite (South Asia, Afghanistan —1), Eberhard notes that the new elite is being drawn in great part from the traditional elite and from urban areas. In addition he notes that many leaders of the future are coming from the bureaucratic elite and the educational elite, both sources of social mobility. In this case education serves as an agent of change in the formation of elites. In another area, on the other hand, (Near East, Egypt—13), the situation is different. Egyptian society is not homogeneous and the children of the well-to-do, the old aristocracy, tend to become rigid and hold extreme views concerning westernization and political ideologies. In this case the children of the growing middle class are more flexible and are being drawn upon for the positions which will determine the leaders of the future. The children of the peasant classes, here as everywhere, have only limited avenues of mobility and remain detached from the mainstream of Egyptian life.

A number of articles on Ceylon also deal with the area of education and culture change. (South Asia, Ceylon—1, 4, 7, 8.) In one article, the author (Ceylon—1) discusses value systems, transmission of values, barriers to acculturation, and the content of the educational program. This author maintains that the development of the British missionary school system led to a large middle- and upper-class group which was English educated and whose social position led them to an overt rejection of the indigenous culture. In this educational system subjects of academic value rather than subjects of cultural or practical value have been emphasized. Another article (Ceylon—7) makes a similar point with regard to performance on intelligence tests. Thus, membership in a social class which provides children with a university education has meant that these children tend to disdain manual, practical, and mechanical tasks. This leads to a relatively low performance on intelligence tests of the nonlanguage variety. The traditional values, high status for government work, distaste for agriculture, and the rejection of manual work among the educated are repeated in the Ryan article (Ceylon—4).

Investigating the effect of urban and secular contact on family and fertility values, Tambiah and Ryan (Ceylon—8) expected that the jungle village would reveal more traditional values than the urban areas. This was supported for individuals, the more urban oriented tended to be less traditional, but considering communities as a whole they were unable to support their hypothesis.

Moving to India (South Asia, India—27, 74, 80, 94, 107, 116), one author, discussing the educational differentials in South India (India—27), notes that changes in one part of the social system are likely to cause changes in other parts. He anticipates that, as the lower classes in India become educated, they will realize the injustices under which they labor and will become even more dissatisfied. Among the educated, Taylor (India—107) notes differential rates of change for Hindu attitudes in a situation of culture conflict. The rate of change and resistance to change depends upon the area of belief under examination. Those beliefs which reveal the most change center on Hindu attitudes toward social problems. Taylor also notes that the external influences which tend to promote change are usually not as complex as the local influences which work to resist change.

In another area, the specific topics of attitude change are revealed by Rath (India—74). His investigation of 800 university students showed that they generally favor the emancipation of women, the joint family system, a classless society, basic education, and the mixing of the sexes in schools. Many of the students were not favorably inclined toward the present system of education. Another investigation which generally supports Rath was done by Shukla (India—94). This investigator found a general dislike toward communalism, untouchability, polygamy, prostitution, and blind religious faith. He also found that while many students favored democracy, there was some attraction to communism in spite of the fact that many of the students had little awareness of the actual nature of communism.

In some respects the reaction of the students noted above are explicated and illustrated by Eells (South Asia, General—2), in his discussion of communism in education. The strategy of the student Communist leaders in manipulating a popular issue for their own ends such as capitalizing on the poor student living conditions, lack of student autonomy, and academic freedom, appeals to a number of students regardless of their information of the actuality of the Communist position.

A 1960 article by Ray (India—80) in the *New Leader*, aptly illustrates the interaction between education and cultural dissatisfaction. In this article, Ray notes that two universities had to close their doors for a period and other universities are threatened by student strikes, demonstrations, and vandalism. He feels that the unrest of the students is due to the great disparity existing between the new aspirations arising in India and the actual present conditions which, in many cases, preclude the fulfillment of these aspirations. Here, in effect, the student perceives desired goals which have few available avenues of approach. He is unable to identify significant referents which will be of assistance in the accomplishment of his goals. Ray places responsibility on the government and its plan for free and compulsive education which has placed an undue strain on the educational system and has driven many teachers into other areas. The unrest of the students then is a sign of a desire for education and knowledge, expressed in one available means of communication open to the students.

Moving to East Asia, namely Japan, we note a 1956 article on the problems of the implementation of the Fundamental Law of Education (1947) (East Asia, Japan—153). The authors note social tension between the public and the new educational policy as well as internal problems in the policy. With education being viewed as a means for improving socio-economic status, the demand for education increased rapidly. A strain was placed on the development of facilities and the maintenance of educational institutions. In addition, job opportunities could not keep up with the increased number of college graduates. In another area, the value of vocational courses was reduced to the point where they were not viewed as important by the public in comparison to the college preparatory courses.

A 1950 article by Cole (East Asia, Japan—20) reflects the dissatisfaction of the youth of Japan with the existing order. Cole notes that the results of opinion polls suggest that youth are more ready for change than are the elders. The youth are described as being in a state of revolt against parents, professors, social mores, and frequently traditional religious values. The activity of the Communist students is also noted here as it was in Ceylon. This orientation is also reflected in (East Asia, Japan—33).

Discussing postwar cultural change in communities in northeastern Japan, Norbeck (East Asia, Japan—119) notes that social change in the examined communities is characterized by a weakening of kinship bonds, a weakening of personal ties, and changes in authority patterns resulting in the weakening of the hierarchial family structure. Rural and cooperative associations have, to a large degree, taken over many former duties of the kinship group. Directly applicable to the youth is the finding that, while legal primogeniture has been abolished, it is continued in practice. This places the eldest son in a poor position since the youngest are likely to receive the education necessary for them to move into new areas while the eldest must stay on the farm or go into the traditional parental occupation. This also puts the eldest son at a disadvantage in the area of marriage since many young girls would rather marry a younger son than be tied to the eldest with little hope of ever leaving the farm and its hard work. Implied in this is the notion that the "love marriage" is to some degree replacing the traditionally arranged marriage.

When we look at China (East Asia, China—21, 30, 83) we see a similar pattern. In an early article (China—21) Chin notes that the personal problems developing in a period of social change may not be a result of conflicting behavior patterns but may rather be a result of the lack of appropriate behavior patterns and cues. He notes the destruction of generational continuity as a result of social mobility based on occupational achievement and discusses the adolescents' problem in the discrepancy between the parental role model and their own conception of masculine and feminine roles. Chin feels that, while the original effects of the Shanghi period were felt among the students, by 1948 the effects had generalized to a second group comprised of white-collar workers and high school students. Another 1948 study (China—83) notes that students in the study rejected traditional landlordism and private capitalism as a possibility for Chinese economy. These students revealed a strong desire for democracy and equality in both the political and social areas.

Complaints concerning the discrepancy between education and occupation are not restricted to non-Communist countries as witnessed by a 1957 article (East Asia, China—30), in which the author specifically refers to Communist China and students' objections that their jobs are not consistent with their levels of education. This article also notes a confusion among these students regarding the differences between socialist democracy and bourgeois democracy.

Occupational interests and attitudes of both adolescents and adults have been the subjects of several works in this section. Ramsey and Smith (East Asia, Japan—138) note striking similarities between Japanese and American samples with regard to the general ranking of occupational prestige and the social importance of occupations. More directly to the point of occupational aspirations and formation of occupational interests is the article by Goodman (East Asia, Japan—43) in which occupational aspirations of elementary school children in Japan and America were examined to get at value-attitude-concept systems. With the exception of the higher level of sophistication exhibited by the American children, both samples revealed a high degree of similarity of aspiration for given age levels. The American's sophistication centered in knowledge of the occupational requirements of an urban technological society. Japanese children showed more interest in political and mass media occupations. American children revealed more interest in the "glamour" type occupations, but the emphasis of professional occupations was general in both samples. The differences in cultural content of the two samples was also reflected in the comments made by the children in their responses.

Students from rural schools in India (South Asia, India—116) do not seem to have especially defined occupational goals. However, most do not want to be engaged in the occupations which their fathers hold. This reflects the changing cultural patterns and the shifting structure of opportunity which affects the younger and older generations differently. Several articles stress the differences between foreign-born and native-born youth and their occupational aspirations. An article by Green (Southeast Asia, General—5) specifies the occupational differences in aspirations and goals between the East and the West. The author relates these differences to the structure of occupational aspirations among 1365 Ceylonese students. One article from Israel (Near East, Israel—9) notes that both Yemenite and non-Yemenite youth desire to "climb the social ladder" occupationally. This article also notes differences in these groups with regard to reading matter and school performance. It is shown that, generally, Yemenite youth prefer historical works while non-Yemenite youth prefer fiction. Articles from both India and Japan indicate a similarity between the reading interests of youth from different lands. (South Asia, India—9, 71; East Asia, Japan—80).

With regard to the interest and influence of foreign films, Cressey (South Asia, India—12) concluded that the interests of Indian students paralleled the interests of United States students. However, he did note that cultural differences and a feeling of social distance tended to limit the influence of foreign films among the Indian students. Much of this reaction was attributed to the growing feeling of nationalism prevalent in India in 1935.

One area in which the American student seems to perpetually take second place to his counterpart in other nations is the area of politics. Such comparisons of student political activity, are far from rare. While many of the articles make mention of political activities, four make special note of the role of the student in the politics of Asia.

Spector (Southeast Asia, Malaya—3) notes a great number of Chinese youth in schools. This, coupled with the traditionally high status of the student leads him to believe that these students are the intellectual cadre of the present and the future. At the time of the article (1955), the active students in politics were identifying themselves with the Chinese Student Movement and were in close association with revolutionary movements in mainland China. Llewellyn (South Asia, India—48) also notes the formidable force of the student in countries from Egypt to China. While many of the students in East Pakistan are politically active, relatively few are Communists (1954). The small number of Communists, however, are very active and tend to leave the more idealistic type leaders behind in their drive for influence among the students. Llewellyn feels that the pull to the left is inevitable.

A recent article by Lifton (East Asia, Japan—92) discusses the psychological patterns of Japanese youth with reference to their political activities. He notes that the role of the student in social movements in Japan is not atypical of students over the world. The student has always played an important role in social change and revolutions. The political actions of Japanese youth, according to Lifton, can still go either to the moderate course or to the totalist camp. He gives an excellent discussion of the totalist and the moderate positions. One further article (Southeast Asia, Burma—1) notes the role of the Student Union in the development of future leaders. In this case the union acts as a forum in which student opinions and communication development can begin to forge the traits of the leaders of the future years.

With regard to opinions of students toward the United States, a range of conclusions can be noted. Adams, for example (South Asia, Pakistan—1), notes a great desire on the part of Pakistani high school students to get information about the United States. She is impressed by the similarities between the Pakistani and the American student with regard to their interests and desires. A 1955 article by Conroy (East Asia, Japan—21) notes a great ambivalence among the students toward American policies and personnel. This ambivalence centers in the political arena with their dissatisfaction with United States foreign policy.

The majority of articles examined for this review concentrated on the attitudes of foreign students toward the United States during or after their stay here as students. One article of general interest (South Asia, India—38), written in 1951, notes the general reaction of Indian students upon their return to India. Examination of a group of 100 students revealed that, prior to coming to the United States, 68 per cent had favorable opinions of the United States. After a short while in this country 89 per cent had favorable opinions. However, after being here between 4 and 40 months 22 per cent of the group still had favorable opinions, 21 per cent had mixed views and 57 per cent had definitely unfavorable opinions. Among objectionable items were noted the lack of true democracy, especially in treatment of races, and the lack of awareness of spiritual values in Americans.

One examination of Indian students' attitudes toward the family life, political activity, and race relations in the United States revealed that the Indian student examines the United States through Indian-colored glasses. That is to say the Indians' attitudes are directly related to his degree of Indianness. The results of such observations are useful in structuring foreign students' visits (South Asia, India—47). In the same area, it was found by Gezi (Middle East, General—7) that the adjustment of the Arab student to American life was highly associated with his perceptions of the willingness of Americans to interact with Arabs and also to meet them socially. Davis (Middle East, General—4) also notes surprise, ambivalence, and intragroup uncertainty among middle eastern students in the United States. Contrary to his expectations, the length of time the student had been in this country did not greatly influence his attitudes toward America. Length of stay did not influence cultural perspectives in a consistent manner.

Turkish students express surprise at the amount of racial discrimination found in the United States. This group revealed few sex differences in the attitudes toward racial discrimination. In this case (Davis, Near East, Turkey—3) a small relationship was found between the length of stay in the United States and the formation of negative attitudes toward racial discrimination.

With regard to Japanese students Passin and Bennet (East Asia, Japan—135, 136) note that the period of study in the United States is intense and the return to Japan is sometimes difficult for the student, but the formation of unfavorable reactions to the United States is far from inevitable. These authors specify three student types which react differently to the United States and differently to their return home; the Ideologist who is perpetually dissatisfied; the Adjustor who comes for skills and returns with anticipation; and the Nationalist who is negatively oriented to the United States and includes both the extreme rightwing and Communist students.

Moving from the area of occupations and politics to the area of parent-child relationships and the structure of families we find the following: as child-rearing practices vary from one culture to the next, so do parent-adolescent relationships. In one area they may be consistent and traditionally oriented, in an area of rapid social and technological change they may be relatively inconsistent and often antagonistic and present and future oriented. Among the articles examined which are applicable here are the following: (East Asia, Japan—38, 98, 137, 161, 206; East Asia, China—15, 17, 56; Near East, Israel—21, 68).

In an examination of 1054 Japanese high school students in Nogoya City, Japan, Yoda and Kuse (East Asia, Japan—206) come to the conclusion that the acquisition of independence by the adolescent is a gradual process which accelerates with age. Within the adolescent group the feelings toward independence vary. Generally, the adolescent desires independence but retains the hope that the parent will be supportive and helpful in the future when the adolescent is facing family problems of his own.

One 1947 article (East Asia, Japan—98) discusses the effect of industrialization on the family structure and the composition of the population. This author notes that urban areas are becoming heavily populated by single individuals and independent family groups. Poor families in the cities strive to keep the size of the family to a minimum and the removal of single individuals from the rural setting to the urban contributes to the breakdown of the traditional family system. This is traceable to the introduction of new productive techniques which removed home industry workers and put them in the factory. The author sees the disintegration of the traditional family system as having a grave effect on the structure of national life and the potential changes it includes.

Articles out of China indicate that the problem of parent-adolescent relations does not respect ideological boundaries. One 1953 article (East Asia, China—56) by Lee notes that modern education and Western influences have weakened the traditional family ties, resulted in the decline of the large family system, increased emphasis on the conjugal family, and have gradually emancipated women. The change in values and orientation has taken place mainly among the youth, due to the programs of the Peking regime. A more recent article (1959) elaborates on this theme (East Asia, China—15). Chen and Chen discuss the changing attitudes toward parents in Communist China. This discussion, based on secondary sources, notes that at an earlier time the Peking government encouraged youth to rebel against traditional family ties and filial loyalty as a part of the social reorganization of China. This program fostered neglect of aged people and the breakdown of discipline of the youth and cost the state the support of many of the older generation. Under the new program loyalty to the state is still emphasized, but loyalty to the parents and a respect for the traditional ways is also being recaptured. The program of the people's republic appears to focus on the notion that the adolescent looks to his parents for support and aid. If then the parents can be discredited as sources of assistance the state can step in as a substitute parent and mold the adolescent into a more useful tool. In an extremely oversimplified fashion this reflects our thesis, discussed earlier, that the adolescent recognizes as valuable referents those whom he evaluates as having both the power and the interest to assist him in the accomplishment of his goals. The fact that the Peking program did not achieve full effectiveness is not to say that the theory behind it is faulty. This is not to condone the theory and the program, but only to illustrate the availability of reasonable explanations for the activities of adolescents.

A number of studies have been done in Asia on the role of the adolescent in the school, teacher-student relations, and the performance of the student in the academic classroom. Amng those listed we see (South Asia, Pakistan—3, 4, 5, 6, 7; South Asia, India—29, 43, 57, 59, 99, 112; East Asia, China—10, 13, 14, 16; East Asia, Japan—81, 154).

Two articles from India reveal that student evaluations of teachers do not seem to differ greatly from the evaluations made of teachers by American students. (South Asia, India—29, 112). In one study it was found that the top five teacher traits preferred by students were knowing how to teach, making the work interesting, a lack of partiality, a knowledge of the subject matter, and being on time to classes. The other study reveals a liking for teachers who like their pupils, do not punish students, are good natured, simple, punctual, and interesting. One of the problems in education in many countries is getting the student in the school. It was found in Pakistan (South Asia, Pakistan—4) that low income was related to whether or not rural parents sent their children to school. The role of education did not seem too great when income was low and the child was needed in the hereditary occupation. A comparison of rural and urban Japanese youth (East Asia, Japan—81) found that the urban youth did much better in school than did the rural children. This was particularly true in the areas of Japanese, science, and mathematics. The role of the technical school in the preparation of the student for useful existence is illustrated in Vietnam where more and more students are preparing themselves for occupations through trade school attendance (Southeast Asia, Vietnam—2). Again and again one finds reference to the poverty of the schools in many countries, particularly Pakistan (Pakistan—7). This is not to point a finger at Pakistan for the specter of poverty haunts many educational systems, even in the United States, where all students are believed to have great advantages of education which are not available to other peoples. Attitudes toward education are also reflected by articles such as Pakistan—5 and Pakistan —6. Differences in political orientations, occupational possibilities, and the paucity of leisure activities as well as the cultural limitations set on the activities of students serve to drastically separate the American student from his Asian counterpart.

Deviant behavior in the schools is far from an unknown phenomenon. Among Indian adolescents, withdrawing and nervous habits are regarded as serious problems while lack of discipline and transgression of authority are felt to be least serious. Overcuriosity about sex is seen as a major transgression by youth. Another Indian study (India—99) presents the problem of truancy in the schools. In the study it was found that no correlation existed between truancy and family and home factors. What was correlated was truancy and the student's failure in examinations and also the lack of enthusiasm on the part of teachers.

The specter of deviant behavior raises the question of juvenile delinquency and its relation to the adolescents of various areas of Asia and the world. Going first to a statement on delinquency in primitive society we note an article by Singh (South Asia, India—97) concerning the aboriginals of India. This author notes causes of delinquency in urban India are not unlike those noted for the urban United States. However, he proposes that, as a result of more effective control of the child's education and behavior, there prevails a high degree of discipline. The appropriate patterns are well defined and tradition has such a firm hold in the aboriginal group that delinquency has little room to flourish. Gokhale also notes similar causes of delinquency in India and the United States. Specifically he notes the importance of significant adults in the adolescents' environment (South Asia, India—28). Hamza (Near East, Egypt—10) in noting that Egyptian delinquents are far from a homogeneous group and specifying contributing factors to their formation also supports the foregoing comments.

Eisenstadt, discussing the delinquent activities among immigrant youth (Near East, Israel—27), notes that, among these youth, social stability is low; social organization is low; communication and identification with the community are low; and there often is a discrepancy between the parents' aspirations and the possibility of the adolescents' achievement of these aspirations.

Both Lunden (East Asia, Japan—94) and Shimizu (East Asia, Japan —151) have discussed the increase in the rates of juvenile delinquency in Japan during and after the war. Lunden interprets the great increase in delinquency over the prewar period in terms of the postwar conditions of the country. Both the social and the economic conditions contribute to the increase. The prevailing conditions lead the youth to acts which would, hopefully, never have been committed in normal times. Lunden holds that a return to normal social and economic conditions will reduce the delinquency rate with the same rapidity with which they caused the increase. Shimizu attempts to establish that a rise in delinquency occurs both in times of social change and after great catastrophe. He offers a distinction between crime following catastrophe and crime in a period of modernization. He feels that the delinquency rate in Japan is a pathological symptom of the distorted social system of Japan.

A recent study on juvenile delinquency by Devos and Mizushima (East Asia, Japan—29) attempts to get at cultural perspectives on delinquency by the comparison of American and Japanese lower-class males. They were interested in seeing if delinquency and nonconformity in general were functions of the adolescents' attitudes toward the goal-attaining opportunities in a given culture (the Merton paradigm) or if it arose as a result of early training. It is the validity of the various views of delinquency which are in question in the article. Among the many findings it was shown that truancy in Japan as well as the United States was an early manifestation of delinquent attitudes or an inability to operate effectively in the school situation. The conclusion reached by these authors shows the heavy reliance placed by both the United States and Japan on the school as a critical social institution and emphasizes that the schools will be forced to play a more central role in the correction and prevention of delinquent activities among the adolescents of both countries.

One specific article concerns itself with a comparison of two types of delinquent youths in Chinese society (East Asia, China—60). The author maintains that there are two types of peer groups in Chinese adolescent life. These two peer groups and the attendent subcultures connected with them are seen as two different adolescent reactions to the modernization and Westernization of Japan. Each of these peer groups has its own attitudes, structure, and behaviors.

The relationship between the sexes is discussed in a number of investigations. Among many industrializing and modernizing nations the trend toward the liberation of women is reflected in the attitudes toward dating and marriage (South Asia, India—89; Pakistan—8). It was found for example, that among married and unmarried college students in India, the married students were the best adjusted. This is analogous to the reported situation in the United States.

Several articles on Japan treat this area (see Japan—8, 9, 27, 181, 199, and 201). Asayama (Japan—8) notes that the development of the Japanese adolescent with regard to sexual development and heterosexual adjustment was not very different from that of the American youth as reported by Kinsey. The democratization of family life and the emancipation of women is being strongly felt (East Asia, Japan—81). The provisions of the new civil code allow that the bride and groom should determine the match, but the weight of the arranged marriage as a traditional form lingers on. Even so it is not dysfunctional as illustrated by Vogel (Japan—199) when he discusses the role of the marriage arranger. The go-between has a functional purpose in a society in the process of industrialization where mobile workers have a hard time finding brides. He is, in effect, a substitute for dating and a referee for assuring a good match where personal ties are important. To this extent the go-between serves as a buffer to rapid social change by integrating the traditional concerns of the parents and the desires of the youth in a greater degree of freedom in mate selection. Baber reveals some figures in his 1961 article on the attitudes of Japanese youth toward mate selection. He found in a sample of 5,000 Japanese youth that 75 per cent say they believe in sexual equality *theoretically*, but *practically* they have doubts; 80 per cent of the males felt that the "love match" was the ideal type; more than 80 per cent of both males and females felt that, in cases of parental conflict, the desires of the youth should prevail; and 80 per cent felt that the go-between was a nice convention. Baber concludes that the Japanese youth are breaking away from the traditional attitudes toward marriage. For a discussion of the attitudes toward arranged marriages in rural Japan see East Asia, Japan—201.

One final area we should touch on is a general area which includes the attitudes of adolescents, their activities in groups, and the presence or absence of youth groups and peer-group behavior. In a popular magazine presentation Gray notes that to some extent the Japanese youth are becoming a cheap copy of American teen-agers. In spite of the fact that the Japanese youth are intellectually sophisticated they fail to have many of the social skills which are found in the youth of the United States. In direct opposition to previous remarks the author emphasized the low rate of delinquency in Japan. He notes that, for a modern industrial country, 1 per cent of the youth involved in delinquencies (recorded) is a very small number (East Asia, Japan—46).

Vogel and Vogel (East Asia, Japan—200) note that by American standards the Japanese child is very dependent on his parents. They are slow to adjust in school and they are more reserved than Americans in new groups. With American children the push for independence comes from the child himself, but with the Japanese the parents must provide the push to independence. It was felt that the Japanese more than the Americans prefer the structured situation.

Rural-urban differences in adolescents' attitudes are illustrated by the situation in Egypt (Near East, Egypt—6). This is a study of the characteristics of rural and urban adolescents in Egypt. The author notes that the degree of culture lag in a country such as Egypt is marked. The rural adolescents strongly reflected the dominant culture, the traditional culture. Acceptance by the peer group was found to be a strong theme among urban adolescents but this goal was relatively weak among the rural adolescents.

One section in *Village Japan* (East Asia, Japan—13) concerns itself with the behavior of adolescents prior to marriage. It was apparent in Niike that there was no separate age-group organization for the youth, no basis for the functioning of any type of adolescent culture. No evidence of stress or strain was found among the youth of this village, stress and strain usually associated with adolescents in America. The explanation offered for the absence of an adolescent subculture is the traditional nature of the culture in Niike. In the United States the child is expected to be an individual, to make decisions for himself. He behaves therefore within a loosely structured set of limits differentially enforced. In Niike, however, with its narrowly defined behavioral limits, the emphasis is not on individuality but on the acceptance of and behavior within a rigidly defined normative pattern. Since there is no conflict between the child and the adult, because the child's role does not bring him into conflict with the adult world, there is no adolescent culture. There is instead a definite break between childhood and the assumption of the adult role at about age 15.

Quantitatively, the number of articles, books, and discussions coming out of Israel exceeds that of any other country save the United States in this area. Perhaps the conditions under which the state of Israel was formed contribute to their great interest in the absorbtion of immigrants, the adjustment of individuals, and the effect of kibbutz life on the youth of the country. Some of the most significant work on youth behavior to come out of Israel has centered on the writings of Eisenstadt. One of Eisenstadt's main points is that specific age groups are present in a society in which the family or wider kinship group is not the basic unit of the social division of labor. Modern society is a prime example of a nonfamilistic society (Near East, Israel—29).

Another article, which eventually led to the writing of *From Generation to Generation,* is Eisenstadt's 1951 article in the *British Journal of Sociology.* In this article Eisenstadt discusses typical patterns of the social life of the youth in Israel. He notes that a number of youth cultures exist in Israel and attempts to show that they can be related to the social structure in Israel. Again the hypothesis that the emergence of youth culture is related to the place of the family in the social division of labor is promoted and substantiated. Among the conclusions reached in the article are the following: (1) the emergence of the youth culture is closely correlated with the loss of the family's function as the basic unit of the social division of labor; (2) despite a long preparation for adulthood within the context set by the adults, the youth is generally not prepared for the assumption of adult roles; (3) the high degree of specialization in society and the state of childhood socialization create a definite interruption in the identification transference of the adolescent from child to adult environments.

For additional information as to the type of material coming out of Israel see Near East, Israel—12, 57, 85, 91.

One final note in the annotations in this section. Special acknowledgment is due to C. S. Brembeck and E. W. Weidner and their publication *Education and Development in India and Pakistan,* Michigan State University Education in Asia, Series I, College of Education and International Programs. Several of the annotations were selected from this publication and adapted for inclusion here.

SOUTH ASIA

AFGHANISTAN

1. Eberhard, Wolfram, "Afghanistan's Young Elite," *Asian Survey,* I (February, 1962), 3-22.

   The author asks where the future leaders come from, what is their social background, and does the trend indicate a new and strong mobility pattern. He notes that the coming elite was recruited largely from urban circles and drawn heavily from the old elite. He also notes a great mobility through government-type jobs and that the future leaders are being drawn from the bureaucratic elite and what is coming to be the educational elite.

CEYLON

1. Green, T. L., "Cross-Cultural Educational Adaptation in Ceylon," *Journal of Educational Sociology*, XXIX (January, 1956), 292-302.

   A descriptive discussion of culture change and the field of education in Ceylon. The author discusses the value system, the transmission of values, the psychology of childhood, barriers to acculturation, and the content of the educational program.

   It is noted that in Ceylon the British development of the missionary-originated educational system led eventually to a large English-educated middle-class and upper-class elite whose social position led them to a strong rejection of the indigenous culture.

   The family organization is patriarchal with the women and children subservient to the men. Children are expected to be submissive to authority, to conform to parental demands and the social mores, and to be dependent. The social climate of the educational system is authoritarian in its conformity.

   With regard to the psychology of the child, it is noted that occupational ambition stems from status factors rather than persistence and interest. Manual skill and dexterity are high but, while the youth perform well on tasks demanding verbal skills, they perform poorly when faced with tasks demanding non-language skills.

   The author concludes that social and economic pressures have emphasized academic subjects rather than those of cultural or practical value. In the future educational development of Ceylon this problem must be dealt with by close attention to the development of educational curricula.

2. Ryan, Bryce, "The Sinhalese System in Transition," in *Caste in Modern Ceylon* (New Brunswick, N. J.: Rutgers University Press, 1953).

   An article discussing the traditional caste system of Ceylon and the present situation of change which is leading to the disorganization of the caste system. Caste as a prestige factor is losing its potency in favor of occupational, political, and economic factors.

3. Ryan, Bryce, "Socio-Cultural Regions of Ceylon," *Rural Sociology*, XV (1950), 3-19.

4. Ryan, Bryce, "Status, Achievement and Education in Ceylon; An Historical Perspective," *Journal of Asian Studies*, XX (August, 1961), 463-476.

Some of the traditional values held in Ceylon include high status associated with government work, the denigration of agriculture, the value of wealth in land, and an attitude which says that work is not an end in itself. Thus parents and university students are most interested in government jobs. Middle-class children denigrate manual work.

In the area of education, the curriculum is European oriented. Agriculture is being introduced into the schools. Education in English, a high status factor, has been closed to the rural youth. Thus 49 per cent of all university students were children of government employees.

The author concludes, "Insofar as meeting the issue of a functional curriculum and realistic status striving, it is conceivable that recent trends have moved in reverse, despite some attention given to vocational training in the schools." (475) The new trend has been to preserve Sinhalese culture and Buddhist tradition.

5. Straus, M. S., "Childhood Experience and Emotional Security in the Context of the Sinhalese Social Organization," *Social Forces*, XXIII (December, 1954), 152-160.

A study dealing with childhood training, care, and emotional security among a sample of 48 third-grade children in the village of Pelpola, Raiygam Koralle, Ceylon.

6. Straus, M. S., "Family Characteristics and Occupational Choice of University Entrants as Clues to the Social Structure of Ceylon," *University of Ceylon Review*, IX (1951), 125-135.

7. Straus, M. S., "Mental Ability and Cultural Needs: A Psychocultural Interpretation of the Intelligence Test Performance of Ceylon University Entrants," *American Sociological Review*, XVI, 3 (June, 1951), 371-375.

A study investigating the reactions and performance of Ceylonese University students to an intelligence test. The test utilized was the California Test of Mental Ability (Advanced, Short Form), in English. The sample consisted of a 50 per cent interval sample of university entrants for the year 1950. 212 students were examined. The test was standardized on an American or English population so as to permit cross-cultural comparison.

Among the findings it was noted that the Total Mental Factors score for the male students was 57, which was 7 centile points above the average for American university entrants. The women scored 44.4, 5.6 centile points below comparable scores in the U.S. The Nonlanguage Factors scores were far below the Language Factors scores.

The author concludes, "In Ceylon, as in many Eastern cultures, membership and participation in the social strata which provide children with a university education has traditionally meant a divorce from and a disdain of the type of manual, practical, and mechanical tasks which are known to be positively correlated with performance on nonlanguage tests of intelligence. There is undoubtedly a carryover of this tradition in modern Ceylon." (374)

8. Tambiah, S. J. and Ryan, B., "Secularization of Family Values in Ceylon," *American Sociological Review*, XXII, 3 (June, 1957), 292-299.

The authors examine three samples from Ceylon in an investigation of family values and fertility values. The hypothesis is that strong family and high fertility value are weakened by expanding contacts with the more urban and secular worlds.

The authors conclude that, "The original expectation, that an isolated jungle village would preserve more traditional value positions than communities in the same culture but under secularizing influences, was not supported." (298) They note a tendency toward emancipation from traditional values but, in the urban areas, contacts influence individuals not communities.

Tables are given which show responses to the daughters marrying out of caste; ideal number of children; and son's selection of occupation.

9. U.N. Department of Social Affairs. Division of Social Welfare, *Comparative Study on Juvenile Delinquency: Part IV. Asia and the Far East* (New York: United Nations, 1953).

A comparative appraisal of current practices in the treatment of juvenile delinquency in Burma, Ceylon, India, Japan, Pakistan, Philippines, and Thailand.

INDIA

1. Ansari, Anwar and Bharati Ghose, "A Study of Family Attitudes of Children with Contrasting Socio-Economic Background," *Education and Psychology*, IV, 2 (Delhi: 1957), 90-102.

To test the asumption that children from differing socio-economic backgrounds differ in family relations a TAT type test portraying 11 different semistructured family situations was constructed. Results revealed the following general trends: 1. Lower socio-economic children assume adult roles early in life;

2. The two groups differ in "sense of transgression"; and 3. Higher socio-economic children begin earlier to repress and sublimate basic emotions toward family members. Reproductions of the 11 situations are included.

2. Asthana. Hari Shanker, "Some Aspects of Personality Structuring in Indian (Hindu) Social Organization," *Journal of Social Psychology*, XLIV (1956), 155-163.

3. Bardis, Panos D., "Attitudes toward Dating among Foreign Students in America," *Marriage and Family Living*, XVIII (1956), 339-344.

4. Bohlke, Robert, "Authoritarianism and Attitudes of College Students Toward India," *Journal of Educational Sociology*, XXXIV (September, 1960), 145-160.

5. Brown, F., "British Youth and India's Problems: Peterborough Youth Conference in India," *Asiatic Review*, XLI (July, 1945), 289-291.

6. Brown, James, "History of the Origin and Progress of the Sicks," *Indian Studies Past and Present*, II, 4 (July/September, 1961), 349-383.

7. Carstairs, George Morrison, "Hinjra and Jiryan: Two Derivations of Hindu Attitudes to Sexuality," *British Journal of Medical Psychology*, XXIX (June, 1956), 128-138.

8. Chand, Tara, "The Educational Problems of India," *Asiatic Review*, XLVI, 166 (April, 1950), 986-995.

9. Chander, Ram, "General Reading Interests of High School Students," *Vidja Bhawan Studies*, V (1956-57), 16-33.

A study of 300 students showed interest in reading material available in Hindi only. Few students read newspapers daily, and still fewer were interested in magazine reading. Stories were most liked, followed by novels, religious themes, patriotic themes, drama, and poetry. Some recommendations are given.

10. Chandra Das, Tarak, "Tribal Life in India and its Problems," *Indo Asian Culture*, I, 1 (July, 1952), 284-293.

11. Collver, Andrew, "The Family Cycle in India and the United States," *American Sociological Review*, XXVIII (February, 1963), 86-96.

A study in which the stages of the nuclear family's life are differentiated by data which indicate that the nuclear family's life is much less clearly defined in rural India than in the United States. The basic study was conducted by S. N. Singh in 60 villages near Banaras. Selection of villages was random within three sizes (under 500, 500-1,500, and over 1,500). Twenty-five per cent of the households were selected at random from each of the 60 villages for a total of 1,999 households (7,598 persons including 1,689 couples, 231 widowers, and 418 widows).

The author concludes that, "The stages of the nuclear family's life are much less clearly defined in rural India than in the United States. The extremely young age of marriage in the villages studied accentuates the couple's dependence on the joint household. One consequence of a long childbearing period and high mortality is a large proportion of orphans and widows with dependent children. This again demonstrates the importance of a larger kinship group in providing the stability and continuity the nuclear family lacks. Despite high fertility, the average size of the nuclear family at its maximum, when the mother is 45 years old, is only 5.39, including the parents. Evidence is presented to show that the probability of death for any member of a family is contingent on the survival of other members, and that the mortality of widows, widowers, and orphans is much higher than that of the general population." (86)

12. Cressey, Paul F., "The Influence of Moving Pictures on Students in India," *American Journal of Sociology*, XII, 3 (November, 1935), 341-350.

An investigation of the influence of foreign films on students in India, the frequency of attendance and the type of films most frequently visited. The sample consisted of 233 Indian college students, 148 men and 85 women, in Bombay, Madras, Nagpur, Lucknow, and Lahore in the Spring of 1931.

Questionnaires were used to determine the types of pictures which were of most interest to the students. The influence of pictures on their lives was assessed by means of responses to direct statements about the influence of films in particular situations.

The following findings are discussed: (1) men attend movies more often than women; (2) the most popular films furnished general entertainment (comedy, adventure, and travel); (3) films dealing with American life were popular among the high attenders; (4) Indian films were popular with those who attended only occasionally; (5) the men showed more interest in the romance films than did the women. It was concluded that the interests of Indian students were similar to the interests of American students.

With regard to the influence of the films, it was noted that (1) the frequency of attendance affects the influence of films in general; (2) foreign films make the students aware of their shortcomings but also instill a sense of national pride; (3) as attendance increased, more men desired to become actors. This was not true among the women.

The author concludes that cultural differences and a feeling of social distance tended to limit the influence of foreign films in India. "Their consciousness of being Indians and a growing sense of nationalism introduced a barrier which limited their desire to imitate these non-Indian ways of life." (350)

13. Dass, Ajit Kumar, "The Effect of Westernization on University Students' Attitudes toward Co-Education," *Education and Psychology*, V, 5 (Delhi: 1958), 65-70.

Using a questionnaire and self-rating scale to study the relationship between westernization and attitudes toward co-education, the author obtained a low *r* of .0391 between the two instruments. He concludes there is no definite relationship between the two variables.

14. Dent, H. D., Educational Problems of India," *Asiatic Review*, LI, 185 (January, 1955), 29-39.

15. Deshmukh, Durgaliar, "Education of Girls and Women in Third Plan," *March of India*, XIII (August, 1961), 47-49.

16. Deshpande, A. R., "Education for Social Change," *Journal of Education* (September, 1957), 378-381.

The problem of social change within community development? What to change?

How to transfer skills, practices, movements and institutions developed in one cultural, economic, social, and political context to another has always been the formidable question confronting technical assistance programs.

Improvements in one aspect of life only will not be successful.

Mistake of concentrating technical assistance and resources in one compact area only.

In India, the technical expert and the educator should plan on "how all change can take place."

Chang for progress has to be first born in the minds of the the people.

17. Dhebar, U. N., "Youth and National Reconstruction," *Youth Congress Series*, I (All India Congress Committee, Publications Department, 1956).

18. Dumas, J., "A Study of Fears Among the Children of Three Indian States," *Manasi*, II (1955), 16-22.

Fears of 2,100 children in the Indian States of Gujaret, Rajasthan, and Assam were studied. Fears reported by the children are discussed in relation to the following variables: sex, religion, socio-economic status, and subculture. The three most common fears for the total group were of bhuts, thieves, and fire.

19. Eells, Walter C., *Communism in Education in Asia, Africa and the Far East* (Washington: American Council on Education, 1954).

20. Ehrenfelo, U. R., "Matrilineal Family Background in South India," *Journal of Educational Sociology*, XXVI (April, 1953), 356-361.

21. Elwin, Verrier, *The Muria and Their Ghotul* (Bombay: Oxford York: B. W. Huebsch, Inc., 1924).

22. Floris, G. A., "India's Women on the March," *Contemporary Review*, CCI (January, 1962), 21-23.

23. Gandhi, Mohandas Karamchand, *Young India, 1919-1922* (New York: B. W. Huebsch, Inc., 1924).

24. Gandhi, Mohandas Karamchand, *Young India, 1924-1926* (New York: The Viking Press, Inc., 1927).

25. Ghosh, Molina, "Fantasy Life of Girls at the Pre-Adolescent and Adolescent Stages," *University of Rajasthan Studies* (Education), III (1958), 54-82.

26. Ghoshal, Dr. U. N., "The Spirit of Indian Civilization," *Indo Asian Culture*, III, 3 (January, 1955), 225-245.

27. Gist, Noel P., "Educational Differentials in South India," *Journal of Educational Sociology*, XXVIII (March, 1955), 315-324.

A study attempting to identify the relationship between educational attainment and other social factors such as language group, occupational status, demographic characteristics, and the caste system. The study was conducted in two large urban areas in Mysore State in 1951-52. Over 5,000 interviews were taken in the two areas.

Among the findings we note: a relationship between the educational level of the household heads and the mother tongue; the highly educated tend to hold the high status positions. About one-fifth of the university people were in clerical positions; those with higher education tended to have more children living.

The author concludes that changes in one part of the social system are likely to cause changes in other parts. Thus, as the masses are educated they may become more dissatisfied as they realize the social injustices against them.

28. Gokhale, S., "Juvenile Delinquency in Relation to Social Influences," *Indian Journal of Social Work*, XV (1954), 6-11.

Juvenile delinquency is not the result of any one factor but of various social and environmental factors. Emphasis is placed on the example of significant adults in the juvenile's environment and fostering of law-abiding attitude and faith in justice. Newspapers, literature, films, and music are also felt to be important factors in shaping the child.

29. Goyal, Jagdish Chandra, "An Investigation into the Attitudes of Adolescents towards Teachers and Their Bearing on Teacher Education," *Studies in Education and Psychology*, IV (Delhi: 1955), 51-54.

A survey blank of traits was circulated personally among 400 adolescent boys and girls for checking. The traits most frequently mentioned are grouped into (a) professional and dispositional equipment and (b) personal and social equipment. In the first group, those teachers are liked most who have love for their subjects, do not punish students, are good natured, are refined, make the lesson interesting, and are approachable. In the second group are listed teachers who are impartial, give moral teaching, entertain pupils, are simple and punctual.

30. Hause, E. M., "India under the Impact of Western Political Ideas and Institutions," *Western Political Quarterly*, XIV (December, 1961), 879-895.

31. Hogg, L. A., "Indian Youth and the YMCA," *International Review of Missions*, XXXIII (June, 1944), 280-286.

32. Hussain, Dr. Zakir, "Future of Education in India," *Indo Asian Culture*, II, 4 (July, 1953), 319-328.

The article discusses the Indian dream of education and the future plans for education reform and facilities. Of interest are figures indicating the percentage of eligible children in the educational system.

1. Over 40 per cent between ages 6-11 attend school.
2. Over 10 per cent between ages 11-17 attend school.
3. Over 1 per cent between ages 17-23 attend colleges (1953 figures).

33. Inamdar, S. V., "The Congress Seva Dal," *Indian Affairs*, II (October, 1949), 41-46.

34. Jones, Charles F., "Notes on Indian Education," *Journal of Educational Sociology*, XXVII (September, 1953), 16-23.

35. Kabir, Humayum, "Secondary Education in India: An Overview," *Journal of Educational Sociology*, XXVIII (January, 1955), 194-199.

36. Kapadia, K. M., *Marriage and Family in India* (Bombay: Oxford, Indian Branch, 1958).

37. Kathurkar, V. K., "Stereotypes," *Indian Journal of Psychology*, XXIX (1954), 75-78.

A group of 256 junior and senior college students at Poona and Bombay who volunteered as subjects were asked to supply adjectives which might be used to characterize Maharashtrians and Gujaratis. These adjectives were made into a check list and given to the group, which was made up of partly Maharashtrians and Gujaratis. Each group received a number of favorable adjectives from most of the subjects. There was an additional set of favorable adjectives assigned to the Marashtrians by themselves, and a different but favorable set by the non-Marashtrians. The Gujaratis assigned themselves an additional set of favorable adjectives, but the non-Gujaratis assigned them an additional set of unfavorable ones.

38. Keill, Norman, "Attitudes of Foreign Students," *Journal of Higher Education*, XXII (1951), 188-194, 225.

The student exchange program is now an integral part of our foreign policy, and the fact that foreign students upon their return home will be looked upon as authorities on America emphasized the importance of their attitudes. The attitudes of 100 Indian students were surveyed. Before arrival, 68 per cent had definitely favorable opinions of the United States; after they had been here a short while 89 per cent had such opinions after living here from 4 to 40 months, 22 per cent were still favorably inclined, 21 per cent had "mixed" views, and 57 per cent had definitely unfavorable opinions. The students objected particularly to the lack of true democracy, especially in treatment of races, and to the lack of awareness of spiritual values on the part of the Americans.

39. Kennedy, Beth C., "Rural-Urban Contrasts in Parent-Child Relations in India," *Indian Journal of Social Work*, XV (1954), 162-174.

40. Keremar, Laksh, "Vastugat Jyamit Yogyata Parikshan" (An Achievement Test in Geometry), *Education and Psychology*, II, 3 (1955), 41-46.

41. Khan, Yusuf Husain, "The Educational System in Medieval India," *Islamic Culture*, XXX, 1 (April, 1956), 106-125.

42. Khanna, Aporsh, "Friendship in Adolescents: A Review of Studies," *Journal of Education and Psychology*, XVII-XVIII (1960), 247-250.

Most of the work in this field has been done in the United States and reveals friendship patterns and factors conducive to social acceptance and rejection. The main emphasis in Indian studies has been on the nature and pattern of friendships.

43. Krishnan, B., "Need for Vocational and Educational Guidance at the High School Level," *Journal of Vocational and Educational Guidance*, III (1957), 153-158.

Results from a questionnaire study of 615 high school males in the Mysore area (India) are presented concerning further plans for education and career choice. Most of the subjects state a preference for science training (where most of the examination failures occur). Most students depend on advice of parents—only 18.6 per cent of whom received university education; 31 per cent illiterate. These results indicate a clear need for guidance at the high school level.

44. Kuppusamy, B., "Measurement of Social Distance," *Indian Journal of Psychology*, XXVII (1952), 39-43.

45. Lajpat Ral, LaLa, *Young India, an Interpretation and a History of the Nationalist Movement from Within* (New York: B. W. Huebsch, 1917), Revised.

46. Lambert, Richard D. and M. Bressler, *Indian Students on an American Campus* (Minneapolis: University of Minnesota Press, 1956).

47. Lambert, Richard D. and M. Bressler, "Indian Students and the United States: Cross-Cultural Images," *Annals of the American Academy of Political and Social Science*, CCXCV (1954), 62-72.

This study examines the cross-cultural images of the Indian student with reference to the United States. The authors are interested in ". . . how the 'Indianness' of the student affects his image of the United States." (63) The study was conducted upon Indian students who attend American universities. Three areas of American life were included; family practices, political behavior, and race relations.

Due to the effect of the joint family in India, many students feel that the home has a relatively small degree of importance in American life. Many disapproved of the inferior status accorded old people here. The average Indian student is more attentive, interested, and concerned in politics than the American. He is not generally well informed about American political life. The results of race relations which he encounters in his stay tend to mitigate the criticisms of racial practices in India.

In general, the Indian student observes the United States

through the values of his own country. This should be considered in any program of assistance aimed at the exchange or foreign student.

48. Llewellyn, B., "New Look in East Bengal," *Contemporary Review,* CLXXXVI (October, 1954), 231-234.

An investigation of student political activities in East Bengal based on secondary publications and discussions with teachers and professors. The author notes that students in politics are a formidable force from Egypt to China. In East Pakistan the students are generally against the government (1954) but the number who are Communists are a small percentage of the student body. Many of the students become known and move on to bigger things. The more altruistically motivated and politically oriented students are generally left in the rush and are not as numerous or as visible as the action oriented agitator type. The author feels that the long run will show that neither military aid, nor pacts, nor stronger government rule will be able to halt the political movement toward the left.

49. Loeffler, Rebecca W., *Our Country Is India: By Young Indians and Their Leaders* (New York: Friendship Press, 1946).

50. Loomba, Ram Murti, "Moral Judgments of University Students of Philosophy," *Indian Journal of Educational Research,* III (1951), 8.

51. Mandelbaum, David G., *Materials for a Bibliography of the Ethnology of India* (Berkeley, Calif.: University of California Press, 1949).

52. Mayer, Adrian C., *Caste and Kinship in Central India* (Berkeley, Calif.: University of California Press, 1960).

53. Ministry of Education, A *Review of Education in India: 1956-57, Submitted to the XXth International Conference on Public Education, Geneva, July, 1957,* No. 287 (Kaslmere Gate, Delhi, India: Albion Press, 1957).

The report reviews basic and social education, audiovisual and technical education, art culture, development of Hindi, cultural relations with foreign countries, and youth and child welfare. Statistics show number of institutions, enrollments, expenditures, number of teachers, number of classes, in different stages of school education, and statistics on compulsory primary education.

54. Mujeeb, M., "Indian Education Retrospect and Prospect," *Pacific Affairs,* XXVI, 208-219.

55. Mukerji, M. J., *Indian Adolescence: A Study of the Problems of Adolescence in India* (Lucknow, India: Teachers' Co-Operative Education Journals, 1945), 156.

This book is designed to help all parents, teachers, and all social workers who have to deal with youths during this period. The text presents general points of view on adolescence and education without bibliography or direct citation of research. The chief purpose is to present to an Indian audience "in as simple a manner as possible the changes that take place, physically, mentally, morally, and sexually during the period of adolescence."

56. Mukerji, M. J., "Provincial Stereotypes of University Students," *Manasi,* I, 1 (1954), 42-47.

By questionnaire the uniformity, direction, intensity, and quality of stereotypes of natives of four provincial regions of India held by students at Lucknow University were studied. Men and women students from the four provinces were included in the 100 subjects. Data are presented on typical traits, sex differences, self-images, and images by others, and degree of perceptual uniformity.

57. Nanda, Anant, "School Problems as Adolescents See Them," *Studies in Education and Psychology,* I (Delhi: 1952), 9-14.

A list of 60 common school problems, grouped into five categories (aggressive behavior problems, indiscipline, nervous behavior, personal problems and study problems) was checked by 200 adolescents on a five-point scale. Quantitative scores were converted into ranks. The findings show that withdrawing and nervous problems were regarded as very serious. There is a high degree of agreement between sexes. Some steps are suggested to improve the conditions of work and play for adolescents.

58. Nelson, Lester W., "Notes on Problems of Indian Secondary Education," *Journal of Educational Sociology,* XXVIII (January, 1955), 200-202.

59. Nigam, S. P., "Model High School, Jabalpur, Madyha Pradesly, India," *Journal of Educational Sociology,* XXVIII (January, 1955), 230-231.

A description of a model government high school in India. This particular school is much above the average Indian high school. The article discusses the organization of student-faculty committees on curricula. It is noted that of the 100 students taking exams under the system 95 passed. The author concludes that "This has shown that the co-curricular activities if properly organized, add to the academic career of the students."

60. Nimkoff, M. F. and M. S. Gore, "Social Bases of the Hindu Joint Family," *Sociological and Social Research,* XLIV (September, 1959), 27-36.
61. Oad, L. K., "Buniyadi Tatha Paramparit Shiksha-Prapta Chhatron ki Hanovritti Parikshan Vishayak Anusandham" (An Investigation into the Attitudes of Basic and Traditionally Educated Pupils), *Shilsha,* VII, 5 (1955), 21-31.
62. Oad, L. K. and B. B. Chatterjee, "Influence of Camping on Shifting Social Attitudes," *University of Rajasthan Studies* (Education), III (1958), 19-53.
63. Orenstein, Henry, "The Recent History of the Extended Family in India," (Relationship of Urbanization and Industrialization), *Social Problems,* VIII (Spring, 1961), 341-350.
64. Panikkar, K. M., *Hindu Society at the Crossroads* (New York: Institute of Pacific Relations, 1956).
65. Parameswaran, E. G., "Social Adjustment of a Group of Early Adolescent Boys," *Journal of Psychological Researches,* I, 3 (September, 1957), 29-45.
66. Pareek, Udai (National Institute Basic Education, New Delhi, India), "Studying Cultural Differences in Personality Development With the Help of Rosenzweig, P-F Study," *Journal of the All-India Institute of Mental Health,* I, 2 (1958), 115-123.
67. Patel, A. S., "Attitudes of Adolescent Pupils toward Cinema Films," *Journal of Education and Psychology,* IX (1952), 225-230.

    Children in the eleventh grade of Baroda schools were employed for this investigation—109 boys and 47 girls between 15 and 18 years of age. The results were analyzed and it was found that the boys were more favorably impressed with the films than the girls. "We have not yet realized that in expert hands the film is capable of doing great service and in raw hands it may do a great harm."

68. Prasad, Laksham and Latka Ghosh, "Field Experience in Family Planning," *Journal of Family Welfare,* II (March, 1956), 98-100.
69. Pressey, S. L. and L. D. Pressey, "Comparative Study of the Emotional Attitudes and Interests of Indian and White Children," *Journal of Applied Psychology,* XVII (1953), 227-238.
70. Princess of Berar, H. H., "The Women of India," *Asiatic Review,* XLIII, 166-167.
71. Rao, Leela, "Interests in Reading of Newspapers and Magazines

of High School Pupils in Some English Medium Classes in Madras," *Journal of Psychological Research, Pakistan,* II (1958), 53-59.

As far as newspaper reading is concerned, the general trend of pupils' interests is similar for both sexes, though minor sex differences are there. Magazines containing short stories are popular with both sexes, though science sections are more attractive to boys and crossword puzzles and women's sections are more appealing to girls.

72. Rao, G. P. Krishna, "Problems of Student Discipline," *Indian Journal of Social Work,* XVI (1955), 176.

73. Rass, Aileen, *The Hindu Family in Its Urban Setting* (University of Toronto Press, 1961).

74. Rath, Radhanath, "Attitudes of University Students Towards Some Socio-Cultural and Educational Issues," *Journal of Education and Psychology,* XIV (1957), 214-225.

The age-old ideologies in India are in transition. The attitudes of 800 university students toward some issues affecting their daily life were evaluated by means of statements graded on a five-point scale. In order to break the monotony, the language of the statements for different issues was changed slightly keeping the meaning and spirit constant. The students tended to favor the emancipation of women, joint family system, classless society, Ghandian principles, religion, Indian culture, coeducation, and basic education. They did not, however, approve of the present system of education. The role of family occupation and economic status was also investigated.

75. Rath, Radhanath, "A Comparison of Attitude Scores of Some Politico-Economic Issues between Two Samples of College Students in Orissa, India, after an Interval of Four Years," *Journal of Social Psychology,* XLVII (1958), 361-371.

76. Rath, Radhanath, "A Comparison of Attitude Scores on Some Socio-Cultural and Education Issues between Two Samples of College Students after an Interval of Four Years: India," *Journal of Social Psychology,* L (1959), 57-64.

77. Rath, Radhanath and J. P. Das, "Study in Stereotypes of College Freshmen and Service Holders in Orissa, India, towards Themselves and Four Other Foreign Nationalities," *Journal of Social Psychology,* XLVII (1958), 373-385.

78. Ray, P. C., "The Children of the Abor and Gallong," *Education and Psychology,* VI (1959), 1-72.

This monograph reports the Rorschach reactions of boys in

three villages in the jungle and mountain valleys near the Indo Tibetian border. Primary schools have just begun, and the 64 subjects of the study, aged 8 to 17 years, comprised all testable school-going children in the three villages. Rorschach tests were administered through an interpreter, and the subjects also made self-ratings on 15 statements defining three personality traits, extratension, anxiety, and aggression. Mean scores for each village group on 23 Rorschach variables were used to draw up composite descriptions of the characters of each village. It appears that extrasensitive trends vary directly, and the rigidity and compulsiveness vary inversely with culture contact with the outside world. Three Rorschach measures were hypothesized to correspond with the three self-ratings variables. Extratension ratings showed significant correlations (.50 to .70) with the M:sumC scale. Anxiety ratings showed no relationship to the number of shadowing scores. Aggressiveness ratings showed significant correlations (.35 to .75) with the FC:CF+C index.

79. Ray, P. C., "Differences in Concrete Intelligence Among the Bhils of Central India," *Indian Journal of Psychology*, VI (1951), 73-77.

80. Ray, Sibnarayan, "The Ferment Among India's Students," *New Leader*, XLIII (June 27, 1960), 10-11.

The problem of student discipline has recently become so acute that two universities had to close for two months and other campuses are constantly threatened by student strikes, demonstrations, and vandalism. Fundamental to the unrest is the great disparity existing between India's new aspirations and her actual present condition. Many short-sighted officials do not realize this, as evidenced by their proposed remedies. The Five Year Plan has placed a severe strain on Indian resources and leadership, one which India had not experienced before independence. The free and compulsory educational goal has brought to the schools many classes which have never before been exposed to education. Overcrowdedness is the result. There is a shortage of facilities for activities in which students could develop initiative, responsibility, and self-expression. Low salaries have driven the most qualified teachers to other professions. The decline in academic standards has produced a cynicism among the students and teachers toward the whole situation. The lack of discipline is a sign of the desire for knowledge and education.

81. Razdan, P. N., "Bribed Discipline and Perverted Gaines," *Education*, XLI, 4 (April, 1962), 19-23.

It is the author's contention that sport competitions breed

indiscipline. By refusing to play for the school, athletes are able to obtain many favors and concessions in the form of bribes. Thus the players get a feeling of unwarranted importance and conceit. To remedy the situation, it is best to let a player not play when he refuses in hopes of getting a bribe. Bribes are emotionally bad for a player, for they reduce him to nothing but a wage earner, rather than a sportsman. The whole spirit of the sport may be destroyed for those honestly participating by making after-game promises. The author includes a real-life incident as illustration.

82. Roy, D. M., "Survey of Living Conditions of Meerut College Students," *Agra University Journal of Research*, V, 1 (January, 1957), 111-143.

83. Rufenaufer, H., "Wachtraume Indischer Jugendlicher" (Daydreams of Youths in India), *Zeitschrift fur Angewandte Psychologie und Charakterkunde*, LIX (1940), 319-350.

84. Rungachery, Santha, "The Family in Transition," *March of India*, XII (August, 1960), 63-65.

85. Ruth, R., "Attitudes of University Students towards Some Politico-Economic Issues," *Indian Journal of Psychology*, XXX (1955), 43-54.

86. Saiyidain, K. G., *Education, Culture and Social Order* (Bombay, India: Asia Publishing House, 1958).

A philosophical treatise on education in India and how it can fulfill the social and cultural aims of the country. The book discusses the future role of teachers and institutions of learning in the growing nation. The author takes into account the changing times and their impact on education.

The concept of "New Education" which has been in Indian thinking for some time is explained by the author through these headings: (1) reverence for childhood, (2) culturation of uniqueness, (3) development of individuality in a social medium, (4) freedom for the child, (5) the release of the creative impulse, and (6) education for happiness.

87. Saiyidain, K. G., "Nationalism and Internationalism in Eastern Education," *Journal of Educational Sociology*, XXVI (April, 1953), 369-373.

88. Saxena, M. S. L., "A Comparative Study of Personality Adjustment and Attitudes towards Marriage among College and University Students," *Indian Journal of Psychology*, XXVII (1952), 117-126.

A study utilizing questionnaire responses of 120 male students at Benares Hindu University. Married and single, graduate and undergraduate students were questioned. Responses were taken to two questionnaires: a personality adjustment questionnaire, and a psychosocial questionnaire on attitudes toward marriage (incaste and intercaste, divorce, dowry).

It was found that the married were the best adjusted while the younger students were the least adjusted. Most of the subjects felt that intercaste marriages do not usually bring the participants a greater degree of happiness than do incaste marriages.

89. Schlinger, Ben, "Changing Patterns in the Hindu Joint Family System of India," *Marriage and Family Living,* XXIII (May, 1961), 170-176.

An article discussing the changes in the traditional family pattern in India. The traditional form is the joint family. With the coming of the British and the emancipation of women in conjunction with the growing industrialization which increased rural-urban population shifts the traditional ideal of the joint family is being threatened by a new form, the nuclear family. While the nuclear family is coming into being physically, obligations and commitments to the joint family still exist. The end product of this conflict may be a new form of the nuclear family, a form which differs from the individualistic pattern of the West.

90. Shah, M. H., "Fundamental Rights in Baroda," *Asiatic Review,* XLIII (n.d.), 246-247.

91. Shanmugam, T. E., "Characteristics of Adolescent Boys' Fantasies," *Journal of the Madras University Human,* XXVI, 1-2 (July, 1954/January, 1955), 57-73.

92. Shils, Edward, "Indian Students: Rather Sadhus Than Philistines," *Encounter,* XCVI (September, 1961), 12-20.

93. Shukla, S., "Students' Perceptions of Indian Problems and the Future of India," *Manasi,* II (1955), 23-28.

Investigates student responses to a series of thirty incomplete statements dealing with five areas of Indian life in which there are problems. 75 students were polled on the following fields: politics, economics, social life, religion, and education. Analysis of the statement completions indicated that, while most favor democracy, there is some attraction to communism as an ideal state. In spite of the attraction many students seemed to lack comprehension of the actual nature of communism. Many students desired a redistribution, an equal redistribution, of wealth and property. It is noted that general dislike was found toward communalism, the mores of untouchability, polygamy, dowry system, prostitution, and blind religious faith.

94. Sinha, A. K. P. and O. P. Upadhyay, "Stereotypes of Male and Female University Students in India toward Different Ethnic Groups," *Journal of Social Psychology,* LI (February, 1960), 93-102.

95. Sinha, Durganand and Usha Niwas, "Vocational Interests of Men and Women," *Education and Psychology,* V (1958), 35-48.

96. Singh, Brij Nath, "Delinquent and Juvenile Pattern in Primitive Society," *Eastern Anthropology,* II, 2 (1948), 107-114.

    A discussion of the phenomena of juvenile delinquency among aboriginals in India. The author notes that, in urban areas of India, juvenile delinquency may be caused by disturbed family relationships, lack of employment, and the lack of suitable companions. In the aboriginal group, however, strong discipline prevails as a result of more definitive control over the child's education and behavior. Approved behavior patterns are more clearly defined and more readily followed in the aboriginal groups. The stronghold of tradition in these groups effectively precludes the existence of delinquent patterns of behavior.

97. Singh, Dalgit, "Vocation Interests of the High School Boys," *Vidya Bhawan Studies,* IV (1955-56), 36-44.

    The author found that the ordering of occupational interests was based on ability, interest, and the apparent needs of the society. 300 students in Indian high schools were examined and the interests revealed included business, engineering, medicine, and trade.

98. Singh, Harnam and Suresht Singh, "Truancy," *Journal of Correctional Work,* II (1955), 118-126.

    A discussion of truancy in the schools of Lucknow. The authors questioned a random sample of 790 students in the 8th and 9th classes at various schools in Lucknow. 67 persistent truants were also interviewed as well as the teachers of the classes. It was found that the peak age for truancy was 15 years old. The authors were able to establish no relationship between truancy on the one hand and any of the following factors, distance of school from home, position among siblings, or the presence of a stepmother in the family. They did establish a correlation between truancy and teacher lack of enthusiasm and failure in examinations.

99. Smith, Marian W., "Wild Children and the Principles of Reinforcement," *Child Development*, XXV (1954), 115-123.

100. Srinivas, M. N., *Marriage and Family in Mysore* (Bombay: New Book Company, 1942).

101. Srivostava, Champa, "Some Asepcts of Growing of Adolescent Rarela Girls," *Vidya Bhawan Studies*, V (1956-57), 76-81.

102. Subrahmanyam, R. S., "Gandhi's Philosophy of Education," *Indo Asian Culture*, VIII, 1 (July, 1959), 75-76.

103. Tagore, Rabindranath, "Woman and Home," *Indo Asian Culture*, III, 1 (July, 1954), 11-17.

104. Tayal, Shanti, "Shahari our Gramin Balkon ka Matkon Adhayan (A Study of Attitudes of Rural and Urban Boys)," *Education and Psychology*, II, 2 (Delhi: 1955), 44-51.

105. Taylor, W. S., "Basic Personality in Orthodox Hindu Culture Patterns," *Journal of Abnormal Psychology*, XLIII (January, 1958), 3-12.

106. Taylor, W. S., "Changing Attitudes in a Conflict of Cultures," *Character and Personality*, X (1941), 87-108.

In this study the author investigates the ways in which, ". . . the attitudes of individuals change under pressure from conflicting cultural influences. It is concerned with changes in patterns of interrelated attitudes, rather than with degrees of change in any specific attitude. It deals with such changes as found among students in colleges in India."

Fifty-two item questionnaires were applied to students from five colleges, two in the north, two in central, and 1 in south India. Only Hindu students were selected.

It was found that the facets of the orthodox Hindu culture pattern are subject to change at varying degrees of speed depending on the pressure. Beliefs which showed the most change revolved about Hindu attitudes toward social problems. It appears that the acquisition of new non-Hindu attitudes is related to the need for security. It was also noted that the foreign influences tending to promote change were generally not as complex as the local influences which worked to resist change.

107. Thakar, R. S., "Social Acceptability among School-Going Adolescents," *Education and Psychology Review*, I (1961), 29-31.

108. Tutto, D. N., "Maladjustment Among Adolescents," *Vidya Bhawan Studies,* V (1956-57), 105-111.

The author investigated a group of 100 17-year-old students who had been evaluated as maladjusted and found that 90 per cent of them had behavioral and moral disorders. A great many were also truants. Generally, the maladjusted came from poor homes, had no regard for their teachers, and were not interested in their work.

109. U.N. Department of Social Affairs. Division of Social Welfare, *Comparative Study on Juvenile Delinquency: Part IV: Asia and the Far East* (New York: 1953).

110. Useem, John, *The Western Educated Man in India: A Study of His Social Roles and Influence* (New York: The Dryden Press, Inc., 1955).

111. Vedavalli, H. C., "Study Habits of College Students at Tirupati," *Education and Psychology,* III, 3 (Delhi: 1955), 42-50.

112. Verma, Kaushalya, "Teacher's Traits as Ranked by Students," *Studies in Education and Psychology,* II (Delhi: 1953), 17-20.

The author administered a questionnaire containing 18 teacher traits to 200 pupils, 100 males and 100 females, in the schools of Delhi and Pathankote. The rank-order method was utilized with tabulation being done by location, school, and sex. It was found that the top five traits of teachers preferred by students were: knowing how to teach, making the work interesting, lack of partiality, knowledge of the subject matter, and is always on time to classes.

113. Verma, R. M., "Sociological Variables and Intelligence of the School-Going Population," *Education and Psychology,* V (1958), 165-170.

Using Mohsin's test of general intelligence (in Hindi), the author examined 286 seventh-grade boys in the rural elementary schools of Bihar. While the scores did not vary with socio-economic level, they did vary for different occupational groupings. The size of the family did not generally affect the results of the test.

114. Williams, R. and J. M. Smith, "India Students," *New Statesmen and Nation,* XXI (June 14, 1941), 605.

115. Yoganarasimiah, M., "Adolescent Work Attitudes," *Psychological Studies,* II, 2 (Mysore: 1957), 31-41.

116. Zernov, N., "Life in a University College," *The Times Educational Supplement* (1956), 921.

The author of this item was the principal of a university college in a rural district in central Travancore during 1945-54. His observations cover the educational aspect of the cultural revolution in modern India.

He notes that the students in his district came generally from mud huts and were the first generation in rural India to reach the level of higher education. To reach this level they had to pass a series of difficult examinations which often required several attempts.

Most of the students did not know what they wanted to do after graduation, but most did not want to work at the same jobs their fathers did. Some were interested in social service programs, some were interested in the field of missionary work, and some were most interested in government jobs with a high degree of security and a fixed income.

NEPAL

1. Barnouw, Victor, "Eastern Nepalese Marriage Customs and Kinship Organization," *Southwest Journal of Anthropology*, XI (Spring, 1955), 15-30.

The Jimdars were once a tribe in the Eastern Nepalese Kirat. They now refer to themselves as a caste. The author focuses on the Jimdar marriage customs and kinship organization. The Jimdars are atypical in their area with regard to marriage and kinship.

It was found that the age of marriage was later for the Jimdars than for their neighbors. There is no child marriage. They have a relatively free courtship system, which from the Western viewpoint, they are not prepared for in childhood. Boys and girls are segregated from the age of five or six. Courtship takes place secretly.

The author notes, "The average Jimdar does not seem to be remarkedly restricted by either family or caste in his social relationships. He is allowed areas for self-assertion and free choice which are not similarly available in the plains."

PAKISTAN

1. Adams, Effie Kaye, *Experiences of a Fulbright Teacher* (Boston: Christopher Publishing House, 1956).

A two-part book, the first part describing the author's experiences as a teacher at the Armenitola Government High School for Boys. The second part tells of her travels in the Far East.

The author found that Pakistani pupils were eager to learn about the U.S.A., in spite of the somewhat exaggerated and distorted notions they had about the country. She noted that the students' interests and desires were not different from those of students in America.

2. "The Education Plan for Pakistan," *Asiatic Review*, XLVIII, 175 (July, 1952), 211-215.

3. Jilani, Ghulam, *Teacher-Student Relationships at the Dacca University* (Dacca: University of Dacca, 1961).

   A report on a research project which studied students' problems at Dacca University. The sample consisted of 192 male and 46 female students out of a resident population of 1,089, exclusive of freshmen. A questionnaire was used which illicited information on student-teacher relationships in the following categories: the method of teaching, the person of the teacher, teachers' attitudes toward the student, the relationship of the teacher to the student, the students, accommodations, environment, and miscellaneous factors.

   Among the findings noted we see: (1) 23 per cent of the males and 25 per cent of the females wanted to enter the teaching profession, (2) many of the students felt that teaching was an easy life, (3) the greatest dissatisfaction was seen with the physical conditions at the university.

4. Kiani, Aquila, *An Inquiry into the Factors That Impede Formal Education of Children in Rural Areas* (Peshawar: Academy for Village Development, Pakistan, 1961).

   A group of researchers in Pakistan found that (1) insufficient income has a considerable influence on rural parents sending their children to school, (2) education does not rate high when it is a question of education or occupying a hereditary occupation, (3) 133 out of 135 subjects felt that education served a useful purpose but 82 per cent preferred that their children attend both the mosque and the government schools.

5. Kibbee, Robert J., "Higher Education in Pakistan," *Journal of Higher Education*, XXIII, 6 (April, 1962), 179-189.

   Rather than a specific analysis the author offers a broad picture of student life, student attitudes, and student values in Pakistan. With 83 million people, Pakistan has but six universities. Only half of the high school (secondary school) students go on to higher education of some kind.

   The involvement of the teachers and students in the intense political activity has effectively destroyed the independence of the universities. The relationship between the teacher and the student has historically been a personal relationship. This too is deteriorating.

The social life of the Pakistani students is limited not only by the activities available to him but also by those that are acceptable in his culture. The activities of females are carefully circumscribed. This situation has implications for the social life of the students. In effect, the Pakistani is left with a great deal of time, time which the American student uses for dating, etc. This time is generally taken up with political activities. The economic situation also contributes to the students' political activities and interests.

6. Owen, John E., "American and Pakistani Students; A Study in Contrasts," *Journal of Higher Education,* XXX (February, 1959), 82-86.

A discussion of the differences in attitude and behavior of American and Pakistani undergraduates. The American student usually feels that a college education is his right while the Pakistani is aware of the highly competitive nature of the college system and the economic hardship involved in his attendance.

There is really no comparison between the physical facilities enjoyed by the American student and the Pakistani student.

In the area of political attitudes the American is generally ignorant and apathetic while the Pakistani is usually intensely involved in politics.

While the American student can expect a good job upon graduation, the Pakistani student realizes that the competition for the few jobs is even tougher than the competition for entrance into higher education.

The author's view is that the American student, in general, loses in the comparison with the student in Pakistan.

7. Owen, John E., "Student Dreamers of Pakistan," *Universities Quarterly,* XIV (February, 1960), 144-149.

Pakistan's university students reflect the problems of a new nation born in chaos and conflict, a land that has been marked by instability, lack of direction, and ubiquitous poverty.

Although they are Muslim, religion is of little importance to the students. Politics are of more concern, and a typical attitude is one of condescension toward America. Poverty is the greatest problem of the students. In many cases, it is extreme. The universities themselves reflect the poverty . . . buildings are dilapidated, facilities limited, and the equipment and books few. Yet, in spite of these drawbacks, the students are being educated, though the system is too exam-oriented, and an education does not promise a job upon graduation.

Despite drawbacks, the future has some promises. Pakistan has made great progress in the last few years and all signs indicate she will continue to do so in the future.

8. Shah, K., "Attitudes of Pakistani Students toward Family Life," *Marriage and Family Living,* XXII (May, 1960), 156-161.

An investigation designed to discover if specific attitudinal differences exist between male and female Pakistani students toward family life. The author distributed questionnaires covering student background, family life, and secular education to 200 subjects in five colleges in Lahore, West Pakistan. The majority of the students were from middle-class families.

It was found that 86 per cent of the sample had some objections to premarital arrangements, the women preferred the modern type marriage while the men were more traditional. 95 per cent were against polygamy. While the men were in favor of employment of women, they did feel that women should not be allowed in "male" professions. In addition, the men felt that the education of the woman should end at marriage. The women did not hold this view.

The author points out that there are significant differences between men and women college students with regard to family life and marriage. He feels that the liberal attitude of the women relates to their being college students and noted the strong female emphasis on equality.

9. Smitter, Faith, and Iqbal Dar, *Growing Up in Pakistan* (Karachi, Pakistan: International Cooperation Administration, 1958).

10. Spear, Percival, "Cultural Heritage of Pakistan," XXX, 4 (October, 1956), *Islamic Culture,* 413-414.

11. U.N. Department of Social Affairs: Division of Social Welfare, *Comparative Study on Juvenile Delinquency: Part IV. Asia and the Far East* (New York: United Nations, 1953).

12. Zaidi, S. M. and Mesbahuddin, "National Stereotypes of University Students in East Pakistan," *Journal of Social Psychology,* XLVII (1958), 387-395.

The authors study the national stereotypes of 97 Pakistani students (average age 21) and discuss the implications of these stereotypes. They note that the students characterize the Turks as *patriotic* and *brave* while the Indians are seen as *superstitious, religious,* and *emotional.* In addition the Turks scored highest and the Indians lowest in the choices. They relate this to the military and political pacts between the Pakistanis and the Turks and the old feudal problems between India and Pakistan.

GENERAL

1. Coonan, John L., "Asian Overseas Students in England," *Asia*, XII (September, 1960), 684-690.

2. Eells, Walter C. *Communism in Education in Asia, Africa, and the Far East* (Washington: American Council on Education, 1954).

   This book deals, in part, with Communist efforts to infiltrate all aspects of the educational system in the subject countries. Among the students the typical strategy is for the Communists to take a popular issue and manipulate it to their own ends. To the students communism promises academic freedom, autonomy for the student, and improved intellectual environments. The student cell leaders, who run well-organized and efficient cells, are intelligent, aggressive, and alert. They know, for example, that the generally poor student living conditions in Asia and Africa are a potential source of discontent and they play heavily upon this theme. With the changing political climate in many of these countries, that is, with students and teachers taking a more decisive and predominant role, the potential for Communist activities is ever widening.

3. Keehn, J. D. and E. T. Prothro, "National Preferences of University Students From 23 Nations," *Journal of Psychology*, XLII (1956), 283-294.

4. U.S. Department of State: Public Services Division. *Southeast Asia, Area of Challenge, Change and Progress* (Washington: Department of State, 1959).

SOUTHEAST ASIA

BURMA

1. Ba, Kyaw, "Burma: Redoubtable Spirits," *IIE News Bulletin*, XXXIV (January, 1959), 10-12.

   Due to its emphasis on the humanities the University of Rangoon has strongly influenced its students to participate in political activity and to aspire to political and governmental positions. "It is truly remarkable that in just one generation after the University opened, its students have restored national freedom to the country." Though the founders of the University intended it to be the producer of technicians and office workers the principles of freedom of the intellect which they established had the effect of producing a politically dynamic student body.

The leader in student politics and the media in which students gain the experience necessary for political life is the Student Union, which ". . . developed into a student forum where fiery sentiments on local, national, and sometimes international issues were vociferously expressed."

The increase in emphasis on nonacademic activity has, however, caused the deterioration of previously high academic standards. The exaggerated prestige given to students by parents and the public must be decreased if the university is to fulfill its true purpose of producing citizens responsible to, and integrated with, the society. An attempt to teach at the University in the national language might serve to lessen the gulf between the students and graduates and the rest of the populace.

2. Cruttwell, P., "Maung Tin and Tin Maung" [Burman Students Before the Japanese Invasion], *20th Century,* CLIX (April, 1956), 332-337.

   The author describes how the Burmese students acted under foreign rule before the Japanese invasion and suggests what caused their behavior in order to show that national passions inevitably conflict with alien rule. In looking at the events taking place in Cyprus in 1956, he sees this occurring again.

   He tells of a student strike at one of the schools. He observed that for students, nationalism was stronger than their desire to do well on the examinations so that they could qualify for becoming government servants. In a chaotic society, the young share in the chaos not really knowing what they do or what they want.

3. U.N. Department of Social Affairs. Division of Social Welfare, *Comparative Study on Juvenile Delinquency: Part IV. Asia and the Far East* (New York: United Nations, 1953).

   Comparative appraisal of current practices in the treatment of delinquency in Burma, Ceylon, India, Japan, Pakistan, Philippines, and Thailand.

CAMBODIA

1. Makhali-Phal, *The Young Concubine,* Translated from French by Edward Weismuller (New York: Random House, Inc., 1942).

   A novel revolving about the life of a Eurasian Cambodian princess. The author's real name is Pierette Guesda, herself a Eurasian princess.

2. Tabellini, M., "Fundamental Education and Youth Problems in Cambodia," *Fundamental and Adult Education,* X, 2 (1958), 62-65.

INDONESIA

1. Danziger, K., "Choice of Models among Javanese Adolescents," *Psychological Reports,* VI (1960), 346.

"Previous studies have indicated that in Europe and the United States the ideal personalities chosen by adolescents are largely taken from the immediate, private sphere of experience, while public and historic figures occupy a relatively minor role in this respect. If this is related to a culturally determined attitude of what Allport and Gillespie have called privatism then one might expect adolescents from societies with marked collectivistic traditions to show a different trend. Javanese society has such strong traditions.

The ideal personalities chosen by 537 Javanese high school students from both urban and rural areas were categorized into personalities drawn from the private world of the adolescent and personalities drawn from the public life. Of the personalities chosen, 35 per cent fell into the former category and 65 per cent into the latter category. There were no marked age changes from 14 to 19 years, except for a tendency for past national leaders to become more frequently chosen than present national leaders.

When the subjects were divided according to family income, it became clear that the highest income group, consisting largely of the children of higher officials, showed a different pattern as compared with all other income groups. In their case the proportion choosing ideal personalities from private life rose to 57 per cent, while those choosing from public life fell to 43 per cent. In other words, this group was closer to the Western pattern than the other groups.

This finding may be related to the marked class differences in child training which have been supported by the author; the highest income group tending to make demands on the child as an independent individual, the other groups treating it rather as a part of the collectivity. The generality of these cultural patterns remains to be established."

2. Eells, Walter C., *Communism in Education in Asia, Africa, and the Far East* (Washington, D. C.: American Council on Education, 1954).

This book deals in part with Communist efforts to infiltrate all aspects of the educational system in the subject countries. Among the students the typical strategy is for the Communists to take a popular issue and manipulate it to their own ends. To the students communism promises academic freedom, autonomy for the student, and improved intellectual environments. The student cell leaders, who run well-organized and efficient cells, are intelligent, aggressive, and alert. They know, for example, that the generally poor student living conditions in Asia and Africa are a potential source of discontent and play heavily upon this theme. With the changing political climate in many of these countries, that is, with students and teachers taking a more decisive and predominant role, the potential for Communist activities is ever widening.

3. Geertz, C., "Ritual and Social Change: A Javanese Example," *American Anthropologist*, LIX (February, 1957), 32-54.

4. Geertz, Hildred, "The Vocabulary of Emotion: A Study of Javanese Socialization Processes," *Psychiatry*, XXII (August, 1959), 225-237.

5. Hazil, "Educational Problems in Indonesia," *Conference*, VI (Spring, 1957), 77-84.

6. McVey, Ruth T., Cornell University Department of Far Eastern Studies, Southeast Asia Program, *Modern Indonesia Project, the Calcutta Conference and the Southeast Asian Uprisings*, III (Ithaca, N. Y.: Cornell University Press, 1958).

   Inquiry into the question: Were Communist instructions for "unrest" passed at the Conference of Youth and Students of Southeast Asia fighting for freedom and independence? Calcutta, India (February, 1948).

7. Moerdowo, Dr. R., "Educational Problems in Indonesia," *Asiatic Review*, LIV, 197 (January, 1958), 62-65.

8. Training Evaluation Section, Participant Training Division, USOM, *An Evaluation of the Participant Training Program in Indonesia* (Djakarta: U.S. Operations Mission, September, 1959).

   Data gathered in a follow-up study of United States educated Indonesians—their experiences before, during, and after study abroad, and views of their superiors, USOM technicians and Indonesian Ministry officials regarding ICA programming.

9. Van der Kroef, J. M., "The Changing Class Structure of Indonesia," *American Sociological Review*, XVII, 4 (August, 1952), 421-430.

10. Van de Kroef, J. M., "Educational Development and Social

Change in Indonesia," *Harvard Educational Review,* XXIV, 4 (Fall, 1954), 239-255.

11. Van der Kroef, J. M., "Patterns of Western Influence in Indonesia," *American Sociological Review,* XVII, 4 (August, 1952), 421-430.

12. Van der Kroef, J. M., "Women and the Changing Marriage Pattern of Indonesia," *The American Catholic Sociological Review,* XVIII (June, 1957), 113-127.

LAOS

1. Halpern, J. M., "Economics of Lao and Serb Peasants: A Contrast in Cultural Values," *Southwestern Journal of Anthropology,* XVII (Summer, 1961), 165-177.

MALAYA

1. Dale, Martin, "Chinese Education in Malaya," *Far Eastern Economic Review,* XXXV (February 8, 1962), 325-328.

2. Dartford, G. P., "Problems of Malay Education," *Oversea Education,* XXIX (April, 1957), 33-37 (quarterly, available from Her Majesty's Stationery Office, York House, Kingsway, London W. C. 2, England).

3. Spector, Stanley, "Students and Politics in Singapore," *Far Eastern Survey,* XXV, 5 (New York: May, 1956), 65-73.

This article is an attempt to understand the political development of the student group and their role and status in society. The data were gathered from field work in Singapore and from work in Penang and Kuala Lumpur (Malaya).

With a great number of the Chinese population under 21 years old and in school, and given the traditionally high status of the student it is felt that the Chinese students constitute the intellectual cadre of the present and the future. Among the activities reported in the article we see: (1) a successful strike conducted in 1945 during which they conducted their own schools, received help from the Chinese Chamber of Commerce, and assisted in forming the Communist-front People's Action Party, (2) in 1955 they assisted workers in their strike which eventually led to many deaths. This activity was undertaken under the banner of the Chinese Culture Preservation Society.

In conclusion, it is noted that the students have a close association with the revolutionary movements in mainland China. The students active in politics at the time of this article

(1956) were identifying themselves with the Chinese student movement and contain the nucleus of future economic and political leaders.

PHILIPPINES

1. Araneta, Francisco, "Some Problems of Philippine Education," *Philippine Studies,* IX (April, 1961), 205-219.
2. Arens, Richard, "Philippines Education in Transition," *Mission Bulletin,* IX (December, 1957), 660-667.
3. Bardis, Panos D., "Attitudes toward Dating among Foreign Students in America," *Marriage and Family Living,* XVIII (1956), 339-344.
4. Firth, Raymond, *We, the Tikopia: A Sociological Study of Kinship in Primitive Polynesia* (New York: The Macmillan Company, 1958).
5. Fisher, M. J., "Filipinos Moving Ahead," *National Municipal Review,* XLIV (May, 1955), 248-252.
6. Hunt, Chester L., "Social Distance in the Philippines," *Sociology and Social Research,* XL (1956), 253-260.
7. Hunt, Chester L. and R. W. Coller, "Inter-marriage and Cultural Change: a Study of Philippine-American Marriages," *Social Forces,* XXXV (March, 1957), 223-230.
8. Stephens, Robert P., "The Prospect for Social Progress in the Philippines," *Pacific Affairs,* XXIII (June, 1950), 139-152.
9. Stoodley, Bartlett H., "A Cross-Cultural Study of Structure and Conflict in Social Norms," *American Journal of Sociology,* LXV (July, 1959), 39-48.

   The author tests two hypotheses concerning the conflict between universalistic and particularistic norms in two samples —American college students and Filipino college students. The first hypothesis stated that Filipinos would exhibit a larger modal response and smaller range with reference to both universalistic and particularistic norms. The second hypothesis: Filipino youth will see particularistic norms as more binding than universalistic.

   The results of the analysis supported hypothesis 1, but rejected hypothesis 2. Proper conduct was seen to be more important by the Filipinos and less conflicts were found among the Filipinos. The Filipinos also revealed a greater conformity of expectations and a smaller range of approved behaviors.

10. Stoodley, Bartlett H., "Normative Attitudes of Filipino Youth

Compared with German and American Youth," *American Sociological Review* (October, 1957) 553-561.

The author's purpose in this study was to compare the attitudes of Filipino youth with German and United States youth. Attitudes examined were those toward "authority and the family," "authority and the state," and "confidence in the average man."

The German and American data were taken from a study done by McGranahan in 1945. This study had a sample of 590 students. The Filipino sample was drawn from the freshmen at the University of the Philippines. It contained 770 Christian Filipinos matched to the American and German samples in respect to urbanization, education, sex, and age.

The comparison between the present sample and the American and German sample of McGranahan indicated that: (1) Filipino youth place higher emphasis on authority and obedience than American youth; (2) Filipino youth attribute less power and prerogative on the one hand and less submission on the other to structural relations of authority and obedience than German youth; (3) Filipino youth see the individual as closely identified with the group and, as a result, make less distinctions between rights and individual rights than either German or American youth.

11. U.N. Department of Social Affairs. Division of Social Welfare, *Comparative Study on Juvenile Delinquency: Part IV. Asia and the Far East* (New York: 1953).

    A comparative appraisal of current practices in the treatment of juvenile delinquents in Burma, Ceylon, India, Japan, Pakistan, Philippines and Thailand.

THAILAND

1. Arens, Richard, "The Thai—Land, People and Culture," *Mission Bulletin*, IX (January, 1957), 4-10.
2. Blanchard, Wendell, *Thailand—Its People, Its Society, Its Culture*, Country Survey Series, edited by Thomas Fitzsimmons (New Haven, Conn.: HRAF Press, 1958).
3. Boesch, Ernest E., "The Bangkok Project, Step One," *Vita Humana*, III (1960), 123-141.

   The author describes a survey investigation dealing with methodological principles and important problem areas in cross-cultural research. Subjects were 285 boys and girls attending school in Bangkok, Thailand. The subjects ranged in age from

5 to 14. Results from group testing, individual testing, and parent interviews were compared with findings from other non-Western and Western cultures. One of the main conclusions was, "Personality development in children in different cultures is not simply parallel but shows areas of retardation and acceleration according to cultural mold." The article ends with a brief discussion of some of the difficulties and significant points of attack in cross-cultural research.

4. Boucher, J. T., "Struggle for Thailand's Youth," *Mission Bulletin* (April, 1959), 325-328.

5. Chandruang, Kumut, *My Boyhood in Siam* (New York: The John Day Company, Inc., 1940).

   In this simply written autobiography, a Siamese provincial official provides a great deal of information about traditional Siamese habits and attitudes.

6. Embree, J. F., "Thailand—A Loosely Structural Social System," *American Anthropologist*, LII (1950), 181-193.

7. Hanks, L. M., Jr., "Indifference to Modern Education in a Thai Farming Community," *Human Organization*, XVII (Summer, 1958), 9-14.

   An essay inquiring into indigenous assumptions regarding education in a community of 1,600 people in Thailand. Presents a history of the community and deals with their attitudes toward education, its institutions, and teachers.

8. Line, W. and Margery King, "Cross-Cultural Research," *Journal of Educational Sociology*, XXIX (1956), 281-291.

   The authors report their experiences in establishing a child-study institute and an initial research program in Bangkok, Thailand. These experiences are carefully organized into several categories of problems that will be encountered in broad and systematic cross-cultural research: differences in cultural values; difficulties in research method, matching and definition of comparability; and problems of specific technique (translation of an instrument such as the TAT involved more than superficial shifting of patterns). No reference is made to earlier anthropological attempts to handle these problems.

9. U.N. Department of Social Affairs. Division of Social Welfare, *Comparative Study on Juvenile Delinquency: Part IV. Asia and the Far East* (New York: United Nations, 1953).

   A comparative appraisal of current practices in the treatment of juvenile delinquents in Burma, Ceylon, India, Japan, Pakistan, Philippines, and Thailand.

VIETNAM

1. Khoa, Le Xuan, "Traditional Humanism and Vietnamese Educational Concepts," *Asian Culture,* II, 3-4 (July/December, 1960), 79-88.
2. Pike, Edgar M., "Public and Private Education in Vietnam," *Asian Culture,* II, 2 (April/June, 1960), 79-116.

   A discussion about education and its improvement over the years in Vietnam. The principal problem faced in this area is the lack of sufficient facilities to make rapid and widespread progress.

   The author notes that the boys begin their schooling at the age of six. The pressure on the elementary school has led to the present operation of 18 technical schools functioning in South Vietnam. The emphasis in education seems to fall on the technical school with more and more students attending to get information regarding technical knowledge about the land and how it can be improved.
3. Republic of Vietnam, *Code of the Family,* Pamphlet including "Preamble of the Bill on the Family," presented by Madame Ngo Dinh Nhu, Deputy of the National Assoc., October 7, 1957; and "Test of the Family Code," Law Number 1/59 of January 2, 1959 concerning "The Family." Available through information office, Embassy of Vietnam, Washington, D.C., 20018 ("Education in Viet-Nam," 32-34).
4. *Viet-Nam: at the Crossroads of Asia,* Press and Information Office, Embassy of Vietnam, Washington, D.C., 20018.

GENERAL

1. Azad, Abul Kalam, Maulana, "The Concept of Man," *Indo-Asian Culture,* IV, 1 (July, 1955), 5-18.
2. Beaglehole, John, *Social Change in the South Pacific* (New York: The Macmillan Company, 1957).
3. DuBois, Cora Alice, *Social Forces in Southeast Asia* (Minneapolis: University of Minnesota Press, 1949).

   A concise analysis of the tensions created by value differences between East and West, with emphasis upon concepts rather than facts and figures.

4. Embree, John F. and Lillian O. Dotson, *Bibliography of the Peoples and Cultures of Mainland Southeast Asia* (New Haven, Conn.: Yale University, Southeast Asia Studies, 1950).

Works in English and European languages on the physical anthropology, archeology, ethnology and religion, cultural history, language, and the folklore of the peoples and tribes of Assam, Chittagong, Burma, Thailand, Laos, Cambodia, and Vietnam are listed. Arrangement is by region and subject. List of periodicals cited.

5. Green, T. L., "Vocational Problems in Education in South East Asia," *Journal of Educational Sociology*, XXVI (April, 1953), 380-391.

An article discussing the differences in vocational ambitions between East and West. In the West motivations to occupational ambitions include; economic reward, tenure, social prestige, etc. In the East (Ceylon) there are class and caste restrictions.

The author sampled 1365 pupils in nine provinces for this study. Results indicate that students in Ceylon have preferences for: courses in religion, shorthand, white collar jobs, government jobs. A dislike for math, agriculture, and an absence of relationship between ambitions and opportunities in the culture were found.

6. Heeble, R. W. J., "A Quick Look at Youth in South East Asia," *Social Service Quarterly*, XXXIV (September-November, 1960), 61-64.

7. Hung, William, "The Closure of the Educated Mission in America," *Harvard Journal of Asiatic Studies*, XVIII (1955), 50-73.

8. Keehn, J. D. and E. T. Prothro, "National Preferences of University Students from 23 Nations," *Journal of Psychology*, XLII (1956), 283-294.

9. Lasker, Bruno, *Peoples of Southeast Asia* (New York: Alfred A. Knopf, Inc., 1944).

A wartime introduction to the life and activities of the various races of the area, their agriculture, industry, trade, politics, and national development.

10. Murdock, George (ed.), *Social Structure in Southeast Asia* (Chicago: Quadrangle Books, 1960).

11. Wedgewood, Camilla H., "The Life of Children in Manam," *Oceania*, IX (1938), 1-29.

A discussion of the socialization process in Manam (South Pacific). The author utilizes data from twelve married couples and their children. The children were under eight years old. The child's environment is affected by several factors including: sex and upbringing, rank and status of parents, polygamous or monogamous households, and patrilocal or matrilocal residence.

EAST ASIA

CHINA

1. All-India Students' Federation, Bombay, *Lessons of China's Student Movement* (Bombay: Printed by J. Ghatt at New Age Printing Press, 1950).
2. Anstice, E. H., "Youthful Radicalism in the Far East," *Pacific Affairs,* VI (August, 1933), 387-393.
3. Bardis, Panos D., "Attitudes toward Dating among Foreign Students in America," *Marriage and Family Living,* XVIII (1956), 339-344.
4. Borg, D., "Students in Kuomintang China," *Far Eastern Survey,* XVII (January 14, 1948), 4-7.
5. Chai, Chiw, and L. Winberg, *The Changing Society of China* (New York: Mentor Books—The New American Library, 1962).
6. Ch'ang, M., "Chinese Education: Force for Democracy," *Far Eastern Survey,* XIV (July 4, 1945), 181.
7. Chang, Samuel S., "The Trend of the Youth Movement in China," *Far Eastern Magazine* (September, 1938), II, 75-80.
8. Chang, Samuel S., "The Youth Movement in China," *Missionary Review of the World,* LXII (December, 1939), 558-561.
9. Chao, C. and I-fan Yang, *Students in Mainland China* (Kowloon, Hong Kong: Union Research Institute, 1956).
10. Chen, T. H., "Collective Learning in Communist China's Universities," *Far Eastern Survey* (January, 1957).

This article was written during a period of time in Communist China when criticism could be heard. The emphasis here is on the objectional aspects of the educational system. These objections centered on (1) the blind imitation of Soviet education; (2) excessive hours of political indoctrination; (3) a lack of the creative spirit among students. The principle objection was the introduction of political indoctrination into every aspect of the educational process. One specific example referred to conformity in study. In this case it was noted that,

"... the self-study schedule specifies the exact time to be spent for each subject regardless of personal interest or aptitude or previous background."

11. Chen, T. H., "Education," *The New Leader*, XLII (May 4, 1959), 16-20.

    A brief survey of educational developments during ten years of Communist rule in China.

12. Chen, T. H., "Education in the Chinese Revolution," *Current History* (January, 1957).

13. Chen, T. H., "Education and Propaganda in Communist China," *Annals of the American Academy of Political and Social Science* (September, 1951).

    This 1951 article discusses the role of education and propaganda in Communist China. Thus education and propaganda is employed before force is used. The comments on the educational aspects of the state system amount to a fair description of the educational philosophy of the Chinese Communists.

14. Chen, T. H., "Salient Characteristics of Education in Communist China," *Education* (February, 1956).

    A short description of education in Communist China. Here education is used as a tool for the attainment of Communist goals. Education is, in effect, indoctrination. One of the primary emphases is speed. The state needs workers and specialists in a short time. Thus students are assigned to fields according to the needs of the state rather than the needs of the student. The emphasis here is on quantity rather than quality. They have even tried to simplify the Chinese language to be able to teach it more rapidly. The state actively promotes the literacy of the working-class party members.

15. Chen, T. H. and W. H. C. Chen, "Changing Attitudes towards Parents in Communist China," *Sociology and Social Research*, XLIII (1959), 175-182.

    A discussion of the changing behavior and attitudes on parental support and respect in Communist China. The author bases his comments on secondary sources. At an earlier time the Communist state in China encouraged rebellion against traditional familial and filial loyalty. This was an integral part of their program of social reorganization. This attitude brought about much disrespect and neglect of aged persons on the part of youth. The situation today (1959) is reversed in that the state is stressing devotion to parents. Devotion to the state is still the primary value, but devotion to parents is making a strong comeback.

The earlier program cost the state the support of many of the older generation and led to disciplinary problems and problems of social maladjustment among the youth. The areas of emphasis in the first program included: attack on filial piety, emphasis on the struggle between the generations, spying on parents for the state, appeals to the youth to help in the changing of society, and a program of public care for the aged.

16. Cheng, J. C., "Half Work and Half Study in Communist China," *Pacific Affairs,* XXXII (June, 1959), 187-193.

A discussion of the reaction of the youth to the Chinese government's program of combining work and study. The discussion is based primarily on articles published by the New China News Agency. Based on a decision of the Central Committee of the Young Communist League in January 1958, all students were required to perform the following types of labor: farm work, subsidiary rural occupations and handicraft, capital construction sites, transportation, service labor, and general industrial labor. The author notes in conclusion, "It seems as if the Communist Chinese are aiming at merging the factory, the commune, and the school all into one."

17. Ch'eng-K'un, Cheng, "Familism, The Foundation of Chinese Social Organization," *Social Forces,* XXIII (October, 1944), 50-59 (bibliography).

A discussion of the roots of familism in China. The origins are traced to the Emperor Shun about 2000 B.C. It grew out of an emphasis on filial piety and the subjugation of the individual to the family. The author notes that the traditional family structure was undergoing drastic change in 1945 due to the results of urbanization and industrialization. He notes, "In spite of the introduction of modern education, the influence of four thousand years of familistic tradition still predominate in practically all phases of their national life."

18. Chi, Tung-wei, *Education for the Proletariat in Communist China* (Hong Kong: The Union Research Institute, 1954).

19. Chiang, Wen-Hen, *The Ideological Background of the Chinese Student Movement* (New York: King's Crown Press, 1948).

20. Chich, Kuo Hui, *Culture and Education in New China* (Peking: Foreign Language Press, 1951).

21. Chin, Ai-Li S., "Some Problems of Chinese Youth in Transition," *American Journal of Sociology,* LIV, 1 (July, 1948), 1-9.

This is a socio-psychological study of the role of youth in social change. It is concerned with certain problem situations confronting youth in China in a period of social change. The study notes that the personal problems developing in a situation of change may not be a result of conflicting behavior patterns but may be a result of the lack of appropriate behavior patterns and cues.

The study was based on 54 cases taken from a volume of published letters to the advise column of a Shanghai periodical. Conclusions were drawn from the analysis of these letters. Though the background of the subjects could not be determined from their letters, the publication from which they were drawn appeals mostly to the urban middle class, including both Westernized Chinese from the port cities and those from non-Westernized small towns who were receptive to social change. The sample consisted of 31 males and 23 females. 50 per cent of the subjects were between the ages of 17 and 26 years old. On the whole the group seemed to be middle class, urban, or urban influenced.

Among the factors reflected in the letters analyzed were the following:

1. Problems of parental conflict, the role of the parent in the economic development of the adolescent and the conflict over early and/or arranged marriages. The problem of mate selection was of high frequency in the letters.

2. Problems involving the absence of appropriate cues and behavior patterns reflected in the questions inquiring after the location of desirable persons.

3. Problems seeking resolutions to the hostility of adults.

The author notes that social mobility based on occupational achievement will be attained at the expense of generational continuity, in contrast to traditional times when the unity of mobility was the entire family. He also notes that there is an increase in the problem of the discrepancy between the parental role model and the adolescent's own conception of masculine and feminine roles.

In conclusion he states, "Anxiety engendered in the revolt is manifested in preoccupation with self-improvement and in an ambivalent attitude toward love and marriage." Also, "It is evident that the process of revolt from the traditional culture has spread beyond the first group of college graduates, returned students, and the residents of treaty ports to a second circle of white-collar workers, and high school students."

22. China Institute in America, *A Survey of Chinese Students in American Universities and Colleges in the Past One Hundred Years* (New York: 1954).

23. China, Ministry of Social Affairs, *Child Welfare Work in China: a Report* (Nanking: 1947).

24. Chung, Shih, *Higher Education in Communist China* (Hong Kong: The Union Research Institute, 1953).

25. Dai, B., "Personality Problems in Chinese Culture," *American Sociological Review,* VI, 5 (October, 1941), 688-696.

26. Dai, B., "Obsessive-Compulsive Disorders in Chinese Culture," *Social Problems,* IV, 4 (April, 1957), 313-321.

27. Dana, R. H., "American Culture and Chinese Personality," *Psychological Newsletter,* New York University, X (1959), 314-321.

28. "Dancing Youth," *New Statesman,* LIII (January, 26, 1957), 87.

A journalistic presentation of the persistence of "bourgeois" recreation. These recreations are seen as a sign of deviation from the doctrine which the state is promoting. Activities in this field are a sign that the individual's indoctrination has not been successful. The author notes, "The young men and women who turn the ballroom into a jungle of swaying and wriggling bodies may perhaps be reacting against too much organization of their private lives."

29. Davidson, Basil, "Education in China," *United Asia,* VIII, 2 (April, 1956), 117-119.

30. "Dissent of the Students" (China), *Commonweal,* LXVI (May 3, 1957), 118.

A general discussion of student complaints in Communist China. In two leading institutions in China, the students have complained that their jobs have not been consistent with their level of education. The students also reflect a confusion between Socialist Democracy and bourgeois democracy. The author notes in conclusion, "When students within Communist countries search for ideas and actions which best serve the cause of democracy and freedom the West should not appear to be empty-handed."

31. Farrington, B., "Education in the New China," *Journal of Education* (London: January, 1953).

32. Fei, Hsiao-Tung, *China's Gentry* (Chicago: University of Chicago Press, 1953). (Essays in rural-urban relations.)

33. Freedman, M., "Family in China, Past and Present," *Pacific Affairs,* XXXIV (Winter, 61-62), 323-336.

34. Freedman, M. and W. Willmott, "South-East Asia with Special Reference to the Chinese," *UNESCO International Social Science Journal,* XIII, 2 (1961), 245-271.

35. Freyn, Hubert, *Prelude to War; the Chinese Student Rebellion of 1935-36* (Shanghai: The China Journal Publishing Company, 1939).

36. Gibson, T., "Students of China," *Spectator*, CLXXX (May 28, 1948), 641.

A discussion of the actions of the Chinese students during times of crisis, namely the Japanese threat, the Kunming Bloodbath, and the Peiping incident. The author discusses the activities of the students and professors in the moving of libraries, etc. These activities are seen as more than ". . . transient exasperations of disillusioned youth." The author feels that there is a growing body of sympathetic Chinese opinion behind these actions. The article was written in 1948.

37. Gillin, D., "Peasant and Communist in Modern China," *South Atlantic Quarterly*, LX (Fall, 1961), 434-446.

38. Goodrich, L. Carrington, "A Short History of the Chinese People" *Harvard Journal of Asiatic Studies*, X (June-December, 1947), 244-245.

39. Grimble, Freda, "Children in China," *United Asia*, VIII, 2 (April, 1956), 102-104.

40. Haleem, A. B. A., "Education in China," *Pakistan Horizon*, XIII, 4 (1960), 284-300.

41. Howatson P., "Youth Group Work in Hong Kong," *Mission Bulletin*, X (March, 1958), 222-228.

42. Hsieh, Ping-Ying, *Girl Rebel, The Autobiography of Hsieh Ping-Ying with Extracts from Her New War Diaries*, translated by Adet and Anor Lin, with introduction by Lin Yutang (New York: John Day, 1940).

43. Hsien, Chin Hu, *The Common Descent Group in China and Its Functions* (New York: Viking Fund Publications in Anthropology, No. 10, 1948).

44. Hsu, F. L. K., "Social Mobility in China," *American Sociological Review*, XIV, 6 (December, 1949), 764-771.

45. Hsu, Yu-chu, "A Case Study of a Farm at Ching-Shiu, Taichung, Taiwan, the Republic of China, 1960." CECA Paper, November, 1962 (The Council on Economic and Cultural Affairs, Inc.).

A descriptive general picture of a typical rice farm in Formosa. The discussion is based on data collected by field interviews using structured schedules. Only one case is discussed in the article.

While it does not deal directly with adolescents, this article gives a fair picture of what the life of an adolescent would be like in this type of cultural situation.

46. Hu, Yao-Pang, "The Role of Youth in National Reconstruction (in China)," *Current Background*, 576 (June, 1960), 11-15.

47. Huang, L. J. *Dating and Courtship Innovations of Chinese Students in America* (Thesis, Chicago: University of Chicago, 1954).

48. Huang, L. J., "Some Changing Patterns in the Communist Chinese Family," *Marriage and Family Living*, XXIII (May, 1961), 137-146.

This paper is a descriptive report on the dating and courtship practices, husband-wife adjustment patterns, and problems of the working mother in Communist China. It is based on items published in the Chinese periodical, *Women of China* included in the issues from the years 1945-1959. Only the items concerned with the youth are reported here.

Since 1949 there have been many laws passed which advanced the position of women. Parents, for example, are no longer permitted to interfere with their children's mates. The increased utilization of female labor has increased the potential for young people meeting on the job. However, the lack of previous heterosexual experience in young people's lives makes it difficult for them to adjust to the new freedom. Contrary to the previous customs, the arrangements and negotiations prior to marriage are now conducted by the parties involved rather than by the parents.

The author notes that the loss of the traditional marriage broker has left many youth helpless, especially the rural and less educated. The phenomena of short courtship and early marriage may be seen as responses to new problems of interpersonal association, problems for which suitable solutions have not, as yet, been found.

49. Koteneu, Anatol M., *New Lamps for Old; an Interpretation of Events in Modern China and Whither They Lead* (Shanghai: North-China Daily News and Herald, 1931).

50. Kuhlen, R. G., "The Interests and Attitudes of Japanese, Chinese, and White Adolescents: A Study in Culture and Personality," *Journal of Social Psychology*, XXI (1945), 121-133. (See Kuhlen, Japan Section)

51. Kwang-Ching Liu, "Early Christian Colleges in China," *Journal of Asian Studies*, XX (November, 1960), 71.

52. Lamson, Herbert D., "The Eurasian in Shanghai," *American Journal of Sociology*, XLI, 5 (March, 1936), 642-648.

53. Lang, Olga, *Chinese Family and Society* (New Haven: Yale University Press, 1946).

54. Lauwerys, J. A., "China's Educational Expansion," *Times Educational Supplement* (June 27, 1957).

55. Lee, S. C., "China's Traditional Family, Its Characteristics, and Disintegration," *American Sociological Review*, XVIII (June, 1953), 272-280.

In this discussion of the Chinese family the author notes that modern education and Western influence have weakened the traditional family ties, resulted in the decline of the large family system, increased emphasis on the conjugal family, and have gradually emancipated women. The change in value and orientation has taken place mainly among the youth, due to the programs of the Peking regime. The traditional patterns of familism and the large family have largely vanished today.

56. Lee, Rose Hum, "Research on the Chinese Family," *American Journal of Sociology*, LIV, 6 (May, 1949), 497-504.

"A review of the literature to date, indicating research trends, methodology, and the misconceptions arising therefrom to clarify some of the distorted pictures of the Chinese family held by most Westerners."

57. Leong, Y. K. and L. K. Tao, *Village and Town Life in China* (London: George Allen and Unwin, 1915).

58. Levy, M. J., *The Family Revolution in Modern China* (Cambridge: Harvard University Press, 1949).

59. Lin, Tsung-Yi, "Tai-Pau and Liu-Mang: Two Types of Delinquent Youths in Chinese Society," *British Journal of Delinquency*, VIII (1958), 244-256.

A description and discussion of Tai-pau and Liu-mang in Taiwan, Formosa. Tai-pau is the nickname of a group of juvenile delinquents and so is Liu-mang. The article focuses on the Tai-pau and utilizes the Liu-mang for comparison purposes. An attempt is made to understand the group dynamics and the socio-cultural backgrounds of the members of these two groups.

The Tai-pau usually come from middle- or upper-middle-class families. Their ages range from 14 to 18. They usually do well in school. There are few girls associated with the group. Petty theft, lying, etc. are favorite activities. The Liu-mang come from the lower classes in the poorer areas of the city. They are usually involved in more serious offences such as gambling, prostitution, and narcotics. The Liu-mang look on the Tai-pau as playboys while the Tai-pau feel the Liu-mang are a group to keep away from. The two groups do have several elements in common: delinquent behavior, ethnocentric systems of values and little interest in change, and the influence of contact with delinquent subculture is important in determining some of the actions of these two groups.

The author concludes, "Two types of peer groups in Chinese society, therefore, they should be regarded as caused by differing reactions of adolescents to the two existing subcultures which have been brought about by modernization or contacts with modern Western culture. Each possesses in terms of behavior, attitude and structure."

60. Lin, Yao-Hua, *The Golden Wing, A Sociological Study of Chinese Familism* (New York: Oxford University Press, 1947).

61. Lindsay, M., *Notes on Educational Problems in Communist China* (New York: Institute of Pacific Relations, 1950).

62. Liu, Hui-Chen Wang, *The Traditional Chinese Clan Rules* (Locust Valley, New York: J. J. Augustin Incorporated Publisher, 1959).

63. Liu, Shui Sheng (pseudonym), "Life in a Chinese University," *The Atlantic Monthly*, CCIV (December, 1959), 89-82.

A journalistic description of the pressures put upon the Chinese students at the University of Peking between 1956 and 1958. The author notes that the foreign students were given better quarters and allowed special permissions. Special reference is made to the results of the Rectification Movement of 1957-1958. The author was a non-Chinese student who was enrolled at the University during this period.

64. MacInnes, D. E., "China in Transition; Refugee School Life and Thought," *Amerasia*, V (December, 1941), 456-463.

65. "Madame Chiang Accepts YWCA Medal As Tribute to Entire Womanhood of China," *China World Review*, XCVI (April 12, 1941), 190.

66. *New Democratic Youth League of China*, Central Committee, Young Builders of China (June, 1953).

Typical achievements of young Chinese workers.

67. Nieh, Ching-Tech, "Problems Concerning Studies and Reform of the Students of the Institute of Socialism," *Current Background*, DCXXVIII (July 22, 1960), 1-7.

68. Osborne, Ernest G., "Problems of the Chinese Family," *Marriage and Family Living,* V (Winter, 1948), 18.

69. Peffer, Nathaniel, *China: The Collapse of a Civilization* (New York: The John Day Company, Inc., 1930).

70. Priestley, K. E., "China," *Yearbook of Education 1952* (London: Evans, 1952).

71. Priestley, K. E., "Higher Education in Hong Kong," *Far Eastern Survey,* XXI (1952), 203-204.

72. "Problems of Educational Policy in Communist China," *Comparative Education Review,* I (October, 1957), 4-6.

A discussion of the operation of the educational system in China based on observations made during a four-week visit to Peking, Sian-fu, Chungking, and Hankow in May, 1957. The author discusses four problems of the educational system: education of the nationalist minorities, organization of secondary education, curriculum and content of secondary education, and mass education.

73. "Rectification of Youth in (Communist) China," *Far Eastern Economical Review,* XXIII (October 3, 1957), 421.

74. "Report of Jen Pi-Shih, Member of the Central Committee of the Chinese Communist Party, at the Congress of the Democratic Union of Chinese Youth," *Soviet Press Translations,* IV (July 1, 1949), 398-401.

75. Rugh, Douglas, "Conduct Standards for Teacher Candidates in the Normal Schools of Communist China." *Teacher Education Quarterly* (State Board of Education, Connecticut), XVII (Fall, 1959), 27-30.

76. Sewell, William Gawan, *China through a College Window* (New York: Friendship Press, 1938).

77. Shih, L., "China's New Educational System," *School and Society* (March 29, 1952).

78. Slater, N., "China's Christian Universities," *Journal of the Royal Central Asian Society,* XXXVI (April, 1949), Part 2, 159-167.

79. Smythe, Lewis S., "The Success of Chinese Families as Families," *Marriage and Family Living,* XIV (November, 1952), 286-294.

80. So, C. F., "Moral Judgments of Chinese Students," *Journal of Abnormal and Social Psychology,* XXXVII (1942), 264-269.

A 1942 effort to secure more evidence on the objectivity and relativity of moral values, and also to supply a basis for the comparison of moral judgments of different racial and cultural groups.

Several groups of Chinese students were asked to rank 15 "vices" and 16 "ideals" in order of importance.

It was found that both the males and the females held similar ideas about vices and ideals. Vices were ranked in the following order: snobbishness, cheating, sex irregularity, stealing, selfishness, lying, dancing, drinking, smoking, swearing, and vulgar talk. It was also found that both Americans and Chinese students regard sex irregularity, stealing, cheating, and lying as serious offenses.

"Honesty was unanimously agreed upon as the most important ideal, while obedience, thrift, and reverence were generally regarded as of small importance. It was also noted that ". . . there do exist social determined ethical standards, and most individual moral judgments tend to conform to such established standards."

81. Spencer, R. F. and S. A. Barrett, "Notes on a Bachelor House in the South China Area," *American Anthropologist*, LIX (July, 1948), 463-478. (Bibliography)

82. Sun, E. Z., "Chinese Student Opinion," *Far Eastern Review*, XVII (August, 1948), 178-181.

An effort to determine and make public the pattern of Chinese student thought in 1948. The author analyzed 660 questionnaires from Chinese born students attending colleges and universities in the United States. These were selected from an original mailing of 2,300 questionnaires. Of the 714 returned, 54 were American-born Chinese.

It was found that the students, who came from many different backgrounds, agreed on economic and political issues. Analysis by religion revealed that the Christian students slightly favored the status quo and were anti-Communist. This was not true for 50.1 per cent who preferred no religion.

It was found that the students had definitely rejected traditional landlordism and private capitalism for the future Chinese economy. A strong desire was seen among the students for democracy and equality in both economic and political areas.

83. Sun, Ien E-tu, "A Poll of Chinese Students in the United States," *Eastern Miscellany*, XLIV, 9, 11-18 (in Chinese).

84. Sze, Szeming, *Chinese Students in Great Britain* (London: China Society, 1931).

85. Ta Chen, "Basic Problems of the Chinese Working Class,"

American Journal of Sociology, LIII, No. 3 (November, 1947), 184-191.

86. Thomas, S. B., "Recent Educational Policy in China," *Pacific Affairs* (March, 1950),
87. "Trials and Tribulations of China's Young People," (Communist Party Programs), *Far Eastern Economic Review*, XVIII (January 27, 1955), 118-119.
88. Wallace, J. A., "Chinese Students in Tokyo and the Revolution," *North American Student* (June, 1913), 171.
89. Wang, Charles K. S., *The Control of Teachers in Communist China: A Socio-Political Study* (Texas: Air Force Personnel and Training Research Center, Lackland Air Force Base, 1955).
90. Wang, Tsu Chang, *The Youth Movement in China* (New York: New Republic, Inc., 1927).
91. Wang, Y. C., "Western Impact and Social Mobility in China," *American Sociological Research*, XXV (December, 1960), 843-855.
92. Webster, James B., *Interests of Chinese Students*, Studies in Education and Psychology, I (Shanghai: Bureau of Publication, University of Shanghai, 1932).
93. Wen-han, Chiang, *The Chinese Student Movement* (New York: King's Crown Press, 1948).
94. Westbrook, C. H. and Y. Hsien-Hwei, "Emotional Stability of Chinese Adolescents as Measured by the Woodworth-Cady-Mathew Questionnaire," *Journal of Social Psychology*, VIII (1937), 401-410.
95. Wu, J. C. H., "Adolescence in China: Its Problems and Aspirations," *China Monthly*, VIII (October, 1947), 339-342.

    Out of the past and from the West, China might well find an educational pattern for herself and the world; her youth problems hold the enlightenment for all educators.

96. Wu Yun-To, *Son of the Working Class; The Autobiography of Wu Yun To*, translated by Huang Pin-Chang and Tank Sheng (Peking: Foreign Languages, 1956).
97. Yang, Ching-Kun, *The Chinese Family in the Communist Revolution* (Cambridge: Center for International Studies, Massachusetts Institute of Technology, 1954).
98. Yang, Martin C., A *Chinese Village: Tactau Shantung Province* (New York: Columbia University Press, 1945).
99. Yap, P. M., "Suicide in Hong Kong," *Journal of Mental Science*, CIV (1958), 266-301.

100. Yen, Ching-Yueh, "Crime in Relation to Social Change in China," *American Journal of Sociology*, XL, 298-308.

101. Ying, Richard, "Harnessing China's Youth to Communism: Peking Hopes to Achieve Absolute Power by Controlling the Thought of the Young Generation," *Far Eastern Economic Review*, XXV (December 18, 1958), 803-804.

A discussion of mass-education methods and indoctrination in Communist China in 1958. The author notes the states' emphasis on the education of mind and body. A doctrine under which thousands of factories have been built and thousands of acres of farmland have been planted. The stress on education for the peasants is also stressed.

102. Yuan, Tung-Li, *China in Western Literature* (New Haven: Yale University Press, 1958), esp. pp. 379-382.

Bibliographic work on China.

JAPAN

1. Akagi, A., "The Survival of Feudal Vestiges within the Family-Parent-Child Relationships Concerning Familism," *Nagoyadaigkukyoikugakubukiyo* 4, Bulletin of the Faculty of Education of the Nagoya University (March, 1958), 123-130.

2. Amano, Makio, "A Study of Factors in the Difference of Achievement between Two Schools in Isolated Villages," *Japanese Journal of Educational Psychology*, V (1958), 73-79.

3. Ando, M., "On the Effect of Reference Group to Growth of Religious Attitude in Female Adolescents," *Journal of Social Educational Psychology*, I (1960), 84-95.

4. Aoi, K., "Social Cures of Crises," *Gendaikazokukoza* 4 (Lectures on the modern family, IV), (Kawade-shobo: 1955), 157-221.

5. Ariga, K., "After the Disorganization of the Large Family System," *Shinano*, 5 (May, 1958), 1-12.

6. Ariga, K., "Contemporary Japanese Family in Transition," *Transactions of the Second World Congress of Sociology*, I (1954), 83-89.

7. Ariga, K., "The Contemporary Japanese Family in Transition," *Transactions of the Third World Congress of Sociology*, IV (1955), 215-221.

8. Asayama, Sin-iti, "Comparisons of Sexual Development of American and Japanese Adolescents," *Psychologia*, I (1957), 129-131.

A brief summary of Asayama's work which is a continuation of Yamamota's research started in 1922. Asayama originally surveyed 1,482 Japanese adolescents in 1948. From this came *Sexual Behavior of Japanese Students,* published in 1949. Subsequent to this 4,888 males and 1,270 females have been questioned. The instrument consisted of a questionnaire with 210 questions covering a range of 19 problems.

The author found, in comparison with United States adolescents, a similarity in the growth curve of nocturnal emissions, but striking differences in the curves for ejaculation, menstruation, masturbation, kissing, petting, and sexual intercourse. Between 1948 and 1953 the Japanese curves for intercourse changed little, but the desire to kiss had increased greatly. This was attributed to the presence of American servicemen and American films.

The author found that the development of the Japanese adolescent was not too different from that of the American youth as represented by Kinsey.

9. Baber, E., "Attitudes of Modern Japanese Youth Toward Mate Selection," *Sociology and Social Research,* XLV (1961), 295-300.

The data for this study were gathered in 1955 while the author was connected with Tokyo University. 5,000 Japanese young people in 47 high schools and universities were questioned with the aid of a 50-item questionnaire. The students were mostly third and fourth year students.

Some of the findings are noted below:

1. 75 per cent say they believe in sexual equality theoretically, but practically they have doubts.

2. 80 per cent of the boys felt the "love match" was an ideal method of mate selection.

3. 60 per cent of the males and 80 per cent of the females felt that the choice of mates should be left to the persons involved.

4. Over 80 per cent of both sexes felt that in parental conflict, the will of the youth should prevail.

5. 80 per cent felt that the use of the "go-between" was "convenient" or a "nice formality."

The author notes that the results of his investigations show that Japanese youth are breaking away from the traditional patterns of thought toward sexual equality, mate selection, family interest, etc.

10. Bacon, A. M., *Japanese Girls and Women* (Boston: Houghton Mifflin Company, 1891 and 1902).

11. Battistini, Lawrence H., *The Postwar Student Struggle in Japan* (The Botham Foundation of New York in cooperation with the

Charles E. Tuttle Company: Tokyo, Japan, Rutland, Vermont, 1956).

A study of the student movement in Japan. This is not primarily a study of socio-economic matters, but rather a descriptive examination of the student movements. The book is based mostly on Japanese language articles; interviews with Japanese students, teachers, and administrators who were involved in the events surrounding the student movements. The student movements are traced through three periods: 1918-1931; 1931-1945; 1945-1956. The third period is further divided into three sections: September 1945 to September 1948; September 1948 to May 1952; and May 1952 to 1956, the year of the writing of the book. The author discusses with great detail the revival and unification of the student movement and the creation of Zengakuren (the Japanese student union today). He also discusses at great length the Communist influence in the student movement and the role of the rightists.

12. Beardsley, R. K., J. W. Hall, and R. E. Ward, *Village Japan* (Chicago: University of Chicago Press, 1959).

Village Japan is an ethnography of Niike, a Japanese fishing village. The section reported here is found on pages 308 to 316 and concerns adolescent behavior before marriage. The study was based on questionnaire data and observational methods. The main tests utilized were: Rorschach, Thematic Apperception Test, Problem Situation, and Authoritarian Personality projective tests. The following paragraphs summarize this section.

"The eighteen or twenty adolescent boys and girls there have no proverbial collective temperament or other peculiarities." Though biological and social maturation obviously occurred, no distinct, separate age-group organization was recognizable, with the exception of the Youth Association for Boys, which, however, seemed to have no basis as a function of any adolescent culture. The process of maturation was slow and stable, integrated into the life stream of both the individual and the village. Unlike the United States adolescent personality, there was no evidence of strife or strain associated with adolescence, existing as a phenomena separable from the general context of the total culture.

An explanation offered for the virtual nonexistence of an adolescent subculture correspondent to that found in the United States is in the traditional nature of the Niike culture. In the United States emphasis is placed on individuality and behavior within loosely defined limits, both in adult life and in adolescence as a preparatory stage for adult life. The child and the adolescent is expected to make a wide range of decisions by himself. "The teenager demands autonomy or finds it thrust upon him." When his decisions and his behavior in the fulfillment of responsibility contrasts with those of his parents and of the adult world, he comes into conflict with them, which leads to the establishment of a distinctive teen-age period.

In Niike, however, where behavior and life are narrowly defined by tradition, the emphasis is not on individuality but on the acceptance of, and behavior within, the limits of a rigidly defined normative pattern.

Since there is little individual autonomy in adulthood, there is no need for a period of training directed toward the development of individual autonomy in adolescence. Because his role does not bring him into conflict with the adult world, but rather is tied traditionally in a fixed pattern relative to it, there is no conflict between the adolescent and the adult and, therefore, no adolescent or teen culture. There is, rather, a definite break, around the age of 15, between childhood and the assumption of the adult role.

13. Befu, Harumi and Edward Norbeck, "Japanese Usage of Terms of Relationship," *Southwestern Journal of Anthropology*, XIV (1958), 66-86.

14. Bennett, John, Herbert Possin, and Robert K. McKnoght, *In Search of Identity: The Japanese Overseas Scholar in America and Japan* (Minneapolis: University of Minnesota Press, 1958).

15. Brinkman, Albert R., "Higher Education in Japan Today," *Harvard Educational Review*, XVI, 3 (Summer, 1946), 167-172.

16. Bureau of Women and Juveniles, Ministry of Labor, *Family Life of Workers—Focusing on the Problem of Provision*, Hujinkankeishiryoshirii-zuchosashiryo 20 (Data of Women Problems Series, Research Material No. 20), September 1957.

17. Candill, W. and G. DeVos, "Achievement, Culture and Personality: The Case of the Japanese-Americans," *American Anthropologist*, LVIII (1956), 1102-1126.

18. Carter, G. W., "Child Care and Youth Problems in a Relocation Center," *Journal of Consulting Psychology*, VIII (1944), 219-225.

19. Cole, A. B., "Children of a Vacuum," *Pacific Spectator*, IV, 2 (1950), 153-159.

This article is based on discussions and observations at an international student conference in Japan. It discusses the youth and the state of affairs in modern Japan. The author notes that the Japanese students are critical of the old ideology and the social order. The results of opinion polls conducted on Japanese youth indicate that the youth are much more ready for change than are their elders. It seems as though the youth of Japan are in revolt, revolt against parents, professors, old social mores, and, occasionally, against organized religion. It is observed that the Communist students, by virtue of the positions they hold in the student world, have a disproportionate share of power.

20. Conroy, H., "Young Japan's Anti-Americanism," *American Quarterly*, VII (Fall, 1955), 247-256.

This article is an attempt to define and discuss some of the opinions held by young Japanese intellectuals concerning Americans and American foreign policy. It is based on conversations held with young Japanese during a field trip to Japan.

While the young Japanese generally likes Americans as individuals, and has adopted many Western customs, he is dissatisfied with American foreign policy. The sudden and unrational policy reversals have caused dissatisfaction among the youth. They resent the refusal of the United States to recognize the advances made by Red China and the support of the dictatorial Nationalist Chinese government. While they disagree with Russian and Chinese political philosophy, they also dislike America's stubborn defense of capitalism.

In short, there is ambivalence of attitude toward American policy and American personnel.

21. "Cool Cats and Samurai," *Senior Scholastic*, LXXVII, 13 (December 14, 1960), 16.

22. Correia-Afonso, J., "Japanese Youth," *Messenger of the Sacred Heart*, XCV (November, 1960), 22-25.

23. Cressey, Earl H., *Daughters of Changing Japan* (New York: Farrar, Strauss & Cudahy, Inc., 1955).

24. Daido, Waichi, *Iyeshi No Kenkyu* (Study of Double Love Suicide) (Dobunkan: 1911), 134.

25. DeVos, George, "The Relation of Guilt toward Parents to Achievement and Arranged Marriage among the Japanese," *Psychiatry*, XXIII (1960), 287-301.

The problem investigated here is ". . . whether the Japanese emphasis on achievement drive and on properly arranged marriage may possibly have its motivational source in the inculcation of shame or guilt in childhood. It is my contention that this emphasis is not to be understood solely as a derivative of what is termed a 'shame orientation,' but rather as stemming from a deep undercurrent of guilt developed in the basic interpersonal relationships with the mother in the Japanese family."

Data pertinent to this study were gathered in Niike, an agricultural village of central Honshu. The TAT results are particularly important.

The author notes that, while shame is a more apparent behavior influencer, guilt may, in many cases, be more basic an influence. The roles of both shame and guilt are discussed with relation to the marriage and child rearing patterns, the sexual patterns, and the intergenerational conflict.

26. DeVos, G., "Value Attitudes toward Role Behavior of Women in Two Japanese Village," *American Anthropologist,* LXIII (December, 1961), 1204-1230.

While this article does not deal directly with the behavior or attitudes of adolescents in Japan it does present the results of a study which can be interpreted as reflecting the atmosphere in which adolescents develop. The author is interested in demonstrating the value of the Thematic Apperception Test in the study of intercommunity differences. The sample for the investigation consisted of Niike, a rural farming village in Japan, and Sakunoshima, a Japanese fishing village. The discussion is based on the analysis of 807 TAT stories from 80 subjects in Niike and 385 stories from 35 subjects in Sakunoshima. Four areas were selected for investigation in this paper: (1) the differences in attitudes toward arranged marriage and a love marriage; (2) the differences in attitudes toward sexual relationships; (3) the differences in the fantasies of self-assertion and the expression of violence in conflicts involving women and (4) the differences in concern over conflict between wife and husband's mother.

The author notes, ". . . it is apparent on the basis of the TAT material that the farming village still harbors attitudes suggesting that marriages other than an arranged marriage cannot be considered proper in nature." In Sakunoshima, however, the attitude toward marriage is freer and people are more optimistic about the success of marriages based on love. In the farming village love relationships are seen as leading to conflict with parents. There is no particular concern with this in the fishing village.

In conclusion, the author notes that no dominant pattern of traditional sex-role attitudes was found to exist in the area of Japan studied. The emphasis placed on traditional values and values of love in marriage varies with regional subcultural variation.

27. DeVos, George and Hiroshi Wagatsuma, "Recent Attitudes toward Arranged Marriage in Rural Japan," unpublished manuscript, 1958.

28. DeVos, George and Keiichi Mizushima, "The School and Delinquency: Perspectives from Japan," *Teachers College Record*, LXIII, 8 (May, 1962).

This research is to gain some cultural perspectives on delinquency by comparing American lower-class males with Japanese males of the same class, in this case. The authors are interested in exploring the validity of the various views on delinquency. They are especially interested in: "whether there are socially induced personality adaptations that are related to delinquency regardless of cultural patterns. Are delinquency and other forms of nonconformity a matter of adolescent attitudes toward the opportunities available in any particular society for achieving its prescribed goals, or does delinquency possibly result from faulty early training or the internalization of social norms within the primary social group, the family, whatever cultural milieu? What roles do peer group and neighborhood problems play in delinquency formation?"

The authors use data from existing research to support or question hypotheses.

In 1956, 23 per cent of all crimes were committed by juveniles. Amount of delinquency varies with the neighborhood. It was found in a study conducted by the Japanese Supreme Court, that delinquency occurred most frequently in urban areas where entertainment centers are concentrated.

Specialists in electroencephalography in Japan have come up with conclusions which "indicate an all-over tendency for delinquents to show more evidence of a variety of personality disturbances than appears in the normal."

Findings have shown that parental neglect or rejection are related to delinquency, also lack of parental consistency toward children, and lack of presence of parents at home in early childhood.

Findings suggest that truancy in Japan as well as the United States is an early manifestation of delinquent attitudes or an incapacity to meet the school situation.

It seems that poor school records are related to delinquency because of factors other than poverty. It seems to be the trend in families with delinquents to encourage part-time work in their children, whereas other families of the same economic background try to avoid having their children work on a job and be away from their studies, which suggests that family attitudes have an affect on delinquency. 60 per cent of delinquents work part-time, only 14 per cent of nondelinquents do.

There seems to be two types of delinquency: that which shows evidence even before junior high and that which is the result of group or other immediate social situation factors.

In reviewing the American educational system and its relation to delinquency and recognizing the "heavy reliance on the school as a crucial social institution" in both Japan and the United States, the authors conclude that "to solve the problem presented by delinquency, the school may be obliged to play a more centrally active role in community-wide prevention than it has to date."

29. Doi, M., "A Scientific Analysis of Conflicts within the Family," *Kateisaibangeppo* (Domestic Court Monthly), 4:1 (January, 1952), 1-65; 4:2 (February, 1952), 1-62; 4:3 (March, 1952), 1-52; 4:4 (April, 1952), 1-62; 4:5 (May, 1962), 1-71.

30. Drucker, Peter, "The Baffled Young Men of Japan," *Harper's*, CCXXII, 1328 (January, 1961), 65.

31. Durgin, Russell, "Japan Thumbs Freedom's Pages," *Christian Science Monitor* (July 3, 1948).

32. Durgin, Russell, L., "What about Japan's Youth?" *Reader's Digest*, LIII (August, 1948), 127-130.

The author was a representative of General MacArthur and conferred with many of the local youth organization leaders in the prefectures of Japan. He noted that many of the youth were asking how they could change, how they could keep from being fooled by new rules. They were also interested in promoting more interaction between boys and girls. This was the Western influence. Reflecting on the author's religious orientation he says, on a deeper level, the issues which confront Japan's youth are spiritual. Democracy requires not only the procedures of freedom, but faith to give it life. "This, I think, is what General MacArthur meant when he said: 'The problem, basically, is ideological.' I believe he would agree that the problem, basically, is Christian."

33. Editorial—"Educational Sociology and Japanese Reconstruction," *Journal of Educational Sociology*, XXVI (September, 1952), 7-9.

34. Eells, Walter Crosby, *Communism in Education in Asia, Africa, and the Far East* (Washington: American Council on Education, 1954).

35. Ema, S., "Chiiki Shakai to Seinen tono Taiketsu" (How Rural

Youth Confronts the Local Community), *Seishonen Mondai,* VI, 2 (1959), 6-15.

36. Emori, I., "On the Custom of 'Premarital Sexual Freedom'—Its Nature and Norms," *Kazokuseido-no-kenkyu,* II (1957), pp. 233-300.

37. Ezra, F. and Suzanane H. Vogel, "Family Security, Personal Immaturity, and Emotional Health in a Japanese Sample," *Marriage and Family Living,* XXIII (May, 1961), 161-166.

    A study of the impact of security upon child-rearing and behavior in Japan. The authors utilized participant observation for 21 months, intensive weekly interviews with a group of six normal families in a small city within commuting distance of Tokyo. Another group of six families with emotionally disturbed children were examined for a period of six months. Interviews with teachers were also taken.

    The authors found that Japanese children were more dependent on the family than were American children. The Japanese children are treated differently with regards to breast feeding and the responses to crying. The child in Japan develops increasing independence with age, but his desires for dependence are more socially approved. Considerable family security was found among the Japanese as well as considerable child dependence. It was also seen that there is much positive affect between husband and wife and satisfaction in the marriage. The author concludes that there is ". . . not a bad fit between the personal immaturity and the social structure which exists in contemporary Japan despite the very rapid changes which are taking place in all sectors of the society."

38. Fukui, Fumio, "Mutual Obligations of Society and University," *Contemporary Japan,* XXI, 1-3 (1952-1953), 117-120.

39. Fukuo, Takeichino, *Nippon Kazoku Seido Shi* (A History of the Japanese Family Institution) (Tokyo: Yoshikawa Kobunkan, 1959).

40. Fuse, T., "Two Types of Modern Japanese Families and the Modernization of the City—Introduction to the Sociological Study of the Japanese Urban Family," *Shakaigaku Hyoron* 31 (*Sociological Review*) (May, 1958), 28-51.

41. Gillespie, J. M. and G. W. Allport, *Youth's Outlook on the Future* (Garden City, New York: Doubleday and Company, Inc., 1955) (1,819 case studies from ten countries).

42. Goodman, M. E., "Values, Attitudes and Social Concepts of

Japanese and American Children," *American Anthropologist*, LIX (December, 1957), 979-999.

By investigation of the occupational aspirations of Japanese elementary school children the author attempts to get at the value-attitude-concept systems. The sample consisted of 1250 Japanese children in grades 1 through 8 in four schools in Central Honshu and 3750 American children in grades 1 through 8 in eight American schools in Northeastern United States. Both samples were urban or suburban and middle class. The responses were classified by age and sex. The instrument consisted of essays written on the subject, "What I want to be when I grow up, and why."

The author immediately found that the value-attitude-concept systems of the children were more complex than she had expected. The American children revealed a high level of sophistication on the vocations characteristic of an urban technological society while the Japanese were not too familiar with these roles. With this exception the structures of occupational aspirations were quite similar between the two samples. It was found for instance, that it is mainly the younger child in both groups who desires to be a policeman, etc. These desires are explained in terms of identification rather than true aspiration. The traditional American sexual differentiation of aspiration was also found in the Japanese students. Professional occupations were popular among the boys in both countries, but the American children revealed a higher desire for "a glamorous and exciting" occupation. The Japanese child sees himself in occupations aligned more with traditional Japan and recent Western importations. The Japanese children showed more interest in the political and mass-media occupations. They totally ignored all occupations dealing with the military. (This was not true of the American children.)

In conclusion, the author feels that a complete reversal has taken place since the Second World War. The Japanese children are more other-directed in occupational choices and reflect more family influence in the choice of occupations. The American children seem to be more realistic and self-oriented due to the cultural value placed on individualism and independence. The different cultural backgrounds of the two groups was evident in all the responses of the two groups.

43. Gorer, Geoffrey, *Themes in Japanese Culture* (*Transactions of the New York Academy of Sciences*), V (1943), 106-124.

44. Gould, Rowland, "U.S. Students in Japan," *This is Japan*, 7 (September, 1959), 46-49.

45. Gray, John M., "Japan's Young Moderns," *Saturday Evening Post*, CCXXXIV, 37 (September 16, 1961), 81.

A journalistic presentation which asks the question "Has Westernization made Japanese youngsters a cheap copy of our own teenagers? Or have they preserved their traditional Oriental values?"

The discussion is based on the author's observation as Fulbright Exchange teacher in Japan.

The author notes that the student in Japan is a respected person. Far from being spoiled, however, they are thoughtful, pleasant, and hard working. He notes an unquestionable trend toward youth-centered attitudes in Japan. While they are intellectually sophisticated, he notes that they are lacking in many of the social skills common to the teen-ager in the West. They have little conception of how to act on a date.

While suicide is not unknown to the Japanese adolescent (721 suicides in 1960), they are shocked at the pregnancy rate of unmarried girls. In the Japanese high school there is little contact between the sexes.

The author makes a particular point of the low rate of delinquency. In Japan, the criminal offense record is less than 1 per cent among the youth. Only 5,000 per year become involved in physical violence. This is a very low rate for a modernizing industrial country.

46. Griffith, Richard M., Otoya Miyogi, and Akira Tago, "Universality of Typical Dreams: Japanese Versus Americans," *American Anthropologist*, LX (1958), 1173-1179.

The authors collected data on the occurrence of typical dreams and dream contents from 250 American college students and 223 Tokyo college students. The questionnaire contained 50 items on frequency and content of dreams, sleep and dreaming, and neurotic symptoms. The author concluded that there are recurrent themes in dreams which seem to have the same significance for every dreamer and to denote his membership in clan, culture, or society.

47. Hamada, Y., "Influences of Home Environment Upon Education —A Sociological Study," *Nomakyoikukenkyushokiyo* (Bulletin of the Noma Institute of Education), 10 (December, 1953), 131-176.

48. Haraoka, K., "On the Attitude to Movies in Pupils," *Journal of Social Educational Psychology*, I (1960), 23-24.

49. Haraoka, K., "Relations between Efforts for Academic Records and

Home Environment," *Japanese Journal of Educational Psychology,* IV (1957), 159-170.

50. Haraya, T., et al., "Attitude to Foreign People in Children and Adolescents," *Journal of Japan Educational Psychology,* XVIII (1960), 1-7.
51. Haring, D. G., "Japan and the Japanese," in Linton, R. (ed.), *Most of the World* (New York: Columbia University Press, 1949).
52. Haring, D. G., "Aspects of Personal Character in Japan," *Far Eastern Quarterly,* VI (1946), 12-22.
53. Hasegawa, Nyozekan, *Educational and Cultural Background of the Japanese People* (Tokyo: Kokusai Bunda Shinkokai (The Society for International Cultural Relations, 1937).
54. Hayashi, Y., "Juvenile Delinquency and Home Environment," *Kateisaibangeppo* (*Domestic Court Monthly*), IX, 5 (May, 1957), 38-58.
55. Hazama, H., "Factory Workers and Their Family Life," *Hujin to Nenshosha* (*Women and Juveniles*), 19 (November, 1954), 8-11.
56. Honde, S., "Only Child and His Family Environment—A Case of a Grown-up Only Child," *Osakashiritsudaigakukaseigakubukiyo* (Bulletin of the Faculty of Domestic Science of the Osaka City University), II, 1 (March, 1955), 74-84.
57. "Hopes, Heartaches and Hara-Karai," *Senior Scholastic,* LXXVI, 1 (February 3, 1960).
58. Hujiwara, Y., "On the Analysis of the Educational Function of the Family Group," *Kyoikushakaigakukenkyu* (*Study of Educational Sociology*), 6 (October, 1954), 98-109.
59. Huziwara, H., "Sengo Seinen no Seishinkeitai" (Young People's Thinking after World War II), *Shiso,* CCCLXCVI (June, 1957), 115-36.
60. Iga, Mamdru, "Cultural Factors in Suicide of Japanese Youth with Focus on Personality," *Sociology and Social Research,* XLVI (October, 1961), 75-90 (Bibliography).

An investigation of the suicide of Japanese youth in the context of Durkheim's comments on suicide. The author, realizing the number of replications and investigations available concentrates on an oriental area. The discussion is based on secondary sources of both theoretical and empirical nature. Among the findings it is noted that suicide is the leading cause of death among Japanese between 15 and 24. The rates for males of these ages is ten times the rate of the same group in the United States. The rate for females is twenty times greater than in the United States. These rates increased following the war. The love-suicide pact accounts for a great percentage of the acts committed: "The leading causes for suicidal attempts in Tokyo in 1948 were weariness of the world, 28.3 per cent; family trouble, 14.4 per cent; unrequited love, 13.1 per cent; and worries about the future, 10.9 per cent." Some of the author's conclusions are noted below:

"The psychological characteristics of Japanese youth are (1) insecurity with floating aggression; (2) a sense of inadequacy and shame as a consequence of discontinuous cultural conditioning, overhasty and inconsistent imposition of self-control, wide goal means, disparity, and stress on competition; and (3) the false sense of power, coexisting with a feeling of helplessness, owing to an 'immature' personality and overwhelming difficulty in attaining one's dreams."

The cause of suicide of Japanese youth seems to be a combination of homicidal aggression, masochistic, submissive attitudes, and the wish to die. Though they are loosing many traditional values, Japanese youth have retained a strong sense of shame. When this shame is combined with the latter factors, ". . . the most likely result for the individual is frustration, resentment, aggression, and correlative rise in delinquency and suicide."

Though calling for some alteration of Durkheim's hypothesis, the study supported it in general and in that ". . . this type of individual phenomena can be explained adequately only in terms of the social milieu."

61. Imamusa, Ken-ichiro, "Chugakusei no Dotoki Ishiki ni Tsuite" (On Conscience of Japanese Junior High School Students: Their Moral Awakening), *Japanese Journal of Educational Psychology*, VII (September, 1959), 19-83.

62. Institute of Education of Kyoto City (ed.), "Parent-Child Relations of Pupils of Junior High Schools and Their Personality," *Kyotoshikyoikukenkyusho* (Institute of Education of Kyote City), 1957.

63. Isomura, Eiichi, *Shinju-ko* (*Study of Collective Suicide*) (Tokyo: Kodansha, 1959).

64. Ito, Nobufumi, *New Japan; Six Years of Democratization* (Tokyo: Japan Peace Study Group, 1952).

65. Ito, Ryoji, "Education in Japan," *Education Abstracts*, VIII, 4 (April, 1956), 1-12.

This selected bibliography of literature on Japanese education by a Ministry of Education official, includes a 3-page bibliographical essay, 31 annotated entries of English and Japanese books and periodicals, and a list of 13 recommended Japanese educational journals. Most entries date from 1950-1955.

66. Ito, Ryoji, "Reforms in Education," *Contemporary Japan*, XXIII, 10-12 (1954-1955), 650-668.

67. Iwai, K., "The Impact of Modern Technology on Family Life," *Jimbungakuho Tokyotoritsudaigaku* (Bulletin of Humanities of the Tokyo City University), 21 (September, 1959), 135-202.

68. Japan, National Commission for UNESCO, *Youth Work in Japan, 1955* (Tokyo, 1956).

67. "Japanese Laud Gallantry of Student Warriors," *China World Review*, XCIII (July 1, 1940), 24.

68. Kaigo Tokiomi, "The American Influence on the Education in Japan," *Journal of Educational Sociology*, XXVI (September, 1952), 9-16.

69. Karasawa, T., *Nihon no jyoshi gakusei* (*The Female Student in Japan*) (Tokyo: Kodansha, 1958).

70. Katayama, Y., "The Family Group and Education," *Kyoikushakaigakutsuron* (*Textbook of Educational Sociology*) (June, 1952)

71. Katsura, H., "Young People and Their Parents," *Jidoshinri*, III, 3 (*Child Psychology*) (March, 1949), 55-56.

72. Kawagoo, J., "Traditional Norms and Their Breakdown within the Family," *Bungakuronso* (*Bulletin of Literature of the Aichi University*) (March, 1957), 95-122.

73. Kawashim, T., *Nippon Shakai No Kayokuteki Kosei* (*Familistic Composition of Japanese Society*) (Tokyo: Gakuṣei-Shobo, 1946).

74. Kawashim, T., *Wagakumi Shakai No Kazokgu-teki Kosei* (*Familial Structure of Japanese Society*) (Tokyo: Nippon Hyoronsha, 1948).

75. Kikuchi, Y., "The Process of Change in the Structure of Agricultural Villages and in Family Forms in Modern Times," *Komazawa-shigaku* (*Komazawa History*), 7 (December, 1959).

76. Kirihara, L., "Seinin No Dokusho Ni Kansuru Chosa, 1. Rodo Seinen no Yomimono" (A Study of the Reading of Youth, 1. Readings of Young Laborers), *Journal of Science and Labor*, XVI (1939), 627-636.

In general the young laborer reads a small variety of publications. They do reflect a broad general interest in topics of current interest, local, national, and international, but the scope of their reading is pretty much limited to the newspapers and certain restricted types of journals.

77. Kitano, Eimasa, "A Study on the Achievement of School Children in Isolated Areas," *Japanese Journal of Educational Psychology*, IV (1957), 215-218.

A comparison of the performance of rural-area young people with urban-dwelling young people in Japan. It was generally found that the rural children do poorer than the urban dwellers, especially in the area of Japanese, mathematics, science, and social studies. This was particularly true of the males tested. The children in the isolated villages did far below the national average while the urban children did far above the national average.

78. Kobarjashi, Saeko and Michiko Saito, "An Experimental Study of Leadership Function in Young Children's Groups," *Japanese Journal of Educational Psychology*, V (1958), 195-199.
79. Kojima, G., "Japan's Need Today: A Democratic Philosophy of Education," *Confluence*, VI (Summer, 1957), 176-183.
80. Kondo, T., M. Ota, and H. Hayashi, "Junior High Pupils' Relations to Family Members in an Out-of-the-Way Place," *Nagoyadaigaku-kyoikugaku-bukiyo* (*Bulletin of the Faculty of the Nagoya University*), 5 (March, 1959), 208-212.
81. Koyama, T., "Bibliography of the Family Research in Japan," *Kikan shakaigaku* (*Sociological Quarterly*), III (October, 1949), 95-101; IV (May, 1950), 77-84.
82. Koyama, T., "The Changing Social Position of Women in Japan" (New York: Unesco, 1961).
83. Kuhlen, R. G., "The Interests and Attitudes of Japanese, Chinese, and White Adolescents. A Study in Culture and Personality," *Journal of Social Psychology*, XXI (1945), 121-133.

A contribution to the understanding of the effects of race and culture on personality. The author utilized an Interest-Attitude Test (Pressey) and applied it to a sample of 1,589 Japanese adolescents and 690 Chinese adolescents in the McKinley High School, Hawaii. The American sample consisted of 1,547 white American adolescents of grade and age level similar to the Japanese and Chinese adolescents. The ages ranged from 15 to 18.

Among the findings are noted the following:

1. The Oriental adolescents proved to be relatively "immature," ". . . on subtests dealing with disapprovals and worries . . ." and about equal to the whites in interests and admira-

tions. The Chinese were closer in score to the whites than were the Japanese. Their longer residence, and therefore greater degree of acculturation, might account for this.

2. The Orientals checked "worries" about twice as frequently as did the whites, possibly indicating emotional stress resulting from acculturation.

3. There appeared to be little difference between the Chinese and Japanese on most subtests. The American and Oriental children were most alike in the type of people liked. The sexes were alike in disapprovals, worries, and admirations but different in interests. "Sex differences in interests . . . are greater than racial differences."

4. "Analysis of responses to individual items supports the above findings and suggests that a new culture makes its impact rather early through those taboos and moral wrongs which are sufficiently crystallized in that culture to be taught as such. It seems reasonable that these should most quickly be passed on to newcomers, and at an early age inculcated in children native to that culture."

The author concludes, "The total outcomes of this study, using broad survey procedures, indicate the value of available instruments for obtaining quantitative evidence regarding the contest of cultures and the outcomes of cultural influences."

84. Kuwabata, Y., "Family Disorganization in Cities," *Toshimondai* (*Urban Problems*), XLVI, 2 (February, 1955), 9-17.

85. Kuze, T. and S. Ohnishi, "The Relation between Pupils of Junior High Schools and Their Mothers," *Seinenshinri* (*Psychology of Youth*), V, 2 (June, 1954), 103-111.

86. Kuzuya, T., "On the Attitudes of Youths and Adults toward Marriage and the Problems Accompanying It," *Kumamotodaigaku-kyoikugakubu-kiyo* (*Bulletin of the Faculty of Education of the Kumamoto University*), 4 (March, 1956), 44-66.

87. La Barre, Weston, "Some Observations on the Character Structure in the Orient: The Japanese," *Psychiatry*, VIII (1945), 310-342.

88. Lifton, R. J., "Japanese Youth: the Search for the New and the Pure," *American Scholar*, XXX (1961), 332-344.

The author discusses the psychological patterns of Japanese youth with reference to political activities. The discussion is based on personal observation and secondary sources. One of his primary interests lies in cross-cultural research concerning the interplay between individual character and historical change.

Concerning the attitudes of the students the author notes the general attitudes of the population toward the police, an attitude which had its formation in past abuses and instances of governmental authority. The people are overly sensitive and negative in this area. He notes that even the most moderate of the students is most likely to have an aversion to authority in general and particularly an aversion to the authority in his recent past. The role of the student movement in the social change in Japan is not atypical. Youth has always played an important role in social revolutions. In this case the student movement can, in the author's opinion, go in either a moderate direction or in the totalist direction. The future is yet to be decided.

The author suggests a distinction between Japanese students with totalist psychological tendencies and those with more moderate inclinations. His composite of the totalist includes: middle-class background, some tendency as a child toward leadership, the formation of political radicalism during the first two years at the university, strong influences in the dormitory life, and the theoretical Marxism of his favorite professors.

The composite moderate includes: searching, confused and worried, particularly about democracy, also middle-class background, less likely to show signs of leadership, belongs to rank and file. While some members are able, they do not become leaders. His emotional makeup tends toward moderation, compromise, and conciliation.

Both of these types have much in common. They both rely on self-expression via the group. The group is very important to them. It seems that the Japanese needs the group much more than the Westerner. This is largely due to his traditional relationship to it both in and out of the family. He is also drawn to the ideal of democratic individualism and therein lies the conflict. In Japan at the present time both the ties to tradition and the rebellion against tradition are particularly strong. The student is affected by the training of his parents and also by the incoming forces of America, Russia, and China.

The author concludes that there is a need to avoid the static labels and, instead, to see psychological tendencies in relation to the direction in which they are heading.

89. a. Lloyd, Wesley P., *Student Counseling in Japan: A Two Nation Project in Higher Education* (Minneapolis: University of Minnesota Press, 1953).
    b. Lloyd, Wesley P., *Student Counseling in Japan* (American Council on Education, Washington, D.C., 1957).

90. Lunden, Walter A., "Juvenile Delinquency in Japan: Pre-War, War, and Post-War Years," *Journal of Criminal Law and Criminology*, XLIV (1953), 428-432.

A discussion and interpretation of juvenile delinquency in Japan in the prewar, war, and postwar periods. The data for the analysis came from the unpublished records of the Criminal Affairs Bureau, Supreme Court of Japan.

The statistics on total delinquency, postwar juvenile arrests —revealed that major violations were up 160 per cent above the five-year prewar average. Lesser offenses had advanced to more than six times the annual prewar average. By age, the under-14 age group increased 66 per cent, the 14-18 age group rose 127 per cent. The 18 to 20 year group rose more than any of the others.

By offense, robberies increased 800 per cent, rape 275 per cent, homicide 108 per cent, theft 194 per cent, obscenity 193 per cent, and gambling 123 per cent.

The author interprets these increases primarily in terms of the general postwar conditions in the country. The social conditions and the economic conditions contributed to the increase. Extreme privation, food shortages, and the lack of basic necessities leads to the commission of acts that in more normal times would have never been committed. The author feels that if social and economic conditions ever "return to normal" the rates of juvenile offenses will decline with the same rapidity that they increased.

91. Makino, Tatsumi, "Educational Sociology in Japan," *Journal of Educational Sociology*, XXVI (September, 1952), 37-42.

92. Makino, Tatsumi, "Japanese Education," *International Social Science Journal* (UNESCO), XIII, 1 (1961), 44-51.

This is primarily an article discussing the educational reforms in Japan between 1945 and 1949 and again from 1950 to present. The emphasis is on the structure of the educational system, the curricula, and the administrative problems of the reconstruction. The author notes in conclusion that while many of the changes instituted by the occupation forces were eliminated by the conservative elements in the educational reconstruction, some of the changes still are in effect. Namely, the improvement in the teacher-student relationship, the absence of supernationalism in education, the introduction of instruction in fundamental human rights, and the prevalence of mass as opposed to elite education.

93. Matsmuto, Yoshikora Scott, *Contemporary Japan: A Review of Japanese Affairs* (Tokyo: The Foreign Affairs Association of Japan, 1962).

94. Matsumiya, Kazuya, "Family Organization in Japan," *American Journal of Sociology*, LIII, 2 (September, 1947), 105-110.

One of the effects of the industrialization of Japan is to create problems of nonfamily population. Economic depression induces young men in rural districts as well as members of proletarian families to leave their homes and live independently in other places.

Although the tendency for rural dwellers to leave their villages is world-wide, it is particularly fateful for Japan which has been chiefly dependent upon agriculture. For the proletarian families in the cities the economic pressure is so strong that they always try to keep to a minimum the number dependent upon the family income.

1. There are more nonfamily members among the younger group, which means that they are not living under the authority of the family head and are not directly receiving family influence and consequently are not likely to be as loyal to family tradition as in previous times.

2. There are more men than women who do not live in their own families. This means that the women are more restricted by their parents than the men; as a result, they are more dependent upon family life. Also, the women in Japan have fewer economic, vocational, and educational opportunities than the men.

3. There are more nonfamily members in the larger cities. This fact indicates that in the future the number of nonfamily members will be increased, and this circumstance will be one of the most influential causes of the disintegration of the patriarchal family organization in Japan.

The size of the family under the patriarchal system is due to the fact that the patriarchal family strongly desires to continue the family line permanently.

The recent development of industry brought about great changes in productive procedure and transferred family members from home industry to that of the factory. This is also true in trade, commerce, education, and amusements, and even in the fields of art and religion.

This is, on the one hand, a hopeful sign for the creation of new Japan by the free expression of individuals, but it is a serious problem because the disintegration of the patriarchal family system, which has been and is the basis of the national life of Japan, will effect a grave change in the national life.

95. Matsunage, S., "A Study of the Breaking Off of Parent-Child Relations in Japan," *Gihujoshitankidaigakukiyo* IV (*Bulletin of the Gihu Women's College*), 1954.

96. Matsushima, M., "Home Backgrounds of the Child Problems of Recent Times," *Shakaijigyo* (*Social Work*), XLI, 6 (June, 1958), 3-11.

97. Matsushita, K., "Sengo Sedai no Seikatsu to Shiso" (Life and Thought of the Post-War Generation), *Shiso,* CDXXI (July, 1959), 12-27.

98. Matsuura, K., "An Analysis of Problem Families," *Kozakyoikusha-kaigsku* (*Lectures on Educational Sociology*), III (September, 1953 , 180-191.

99. Matsuura, K., "The Significance of the Broken Home to the Problem Child—A Reflection on the Controlled Sample Method," *Tokyogaku geidaigakukenkyuhokoku* (*Bulletin of the Tokyogakugei University*), V (December, 1953), 39-44.

100. Michio, Takeyama, "Tradition and Japanese Youth," *Japan Quarterly,* VII (July/September, 1960), 274-280.

101. Minoru, Tachi, "The 'Baby Boom' and After," *Japan Quarterly,* VIII (1961), 295-301.

An examination of the postwar baby boom in Japan and a commentary on the reasons for its sudden termination and the effect of this termination. The author utilized the records of survey reports and personal observation in the writing of this article.

After the Second World War the baby boom in Japan has dropped sharply. Part of the explanation is due to the adoption of abortion acts which allow abortion under certain circumstances. The drop in the number of birth has left its mark on the schools. The upper grades are overfull while the lower grades are all but empty.

102. Mishima, Sumci Seo, *The Broader Way* (New York: The John Day Company, Inc., 1953).

103. Morita, S., "Family Tensions As Seen through Juvenile Cases," *Shakai-tekikincho-no-kenkyu* (*Study of Social Tension*), V (Yjgikaku: 1953), 27-61.

104. Morita, S., "Tensions and Conflicts in Home Life Among Juvenile Cases," *Kateisaiban-geppo* (*Domestic Court Monthly*), V, 1 (January, 1953), 1-26.

105. Naito, K., "On Parent-Child Relationships—Their Meaning in

Japan," *Kyoiku to igaku* (*Education and Medicine*), III, 9 (April, 1955), 22-27.

106. Nakano, S., "Modern Trends in the Family Group and Children," *Gakkakyoi-ku* (*School Education*), 429 (March, 1953) 16-21.

107. Nakano, T., "Methods of Social Research in Cities," *Shakaichosa no hoho* (*Methods of Social Research*), T. Fukutake (ed.) (Yuhikaku: 1954), 71-110.

108. Nett, Martha, "An American Girl in a Japanese Home," *This Is Japan*, 6 (September, 1958), 79-81.

109. Nishida, Kikuo, "Students' Movement," *Contemporary Japan*, XXI, 10-12 (1952-1953), 555-572.

An article from the early 1950's which attempts to explicate the student movements in Japan. The relevance of the comments for understanding the youth of Japan in 1963 may be seen in the continued activity of the student population of that country.

An important factor is the psychological background of these students. That they were completing their primary education during the Pacific war is significant in that the war strangely affected them and their school systems. Military training and labor mobilization cut into their secondary education. Added to this is the psychological confusion caused by the postwar social and economic anomalies. This is probably the most important factor.

The end of war disillusionment and confusion has a tendency to instill an appetite for the high-spirited life, although they were abhorred by thoughts of violence and/or war. Furthermore, there seemed to be a general inferiority complex that eventually developed with an antialien orientation.

There are five primary characteristics of these students' movements. They are as follows: (1) they work for self-protection; (2) there is a trend away from local, autonomous units toward national politics; (3) they dislike de facto political power; (4) they are becoming eager to affiliate with a "certain internationally organized political power"; and (5) they are led by a despotic minority.

Their objectives today can be summarized in five points also. They are working for: (1) place and independence; (2) economic improvements for their own lives; (3) the protection of democratic rights; (4) the formation of a joint front with organized labor; and (5) the denunciation of the Anti-Subversive law.

These students' movements exhibit five basic weaknesses also: (1) they are abusing their free-speech right; (2) they are attempting to impose their purposes on others (just as they see the government attempting to do with them); (3) they have no real justification for their violence; (4) they are abusing the universities who are letting them exist; and (5) by nature and organization they are falling outside of the university milieu.

110. Nishihira, Naoki, "Okinawato Seinen no Seikatou Kukan no Bunseki: Shakai Shinrigakuteki Wakugumi" (Analysis of Life-Space of Adolescents on Okinawa Island: Sociopsychological Frame of Reference), *Japanese Journal of Educational Psychology,* V (1958), 171-177.

A proposal for the study of adolescent psychology on the basis of their environment. The behavioral patterns are felt to be understandable only in relation to the environmental background of the individuals. In this case, 4,000 adolescents on Okinawa were interviewed and six aspects of their life-space were examined. The aspects examined were difficulty of adjustment, freedom, stability, health, integration of value system, and differentiation of the time perspective.

111. Nishimoto, Mitoji, "Educational Change in Japan after the War," *Journal of Educational Sociology,* XXVI (September, 1952), 16-27.

112. No Author: *Japan Quarterly* (Basic Trends: Social)
III, (1956), 12-16.
III, (1956), 271-275.
V, (1958), 412-417, "The Faces of Violence."
VII, (1960), 137-141, "The Red 'Thunder Tribe.' "
VIII, (1961), 10-13, "Crime on the Increase."

113. Nobechi, Masazuki and Teiji Kimura, "Study of Values Applied to Japanese Students," *Psychologia,* 1 (1057), 120-122.

A brief report on two studies of Japanese students using the old and the revised form of the Allport, Vernon, and Lindzey studies. The first study utilized the old form in 1954 on a group of 410 males and 96 females at Nihon University. It was noted that the value orientations of these students corresponded very well with their special fields of study.

The second study (Nobechi, 1955, revised form), dealt with males and females at Deshisha University. Again the high and low scores corresponded well with the subjects' special fields. It was found that women were more religious than men; less theoretic; and less economical. In an area where the American groups do not score very high (aesthetic values) both males and females in this Japanese group scored very high. While American students place high emphasis on social values the Japanese students place much less emphasis on social values.

The author concludes, "As to the difference between the evaluations of Americans and Japanese students in the religious and the aesthetic, Nobechi presumes that the religious experiences in Japan are quite different from those in the United States, and moreover, they are not so common and ordinary for the Japanese people as for the American people, and wonders why the preference for the aesthetic value was not formed in American male students, in spite of the notion that adolescence is a period in which one longs for beauty increasingly."

114. Norbeck, E., "Age-Grading in Japan; Adolescence and Early Maturity," *American Anthropologist*, LV (August, 1953), 376-379.

Associations for single men and women are in a sense an example of age-grading. The nationally organized associations are supposed to promote community welfare and help out in emergencies. They are also social, recreational, and educational organizations.

Traditional organizations are subdivided often into three age classes. Special feelings of attachment are experienced between those initiated in the same year. In some communities members feel a joint responsibility for another member's misbehavior.

Puberty ceremonies are closely linked with initiation into the age-class youth organizations.

A few rural communities observe coming-of-age ceremonies.

When a boy enters into the youth age class (14 or so) he accepts an adult's share of labor in the community.

115. Norbeck, E., "Postwar Cultural Change and Continuity in Northeastern Japan," *American Anthropologist*, LXIII (April, 1961), 297-321. (Bibliography)

Social change in the communities studied is characterized by a weakening of kinship bonds, a weakening of personal ties, changes in authority patterns resulting in the weakening of the hierarchical family structure. Though the family group living under the same roof is still fairly unified affective ties to extranuclear family kin have weakened and reliance on these relatives for economic assistance is not desirable.

An increasing stress has been placed on cooperative associations and these often have an extracommunity organization. Property redistribution legislation, passed after the war, has produced more democratic intrapersonal relationships. Economic reforms and programs have been the most influential factors in bringing about the social changes.

Rural associations have taken over many of the functions previously associated with the kinship group. During the war, membership in these associations was required and enforced. Though this is no longer the case the social pressure on the family and on the individual to join these associations is very strong.

Though legal primogeniture has been abolished the eldest son usually still succeeds the father in the patriarchal succession. Because of this the eldest son has lost a considerable amount of status in modern times. Since he will assume the paternal occupation, usually farming or fishing, and inherit the family lands he is not given the education which younger sons receive. The younger sons leave the household, and usually the village, and establish their own business, trade, or profession. It was reported that the eldest sons had difficulty finding brides. Girls prefer the younger, better-educated sons rather than live with the husband's parents until he inherits their land and then be consigned to a life of household, and farming drudgery. Though most marriages are still arranged, "love marriage" is becoming more popular than it was in the prewar era.

116. Noboru, Ito, "Full Cycle in Education," *This Is Japan,* 10 (September, 1963), 90-93.

117. Noboru, Ito, "'New Education' Suffers Growing Pains," *This Is Japan,* 5 (September, 1957), 84-85.

118. Noboru, Ito, "The Reform of Japanese Education," *Japan Quarterly,* III (1956), 425-430.

119. Ogawa, Kazuo, "A Study of Teacher's Attitude toward the Social Structure of Children in Classroom II," *Japanese Journal of Educational Psychology,* IV (1956), 46-54.

120. Ogawa, T., "Parent-Child Relations and Education in Modern Society," *Jidoshinri* (*Child Psychology*), VII, 9 (September, 1953), 1-9.

121. Ohama, H., "Family Tensions and Juveniles," *Seishonenmondai* (*Problems of Juveniles*), I, 4 (October, 1954), 6-12.

122. Ohta, T., "Familism and Youth," *Seinenshinri* (*Psychology of Youth*), V, 3 (September, 1954), 102-106.

123. Oi, Heiichiro, "Daigakusi No Aino-jin ni Taisuru Nonkirigata no Henken ni Tsuite" (The Stereotyped Prejudices of College Students on the Aino), *Tohoku Journal of Experimental Psychology,* I, 3 (1955), 86-91.

A study of the patterns of stereotypes of 420 college students in Japan. The group used as objects of evaluation were the

Aino. The students were asked to select, from a list of seventy items, the five most outstanding characteristics of the Aino. In order of frequency the five selected as most characteristic were: traditional; superstitious; artistic; seclusive; brave. The general student reaction was that the Aino are uncivilized and barbarous. It was felt that these prejudices were the result of false information in irresponsible periodicals, radio programs, movies, and the other mass media rather than the result of personal observations and rational conclusions.

124. Okada, Y., "Family and School," *Shakai to gakko* (*Society and School*), III, 3 (March, 1949), 1-6.

125. Okada, Yuzuru, "Kinship Organization in Japan," *Journal of Educational Sociology*, XXVI (September, 1952), 27-32.

126. Okaji, Ichiro, "Seinen no Seikatsu ni Taisuru Taido no Tokushitsu ni Kansuru Kenkyi" (Studies on Characteristics of Adolescents' Attitudes toward Life), *Japanese Journal of Educational Psychology* (July, 1958), 7-13, 61-62.

A factor analysis was done on the responses of a sample of 157 college students and 58 adults to a questionnaire on the values of adolescents. Generally, the two groups revealed similarities of attitudes. Half of the adolescent group were then instructed in efficient ways to live in the modern world. The instruction proved effective in altering the attitudes. The author concludes that the adolescents' attitudes are indefinite and subject to change.

127 Okamoto, K. and I. Sakamoto, "On the Attitude Change by Reading a Biography in Pupils," *Reports of Annual Meeting of Association of Educational Psychology* (1957).

128. Okubo, M., "On Problem Children and the Attitudes of Their Parents," *Shakaijigyo* (*Social Work*), XXXVII, 6 (July, 1954), 37-39, 79-90.

129. Oura, K., "A Study of the Family through Juvenile Cases—Juvenile Delinquents and Home (2)," *Kateisaibangeppo* (*Domestic Court Monthly*), IX, 7 (July, 1957), 59-101.

130. "Parent-Child Relationships within Urban Families—Comparison of Salaried Families and Merchant Families," *Konanjoshitankidigakuronso* (*Bulletin of the Konan Women's College*), 1, 1956.

131. Passin, Herbert and John Bennett, "The American-Educated Japanese, I. The Student in America: Theory; Background; Images," *Annals of the American Academy of Political and Social Science*, CCXCV (1954), 83-96.

A 1954 article which reports on an intensive study of 100 Japanese students in the United States. The author is interested in the culture and images of the Japanese students, how they change when they return home, and what factors are responsible for this change.

It was noted that the contemporary Japanese student holds a great deal of ambivalence toward the United States. The author notes several types among the students: (1) Ideologist—this group is found mostly among students in Japan. His experience is ". . . pressed by his internal needs and hoping to find much in America, the expectations of the ideologist are very high, perhaps too high for reality." (2) The Japanese Oriented—the Adjustors—they are mainly oriented toward their own society. While some negative attitudes toward the United States can be found, most are here to obtain skills and manage to display friendly adjustment strategies. (3) The Nationalist—is negatively oriented toward the United States. Few are interested in coming here. This group includes both the extreme right wing and the Communist students.

The author notes that the period in America is intense and the return sometimes difficult but an unfavorable reaction to the United States is far from an inevitable response.

132. Passin, Herbert and John Bennett, "The American-Educated Japanese, II. Images after Return to Japan; Conclusions," *Annals of the American Academy of Political and Social Science*, CCXCV (1954), 97-107.

A continuation of the above study. In this article the authors discuss the reactions and adjustments of the Japanese student upon his return to Japan. Among the questions noted by the returning students were: How to achieve reintegration in Japanese life? What to do about new habits of life? How to secure the acceptance of the value of their American education?

Among the postwar types discussed are the following: (1) The Woman Rebel—her images of America, whatever they are, will be reinforced and confirmed. (2) The Ideologist—he will remain dissatisfied and in search of new values. His memberbership in various groups will demand that he select his images of America with care. His equal treatment in America makes his treatment as an inferior at home particularly hard to bear. (3) The Adjustor—returns with a feeling that he has had a worthwhile experience which he can now use. He is glad to be home. His image of the backward and rigid facts of life in Japan will be strengthened.

133. Pease, Damaris, "Some Child Rearing Practices in Japanese Families," *Marriage and Family Living*, XXIII (May, 1961), 179-181.

A discussion of the child-rearing practices of the Japanese family. The author comes to the conclusion that the Japanese family is child-oriented.

134. Ramsey, Charles E. and Robert J. Smith, "Japanese and American Perceptions of Occupations," *The American Journal of Sociology*, LXV, 5 (March, 1960), 475-484.

A comparison of Japanese and American samples which leads the authors to note the similarities between the two areas with regard to general rankings of occupational prestige and social importance of occupations. The emphasis here is not so much on the similarities of ranking but on the relationship of the rankings to other variables (age, sex, residence, and social importance).

135. "A Research on the Attitude of Working Adolescents," *Research Association of Education* (Tokyo: 1962).

136. Sakanishi, Shio, "Women's Position and the Family System (in Japan)," *The Annals*, CCCVIII (November, 1956), 130-139.

137. Sanada, Z., "The Family Composition of Urban Lower Classes—from the Survey of Nittoh Area of Osaka City," *Shakaimondai-kenkyu* (Study of Social Problems), V, 7 (December, 1955).

138. Sano, Katsuo, "College Students' Attitudes toward Literature," *Japanese Journal of Psychology*, XX, 3 (1950), 27-32.

139. Sasabe, T., "Amaasaki-shi ni okeru Yakan Chugakusei no Jittai," (Children Who Work by Day and Go to School at Night), *Ronshu*, IV, 3 (1958), 19-54.

140. Sato, N., "Nihon no Mishushugi to Sengo Sedai" (Japanese Democracy and the Post-War Generation), *Shiso*, CDXXI (July, 1959), 1-11.

141. Schmid, P., "Japan's Lost Generation," *Commentary*, XXIII (May, 1957), 466-470.

142. Schwantes, Robert S., "Educational Influence of the U.S.A.," *Contemporary Japan*, XXVI, 3 (1959-60), 442-485.

143. Seki, K., "Destitute Stratum of a City and the Structure of Their Life—a Study of the Association between Poverty and the Group Structure of the Family," *Hokkaidodaigakubungakubkuiyo* (*Bulletin of the Faculty of Literature of the Hokkaido University*), IV (1955), 26-75.

144. Seki, K., "Patterns of Family Disorganization and Poverty—a Sociological Study of the Measurement of the Standards of Living," *Shakaigaku Hyoron* (*Sociological Review*), XX (April, 1955), 10-32.

145. Shimada, K., "The Study of Value in Students," Doctoral Thesis, Tokyo Educational University.

146. Shimizu, Y., "Home Education in Time of Crisis," *Kozakyoikush-akaigaku* (*Lectures on Educational Sociology*), II (December, 1953), 121-143.

147. Shimizu, Y., "The Problems of Juvenile Delinquency in Post-War Japan," *Journal of Educational Sociology,* XXVI (September, 1952), 32-37.

An article from the early 1950's discussing the problem of delinquency in Japan. Utilizing the statistics on youth crime in Japan the author attacks the problem by noting the rise and presenting the figures. He attempts to establish that the rise in delinquency occurs both in times of social change and after great catastrophes (such as World War II). On the basis of 1936 he notes that the increase in crime in 1946 is 240 per cent and in 1950 the increase is 340 per cent. Noting the trend toward lower ages, taking 1945 as index 100 he notes the following figures: under 14, 408; 14-18, 288; 18-20, 245. Burglary, rape, assault, and theft are all over 700 per cent higher than they were in 1936. He also notes an increase in female delinquency, delinquency in the schools, and sexual delinquencies.

In explanation of these rates he offers a distinction between crime following catastrophe and crime in a period of modernization. Following the war there was economic impoverishment in general and a general distortion of the social structure. He feels that delinquency is ". . . a pathological symptom of distorted social structure of Japanese society."

148. Shioda, Y., Y. Murakami, and M. Ohashi, "Parental Expectations and Children's Wishes," *Nagoyadaigakukyoikugakubukiyo* (*Bulletin of the Faculty of Education of the Nagoya University*), I (March, 1955), 87-100.

149. Shunsuke, Murakami and Ivahashi Bunkichi, "Post-War Reconstruction of Japanese Education and Its Social Aspects," *Journal of Educational Sociology,* XXIX (January, 1956), 309-316.

"The Fundamental Law of Education in 1947 declares that the purpose of education in new Japan is 'to aim at the full development of personality, striving for the rearing of the people, sound in mind and body, who shall love truth and justice, esteem individual values, respect labor, have a deep sense of responsibility, and be imbued with an independent spirit, as builders of a peaceful society and state."

There has been some social tension between this new educational policy and the public, as well as internal difficulties in the system.

Some problems were: education was seen as a means of improving socio-economic status and caused great number of college applicants; difficulty arose in trying to handle so many; there is criticism because of the financial burden of supporting more institutions; the present difficult situation of the employment of college graduates.

There is a problem in that vocational subjects, essential to a democratic nation, are not viewed as important by the public. They emulate the college preparatory course.

In trying to educate working youth, the employers are indifferent and public doesn't provide enough financial support, causing difficulty in this area of education.

150. Skillman, John H., "A Study of the Relationship between Participation in Various Types of Extra-Class Activities and Academic Performance in Three Private Japanese Secondary Schools" (Ann Arbor, Michigan: University Microfilms, 1959). Collation of the Original: vi, 110. l. forms. Abstracted in *Dissertation Abstracts*, V. 19 (1959), N. 8, 1958-1959.

This dissertation investigated the relationship between participation in extra-class activities and academic achievement with intelligence factors controlled. The sample consisted of 194 third-year students from three private Japanese high schools in Tokyo. Subjects were matched for intelligence, age, year in in school, and socio-economic background.

The following hypotheses were examined:

1. There is a significant difference between the academic achievement of the participants in some types of the extra-class activities in which students engage and the academic achievement of nonparticipants with intelligence controlled.

2. The academic achievement of participants in extra-class activities is significantly different for the various types of extra-class activities in which students engage when intelligence is controlled.

3. Academc achievement is significantly higher for the participants in those types of extra-class activities in which improved academic achievement is a more important objective than for the participants in those types of activities in which it is a less important objection.

4. There is no significant difference between the mean achievement of all participators in extra-class activities and the mean achievement of all nonparticipators.

Hypotheses 1, 2, and 4 were supported by the analysis. Hypothesis 3 was rejected.

151. Smith, R. J., "Japanese Rural Community: Norms, Sanctions and Ostracism," *American Anthropologist*, LXIII (June, 1961), 522-533.

Discussion of intrafamily and intrapersonal normative interaction within a Japanese hamlet. Applies to youth, in general, as members of the larger family and community.

152. Smith, R. J. and Charles E. Ramsey, "Attitudes of Japanese High School Seniors toward the Military," *Public Opinion Quarterly* (in press).

153. Smith, Thomas C., "The Introduction of Western Industry to Japan during the Last Years of the Tokugawa Period," *Harvard Journal of Asiatic Studies*, XI (1948), 130-152.

154. Smythe, H. H. and S. Kono, "Social Distance Test of the Eta Caste of Japan," *Sociology and Social Research*, XXXVIII (September, 1953), 26-31.

155. Soto, K. and F. Nakano, "Nationality Preferences of Japanese Students After World War II," *Journal of Social Psychology*, XXVIII (August, 1949), 165-166.

A 1949 study of the social attitudes of 917 Japanese boys and girls in high schools and junior colleges. Nationality and racial differences were investigated and compared with an earlier study by Kusunoki done before and after the Sino-Japanese War (1937).

The later study revealed a strong preference for Western nationalities as compared to Asiatic groups. In comparison with the Kusunoki study, Americans, Chinese, and Russians made large gains in standing and Koreans and Italians declined. It was noted that the low ratings received by the Negro and the Jew were unusual due to the lack of contact between the Japanese and these groups.

156. Spinks, C. N., "Indoctrination and Reorientation of Japan's Youth," *Pacific Affairs*, XVII (March, 1944), 56-70.

157. Steiner, Kurt, "The Revision of the Civil Code of Japan: Provisions Affecting the Family," *The Far Eastern Quarterly*, IX (February, 1950), 169-184.

As a result of their commitment to the Potsdam Declaration, the Japanese were forced to revise their civil code which had been in existence since 1896. This code was one which embodied the customs prevailing in Japan at that time. The emphasis was on the patriarchic family which was an expression of the traditional Japanese devotion to ancestors. Furthermore, in this family system ". . . the family is the symbol and sample of all other social units including the state. . . ." The family, then, was stressed as the basic social unit.

The "new code" came into effect January 1, 1948. It was an attempt to democratize this almost feudal system. Two of its outstanding features were the raising of the legal status of women and the weakening of the authority and power of the family. Hereafter, the individual of either sex was to have legal status and rights (formerly, there had only been duties) which had formerly been the prerogatives of the family: men and women could freely choose their own spouse; women were to be given equal rights in regard to property and inheritance; the newly married couple could choose their own place of dwelling, irrespective of the wishes of a family head; and more equal rights were established in regard to divorce.

The author concludes by mentioning that it is a simple matter to write a new code, but adherence will probably be a less simple matter. The importance of the family has strong social, economic, and psychological bases, and it will take some time for the Japanese people to adjust to, and appreciate, their new democracy.

158. Stoetzel, Jean, *Without the Chrysanthemum and the Sword: A Study of the Attitudes of Youth in Postwar Japan*, A UNESCO publication (New York: Columbia University Press, 1955).

No attempt will be made here to summarize this significant contribution to the understanding of the youth of Japan. Let it suffice for us to note one short passage which will illustrate the tenor of the work.

"In fact, 20 is the official age for attaining majority in Japan, and is marked by a solemn coming of age ceremony newly instituted by the State. Coming of Age (January 15) is one of the nine national feast days of the new order, and on that day ceremonies and meetings are held throughout the country at which young people are required to take formal cognizance of their new responsibilities. Coming of age is undoubtedly important in the eyes of the individual, and of his immediate circle. But at the age of 20, the individual is far from being, in all cases, mature in the psychological and sociological sense, an adult in the full meaning of the word. The decisive line of demarcation between adolescence and adulthood is marriage, and, even more surely, in a country where marriages are not often registered until after the birth of the first child, parenthood. It is fatherhood that makes a man a full member of the community, and motherhood that converts the wife into a matron entitled to the privileges of smoking, drinking, and of making, not merely laughing at, coarse sexual jokes. . . ."

159. Sudo, K., *Noson seinen no ikikata* (*The Way of Life of the Rural Youth*) (Tokyo: Nosangyoson bunkakyokai, 1958).

160. Suekawa, Hiroshi, "Educator's View of the Revision of Education Law," *Contemporary Japan,* XXIII, 1-3 (1954), 199-202.

161. Suga, S., "On the Familial and Social Conditions of Juvenile Delinquency," *Kyoikushakaigskukenkyu* (*Study of Educational Sociology*), IX, 1956.

162. Sugimito, E. I., *A Daughter of the Samurai* (New York: Doubleday, 1925).

163. Sugo, H., "Authority in Home Education," *Jidoshinri* (*Child Psychology*), VI, 3 (March, 1952), 201-205.

164. Supreme Commander for the Allied Powers, Civil Information and Educational Section, *Education in the New Japan* (Tokyo: General Headquarters, Supreme Commander for the Allied Powers, Civil Information and Education Section, Education Division, 1948), 2 vols.

165. Suyama, S. and M. Mochizuki, "Misunderstandings between Senior High School Students and Their Mothers," *Shiso no kagaku* (*Science of Thoughts*), I, 8 (1954), 28-33.

166. Tachi, M., M. Ueda, and H. Hama, "Seinen-ki Jinko no Chiikiteki Bunseki," (Regional Analysis of the Youth Population), *Jinko Mondai Kenkyu* 76, (1959), 1-40.

167. Taeuber, Irene B., "Family, Migration, and Industrialization in Japan," *American Sociological Review,* XVI (1951), 149-157.

168. Takada, Y., "White collar no Sengo Senai" (The Pre-War Gen-*Ecumenical Review,* III (July, 1951), 393-404.

169. Takeda, K., "What Is in the Mind of the Japanese Youth Today?" eration as White Collar Representation), *Shiso* 421 (July, 1959), 39-54.

170. Takenaka, T., "Jogakusei no Goraku ni Kansura Chosa, I" (An Investigation of the Amusements of School Girls, I), *Kyoiku Shinri Kenkyu,* XV (1940), 38-54.

171. Takenaka, T., "Jogakusei no Goraku Cosa, II. Jogakusei no Goraku Toshiteno Eiga" (An Investigation of the Amusements of School Girls, II. The Cinema as an Amusement of School Girls), *Kyoiku Shinri Kenkyu,* XV (1940), 106-129.

172. Takizawa, Matsuy, *The Penetration of Money Economy in Japan* (New York: Columbia University Press, 1927).

173. Tamanyu, M., "Senso to shonen hanzai-koto ni kikikeizai to hanzaisharuikei no kankei o chushin to shite" (Juvenile Delinquency and the War: A Sociopsychological Analysis), *Japanese Journal of Psychology,* XIX (1948), 97-116.

174. Tamon, Maeda, "The Direction of Postwar Education in Japan," *Japan Quarterly,* III (1956), 414-424.

175. Tamura, K., "Family Relationships As Reflected in the Minds of the Students of Our University—Employing the Method of Free Description," *Tokyogakugeidaigaku-kenkyugokou* (*Bulletin of the Tokyogakugei University*), X (1959), 49-64.

176. Tanaka, Kunio, "Shakaiteki Taido No Sokuteironteki Kenkyu I," (The Measurement of Social Attitudes), *Japanese Journal of Psychology,* XXIV (1953), 98-104. (English Abstract, p. 175-176)

177. Tanino, Setsu, "Family Life," *International Social Science Journal* (UNESCO), XIII, 1 (1961), 57-64.

A discussion of the democratization of family life in Japan based on the examination and interpretation of laws and documents.

The author notes that the new family law is based on the principle of respect for the individual and sexual equality. The new civil code stressed the dignity of the individual and marriage as the beginning of life for a new family. The new constitution also stressed sexual equality. The law emphasized that it is the will of the bride and her bridegroom that should prevail about the decision of marriage and not that of the parents. However, tradition was very strong here and parents are still deciding the marriages, but to a lesser extent. Marriages are not recognized by both a social ceremony and an official registration. "The younger women today are quite dependent on husbands. The wider experience of women in public life has promoted the rationalization of daily home life, and the newly emancipated women are making the best effort with not a little success to democratize family life in Japan."

178. Tatai, Kichinosuke, "A Further Study of Suicide in Japan," *Report of the Department of Physiological Hygiene,* VII (The Institute of Public Health), 152-158.

179. "The Rising Sun Tribe," *Time,* LXVIII, 25 (December, 1956), 37.

180. Togawa, Y., "Family Disorganization," *Gendaishakaishinrigaku* (*Modern Social Psychology*), VIII (*Nakayam-shoten,* June, 1959), 119-134.

181. Tokiomi, Kaigo, "The American Influence on the Education in

Japan," *Journal of Educational Sociology,* XXVI (September, 1952), 9-16.

A short discussion of the foreign trends and influences in Japanese education. The author goes back to the eighteenth century and notes the influences up to and including the occupation of Japan after World War II and the educational influences of the occupation forces.

182. Trumbull, Robert, "Children of Japan's Broken Family," *New York Times Magazine,* CVIII (August, 1959), 9.

183. Trumbull, Robert, "Young Love vs. Japan's Old Code," *New York Times Magazine,* CVII (March 9, 1958), 26.

184. Tsugami, M., "Social Classes, Ways of Dealing with Children and Their Influences," *Jidoshinri to seishineisei* (*Child Psychology and Mental Hygiene*), IV, 4 (August, 1954), 60-80.

185. Tsuji, S., "Child-Adult Relations in the Family," *Jidoshinri* (*Child Psychology*), VII, 9 (September, 1953), 30-36.

186. Tsuji, S., "A Study of the Dynamic Structure of Home as Seen by Children—Focusing on Father-Mother-Child Relations," *Jidoshinri to seishineisei* (*Child Psychology and Mental Hygiene*), III, 1 (September, 1952), 12-21.

187. Tsuru, H., "Family Relationships and the Way of Calling Each Other," *Japanese Journal of Educational Psychology,* IV (1956), 12-20.

188. Tsuru, H., "Grandparents and Parents Around Children," *Kyoikushinri* (*Educational Psychology*), III, 7 (July, 1955), 36-38.

189. Tsuzuku, A., and others, "A Study of Adolescent Attitude to Social Life," *Bulletin of Educational Department of Nagoya University,* V (1959), 170-177.

190. Ukai, Nobushige, "Whither Students of Today" (Activities of Zengakuren, the All-Japan Federation of Autonomous Students Bodies), *Contemporary Japan,* XXVI (November, 1960), 675-709.

191. U.N. Department of Social Affairs, Division of Social Welfare, *Comparative Study on Juvenile Delinquency: Part IV, Asia and the Far East* (New York: United Nations, 1953). (Note: See Burma.)

192. Ushikubo, H., "Home Background of Juvenile Delinquents," *Shakaijigyo* (*Social Work*), XXXVII, 9 (November, 1954), 80-94.

193. Ushikubo, H., "Mental Characteristics of Home Environment and Discipline of Juvenile Delinquents," *Shakaigaku Hyoron* (*Sociological Review*), X (February, 1953), 60-70.

194. Ushyima, Y., *Seinen no Shinri (Psychology of Youth)* (Tokyo: Ganshodoshoten, 1940).

195. Vogel, E., "Go-Between in a Developing Society: The Case of the Japanese Marriage Arranger," *Human Organization,* XX (Fall, 1961), 112-120.

Utilizing secondary sources and the results of personal observation, the author discusses the place of the marriage arranger in Japan.

Industrialization means transition in social organization. In Japan the mobile workers had a difficult time finding brides. This problem was filled by the "nakahdo" or marriage arranger who had contacts between the workers and eligible women. The use of the go-between allows detachment and objectivity in making decisions in a society where personal ties are very important.

The go-between is a functional alternative to dating. It has helped to prevent disruptions from rapid social change. The traditional patterns have been somewhat maintained even in the face of industrialization. The youth of Japan want more to say in the marriage decision than they did a generation ago. The go-between has adjusted to the increasing power of children, but considers the parents' wishes also and thereby serves as an integrator.

196. Vogel, S. H. and E. F. Vogel, "Family Security, Personal Security, and Emotional Health in a Japanese Sample," *Marriage and Family Living,* XXIII (May, 1961), 161-166.

The authors utilized participant observation and interviews over a period of 21 months to gather data for this study.

In attempting to use the American definition of maturity in non-Western countries when they do not always value independence the same, one finds personal immaturity but stable families and well-adjusted personalities. In a comparative study of a Japanese and American sample, the Japanese tend to rely more on others and prefer to be under the protection of a superior.

By American standards the Japanese child is very dependent upon his parents. They are slow to adjust in school, to overcome shyness. They are more reserved than Americans in new groups but lose this with time. In America, the push for independence comes from the child himself, but in Japan the parents must provide the push. The Japanese, more than Americans, prefer a structured situation.

197. Wagatsuma, Hiroshi and George DeVos, "Attitudes toward Ar-

ranged Marriage in Rural Japan," *Human Organization,* XXI, 3 (Fall, 1962), 187-200.

An examination of the effects of legal change of marriage laws as related to value attitudes in local settings. The data were gathered as part of larger survey conducted in Japan from 1953 to 1955. The sample consisted of three rural villages and two cities of central Honshu. The city sample contained 2760 individuals, the rural sample contained 435 individuals. The Thematic Apperception Test, Rorschach Test, Insight Tests, and figure drawings were utilized in this survey.

This particular study is limited to the examination of the attitudes toward marriage in the rural areas following the passage of new marriage laws which insure the rights of the individual over those of the parents. Under the new constitution men and women can legally marry without the consent of the parents. The study indicates that marriage by the family is no longer in favor with more than a small minority either in rural or urban areas.

The results indicate that the majority of young people examined felt that the marriage is primarily a concern of the parties involved and not a primary concern of the parents and families. These youth would not be particularly influenced by the lack of parental approval or the presence of active parental disapproval. On the other hand, these attitudes were reflected in response to the idea of a love match *in principle*. The authors note a disparity between what the individual believes in principle and what he does in practice. Thus, many subjects, when faced with the possibility of conflict in the marriage situation, will, in effect, fall back on familial dependence for solution of the problem. The authors note that the men interviewed placed a greater value on assertive behavior than did the women. Thus, it is the women who are most liable to fall back on tradition while the men are in the foreground in asserting the notions of individual independence in marriage choice. The assertive behavior of the males is further supported by the official government position as embodied in the constitution. Thus, the situation is consistent in this society which has committed itself to a new tradition of equality and individual determination.

198. Wagatsuma, Sakae, "Democratization of the Family Relations in Japan," *Washington Law Review,* XXV (1950), 405-426.

199. Wildes, Harry Emerson, *Aliens in the East: A New History of Japan's Foreign Intercourse* (Philadelphia: Univ. of Pennsylvania; London: Oxford, 1937).

200. Yamamota, T., "Parental Discord and Children," *Kyoikushinri* (*Educational Psychology*), III, 7 (July, 1955), 39-43.

201. Yamayaki, S., "The Psychical Attitudes of Youths Toward Death," *Japanese Journal of Psychology,* XV (1940), 469-475.

202. Yoda, A. and T. Kuse, "The Psychological Study of Parent Adolescent Relationships," *Bulletin of the Faculty of Education, Nagoya,* III (March, 1957), 391.

A study of parent-adolescent relationships conducted on 563 male and 491 female students in junior and senior high schools in Nagoya City, Japan. A questionnaire approach was utilized. The results of the analysis led to authors' conclusion that the adolescents' gaining of independence is a gradual process, a process which accelerates with age. The feelings and attitudes surrounding the adolescents' independence vary among the adolescents studied. It is especially noted that the males express more overt independence and attitudes of independence from the parents than do the girls. Regardless of sex, but with the females predominating, the adolescent generally hopes that the parent will be supportive and helpful in the future in the area of family problems when the adolescent reaches the point where he, or she, is in a position to have family problems of his own.

203. Yoda, Arata and Kuze, Toshio, "Seinen-ryoshin Kankei: Shakaiteki Taido ni Okeru Oyako no Kankei" (Parent-Adolescent Relationships and Social Attitudes), *Japanese Journal of Social Psychology,* VI (March, 1959), 229-231.

204. Yoshida, S., "The Types of Character in Delinquent Boys and Their Dynamic Peculiarity," *Japanese Journal of Psychology,* XIV (1939), 408-430.

205. Yoshikawa, Fusae, "Seinenki mi Okeru Jiga No Beisei" (Development of Self-Consciousness in Adolescence), *Japanese Journal of Educational Psychology,* VIII (1960), 26-37.

206. Yuzo, Morita, "The National Income and the Standard of Living of Japan," *Japan Quarterly,* III (1956), 107-117.

KOREA

1. Rettig, Solomon and Benjamin Pasamanick, "Moral Codes of American and Korean College Students," *Journal of Social Psychology,* L (1959), 65-73.

The authors examined 513 Korean students at the University of Seoul and 489 American students at Ohio State University for a comparison of moral values. A questionnaire containing 50 morally prohibited activities was used. The results indicate that the moral codes of American college students are not comparable in severity to the codes of Korean students. The reasons for this may be found in the background of Buddhism and Confucianism and parental training. The conversion to Christianity in many cases is not a religious conversion but a matter of identification with the West.

2. Simos, Irving, "Ethnocentrism and Attitudes toward the Rosenberg Case and the Republic of Korea," *Journal of Social Psychology*, XLIII (1956), 181-185.

3. Wood, C. W., "Secondary Education in South Korea," *The Educational Forum*, XXIV (November, 1959), 99-106.

4. Yu, Chong-Yol, "Korea's Marriage," *Korean Report*, II, 9 (November-December, 1962), 29-31.

MONGOLIA

1. Briggs, Lawrence P., "The Structure of Moslem Society in Inner Mongolia," *The Far Eastern Quarterly*, VIII (November, 1948), 34-44.

2. Miller, Robert, "Education," *A Regional Handbook on the Inner Mongolia Autonomous Region*. Subcontractor's Monograph HRAF-60, Wash-7. University of Washington, Far Eastern and Russian Institute, compiler. New Haven, Conn. Human Relation Area Files, Inc., 1956.

   Describes the cultural and educational systems of Inner Mongolia, with specific attention to efforts of the National Government and of the present regime to deal with problems of minority groups, multiple languages, illiteracy, and the teacher shortage.

TAIWAN

1. Chang, Siao-Sung, et al., "A Study of the Interests of the 1957 Freshman Class of National Taiwan University," *Acta Psychologia*, 1 (November, 1958), 85-98.

2. Marsh, Robert M. and Albert R. O'Hara, "Attitudes toward Marriage and the Family in Taiwan," *The American Journal of Sociology*, LXVII, 1 (July, 1961), 1-8.

   The authors utilized questionnaires on six aspects of marriage and family attitudes in investigating Nationalist Chinese attitudes on marriage. The questionnaires were applied to 651 undergraduate students in two universities in Taipei and Taiwan. 651 University of Michigan students were examined in 1959 for purposes of comparison. The results generally indicate that certain attitudes have gained almost as much acceptance in Formosa as they have in the United States. The figures below indicate the responses to some of the items.

	Taiwan	Michigan
1. Marriage should be based on love; there should be love before marriage	92	98
2. I want to choose my mate independently	87	—
3. The new (Western) style marriage is better than the old-style Chinese marriage	87	—
4. Sexes should not be separated at social gatherings	87	96
5. Sexes should not be separated in a university	87	94
6. Sexes should not be separated in primary school	84	94
7. Young people should be engaged before marriage	84	93
8. Newlyweds should not live with parents	59	99
9. I expect to be able to choose my mate independently	58	98
10. Sexes should not be separated in middle school (7-12)	45	95
	N = 651	238

It was also noted that the respondents whose parents had received more schooling (college) were not significantly more modern in their attitudes than were the students whose parents had had no college training. This is interpreted in light of the fact that the college educated elites were the groups who originally exerted the greatest control over their children in the matter of mate selection.

The free choice of mates presupposes some form of dating or courtship, but the contact between the sexes, with exception of graduate students, is very slight. In the middle school, the sexes are almost totally separated. While group mixing is accepted the unchaperoned pairing off of couples is thoroughly disapproved.

3. Rodd, William G., "A Cross-Cultural Study of Taiwan's Schools," *Journal of Social Psychology*, I (1959), 3-36.

4. Sassani, Abul H. K., *Education in Taiwan: Formosa* (Washington: U.S. Government Printing Office, 1956).

GENERAL

1. "Challenge of Asia's Youth," *Asia*, XXXVIII (July/October, 1938), 414-17; 500-503; 523-525; 587-590: XXXIX (April/May, 1939), 237-239; 300-302.
2. Fraser, J., "Youth in Asia," *Ecumenical Review*, II, 3 (1950), 259-266.
3. Keehn, J. D. and E. T. Prothro, "National Preferences of University Students from 23 Nations," *Journal of Psychology*, XLII (1956), 283-294.
4. Lin, Yueh-hwa, "Kinship System of the Lolo," *Harvard Journal of Asiatic Studies*, IX (1945-1947), 81-100.
5. Taylor, H., "The Student: A Key Man in Asia," *Institute of International Education News Bulletin*, XXXVI, 2 (1960), 4-10.
6. Yamamura, Douglas S., "Attitudes of Asiatic Students to Orientation in Hawaii," *Social Processes Hawaii*, XX (1956), 54-73.

THE NEAR EAST

ALGERIA

1. Blanc, Amedee, "L'Evolution Intellectuelle, Morale et Sociale de la Jeune Fille Musulmane D'Algerie" (The Intellectual, Moral, and Social Development of an Algerian Musselman Girl), *Revue de Psychologie des Peuples*, XIII (1958), 306-323.

   The author discusses the changes in the way of life in Algeria and how these changes are affecting the freedom and altering the personality of the Mussulman girl. The modern-day girl is compared to an earlier counterpart. The author discusses several typical but different girls and reveals the influence of the public school on customs, religion, dress, and intellectual life.

EGYPT

1. Abu-Lu-Ghad, J., and L. Amin, "Egyptian Marriage Advertisements; Microcosm of a Changing Society," *Marriage and Family Living*, XXIII (May, 1961), 127-136.

   A discussion of the marriage advertisements appearing in Egyptian newspapers. The article discusses the qualities revealed in the ads and notes the marginal status of many of the women.
   The authors conclude that women who advertise, on the whole, desire older men with college educations, respectable

positions, and high incomes. Marital status, physical status, and personality seemed to be relatively unimportant items. For the men, the desirable women are five years younger than themselves, unmarried, beautiful, and tall. Education and skill in the home seem to count for little in their appeals.

2. Al-Meligui, A., "Psychology of Adolescence through Diaries," *Egyptian Journal of Psychology*, VI (1950-1951), 173-184.

A discussion of the value of diaries as a source of information in the understanding of the adolescent. The author holds that diaries are a valuable source of data and presents excerpts from several diaries of well-known men in illustration. He notes that the adolescent first rebels against parental authority and next against that of the school. It is in the later stages of adolescence that the rebellion is directed against the society and its institutions in general.

3. Ammar, Hamed, *Growing Up in an Egyptian Village* (London: Routledge & Kegan Paul, 1954). (223 item bib.).

A study of Silwa, an Egyptian village in the province of Aswan. The author discusses the social organization of the village, social change, and the socialization process as it relates to the formal and informal education of the young.

4. Bogardus, E. S., "Social Change in Egypt," *Sociology and Social Research*, XXXIX (May, 1955), 328-333.

5. Craig, A. J. M., "Egyptian Students," *Middle East Journal*, VII, 3 (1953), 293-299.

6. El Koussz, A. H. "The Characteristics of Rural and Urban Adolescents in Egypt," *Vita Humana*, III (1960), 219-26.

A study of the characteristics of rural and urban adolescents in Egypt. The author questioned 800 students in Port Said and in rural areas in North and South Egypt with regard to their values and attitudes. The author notes that the degree of culture lag in a country such as Egypt is very apparent. The findings indicated that among the rural adolescents themes of the dominant culture prevailed. Traditional standards such as approval of God, parents, teachers, and older people predominated in the rural areas, whereas they were relatively absent in the urban setting. While acceptance by the peer group was a string theme in the urban area, it was relatively weak in the rural areas.

7. El-Melcegy, A. A., "Alshwoor'el Dini Endal Mourahik" (Religious Feeling in Adolescents) *Egyptian Journal of Psychology*, III (1947), 193-206.

8. Gillespie, J. M. and G. W. Allport, *Youth's Outlook on the Future* (Garden City, New York: Doubleday and Company, Inc., 1955).

1819 case studies from 10 countries.

9. Hammad, Salama I., "Some Notes on Educaitonal Change in Egypt," *Journal of Educational Sociology,* XXIX (January, 1956), 305-308.

10. Mahza, Mukhtar, "The Dynamic Force in the Personalities of Juvenile Delinquents in the Egyptian Environment," *British Journal of Psychology,* XLIV (November, 1953), 330-338.

The author is involved in the standardization of the Thematic Apperception Test among Egyptian delinquents. He also discusses the dynamic forces which affect delinquents. The sample consisted of 80 boys, 8-12 years of age who were living in an institution for child welfare and an 80-boy control group of nondelinquents.

The instruments utilized in the study included the Stanford-Binet Test (Arabic Revision), the Drever and Collins Performance Test, the Porteus Maze Test, Alexander's Passalong Test, and the Thematic Apperception Test.

It was found that the delinquents' backgrounds contained many broken homes. There was a high correlation between broken homes, poverty, and low intelligence. Two factors contributing to delinquency were identified: factors within the child and; environmental factors, home conditions, parental relations, and poverty. It was generally found that, as a group, juvenile delinquents in Egypt are far from a homogenous group.

With regard to the TAT, it was felt that, while some of the cards were suitable for an application in Egypt, others could be improved.

11. Husain, Taha, *An Egyptian Childhood; the Autobiography of Taha Hussein,* translated by E. H. Paxton (London: Routledge and Kegan Paul, Ltd., 1932). Revised.

12. Husain, Taha, *The Stream of Days, a Student at the Azhar,* 2nd ed., translated by Hilary Wayment (London: Longmans, Green & Co., Ltd., 1948).

Recollections of his youth by Egypt's famous blind scholar, a leading figure in Egypt's modern literary renaissance.

13. Hussein, Ahmed (Madame), "Egyptian Children in an Era of Awakening," *Journal of Educational Sociology,* XXVIII (March, 1955), 287-294.

A discussion of the problems faced by Egyptian children in a period of social change. It was noted that Egyptian society is not homogenous. For example, the children of the well-to-do but gradually vanishing landlord aristocracy tend to hold extreme views about Westernization and political ideology while the children of the growing middle class are rapidly becoming a source of supply for future leaders. The children of the rural laborers and urban workers, fighting illiteracy, poor food and housing are left almost entirely on their own. The author also discusses the gravity of the economic problems of the country and their impact on the young.

14. Kamel, Maher, "Evaluations of Adolescent Personality by Adolescents and Adults," *Egyptian Journal of Psychology,* III (1947), 33-54 (English translation 147-152).

A sample of 468 boys and 246 girls attending secondary schools in various regions of Egypt were asked to rate their classmates on 44 traits. Some of the students were also rated by teachers. The results show that boys from age 14 to 18 experience a decrease in desire to serve society, and an increase in interest in social life, aggressive behavior, day-dreaming, frankness, materialism, and care for appearance. For the girls, in the same age range, there is an increase in social interest, talkativeness, frankness, and care for personal appearance, and a loss of interest in sports and religion.

15. Lichtenstadter, I., "Arab-Egyptian Family," *Middle East Journal,* VI, 4 (1952), 379-399.

16. Lichtenstadter, I., "Some Aspects of Public Elementary Education in Egypt—a Report," *Harvard Educational Review,* XXIII, 3 (Summer, 1952), 168-183.

17. Melikian, L., "Authoritarianism and Its Correlates in the Egyptian Culture and in the United States," *Journal of Social Issues,* XV, 3 (1959), 58-68.

18. Mouhyi Al-Din Mouhannad, "Les Soucis de la Jeunesse," *Orient,* IV, 14 (1960), 127-137.

19. Prothro, E. Terry. "Arab Students Choices of Ways to Live," *Journal of Social Psychology,* XLVII (February, 1958), 3-7.

One hundred Arab university students (60 Christians and 40 Moslems) rated the thirteen "ways to live," as described by Morris, on a seven-point scale. Compared to students from seven other countries they revealed a preference for ways of life involving activity, group participation, and self-control. The students rejected ways of life characterized by contemplation, solitary living, and carefree enjoyment. The author notes, ". . . the picture which emerges seems to be one of active extroversion coupled with a moderating self-restraint."

The thirteen "ways to live" summarized the most desirable points in the world's leading religious and ethical systems.

20. Prothro, E. Terry and L. H. Molikian, "Social Attitudes of University Students in the Near East," *Egyptian Journal of Psychology*, VIII (1953), 291-298.

Social-distance scales were applied to 232 students at the American University of Beirut to get at attitudes toward various national groups. Analysis of the results revealed that religion, in this case, was an important determiner of attitudes. The authors found that the Christian subjects revealed attitudes more similar to the attitudes of American subjects than to the attitudes of Moslem subjects tested for this study. The study also noted the following preferences: (1) a preference for Near Eastern countries; (2) a preference for other countries whose foreign policies favored Near Eastern countries; (3) a rejection of peoples from backward countries. The author felt that the study showed that lack of understanding and ignorance do not exhaust the explanations for differential and negative attitudes toward other national groups.

21. Riyk, Abdou Mikhail, "Smoking among Adolescents: an Objective Study," *Egyptian Journal of Psychology*, III (1947), 55-67 (English translation, 144-146).

An examination of 268 adolescents between the ages of 14 and 22 on attitudes toward smoking by youth. The author notes that smoking is felt to be a mark of manhood, superiority, and respect by youth. In general, adults object to adolescents' smoking. In spite of adult objection the majority of smoking adolescents are unwilling to give up the practice.

22. Rowlatt, Mary, A *Family in Egypt* (London: Hale, 1956).

23. Sheab, Ibrahim Khali, "Personal and Social Problems as Identified by Egyptian Adolescents," *Dissertation Abstracts*, XIV (1954), 1623-1624.

A discussion which attempts to identify the personal and social problems of Egyptian youth and discuss the implications of these problems for the school system. A questionnaire which covered 94 personal and 20 social problems was administered to 1,035 high school students. The personal problems which bothered the boys included vocational choice, educational opportunities, sex, health, character development, and leisure-time activities. The girls were bothered by essentially the same personal problems. A large percentage of the total sample revealed concerns with social problems such as ignorance, poverty, and disease in Egypt.

24. U.N. Department of Social Welfare. Division of Social Welfare, *Comparative Study on Juvenile Delinquency. Part V, The Middle East* (New York: United Nations, 1953).

    A discussion and comparative appraisal of practices in the treatment of juvenile delinquents in Egypt, Iran, Iraq, Jordan, Lebanon, Saudi Arabia, Syria, Turkey, and Yemen.

25. Zaki, Saleh A., "A Questionnaire Study of the Problem Adolescent Girls in Secondary Schools," *Egyptian Journal of Psychology*, VII (1952), 410-416. (In Arabic.)

IRAN

1. Aliabadi, Dr. A., "Education in Iran, Now and in the Future," *Journal of the Royal Central Asian Society*, XXXVI (January, 1959), Part I, 62-66.
2. Dehquni-Tafti, H. B., "The Church and Its Youth in Iran," *Ecumenical Review*, III (October, 1950), 42-46.
3. Esfandiary, H. A., "Education in Iran," *Middle Eastern Affairs*, II, 6 (June, 1951), 213-225.
4. Hayden, Lyle J., "Living Standards in Rural Iran," *Middle East Journal*, III, 2 (April, 1949), 140-150.
5. U.N. Department of Social Welfare, Division of Social Welfare, *Comparative Study on Juvenile Delinquency. Part V, The Middle East* (New York: United Nations, 1953).

IRAQ

1. Fargo, Adeeb F., *Compatibility of the Cultural Heritage and Education in Iraq*. University of Maryland (1956). (Available as 1957 Publication No. 19,657, University Microfilms, Ann Arbor, Michigan.)
2. U.N. Department of Social Welfare. Division of Social Welfare, *Comparative Study on Juvenile Delinquency. Part V, The Middle East* (New York: United Nations, 1953).

ISRAEL

1. Aeden, Sheva, "Emadt Hanoar Hayisreli K'lapey Averat Hevratiyat" (Israel Youth Attitudes toward Social Delinquencies), *Niv Hak-vatsa,* II (1952-1953), 274-295.

The author applied a list of 12 social delinquencies to 1,277 adolescents from 15 to 18 years of age who lived in communal settlements or in towns. The purpose was to construct a scale of attitudes toward delinquent actions. It was found that the first six selected in the towns were, in order: lying, truancy from social activity, stealing, doing harm to the weaker, property damage, and truancy from work. In the communal settlement the first six selected in order, were: lying, truancy from work, truancy from social activity, stealing, property damage, and doing harm to the weaker.

2. Aeden, Sheva, "Manhigim Umadrihim Banoar Hayisr'eli" (Youth Leaders and Guides in Israel), *Niv Hak'vatsa,* I, 4 (1951-1952), 78-90.

3. Aeden, Sheva, *Manhigim Umadrihim Banoar Hayisr'di* (Youth Leaders and Guides in Israel) (Jerusalem: Youth Department of the Jewish Agency, 1953).

An attempt to scale attitudes toward youth-leader traits among town and communal settlement adolescents. 400 adolescents living in collective settlements and 427 adolescents living in towns were selected. Among the town adolescents the six most preferred traits were: knowledge, sociability, activity, intellect, gaiety, and organizing ability. Among the dwellers in communal settlements the six most preferrred traits were: activity, learning, capacity of expression, sociability, intellect, organizing ability.

4. Arlow, Jacob A., "A Psychoanalytic Study of a Religious Initiation Rite: Bar Mitzvah," in Ruth S. Eissler, *The Psychoanalytic Study of the Child,* VI (New York: International Universities Press, 1951).

5. Arnstein, E., *Al M'didat Han'tiya Hamiktsoit* (Measuring Occupational Interests) (Jerusalem: Hadassah Vocational Education Services, 1955) (English summary).

6. Arnstein, E. (Vocational Guidance Center, Hadassah, Jerusalem) *Al Han'tiyot Hamiktsoiyot Shel Hanoar Hayisr'eli* (About Occupational Interests of Youth in Israel) (Jerusalem: Hadassah Vocational Education Services, 1953).

The author investigated the occupational interests of 583 eighth-grade students in cities, small towns, villages, and communal settlements. The inventory used contained 136 of the most common occupations in Israel. It was found that the differences between the Israel-born and foreign-born adolescents were slight, but the Israel born generally showed more inclination to physical work while the foreign born inclined toward white-collar occupations. (Social Services and Artistic Occupations)

7. Arthur, Julietta, "Youth Goes to the Holy Land," *Asia*, XXXIX (August, 1939), 442-444.

8. Avidor, M., "Education in Israel," *Middle Eastern Affairs*, I, 8 (August, 1950), 229-233.

9. Bakalias-Alon, S., "Kavim lid' muto shel hanoar hatemani" (About the Emotional and Intellectual Features of the Yemenite Youth), *Hahipukh*, XXII (1948-1949), 300-323.

   Basically an examination of preferences among Yemenite and non-Yemenite youth. It is noted that both classes of boys prefer arithmetic and Hebrew as school subjects. Among the girls the Yemenites prefer Bible study and history while the non-Yemenites prefer fiction. In occupations all reflect a desire to climb up the social ladder.

10. Bardin, Shlomo, *Pioneer Youth in Palestine* (New York: Bloch Publishing Co., 1932).

11. Bar-Yoseph, R., "Pattern of Early Socialization in the Collective Settlements in Israel," *Human Relations*, XII, 4 (1959), 345-360.

    A well-done article dealing with the socialization processes in infancy, childhood, and the preadolescent period.

12. Ben-David, Y., "Huhaverut bitnuat Hanoar v'hastatus hahevrati" (Membership in Youth Movement and Social Status), *M'gamot*, V (1953-1954), 227-247.

    In this investigation of membership in youth movements and the status image of adolescents, 116 members of two youth groups were interviewed. One finding indicates that, for those members with family backgrounds which reflect unstable or unclear status positions, the youth group provides a source of relatively stable status which the family is unable to provide.

13. Benedict, Ruth, "Child Rearing in Certain European Countries," *American Journal of Orthopsychiatry*, XIX (1949), 342-350.

14. Ben-Or, J. L., "Arab Education in Israel," *Journal of Educational Sociology* XXVII, (April, 1954), 380-384.

15. Ben-Or, J. L., "Arab Education in Israel," *Middle Eastern Affairs,* I, 8 (August, 1950), 224-229.

16. Benushevski, I., "Ruah haz'man V'gil hayaldut" (Spirit of Time and Childhood), *Ofakim,* V (1948), 24-26.

An investigation of the attitudes, desires, and values of a group of Jewish displaced children in Hungary. All of the subjects were 10 years old or older. It was found that 38 per cent of the children did not feel that they knew a good man, but only 1.7 per cent felt that they did not know a bad man. "Good" men included: Stalin, Tito, Churchill, Russians, Englishmen, Americans, while "bad" men included: Hungarian Fascists, German Nazis, and Hitler. Among other findings it was noted that 34 per cent didn't know joy and 30 per cent will find joy only when their parents return. Thirty-one per cent wanted food, but only 10 per cent wanted toys.

17. Bier, F., "Nigudey arahim etsel olim" (Conflicting Values with Immigrant Children), *M'gamot,* V (1953-1954), 386-391.

18. Blum, Uri, "Generations and Layers of Society in Israel," *American Journal of Individual Psychology,* XII (1956), 128-135.

A discussion of the assimilation of immigrants and layers of society into one homogeneous society. While the comments on the youth are a minor part of the discussion, a few insightful comments are made. It was noted that youth living in the kibbutz encounter less difficulties, less neurosis, and few criminal tendencies. The IQs of immigrant children tend to increase after arrival in the kibbutz.

The children arriving in Israel without parents are generally placed in communal settlements rather than with families to ease their subconscious guilt over having left their parents behind.

19. Blumental, H. E., *Psychological Problems of the Adolescent Immigrant in Israel of Today* (Jerusalem, Israel: Ministry of Labour, Department of Vocational Education, 1958).

A discussion of the "psychic and social crisis," caused by the translation from one environment to another. Among the areas discussed are (1) adjustment problems of new immigrants, (2) socio-educational problems, (3) vocational problems of immigrant youth.

20. Brodersen, A., "Cultural Assimilation of Immigrants: A UNESCO

Project in Israel," *International Social Science Bulletin,* VII (1955), 652-655.

The comment is made in this study of the assimilation of immigrants that the immigrant youth show an increase in delinquency and deviant behaviors. It is also noted that the youth movements do not play a great part in the absorption of these incoming youth. In general, the patterns of intergenerational conflict existing in the prestate period has altered since the formation of the State and the increase of immigration.

21. Caplan, G., "Clinical Observations on the Emotional Life of Children in the Communal Settlements in Israel," in Milton J. E. Senn (ed.), *Problems of Infancy and Childhood* (New York: Josiah Macy Jr. Foundation, 1954), 91-120.

While this is primarily a discussion of infancy and childhood in the kibbutz, it does include some comment on adolescence. The author is interested primarily in the personality effects of kibbutz life and the socialization of the child.

It is noted that the adolescent in the kibbutz appears to be stable, group-oriented, and appears to have goals and behaviors which are in conformity with the norms of the kibbutz. The peer-group influence is very strong and in many cases the individual spends his entire life within their sphere of influence. If he should happen to lose contact with his peer group he attempts immediately to associate himself with another group. It was further noted that the kibbutz youth shows great plasticity and courage in situations of conflict and danger, placing himself in personal danger in order to protect his comrades.

While discussion of sex is open and coeducational, there is peer-group experimenting. Courtship and sexual experimenting is rare in the peer group. Strong incest taboos exist. There is little evidence of sex play or perversion.

One objection often raised by adults toward kibbutz youth is the apparent lack of concern with spiritual, scholarly, and philosophical matters. The elders feel a general lack of the idealism usually associated with the Jewish tradition.

22. Cohen, G. L., "Affluent Kibbutzim," *Commentary,* XXVIII (October, 1959), 292-298.

23. "Din V'heshbon Havaada L'heker Avaryanut Hanoar B'Israel" (Report of the Committee for Studying Juvenile Delinquency in Israel), *M'gamot,* VII (1956), 277-388. (English summary)

24. Dufen, David, "Juvenile Delinquency in Israel's Changing Society," *Jewish Frontier,* Section 2/28 (December, 1961), 25-9.

25. Easterlin, R. A., "Israel's Development: Past Accomplishments and Future Problems," *Quarterly Journal of Economics,* LXXV (February, 1961), 63-86.

26. Edelston, Israel H., "Uprooting and Resettlement: A Survey of the 'Youth Alizah'" (Youth Immigration Department, Jewish Agency, Program in Israel), *Journal of Educational Sociology,* XXXII (April, 1959), 392-401.

27. Eisenstadt, S. N., "Delinquent Group Formation among Immigrant Youth," *British Journal of Delinquency,* II (1951), 34-45.

In this discussion of the delinquent groups among the immigrant youth in Israel the author notes that, among these youths social stability is low, social organization is low, there is a lack of communication and identification with local community, there are conflicts with authority, and there is often a discrepancy between the parents' aspirations and the possibility of realization. The author notes that the tendency toward delinquency is reduced when recognized, and permanent social roles can be established immediately upon arrival.

28. Eisenstadt, S. N., "Hamered Hehadash Shel Hanoar" (The New Youth Revolt), *M'gamot,* IX (1958), 95-102.

29. Eisenstadt, S. N., "Lid'muto hasotsylogit shel hanoar beheva hamodernity" (The Sociological Pattern of Youth in Modern Society), *M'gamot,* II (1950-1951), 52-72.

A discussion which is reflected in his later (1956) book, *From Generation to Generation: Age Groups and the Social Structure.* In this article Eisenstadt discusses the emergence of youth culture in modern society. A cross-cultural hypothesis is presented in which specific age groups are present in societies in which the family or a wider kinship group is not the basic unit of the social division of labor. Modern society is presented as the most complete example of nonfamilistic society. Youth groups in modern society are analyzed with respect to the following factors: degree of formal organization; degree of autonomy; degree of legitimacy in relation to adult society; and the development of aggressive symbols. The content of the article is expanded and reiterated in the book mentioned above.

30. Eisenstadt, S. N., "Youth Culture and Social Structure in Israel," *British Journal of Sociology,* II (1951), 105-114.

Another article which eventually led to the writing of *From Generation to Generation.* In this article Eisenstadt discusses typical patterns of the social life of the youth in Israel. He notes that a number of "youth cultures" exist in Israel and attempts to show that they can be related to the social structure in Israel. Again the hypothesis that the emergence of youth culture is related to the place of the family in the social division of labor is promoted and substantiated. Among the conclusions reached in the article are the following: 1. the emergence of "youth culture" is closely correlated with the loss of the famliy's function as the basic unit of the social division of labor; 2. despite a long preparation for adulthood within the context set by the adult, the youth is generally not prepared for the assumption of adult roles; 3. the high degree of specialization in society and the state of childhood socialization create a definite interruption in the identification transferrence of the adolescent from child to adult environments.

31. Faigin, H., "Case Report: Social Behavior of Young Children in the Kibbutz," *Journal of Abnormal Social Psychology*, LVI, 1 (1958).

32. Foa, U. G., "Hashpaat haeda v'hamatsav hakalkali al hithabrutam shel y'ladim" (The Influence of the Community and of the Economic Status on Grouping of Young Children), *Hahinukh*, XXI (1947-1948), 70-72.

33. Gerson, Menahem, "Arakhim Tenuatiyim Behaye Benot Hakibuts" (Values of the Kibbutz Movement According to the Girls of the Kibbutz), *Ofakim*, XIII (1959), 291-315.

34. Gerson, Menahem, "Yahasey Banat'horim Begil Hahitbagrut" (Daughter-Parents Relationship in the Adolescent Period), *Ofakim*, XI (1957), 469-484.

35. Gesimar, Ludwig L., "Ideology and the Adjustment of Immigrants," *Jewish Social Studies*, XXI (1959), 155-164.

36. Gillespie, J. M. and G. W. Allport, *Youth's Outlook on the Future* (Garden City, New York: Doubleday and Company, Inc. 1955). (1,819 case studies from 10 countries.)

37. Gitlin-Bitensky, Malia, *Hapsihologia Hahevratit Shel Gil Hahitbagrut* (Social Psychology of the Adolescent Age) (Tel Aviv: Yavnek Publishing House, 1954).

38. Golan, S., "Al Beayot Hanoar Beyamenu" (On Youth Problems Today), *Ofakim*, XII (1958), 167-176.

39. Golan, S., "Behavior Research in Collective Settlements in Israel: II, Collective Education in the Kibbutz," *American Journal of Orthopsychiatry*, XXVIII (1958), 549-556.

40. Golan, S., "Collective Education in the Kibbutz," *Psychiatry*, XXII (May, 1959), 167-177.

41. Golan, S., "Lidmuto shel hanoar shelanu" (About the Appearance of Our Youth) in *Dor Lador* (*Generation into Generation: A Record of the Hashomer Hatsari Central School at Mishmar Haemek*) (Merhavia: Sifriat Poalim, 1948), 33-63.

42. Golan, S. (ed.), "Yoman" (A Diary), *Ofakim,* VIII (1954), 258-388.

43. Halpern, H., "Alienation from Parenthood in the Kibbutz and America" (Bibliography), *Marriage and Family Living,* XXIV (February, 1962), 42-45.

44. Herman, S. N. and E. Schild, "Ethnic Role Conflict in a Cross-Cultural Situation," *Human Relations,* XIII, 3 (1960), 215-228. (Bibliography)

The authors investigate multiple group membership and the accompanying role conflict. They are concerned with the ethnic role differentiation (American, Jew, and Israelite) of Jewish-American youth studying in Israel. A questionnaire dealing with the self-concept and ethnic role in specific circumstances was applied to 32 Jewish youths who had been selected for a year of study at an institution in Jerusalem. The relative potency of dissonant roles: the valence and salience of roles and the ethnic identity of the youth are included in the discussion and analysis.

45. Herman, S. N., "American Jewish Students in Israel" (A Social-Psychological Study in Cross-Cultural Education), *Jewish Social Studies,* XXIV (January, 1962), 3-29.

46. Howorth, Herbert, "Youth in the Land of the Bible," *Palestine,* III (October, 1946), 112-115.

47. Huebener, Theodore, "Education in Israel," *Journal of Educational Sociology,* XXVII (April, 1954), 348-352.

A description of the educational system in Israel since 1948 and the progress which has been made toward establishing a national system. Special emphasis is placed on the role of the educational system in assimilating newcomers and assisting immigrants to become integrated. The comment is made that, ". . . tens of thousands of newcomers of highly varied cultural backgrounds have been assimilated in a few years, attest to the effectiveness of Israeli teachers."

48. Infield, H. F., "The Concept of Jewish Culture and the State of Israel," *American Sociological Review,* XVI (August, 1951), 506-513.

49. Irvine, Elizabeth R., "Observations on the Aims and Methods of

Child Rearing in Communal Settlements in Israel," *Human Relations,* V (1952), 247-275.

50. Kaffman, Mordecai, "Evaluation of Emotional Disturbance in 403 Israel Kibbutz Children," *American Journal of Psychiatry,* XVII (February, 1961).
51. Kaneti, Malka, "Hakeria Besifrut Kelokelet" (Reading of Cheap Literature), *M'gamot,* IX (1958), 250-253.
52. Katz, E. and A. Zloczower, "Ethnic Continuity in an Israeli Town: Relations with Parents," *Human Relations,* XIV, 4 (1961), 293-308.
53. Katz, E. and A. Zloczower, "Ethnic Continuity in an Israeli Town," *Human Relations,* XIV, 4 (1961), 293-327.
54. "Kibbutz Adolescents," Paper read at the Annual Meeting of American Orthopsychiatric Association, Chicago, February, 1960.
55. Klausner, Samuel Z., "Immigrant Absorption and Social Tension in Israel: A Case Study of Iraqi Jewish Immigrants," *Middle East Journal,* IX, 3 (Summer, 1955), 281-294.

    A discussion of the social-psychological tensions arising out of the absorption of Oriental Jews into Israel, a predominantly Western society. The study centers on the Iraqi Jewish immigrants and three contexts of tension, namely: (1) family disorganization, (2) clashing concepts of social authority, and (3) emerging social stratification.

    One of the first consequences of the assimilation of the oriental Jew was the breakdown of the extended family. This led to emotional strain for the child, the father losing a great part of his control of the family as the younger sons quickly grasp the new culture and contribute disproportionately to the economic status of the family. The new culture (Israel) did little to support the traditional monosexual relationships of the immigrant youth. Sex roles were further confused by the emancipation of women in the new situation.

    The author concludes that the dominant personality trait among the immigrants is depressive anxiety. Some of them become stoic, some become introverted, and some join marginal movements. Eventually they will become assimilated but, ". . . at the same time, the backwash of the family and social disorganization is straining the economy by lengthening the welfare roles and increasing crime and juvenile delinquency."

56. Langerman, Shoshana, "Ma Koreim Talmidey-kitot Het" (What Pupils of the Eighth Grade Read), *M'gamot,* X (1959-60), 3-11.
57. Levine, Carl, "Israel's Expresso Generation: Inability to Create

Any Contact With Youth Arouses Ire of State's Founding Fathers," *New Leader*, XLIV (January 9, 1961), 13-15.

A popular type discussion of the youth of Israel and how they measure up to the expectations of their elders. The author lived in Israel for several years. With the aid of this experience plus the information from selected secondary sources he reports the following impressions.

Initially he notes the irritation of Israeli leaders at the narrow, self-centered preoccupations of the youth. They feel that the youth show little interest in the tasks the nation faces and that the youth have abdicated the pioneer spirit which characterized their elders.

The disorientation of the *sabra* (youth) is explained in terms of overcompensation for hardships and repression. Thus the parents instill a feeling in their children that they can do no wrong and that nothing is too good for them. The author notes, ". . . in their schools *kibbutz* children are permitted great freedom, self-expression which frequently degenerates into complete indiscipline, and a tendency for the pupils to criticize teachers."

The sudden shift from the overindulgence of childhood to the severe demands of the young adult period have engendered some psychological maladjustments. The youth of Israel will make his contribution, but he will do it in his own way. One of these ways is illustrated in the area of science where the youth are coming to play an ever-increasing role. This is the area in which much "pioneering" is being done.

58. Milo, Efraim, "Netunim Statistiycm al Avaryanut Hanoar Bey-israel" (Statistical Data about Juvenile Delinquency) *M'gamot*, X (1959-1960), 56-64.

59. Ormian, Haim, "The Attitudes of Israel High School Students toward Mendele," *Yivo Annu, Jewish Social Science*, V (1950), 293-312.

60. Ormian, Haim, *Hapsikhologia shel sh'not hayaldut hoahronot* (The Psychology of Later Childhood), 2nd ed. (Jerusalem: Zionist Organization, Youth Dept., 1951).

61. Ormian, Haim, "The Influence of the Society on the Vocational Interests of the Youth in Israel," pp. 435-440, in F. Baumgarten (ed.), *La Psychotechnique dans le Monde Moderne* (*Psychotechnology in the Modern World*) (Paris: Presses Universitaires de France, 1952), 557-561.

62. Ormian, Haim, "L'ofi hahitbagrut shel b'ne adat Hamizrah"

(About the Traits of the Puberty of the Oriental Communities), *Alon Lamore* 2, (1946), 4-9.

63. Ormian, Haim (ed.), *Psihologia Shel Hahitbagrut* (*Psychology of Adolescence*), 2nd ed. (Jerusalem: Union of Hebrew Teachers in Israel, 1952).

64. Ormian, Haim, "Quatre Schemes d'Adolescence en Israel" (Four Schemes of Adolescence in Israel), *Enfance*, VI (1953), 53-60.

65. Patai, R., "Ritual Approach to Hebrew African Culture Contact," *Jewish Social Studies*, XXIV (April, 1962), 86-96.

66. Pincsower-Langerman, Shoshana, "Ma Kore Hanoar" (What Adolescents Read), *M'gamot*, IX (1958), 286-300.

67. Popkin, Zelda, "A New Youth for a New Land: Boys and Girls of Israel Have Endured Much Hardship but They Are Hopeful and Self-Assured because They Know Their Country Needs Them," *Parents Monthly* (September, 1949), 36-37.

68. Rabin, Albert I., "Attitudes of Kibbutz Children to Family and Parents," *American Journal of Orthopsychiatry*, XXIX (January, 1959), 172-179.

    The author investigates the problem of the child-parent relationship in families where the parents are not the main socializing agents or do not have any particular socializing function. Data was gathered from 92 kibbutz-reared and 45 control group children between the ages of 9 and 11. These groups were given sentence-completion tests and analyzed toward the family, the father, and the mother.

    Analysis disclosed that the kibbutz children had more positive attitudes toward the family than did the nonkibbutz children. The girls of the control group had more positive feelings toward the father and the boys of the kibbutz group had more positive attitudes toward the mother.

69. Rabin, Albert I., "Comparison of American and Israeli Children by Means of a Sentence Completion Technique," *Journal of Social Psychology*, XLIX (1959), 3-12.

70. Rabin, Albert I., "Hamitbogrim Bakibuts" (Adolescents in the Kibbutz), *Ofakim*, XIV (1960), 87-92.

71. Rabin, Albert I., "Kibbutz Children: Research Findings to Date," *Children*, V (1958), 179-184.

72. Rabin, Albert I., "Personality Maturity of Kibbutz and Non-Kibbutz Children as Reflected in Rorschach Findings," *Journal of Projective Techniques*, XXI (1957), 148-153.

73. Rappaport, David, "Behavior Research in Collective Settlements in Israel: VII, The Study of Kibbutz Education and Its Bearing on the Theory of Development," *American Journal of Orthopsychiatry*, XXVIII (November, 1954), 587-597.

74. Reifen, D., "Observations on the Juvenile Court in Israel," *Social Service Review*, XXVI (June, 1952), 202-213.

75. Rey, Andre, "Sikum Mehkarim Biladim Onitsfon Afrika" (Resume of Studies Concerning Children from North Africa in Israel), *Ofakim*, IX (1955), 376-382.

76. Rosner, Arye, "Ma Kore Hanoar" (What the Youngsters Read), *Urim*, XV (1957-1958), 352-354.

77. Rufen, David, "Youth Welfare in Tel-Aviv," *British Journal of Delinquency*, IV, 1 (1953), 53-55.

78. Simon, E., "Jugend und Religion in Israel" (Youth and Religion in Israel), *Frankfurter Hefte*, IX, 11 (November, 1954), 823-827.

79. Simon, E., "What Price Israel's Normalcy?", "A Young Nation and Its Ideals" (translated by R. Manheim), *Commentary*, VII (April, 1949), 341-347.

80. Smilansky, Mashe, et al. (eds.), *Child and Youth Welfare in Israel* (Jerusalem: Henrietta Szold Institute for Child and Youth Welfare, 1960).

81. Spiro, M. E., "Education in a Communal Village in Israel," *American Journal of Orthopsychiatry*, XXV (1955), 283-293.

82. Spiro, M. E., *Kibbutz: Venture in Utopia* (Cambridge, Massachusetts: Harvard University Press, 1956).

83. Szczepanski, Y., "Hanoar Baolam Shel Yamenu" (Youth in the Present World), *Ofakim*, XIII (1959), 205-212.

84. Talmon-Garber, Yonina, "The Family in Israel," *Marriage and Family Living*, XVI (November, 1954), 343-349.

85. Teller, S. L., "Spartan Youth of Israel: A Generation Searches for Its Souls," *Commentary*, X (July, 1950), 7-14.

In this journalistic presentation the author notes that the youth, the native-born sabra, have been trained to conform in the kibbutz life and to be of service to the group as the highest individual aim. When they encounter the rest of society, therefore, they are discontent and disillusioned with the attitudes and morality they encounter. Since he has not been taught religion, he cannot turn to this as an outlet. While they were once the instruments for winning a war and constructing a state, they must now search for meaning and a place for themselves in society they helped to create.

86. Tindall, G., "Kibbutz Girl," *New Statesman,* LX (October 29, 1960), 640.

87. Tuma, E., "Hinuh y'ladim bak'far hoaravi" (Child Rearing in the Arab Village), *M'gamot,* VI (1954-1955), 130-138.

88. Weinryb, B. D., "The Lost Generation in Israel" (Conflict of Values Between the Native-Born Second Generation Youth and the Largely Immigrant First Generation), *Middle East Journal,* VII, 4 (Fall, 1953), 415-429.

89. Wolman, Benjamin, "The Jewish Adolescent: A Bibliographic Review of Current Psychological and Educational Literature in the United States and Israel," *Jewish Social Studies,* XIII (October, 1951), 333-344.

90. Wolman, Benjamin, "The Social Development of Israeli Youth," *Jewish Social Studies,* XI (July/October, 1949), 283-306; 343-372.

91. Wolman, Benjamin, "Spontaneous Groups of Children and Adolescents in Israel," *Journal of Social Psychology,* XXXIV (November, 1951), 171-182. (Bibliography)

Specifically the author asks, "Is there a 'gang forming age' "? If there is, what is it? What is the composition of adolescent gangs? Do these gangs necessarily have delinquent orientations? To get at the answers Wolman studied 2,526 boys and girls between the ages of 8 and 20 in and around the area of Tel-Aviv. The educational spectrum covered elementary school through college. The sample was divided into four age groups: 8-12, 12-14, 14-17, 17-20, and a questionnaire was administered in addition to a series of interviews.

In the 8-12 age group the gang seemed to be a characteristic feature. This group had the highest percentage of gang membership. Most of these gangs were formed in the street with self-appointed leaders, a secret language, emphasis on secrecy. In the main the delinquent activities were seen as conforming to a trait of the age group in the need for adventure and independence.

Among the 12-14 year old group, the gang has lost in quantity and quality. Most of the intelligent adolescents leave the gang to enter organized youth groups. Gangs here are usually the result of problems in school. The amount of destructive activity declines and the gangs seem to aim at recreational activities.

Only 11 per cent of the sample were gang members at ages 14-17. Here also the better adjusted individuals leave the gangs to join organized activities. Those who remain are usually maladjusted individuals with bad school records and low intelligence.

92. "World Jewish Youth Convention," (Jerusalem, Israel), July 28-31, 1958 (Minutes, *World Zionist Organization*, 1959), Department of Youth and Hechalutz.

93. Zohar, Zvi (ed.), "Yomana Shel Tamar" (Tamar's Diary), *Ofakim*, XII (1958), 327-420.

JORDAN

1. Harris, George L., *Jordan: Its People, Its Society, Its Culture* (New York: Evergreen Books, 1959).

2. U.N. Department of Social Welfare, Division of Social Welfare, *Comparative Study on Juvenile Delinquency. Part V, The Middle East* (New York: United Nations, 1953).

LEBANON

1. Gulick, John, *Social Structure and Culture Change in a Lebanese Village* (New York: Wenner-Gren Foundation, 1955).

2. Melikian, Levon H., "Some Correlates of Authoritarianism in Two Cultural Groups," *Journal of Psychology*, XLII (1956), 237-248.

   An investigation of the dependency of authoritarianism, anxiety, and hostility upon cultural conditions. The comparison and analysis was based on a sample of 90 Moslem Arabs at American University, Beirut and a group of second-generation American, white, Protestant students in the United States. It was found that the Middle Eastern students were more authoritarian and more hostile, while the American students revealed more anxiety. In both samples it was found that the authoritarian students were more hostile and tended to idealize their parents. With regard to authoritarianism, it was difficult to isolate the specific effect of cultural conditions.

3. Prothro, E. Terry, "Lebanese Stereotypes of America as Revealed by the Sentence Completion Technique," *Journal of Social Psychology*, XL (1954), 39-42.

   An application of the sentence-completion technique to a group of 104 Lebanese girls between the ages of 13 and 18. The girls were students at a British-supported high school. The religious affiliations are noted as: 62 Christians, 40 Moslems, and 2 Jews. The girls were asked to complete the sentence, "America is a country where . . ." The results indicated that industrialization, individual freedom and the equal rights for women were the most frequently mentioned items. Educational opportunities were also mentioned frequently. Unfavorable comments were noted infrequently and then only among the higher school classes. The frequency of certain items was interpreted as a result of the student's interpretation of current problems in her own country.

4. U.N. Department of Social Welfare, Division of Social Welfare, *Comparative Study on Juvenile Delinquency. Part V, The Middle East* (New York: United Nations, 1953).
5. "The Y.W.C.A. of Beirut," *Woman's Preview* (December, 1948), 18-19.

MOROCCO

1. Hart, D., "Notes on Rifan Community in Tangiers," *The Middle East Journal*, XI (Spring, 1957), 153-162.

SAUDI ARABIA

1. U.N. Department of Social Welfare. Division of Social Welfare, *Comparative Study on Juvenile Delinquency. Part V, The Middle East* (New York: United Nations, 1953).

SYRIA

1. U.N. Department of Social Welfare. Division of Social Welfare, *Comparative Study on Juvenile Delinquency. Part V, The Middle East* (New York: United Nations, 1953).

TURKEY

1. Aker, Zubeyir, "Education in Turkey," *Pakistan Horizon*, I, IV (December, 1948), 256-262.
2. Bisbee, Eleanor, *The New Turks: Pioneers of the Republic, 1920-1950* (Philadelphia: University of Pennsylvania, 1951).
3. Davis, F. J., "American Minorities as Seen by Turkish Students in the U.S., *Sociology and Social Research*, XLVI (October, 1961), 48-54. (Bibliography)

   The author is interested in establishing the attitudes of Turkish students in the United States toward the status of racial and ethnic groups in America. A questionnaire approach was utilized. The sample consisted of all the Turkish students in the United States. The response, due to a lack of current addresses, was small (286 returned out of 410 mailed). The final sample included graduate and undergraduate, married and single, male and female students. Among the findings we note the following:

1. Considering racial versus ethnic groups, more Turkish students felt that ethnic minorities were treated fairly than those who felt that racial minorities were treated fairly.

2. Most of the students were surprised to find the quantity of racial discrimination which exists in the United States.

3. Sex differences in the perception of racial discrimination were small. The females had less favorable attitudes toward American discrimination than did the males, and the married students had more favorable attitudes toward ethnic and racial discrimination than did the single students.

4. Students in the fields of natural sciences and engineering had more favorable attitudes toward American discrimination than did those in the social sciences and the humanities.

5. A small relationship was found between length of stay in the United States and the formation of negative attitudes toward discrimination.

4. Hyman, H., et al., "The Values of Turkish College Youth," *Public Opinion Quarterly*, XXII (1958), 275-291.

The authors feel that a study of values may contribute to the study and understanding of the problems in a modernizing country (Turkey), since, in their words, ". . . values may govern the way economic activity is pursued and resources manipulated, and may reflect in turn the economic changes that have taken place."

Students at two colleges in Turkey were chosen for this study. These men represent the elite of Turkish students and society. 259 men at Robert College and 399 men on the faculty of Political Sciences, Ankara University were used. At Robert College the American influence is strong; most of those at Ankara are training to be Turkish civil servants. For comparison the results of Allport and Gillespie's study of values.

Among the findings we note: 33 per cent felt that war was sometimes a good thing, 36 per cent expect war within 15 years; 35 per cent believe that it won't occur at all. Turkish youth are extremely nationalistic in comparison with other countries. Traditional emphasis on family loyalty was seen among the Turks, but Turkish students were only a little more religious than American students and considerably less religious than German or Italian students. These findings apply to the sample at Ankara.

For the Robert College group, we see a group less typical of the Turkish pattern and closer to the American pattern.

They exhibited less nationalism and more internationalism, less authoritarianism, and less religiousness than the Ankara group.

5. Maxwell-Hyslop, A. R. and K. R. Maxwell-Hyslop, "The Development of Education in Turkey," *Asiatic Review*, XLII, 66-73.
6. Ozdil, Ilhan, "Education in Turkey," *Middle Eastern Affairs*, I, 10 (October, 1950), 285-290.
7. Ozinonu, Lamia and Kemal Ozinonu, "Visit to a Turkish High School," *The Clearing House*," XXXI (September, 1956), 11-14.
8. Patel, Manilal, "Adult Education in Turkey," *Indo Asian Culture*, VI, 2 (October, 1957), 191-196.
9. Ramsaur, Ernest Edmondson, *The Young Turks; Prelude to the Revolution of 1908* (Princeton: Princeton University Press, 1957).
10. Spencer, R. F., "Social Context of Modern Turkish Names," *Southwestern Journal of Anthropology*, XVII (Fall, 1961), 205-218. (Bibliography)
11. Stirling, A. P., "A Death and Youth Club: Feuding in a Turkish Village," *Anthropological Quarterly*, XXXIII, 51-75.
12. U.N. Department of Social Welfare, Division of Social Welfare, *Comparative Study on Juvenile Delinquency. Part V, The Middle East* (New York: United Nations, 1953).

YEMEN

1. U.N. Department of Social Welfare, Division of Social Welfare, *Comparative Study on Juvenile Delinquency. Part V, The Middle East* (New York: United Nations, 1953).

GENERAL

1. Arasteb, Reza, "Some Problems of Education in Underdeveloped Countries," *Middle East Journal*, XII, 3 (Summer, 1958), 270-276.
2. Beck, Dorothy G., "The Changing Moslem Family of the Middle East," *Marriage and Family Living*, XIX (1957), 340-347.

A note on the structure of the Moslem family in the Middle East and the results of creeping Westernization. Thus, the Moslem family and the traditional restrictions on women have changed the most in areas where Westernization has been most rapid. The harem and its restricted life for women has passed. There is increased freedom for interpersonal contact and premarital courtship. Moslem law still rules marriage customs and the duties of the wife and other household females. The basic patterns are opposed to Western ways and will be discarded only at the price of conflict and stress between family members.

3. Berque, Jacques, "The North of Africa," Recent Research on Race Relations, *UNESCO International Social Science Journal*, XIII, 2 (1961), 177-197.

4. Davis, James F., "Cultural Perspectives of Middle Eastern Students in America," *The Middle East Journal*, XIV (Summer 1960), 256-264.

At the outset it was expected that Middle Eastern students in the United States would experience surprise upon contact with American life, have mixed views of American life, experience problems of culture contact, and differ within themselves when broken down by sex, marital status, native country, field of study, and length of time spent in the United States. 93 students at the University of Michigan and the University of Minnesota, students from 7 different Middle Eastern countries were questioned on these topics.

The percentage findings show that: 80 per cent were surprised at the amount of religious activity, 60 per cent were surprised at the racial discrimination, there were mixed views on the high standard of living here, 90 per cent felt that Americans are hard-working people, 40 per cent rejected the view that Americans have no purpose in life, 5 per cent said that American government is not democratic, 60 per cent agreed that racial discrimination is the most objectionable aspect of American life, 75 per cent agreed that American youth has great opportunity for education, 75 per cent approved of the informality of the student-professor relationship, 75 per cent agreed that American couples should get parental approval for marriage.

The author concluded that all of the expectations were met with the exception of length of stay which was not related to cultural perspectives in any consistent manner.

5. "Education and Culture in the Middle East," *Middle East Affairs*, VIII (June, 1957), 254.

6. Gezi, Khalil, "The Acculturation of the Middle Eastern Arab Students in Selected American Colleges and Universities," Washington, D.C., Doctoral Dissertation, 1960.

7. Gezi, Khalil, "Arab Students' Perceptions of American Students," *Sociology and Social Research*, XLV (July, 1961), 441-447.

The problem discussed in this article deals with the association between adjustment of the Arab student and (1) his perception of American students' interest in associating with Arabs;

(2) his perceptions of Arab students' interest in associating with Americans; and (3) his perceptions of ease or difficulty in dating Americans. The sample consisted of 62 students from Middle Eastern countries attending college in California. A 20-item question interview schedule with three open-end questions was used.

It was found that 74 per cent felt that ". . . American students, and Americans in general, are friendly and interested in interacting wth Arab students." Twenty-four per cent ". . . thought that American students and Americans in general are unfriendly and disinterested in associating with Arab students."

It was concluded that the adjustment to American life was highly associated with the Arab students' perceptions of the willingness of Americans to interact with them, and, also with their perceptions of the willingness of Americans to date them.

8. Hamilton, M. M., "Social Work in the Middle East," *Journal of the Royal Central Asian Society*, XXXVIII (January, 1951), Part I, 21-28.

9. Holloway, Owen, "University Students of the Middle East," *Journal of the Royal Central Asian Society*, XXXVIII (January, 1951), Part I, 10-20.

10. Holmes, Lt. Col. Fox, "Central Asian Youth Grows Up," *Journal of the Royal Central Asian Society*, XLVIII (July/October, 1961), Parts III and IV, 221-228.

11. Hudson, B. B., "Cross-Cultural Studies in the Arab Middle East and United States; Studies of Young Adults," *Journal of Social Issues*, XV, 3 (September, 1959), 1-75.

12. Joy, C. R., *Young People of the Eastern Mediterranean: Their Stories in Their Own Words* (New York: Duell, Sloan & Pearce, Inc., 1959).

13. Keehn, J. D. and E. T. Prothro, "National Preferences of University Students from 23 Nations," *Journal of Psychology*, XLII (1956), 283-294.

14. Klett, C. James and David W. Yourkey, "A Cross-Cultural Comparison of Judgments of Social Desirability," *Journal of Social Psychology*, XLIX (1959), 19-26.

A cross-cultural test of "social desirability" using the Edwards Personal Preference Schedule. Subjects were 165 male and 33 female students at the American University of Beirut. The median age was 19. The majority of the subjects were from Lebanon, Palestine, Jordan, and Syria. Five other groups, including one from Norway and four from the United States, were used for comparison. One of the United States groups was comprised of Nisei attending college. Considerable agreement was seen in the judgments of social desirability by the six groups.

15. Masuoka, Jitsuichi, "Basic Problems of Asia and Democratic Education," *Harvard Educational Review*, XVII, 4 (Fall, 1947), 228-241.
16. Melikian, L. H. and E. T. Prothro, "Goals Chosen by Arab Students in Response to Hpothetical Situations," *Journal of Social Psychology*, XLVI (August, 1957), 3-9.
17. Melikian, L. H. and Lutfy N. Diab, "Group Affiliations of University Students in the Arab Middle East," *Journal of Social Psychology*, XLIX (May, 1959), 149-159.
18. Melikian, L. H. and E. T. Prothro, "Sexual Behavior of University Students in the Arab Near East," *Journal of Abnormal and Social Psychology*, XLIX (1954), 59-64.
19. Muhyi, I. A., "Women in the Arab Middle East," *Journal of Social Issues*, XV, 3 (1959), 45-57.
20. Perkins, W. A., "Christian Youth in the Middle East," *Ecumenical Review*, VII (July, 1955), 347-352.
21. Prothro, E. T. and L. H. Melikian, "Generalized Ethnic Attitudes in the Arab Near East," *Sociology and Social Research*, XXXVII (July, 1953), 375-379. (Bibliography)
22. Prothro, E. T. and L. H. Melikian, "Studies in Stereotypes, III. Arab Students in the Near East," *Journal of Social Psychology*, XL (1954), 237-243.
23. Qubain, Fahim, "Social Classes and Tensions in Bahrain," *Middle East Journal*, IX, 3 (Summer, 1955), 269-280.
24. Renner, George, "Arab Education in the Near East," *Middle Eastern Affairs*, I, 8 (August, 1950), 215-224.
25. Tannous, A. I., "Social Change in an Arab Village," *American Sociological Review*, VI, 5 (October, 1941), 650-662.
26. UNESCO, Social Science Bibliography, Egypt, Iraq, Jordan, Lebanon, Syria, 1945-1955 (retrospective bibliography of social science works published in the Middle East), United Arab Republic, Iraq, Jordan, Lebanon, 1945-1955. Prepared by the International Committee for Social Sciences Documentation with the co-operation of the United Arab Republic, National Commission for UNESCO, Cairo UNESCO Middle East Science Co-operating Office (1959).
27. "Youth and Politics in the Near East," *World Today*, VII (March, 1951), 102-109.

AFRICA

The countries included in the African section are:

- Angola
- Belgian Congo
- British Somaliland
- Ethiopia
- Ghana
- Guinea
- Kenya
- Madagascar
- Nigeria
- Northern Rhodesia
- Nyasaland
- South Africa
- Southern Rhodesia
- Sudan
- Tanganyika
- Uganda
- General

As much of Africa is in a relatively low stage of industrial development, the research literature is correspondingly underdeveloped. Obviously the more developed nations will have the more adequate resources and skills for the carrying out of scientific research.

African governmental policies nearly always arrogate assimilation of tribal units and traditional structures into larger and more modern forms. There is a concomitant desire to undo the traditional values and institutions. (See Belgian Congo—4, Angola—1, Ghana—4, General—1, General—64, General—65, and General—68.)

The bulk of African social research on adolescence deals with changes in value and social structures, especially in the educational sphere. Within this context, there is a problem of striking a workable balance between traditional socio-cultural patterns, and the new (Ghana—4). Musgrove (Uganda—1) states that the job of the schools is to compensate for the inability of the family to orient the children toward modern demands. A study by Lystad (Ghana—4) experimentally supported the hypothesis that traditional values in 12 to 16-year-old children prevail over the secular. The children were asked to write stories about a boy and a girl in their own town. The relationships they described among actors was essentially nonrational, intimate, group-oriented, and nonhierarchical. The findings also suggested, however, that adolescent thinking has shifted from that of their parents toward the secular and modern. Darke (British Somaliland—1) found that sex-role differentiation and dress patterns were African-European problems to be overcome in Somaliland schools. The success of the school studied was attributed to the Principal, who insisted on mixing home skills and academic work for the girl students.

There is, in general, an attempt to overcome the traditional patterns, which are often considered to be inferior. A contrasting view is presented in Uganda. Page (Uganda—2) reports a desire to maintain a balance between what is needed and what is wanted: in effect, to improve a traditional culture, rather than to transform it. (See also: Swinbanks, Uganda—3 in this connection.) Blanguernon (General—10) discusses the difficulties of offering education to the nomadic Hoggar in the central Sahara. He advises a program whereby education would neither be rushed nor encroach on existing customs and beliefs.

A study of Ethiopian schools by Lewis (Ethiopia—2) examined the "nonscientific beliefs" held by students. He concludes that these traditional values are dysfunctional to modernization, e.g., a belief that manual laborers turn into hyenas at night. Beliefs were found to be changeable by teachers, but an additional problem is that these nonscientific beliefs are held to a considerable extent by teachers as well as by students. (Cf. Barnard's, General—6, study of the Gold Coast.) Here we have a recurrent theme: the teachers are seen in the role of bearers of new cultural patterns, of modernity, and are engaged in an overt effort to transmit skills and abilities to the young, a task which the family can no longer perform.

Omari (Ghana—5) found a reluctance of West African children preparing for college to part with traditional values (cf. Ghana—4). At the same time, there is a preference for Ordinance marriage—a Western type forbidding of polygamy; this is undermining the traditional customs of betrothal and marriage. It can certainly be argued, however, that these adolescents are more secular than their parents.

Musgrove (General—59) found that English teachers became frustrated when African children failed to comprehend obvious truths. He suggests that these truths appear obvious only because of the teachers' unconscious cultural background. The literature supporting the proposition that performance is related to cultural background is extensive and convincing (General—49, 58, 60, 81, etc.).

Of course there is the problem encountered by *any* educational system that would change values and attitudes: namely, that the students return to their original communities and general socio-cultural milieu at the end of the educational process, which results in an *un*learning of the new values. The shift of referents back to family and home community reward different values and attitudes than the significant referents in the academic community. There is a regression to the old behavioral patterns. Banton (General—8) claims that the school is a foreign institution to the community, and has little relevance to community life. In Ghana, Jahoda (Ghana—3) found an example of this phenomenon in male marriage preferences. As age increases, the propensity to select wives of African dress increases relative to that of choosing women of European dress. Younger boys from Westernized homes tended to choose the European type, but the older boys from such homes reverted to the African model. This "regression" occurred in literate, semiliterate, and polygamous families alike.

In Kenya, there is an accelerating breakdown of family patterns. (Kenya—1). Parents have a large role in marriage choices of their daughters (Kenya—2). At the same time, the educational system is striving to educate women (Kenya—5) and to train women as teachers at the primary level. Parents object to this. Here we see parents and referents in the educational system as competing referents, with the educators, as usual, on the side of modernity, and the parents opposed. The strain here is certainly related to strains in the family structure. For a study of the ambivalence created in students between modern and traditional cultural forms, see Banton (General—4).

In Nigeria, the young educated elite faces a dilemma (Nigeria—6, General—86). They are socialized to Western patterns and want to change Nigeria; but they are torn in identification (and involvement) with the old and the new. Money and political office are highly valued. Here we see, to some extent, success defined in terms of peers rather than in terms of traditional referents, and involvement with these new referents.

Roucek (General—74) sees a desire to attain "moral status" in homeland and world as one of the most dynamic of African nationalism. One result is an intense desire for learning (see General—82). Traditional educational forms, such as the "bush school" (see Scanlon, General—75), have disintegrated, and the new competition is between western and African dominated schools and values.

Young Africans, attempting to adjust to the problems of industrialization and secularization, must also come to grips with political independence. Maillard (Madagascar—1) found that more than 100,000 Malagasy boys and girls (ages 8 to 20) are participating in highly organized associations. They are settled in cooperative villages and participating in the National Development Plan dealing with farming, education, public information, health, and nutrition.

An article by Powdermaker (Northern Rhodesia—1) suggests that most adolescents cling to the traditional (rural) way of life as an ideal, though they lean toward Western occupational roles. It is interesting to note that boys felt more disposed to change than girls, e.g., they were more disposed to Europeans. In connection with our general model, this would be expected, as girls have most of their referents centered around home and community, around the business of organizing home activities, such as producing and socializing children, maintaining the home, and so on. By contrast, males are related more to extrahome, and extracommunity activities, such as in the educational and occupational spheres. Omari's study (Ghana—5) reveals a qualified exception to these generalizations. With respect to traditional family institutions, Ghanian women showed greater tradition-breaking desire than the men. They led the men in opposing the avunculate—the main basis of the matrilineal system, as uncle inheritance and other traditional forms of family life have worked largely to their disadvantage. A great majority of the sample preferred polygamy, and *all* the women did.

The support for the generalizations about sex-differential referents in the above paragraph is overwhelming. By way of example, Read (Nyasaland—2) found that in Nyasaland, peer-group compatibility is especially important for males. Adolescent males have dormitories in which they learn the adult roles and occupations. Girls have no corresponding institution and remain in the "womans' world" throughout their adolescence.

Throughout Africa, youth desire to improve their socio-cultural conditions. They are often faced with formidable institutional barriers (see Hodgkin, General—38). For example, in South Africa, Bloem (South Africa—10) found the Negro majority desiring change, but extremely frustrated and discouraged over their inability to bring it about (South Africa—48). The referents with the ability to help them attain their goals do not desire to do so, with the predicted (by our model) result that they are alienated from and hostile to their society, to their uncooperating referents and even to their families. Hellman (South Africa—36) notes the inability of Negro slum parents to deal with their recalcitrant children. On lack of parental control in such circumstances, also see Muller (South Africa—54). Coppens (South Africa—16) notes that youth in the new setting are somewhat lacking in morals and are not developing appropriate social behavior and learning responsibility. The rate of juvenile delinquency is high. South African Negroes are more oriented to change and to broad social goals than are the whites (see South Africa—19). Muller's study suggests that lack of opportunity to attain social and occupational goals produced alienation from society and delinquent behavior. For example, Negroes are barred from most educational opportunities (see Wilson, South Africa—71). This finding is certainly consistent with our model.

We have dealt briefly with sex-role differentiation. Education is more available to men, and the men are more oriented to Europeans. The educated African is seen by Hunter (General—40) as isolated from *both* European and traditional African contacts and fellowships. He is cut off from full integration into both worlds. Hence the adults share an alienation akin to that experienced by their adolescent children. A breakdown in family solidarity is apparently a concomitant of both industrialization and urbanization. For example, Kahl (General—44) found that parental control over adolescent children weakens as the urbanization process continues. This is consistent with the literature on Negro migration to urban areas in South Africa.

As societies industrialize and develop complex institutional frameworks, the socialization of the young begins to slip away from family (see Kahl, General—44) and community (see Hodgkin, General—38), and go to formal organizations. Hence the literature reveals in Africa a rapid growth of youth organizations. Adegbite (General—1) found that State, Islamic groups, civic groups, and churches have provided new avenues of development for the youth of Africa. In Nigeria, there are Scouts and Guides movements, YMCA, 4-H Clubs, and clubs centered around the social life of African adolescents which are social and recreational. Here we see the seeds of the development of adolescent subcultures. It is in the countries that have progressed the most in developing formal socialization institutions, particularly educational, that adolescent subcultures will develop (Davis, General—22).

Special acknowledgment is due C. S. Brembeck and J. P. Keith for their publication *Education in Emerging Africa,* Michigan State University Education in Africa Series I, College of Education, in cooperation with International Programs and African Language and Area Center. Several of the selections appearing in this section were selected and adapted for use in this presentation.

ANGOLA

1. Duffy, James, "Portuguese Africa: Some Crucial Problems and the Role of Education in Their Resolution," *Journal of Negro Education,* XXX (1961), 294-301.

    The Portuguese African policy is one of the assimilation of the primitive African child into Portuguese adulthood. To bring about this evolution two school systems are used. The first, a three-year program, is an initiation system teaching the rudiments of Portuguese. The second is conducted entirely in Portuguese. The majority of Africans are not sufficiently trained to enter this second school system.

    The Portuguese claim they are lowering illiteracy at a rate of 2 per cent per year. 1955 illiteracy tables showed that 98 per cent of Portuguese Africans were illiterate. Duffy states that in the past there has been considerable variation between official pronouncements and what was actually being accomplished. School tables for 1955-1959 are given.

2. Hambly, Wilfrad D., "Tribal Life in Angola," *African World* (April, 1961), 5-7.

BELGIAN CONGO

1. Comhaire-Sylvain, S., *Food and Leisure among the African Youth of Leopoldville* (Cape Town: 1950).

2. Grevisse, F., "Les Perspectives Ouvertes a la Jeunesse Belge au Congo," *Problemes Sociaux Congolais* XLVII (Elisabethville: December, 1959), 3-14.

3. Maquet, Jacques J., "Le Systeme des Relations Sociales dans le Ruanda Ancien," *Tervren, Annales du Musée Royal du Congo Belge,* 1954.

A discussion of the social or cultural categories in to which 11 million Africans in the Belgian Congo can be divided. The author's principal cleavage is based on the character of the political institutions to which the individual is subject. Thus 85 per cent of the people are still living in the tribal tradition with chiefs and elders, while 15 per cent are detribalized and no longer live under traditional political institutions. Solutions are offered for the problems involved in the change.

5. Mernier, J., "The Evolution of African Society in the Belgian Congo," *Zaire*, II, 8 (October, 1948), 835-868.
6. Pons, V. G., et al., "Social Effects of Urbanization in Stanleyville, Belgian Congo," Preliminary Report of the Field Research Team of the International African Institute, *Social Implications of Industrialization and Urbanization in Africa South of the Sahara.* Prepared under the Auspices of UNESCO by The International African Institute, London, Paris: UNESCO (1956), Part III, 229-492.

A series of studies by a psychologist, a sociologist, and a statistician. The areas covered are: socio-demographic structure of Stanleyville; labor problems; aptitudes and training of Africans; work attitudes and stereotypes; social patterns of urban life.

BRITISH SOMALILAND

1. Darke, Marion, "The Education of Girls and Women in British Somaliland," *Overseas Education*, XXX (1959), 160-163.

This article is largely a report of the opening of a girls school among the Somali people. The success of this school was largely due to the Principal who insisted on combining plenty of housecraft and the elementary needlework with academic work.

In the course of time, men began comparing academic attainments of the girls with those of the boys. The girls were by no means behind the boys and as a result the Somali no longer want proof of the girls' ability to learn.

Dress problems were eventually solved by the Somali themselves. They suggested that the school girls dress like their European teachers while in school. This will eventually lead to the overcoming of several cultural problems dealing not only with dress but with problems of mixed company in school.

ETHIOPIA

1. Lewis, W. H., "Ethiopian Empire: Progress and Problems," *Middle Eastern Journal*, X (Summer, 1956), 262-263.

2. Lord, Edith, "The Impact of Education on Non-Scientific Beliefs in Ethiopia," *The Journal of Social Psychology*, XLVII (1958), 339-353.

Perhaps the most important person in any educational program is the teacher. Apart from the disseminating of knowledge, teachers indoctrinate. Therefore in any study of educational problems, it becomes necessary to discover which nonscientific beliefs are held by indigenous teachers.

Over 200 nonscientific beliefs were gathered. Some impede education and others have a lesser value. For example, in trade schools, most students want to study electricity and show no interest in bricklaying or plumbing. The reason is found in a belief stretching back to the Queen of Sheba, that manual laborers in general, and iron and metal workers in particular, can turn themselves into hyenas at night. There is a widespread belief that eating garlic and butter that is 20 years old is the best treatment for malaria.

Of 132 items of nonscientific beliefs, 34 of those items were believed by 50 per cent or more of the 96 teachers. For example, 74 per cent of the teachers believed that gonorrhea first came from a female dog. In a country where venereal disease is a major health problem, the nonscientific beliefs of teachers related to any major health problem becomes of major significance.

Intelligence is not the problem. Both clinical and test evidence exists to support the thesis that Ethiopian children are as heavily endowed, intellectually, as are the children of other lands. Under the present curriculum Ethiopian children are studying the earth's crust, astronomy, physics, and chemistry before they reach Standard 6. These learnings are rooted in the air; they do not take hold, root, bud and blossom. They can be memorized and regurgitated at examination time, but they do not affect changes in attitudes or behavior.

This study has demonstrated that education can have an impact on nonscientific beliefs which motivate attitudes and daily behavior of Ethiopians. The study further demonstrated that over 100 of the superstitions studied proved impervious to modern educational procedures in Ethiopia.

GHANA

1. Bryant, A., "Ghana Eighty Years Ago and Today," *Illustrated London News,* LLXXXIX (December 2, 1961), 954.

2. Hodge, Peter, "Work with Youth in the Towns of Ghana," *West African Journal of Education,* II (1958), 96-100.

The author reviews some of the problems affecting youth in the cities of Ghana, in particular, and West Africa, in general. He makes the following suggestions:

1. Attempts should be made to supplement the basic primary and secondary school education which is all the formal education young people are likely to get.

2. Youth work should aim to assist with the various measures being taken to solve the chronic unemployment of young people having only a middle-school leaving certificate.

3. More publicity efforts and funds must be devoted to those measures which will promote national unity among youth.

4. The training of youth leaders and group workers should be thoroughly reexamined.

3. Jahoda, Gustav, "Boys' Images of Marriage Partners and Girls' Self-Images in Ghana," *Sociologus,* VIII, 2 (1958), 155-169.

This article reports on an attempt ". . . to discover the expectations of boys and girls concerning the roles played by women in adult life." The sample was drawn from six schools in Accra which were felt to contain a good cross section of the primary and secondary school age population. The ages included ran from 6 to 12 years for the primary and 12 to 18 for the secondary students. 44 per cent of the girls' fathers were manual laborers while 59 per cent of the boys' fathers were thus engaged.

The instrument was a projective type test consisting of eight pictures of African women specifically drawn for the test. The pictures varied in skin shade and clothing with both African and European dress represented. The boys were told to choose the women they would most like to marry and the girls were asked to select those they would most like to grow up to be.

It was found that the tendency to choose the women in African dress increased with the age of the subjects. This was true of both the boys and the girls. The results for the girls tended to parallel those for the boys. Younger boys from Westernized homes chose the European type, but older boys from such homes reverted to the African types. There was no significant difference between the choices of boys from literate, semiliterate, or polygenous families. As age increased the choices were made more on personal characteristics rather than on appearance and status.

The author offers an interpretation based on role Westernization and the development of the adolescent in Ghana.

4. Lystad, Mary H., "Traditional Values of Ghanaian Children," *American Anthropologist,* LXII (1960), 454-464.

In Ghana's movement toward independence and self-rule a conscious attempt was made to change many traditional institutions and to alter many traditional attitudes and values. This study examines the youth to see if they have accepted these secular values.

The subjects were 94 secondary students between the ages of 12 and 16. There were 61 boys and 33 girls, 39 of the subjects were from urban areas and 55 were from rural areas. These students were chosen from among 18,000 eligible candidates for college preparatory training. Analysis revealed that the hypothesis that the children would show a preference for traditional over secular values was, to a large extent, supported.

5. Omari, T. Peter, "Changing Attitudes of Students in West African Society Toward Marriage and Family Relationship," *British Journal of Sociology,* XI (1960), 197-210.

An examination of the trend of change as reflected in the marriage attitudes of Ghanian students. A questionnaire was applied to 142 male and 150 female final-year students from teacher-training institutions in Ghana. The ages ranged from 17 to 31 with the mode falling between 21 and 24.

The findings revealed that the majority favored the Ordinance marriage (a Western type forbidding polygamy) over the traditional type. The great majority felt love to be an important factor in marriage and 94 per cent were involved in relationships of their own construction. In spite of this the parents approval is still felt to be desired. If the parents objected to the marriage choice 41 per cent would obey the parents, while 24 per cent would disobey and 31 per cent were undecided. There was a strong rejection of the avunculate.

The author concluded that the women have a more radical attitude toward traditional family institutions than do the men. Additionally he notes, ". . . there seems to be a desire among members of the sample—irrespective of sex—to bear financial responsibility for their own children's upbringing, singly or together with their husbands or wives."

6. United Kingdom, British Information Services, Reference Division,

The Making of Ghana. I.D. 1254 (London: F. Mildner & Sons, 1956).

This account of the Gold Coast, its people, introduction of Western institutions and technology, political responsibility, and economic and social progress, contains data on action taken under the Accelerated Development Plan for Education.

GUINEA

1. Gardeazabal, E. De, "La Proteccion de Menores en Guina," (Youth protection in Guinea), *Africa,* XII, CLXVI (Madrid: October, 1955), 15-19.

KENYA

1. Barnett, A., "Christian Home and Family Life in Kenya Today," *International Review of Missions,* XLIX (October, 1960), 420-460.

A report of a conference discussion at a meeting of the Christian Council of Kenya at which the phenomena and causes of family breakdown in Kenya were discussed. It was noted that the youth problem was an important area for work. More organized leisure time and more trained youth leaders were called for.

2. Kabatu, K., "African Marriage Systems," *Indo Asian Culture,* VI, 3 (January, 1958), 299-309.

A general discussion of African marriage systems with special reference to the systems in Kenya. It is noted that great importance is attached to marriage by the parents. Premarital sexual relations are strictly forbidden and severely punished if discovered. Youth are encouraged to participate in activities such as work projects and dances. While there is some freedom of choice and association, the approval of the parents is always demanded prior to the marriage.

3. Levine, R. A., "Internationalization of Political Values in Stateless Societies," *Human Organization,* XIX (Summer, 1960), 51-58. (Bibliography)
4. Mason, H., "The Training of Social Welfare Workers in Kenya," *Mass Education Bulletin,* I (London: 1950), 65-71.
5. Matheson, Alastair, "Overcoming Tribal Prejudice against Educating Girls in Kenya," *Journal of Negro Education,* XXIII (1954), pp. 481-482.

African girls' education is one of the primary tasks currently occupying the attention of education authorities in Kenya. Generally speaking womens' education in Kenya today stands where boys' education stood 15 years ago.

Government plans call for each school to have two women teachers in the primary level. This will mean a provincial strength of 3,000 women teachers. The Education Department realizes, further, that by having women teachers in every school, the possible objection of parents to all male staffs teaching their girls can no longer be a valid deterrent. Women teachers provided the key to girl education in Kenya.

MADAGASCAR

1. Maillard, Jean-Pierre, "Malagasy Youth and Adult Education Problems in Madagascar," *International Journal of Adult and Youth Education,* (UNESCO), XIV, 2 (1962).

A discussion of the educational and adjustment problems of the youth in a newly independent nation. One avenue utilized is the organized youth movement in which more than 100,000 Malagasy youth are actively involved.

NIGERIA

1. Burness, Helen M., "Women in Katsina Province, Northern Nigeria," *Overseas Education,* XXIX (1957), 116-122.

This author attempted to state the reasons why education of African women is unpopular in certain tribes of Northern Nigeria. Some of these reasons are:

1. Education of girls below the marriage age is unpopular because it interferes with their being trained in the customs and economics of the tribe.

2. Education of girls above the normal age for marrying meets with violent tribal objections for deep-rooted and social reasons.

3. Education of married women is not yet accepted in many tribes. Adult education classes have been attended only by divorcees or widows, hence the unpopularity of the classes for married women.

2. Ellis, Richard W. B., "Age of Puberty in the Tropics," *British Medical Journal* (January 14, 1950), 85-89. (Bibliography)

In order to determine if there is a difference in the age of puberty between children in the tropics and in Great Britain, interviews and medical examinations were held with 300 Nigerian girls and 470 British girls, 333 Nigerian boys and 662 British boys.

It was found that puberty did not occur significantly earlier in Nigeria than in Great Britain although there was a slightly earlier occurrence in Nigeria. The author notes, in connection, that the age of consent in Nigeria is 13 while in Britain it is 16.

3. Faulkner, D., "Social Welfare and Juvenile Delinquency in Lagos," *Howard Journal* (London: 1944-45).
4. Kiernan, Irene S., "Queen's School for Girls, Ede, Western Nigeria," *Overseas Education*, XXXII (1960), 103-111.

   This article reports an interview with Miss Kiernan, the principal of Queen's School for Girls. Miss Kiernan stated that the aim of this 300-girl school was to "fit the girls for life in the community by giving them the best of both Yoruba and European culture."

5. Marris, L., "Slum Clearance and Family Life in Lagos," *Human Organization*, XIX (Fall, 1960), 123-128.
6. Smythe, Hugh H., "Human Relations in Nigeria: the Young Elite," *Journal of Human Relations*, VI, 2 (1958), 54-72

   A discussion of the interpersonal relations, attitudes, and characteristics of the young elite class in Nigeria. The author notes that the members of this group are Western educated or educated in the better African universities. Many have careers in the civil service or the foreign businesses. They wear Western clothes and conduct close primary relations with the elites of United States and British graduates. They live, however, in an area where the people have little in common either educationally or culturally.

   Most are concerned with advancing in their life's work and give little thought to problems of labor, business, and international affairs. Many are cynical toward the present leadership of the country but they hold that high political office is a symbol of highest success. They feel a conflict between the modern and the traditional values.

   One individual felt that money was the dominant value in the class. He also notes that the values of the past play only a small role in the present situation where the goals are significantly different. The removal of the British seems to be a predominant theme.

NORTHERN RHODESIA

1. Powdermaker, H., "Social Change through Imagery and Values of Teenage Africans in Northern Rhodesia," *American Anthropologist*, LVIII (October, 1956), 783-813.

   An attempt to describe the change involved in the westernization of teen-age Africans in N. Rhodesia. The values reflected in the African's self-image and his perception of good interpersonal relations along with his goals and ambitions are used in the analysis. The sample consisted of 106 essays written in two government schools by boys and girls between the ages of 12 and 17. These essays were designed to elicit data on African attitudes toward Europeans, toward Africans, toward occupations, marriage, number of children desired, and the fantasy desires of rebirth.

   Among the findings discussed, the author noted the following: (1) With regard to manner of living, the majority favored the traditional rural setting in spite of the fact that they were urban dwellers. This was more prevalent for the girls. (2) Boys' occupational aspirations were Western-oriented toward white collar, skilled labor, or small businesses. Nursing and teaching were prevalent among the girls. (3) A large proportion of the sample preferred traditional African moral values over European values. The boys were more disposed toward Europeans than the girls. It was noticed that the girls reflected a strong desire for equal status and privileges with new individual goals, goals which cause conflict when they meet traditional goals.

NYASALAND

1. Mitchell, J. Clyde, "An Outline of the Social Structure of Malemia Area," *Nyasaland Journal*, IV (July, 1951), 15-48.
2. Read, Margaret, *Children of Their Fathers* (London: Methuen & Co., Ltd, 1959).

   A description and explanation of the life patterns of children of the Nagoni tribe of Nyasaland. Chapters five and six deal with the period between the eruption of the second teeth until marriage. The discussion is based on observation of the children and adults of the tribe.

   At the age of 6 or 7 both the males and the females begin to assume greater social and personal responsibilities. This applies both to the society as a whole and to the peer group. Peer-group compatibility is a particular goal for the male. He is moved into a dormitory where he lives and learns the responsibilities of an adult and a cattle herder until he marries when he is about 18 years old. The dormitory boys are looked on as a status step ahead of the youths who attend school. Girls have no similar institution but continue to live in the woman's world. There is, however, an attitude which considers the girl in a "girls' circle," but this is not a close parallel to the dormitory. The Nagoni have no "initiation schools," their youth facing an individual ritual at puberty rather than a group initiation.

The author notes that, in general, in the Nagoni society, the ". . . threshold of adulthood is a test of effectiveness of training children and young people to conform to the personality pattern of the culture of the society and for the young individuals themselves a test of their adjustment to that pattern."

3. "The Rhodes Livingstone Institute for Social Research," *Nyasaland Journal*, X (January, 1957), 23.

4. Spoczynska, Joy O., "Health Problems and Progress in Sierra Leone," *African World* (May, 1962), 4-5.

SOUTH AFRICA

1. Arnoldi, J., *The Vocational Choices, Interests and Aptitudes of Secondary School Boys, with Special Reference to the Consistency of These Factors*, Doctor of Education Dissertation, University of Pretoria, South Africa, 1957.

2. Badenhorst, L. T., "The Future Growth of the Population of South Africa and Its Probable Age Distribution," *Population Studies* (London: June, 1950).

3. Badenhorst, L. T., A *Study of the Social Values of Life Goals of White Children in Secondary Schools in Johannesburg* (Johannesburg: University of Witwatersrand, in progress).

4. Barnard, J. S., *'n Empiriese Studie oor die Sosiale Ontwikkeling van 'n Groep Afrikaans-sprekende Middelbare Skoolleerlinge* (*An Empirical Study of Social Development of a Group of Afrikaans-Speaking Pupils in Secondary Schools*), Doctor of Education Dissertation, University of Potchefstroom, South Africa, 1956.

5. Bettison, D. C., "Child Maintenance in a Small South African Town," *African Studies*, 15 (1956), 132-138.

6. Bettison, D. C., "Influence of Social Circumstances on the Attitudes of Educated Africans," *South African Journal of Sociology*, LIII (1957), 309-314.

7. Bettison, D. C., "Mind, Manners and Morals: some Problems in

Cultural Readjustments," *Race Relations Journal*, XXII, 3 (1955), 18-30.

8. Bieshevvel, S., *African Intelligence* (Johannesburg: South African Institute of Race Relations, 1943).

9. Blignaut, J. B., *Die Invloed van Buiteskoolse Aktiwiteit op die Ontwikkeling van die Persoonlikheid van die Laerskoolkind (The Influence of After School Activities on the Development of the Personality of the Primary School Child)*, Master's of Education Thesis, University of Pretoria, South Africa, 1953.

10. Bloom, Leonard, "Self Concepts and Social Status in South Africa: A Preliminary Cross-Cultural Analysis," *Journal of Social Psychology*, LI (February, 1960), 103-112.

An analysis of white and nonwhite groups in South Africa. The author tested 94 political science students in segregated and integrated colleges in South Africa. The instrument consisted of a questionnaire containing background information and five projective-type questions designed to uncover aspirations, attitudes, expectations, and fears between the members of two major ethnic groups.

The analysis uncovered clear differences between blacks and whites. The whites were favorable toward social change in the prospering states, and were satisfied with the current situation in Europe. The nonwhite subjects believed in social change, in rights and equality, and community responsibility. The educated blacks are marginal men with the typical problems of adjustment. They offered many emotional answers revealing their insecurity and sensitivity.

The author concluded, "We cannot avoid stepping out of the sterile role of social scientist to deplore the lack of hope, the wastage of potential in a country with inadequate educational and social services, and few opportunities for the nonwhites who comprise 75 per cent of the total population, and whose slender weight of opportunity is amply overweighted by the heavy and crushing burden of discouragement."

11. Bothma, C. B., "Tsotsi-Bendes in Pretoria" (Bantu Juvenile Gangs in Pretoria), *Tydskrif vir Rasse-aangeleenthede*, III, 2.

12. Centlivres, A. Van de Sandt, *Blundering into University Apartheid* (South Africa: University of Cape Town, Academic Freedom Committee, 1959).

13. Collins, Colin B., *Catholic Bantu Education* (Pretoria: C. B. Collins, 1957).

14. Coetzee, A. J. S., *Die Ontwikkeling van die Sedelike Oordeel by*

Leerings van die Middelbare Skool (*The Development of the Moral Judgment of Pupils in Secondary Schools*), Doctor of Education Dissertation, University of Pretoria, South Africa, 1952.

15. Coetzee, H. H., *Jeug in Betsing: Gedagtee oor Wangedrag en Jeugnisdaad* (*Youth in Conflict: Ideas on Misconduct and Juvenile Delinquency*), Potchefstroom, Pro Rege-pers, 1957.

16. Coppens, B., "Social Work in Urban Areas, with Special Reference to Family Life," (Conditions of change which have led to jobs for the African in South Africa), *International Review of Missions*, XLI (October, 1952), 464-470.

This report given at a conference on social welfare on behalf of the Christian Council of Northern Rhodesia deals with the social conditions which exist in the urban areas and the problems which have arisen. The essential problem is that of the disruption and transition resulting from the transplanting of the African into a European culture.

The author discusses the following problem areas: government, economy, health, family, and youth. The problems for the family arise from the threatened solidarity of the kinship group. Youth in the new setting are somewhat lacking in morals and are not developing appropriate social behavior and learning responsibility. The rate of delinquency is very high.

17. Crause, H. L., *Sosiologiese studie van jeugarbeiders van landelike oorsprong in Johannesburg* (Sociological Study of Adolescent Labourers of Rural Origin in Johannesburg), Ph. D. Dissertation, University of the Orange Free State, South Africa, 1953.

18. Danziger, K., "Self-Interpretations of Group Differences in Values (Natal: South Africa)," *Journal of Social Psychology*, XLVII (1958), 317-325.

19. Danziger, K., "Value Differences among South African Students," *Journal of Abnormal and Social Psychology*, LVII (1958), 339-346.

An examination of the evaluation of whites and nonwhites of the dominant pattern of their society as it exists at the present. 195 students in the colleges of South Africa (34 white, 37 Indian, and 47 African) were administered voluntary questionnaires in classes. The questionnaires dealt with the characterization of white civilization, personal values, and goals.

With regard to personal values, the whites reflected a desire for purely personal satisfactions, while the nonwhites held desires for broader social goals. The characterizations of the white civilization were more unfavorable among the African students than among the Indian students. Among the whites, the technical college students were more favorable than the general university students. The behavior of white university students revealed some conflict between home and university values.

The author notes a deep conflict aided by a legalized dominant minority and a lack of adequate and satisfactory communications. He also notes, "The privatistic (white) and the socially oriented (Negro) individuals are subject to different forms of anxiety. Whereas the latter tends to fear political persecution and a possible loss of moral standing, the latter's great fear is of social isolation in its various forms."

20. Davie, T. B., *Education and Race Relations in South Africa*, South African Institute of Race Relations, Hoernle Memorial Lecture (1955).

21. De Vos, P. J., *Indier-jeugmisdaad: 'n Sociologiese ondersoek na die Probleem an 'n Verkynsel van die Indierbevolking van durban* (*Crime among Indian Juveniles: a Sociological Study of the Problem as a Phenomenon of the Indian Population in Durban*), Unpublished Ph. D. Dissertation, University of Pretoria, 1945.

22. Dickenson, H. M., *Frustration Shown by Various Groups of High School Girls as Evaluated by the Rosenzweig Picture-Frustration Study*, Unpublished Master's Thesis, University of South Africa, 1958.

23. Du Toit, H. B., *Die Na-Skoolse Jeug: Arbeid en Vryetyd* (*Work and Leisure of Youth who Have Finished School*), Ph.D. Dissertation, University of Stellenbosch, South Africa, 1956.

24. Du Toit, H. B., "Work and Leisure Roles of Youth People: An Empirical Study," (Functional Relation between the Way They Spend Their Leisure Time and Their Socio-economic Background: South Africa), *Sociology and Social Research*, XLIV (March/April, 1960), 235-243.

The author is not here attempting generalizations or reporting trends for South African youth as such. Rather he is investigating the place and function of leisure-time activities among diverse groups of South African youth. These groups vary in their place of origin, vocational aspirations, and socio-economic status.

Through various youth organizations the author sampled unmarried white juveniles, both male and female, between the ages of 16 and 25; 403 subjects were from Johannesburg and 402 were from Paarl (mostly of rural background). The range of data were collected by the use of "questionnaires, interviews, participant observation, and published and unpublished reports on youth organizations and clubs."

It was found that the youth studied had much occupational mobility. The group who fell in the lower work categories did not have much enthusiasm for their work. Both positive and negative attitudes toward work were found to be associated with certain groups. While work and leisure were about equal in satisfaction, those who found leisure more satisfying were generally less satisfied with their occupations.

Among the leisure preferences reported we see: (1) a preference for light radio over educational programs, (2) selection of programs varied with socio-economic status, (3) scientific magazines lost out to cultural publications, (4) selection of reading material varied with educational level, (5) attendance at films was highest for the lowest educational levels and the pattern of film preferences varied with the educational level on the subject.

The author concludes, "The solution to some of the problems of leisure time is related not only to the quality of the facilities and activities but also to the sociocultural life pattern."

25. Fouche, J. W. J., *Die Persoonlike en Gesinsagtergrond van 175 Onbeheerbare Kinders was Gedurende 1956/1957 na Inrigtings verwys is* (The Background of 175 Uncontrollable Children Which Have Been Committed to Institutions during 1956/1957), Unpublished Master's Thesis, 1960, University of Pretoria.

26. Fourie, A. B., *The Influence of Participation in Sport on the Process of Socialization with Special Reference to Senior School Boys: a Comparative Study of Participants and Non-Participants in Sport,* Unpublished Master's Thesis, University of Orange Free State, 1954.

27. Garbers, J. G., *'n Ondersoek na die puberteitsbeeld van die moderne jeug* (An Investigation into Adolescence of Modern Youth), in progress, University of Pretoria, South Africa, 1960.

28. Gerber, J. J., *The Personal and Political Ideals of Adolescents,* Master's of Education Thesis, University of South Africa, 1947.

29. Gerdes, L. C., A *Study of the Responsibilities of Adolescent Girls as Revealed by Their Diaries and Rorschach Records,* Unpublished Master's Thesis, University of South Africa, 1957.

30. Gillespie, J. M. and G. W. Allport. *Youth's Outlook on the Future* (Garden City, New York: Doubleday and Company, Inc., 1955).

1,819 case studies from 10 countries.

31. Gous, A. G. S., *Godsdienstige Konflikte in Rypwordingsprobleme by die Adolescent* (Religious Conflicts and Problems of Maturity of the Adolescent), Master's Thesis, University of Stellenbosch, South Africa, 1955.

32. Grieveson, E. T., "Educational Needs of Urbanized Natives in South Africa," *Journal of the Royal African Society* (July, 1937), 321-336.

33. Hartshorne, K. B., "The Background to Education in the Urban Areas of South Africa," *Overseas Education,* XXII, 1 (October, 1950), 26-30.

34. Hartshorne, K. B., *Native Education in the Union of South Africa: A Summary of the Report of the Commission on Native Education in South Africa,* South African Institute of Race Relations, 1953 (U.G. 53, 1951).

35. Hellmann, Ellen, *The Development of Social Groupings among Urban Africans in the Union of South Africa.* UNESCO Social Science Affairs Conference. Paris (1954).

36. Hellmann, Ellen, "Native Life in a Johannesburg Slum Yard," *Africa* (January, 1935), 34-62.

   Report of a year's investigation of a slum yard in Johannesburg. The author observed 100 families and noted that the breakup of the family was one of the first results of residence in the slum yard. The socialization of the child and the inability of the parents to deal with recalcitrant children is thoroughly discussed.

37. Hellmann, Ellen, *Problems of Urban Bantu Youth: Report of an Enquiry into the Causes of Early School-Leaving and Occupational Opportunities Among the Bantu Youth in Johannesburg,* South African Institute of Race Relations, Johannesburg, VI (1940).

38. Hellmann, Ellen, *Rooiyard: A Sociological Survey of an Urban Native Slum Yard* (Rhodes-Livingstone Institute, Cape Town: Oxford University Press, 1948).

39. Heyns, I. de V., A *Quantitative Comparative Analysis of the Response Records of the Rorschach Test Applied to Successful and Unsuccessful Adolescent Scholars,* Master's of Education Thesis, University of Cape Town, 1951.

40. Heyns, M. E., *Die Houvas van Jeugbewegings op die Adolescent* (*The Influence of Youth Movements on the Adolescent*), Master's of Education Thesis, University of Stellenbosch, South Africa, 1948.

41. Jaspan, M. A., "Race and Society in South Africa," *Science and Society*, XIX (1955), 1-22. (See *Social Abstracts*, 1955), III, 1476.)

42. Kaldenberg, H., *Methods of Re-Educating the Juvenile Delinquent in the Constantia Reformatory*, B. Education Paper, University of Cape Town, 1951.

43. Kommissie van Ondersoek Insake die Gesinslewe: *Ongetroude Moeders. 'n Sosiologiese Ondersoek* (*Unmarried Mothers. A Sociological Study*), University of Pretoria.

44. Kriek, J. J., *'n Psigo-Diagnostiese Studie van 'n groep Sosial-wa naan-gepaste jeugdiges* (*A Psycho-Diagnostic Study of a Group of Socially Maladjusted Adolescents*), Unpublished Master's Thesis, Pretoria University, South Africa, 1957. (In Afrikaans)

45. Kriell, R. G., *'n Ondersoek na die Verband Tussen Belangstelling en Bekwaamheid in Afrikaanse Hoerskoolleerlinge* (*An Investigation into the Relationship between the Interests and Abilities of Afrikaans High School Pupils*), Unpublished Ph.D. Thesis, University of Stellenbosch, South Africa, 1955.

46. Le Roux, A. G., *'n Vergelykende Studie oor Bereopsbelangstelling en persoonlikheidseinskappe by n groep Hoerskoolsouns* (*A Comparative Study of the Vocational Interests and Personality Traits of a Group of High School Boys*), Unpublished Master's Thesis, University of Pretoria, South Africa, 1956. (In Afrikaans)

47. Le Roux, W. G., *Die Kleurlingbende in Kaapstad* (Gangs among Coloureds in Cape Town), Ph.D. Dissertation, University of Stellenbosch, 1951.

48. Leyburn, J. G., "Urban Natives in South Africa, *American Sociological Review*, IX, 5 (October, 1944), 495-502.

The author offers a short statement on the conditions of the urban native in South Africa for comparison by the reader with the conditions of the American Negro. Young men leave the native areas for the city to make money, to find excitement, to be free of parental and tribal discipline, or, and this is the prevalent, to avoid the poll taxes on males in their areas.

The author goes on to discuss the educational plight of the native, his recreational facilities, the trials of racial prejudice, and the social injustices perpetrated by the white minority upon the black majority.

49. Longmore, L., *The Dispossessed* (London: Jonathan Cape, 1959).

50. Longmore, L., "Teen-Age Vote in South Africa," *Political Quarterly*, XXXI (1959), 114-119.

A discussion of the South African law permitting white males and females 18 or over the right to vote and the implications of this law for the racial situation. Various arguments are presented. For example the inability of an 18-year-old to marry, to make a legal contract, or to get a passport without parental consent and yet have the vote. With the given tax structure which begins at 21, the youth have, in effect, what is representation without taxation.

The author concludes, "In a country like South Africa where the vote is denied to the bulk of the population on the grounds of color no matter how well qualified some individuals might be to use the vote, the extension of voting rights to white boys and girls of 18 can only aggravate racial discontents and tensions."

51. Malan, M. B., *Die Maatskaplike Betekenis van Jeugsentra; n spesiale ondersoek na die maatskaplike rol en betekenia van die Pretoria Jeugsentrum van die N. H. of G. Kerk van Suid-Afrika (The Social Value of Youth Centres; a Special Investigation into the Social Role and Value of the Pretoria Youth Centre of the Dutch Reformed Church of South Africa)*, Masters of Social Work Thesis, University of South Africa, 1957.

52. Mayer, P., *Townsmen or Tribesmen* (Cape Town: Oxford University Press, 1961). (Conservatism and the Process of Urbanization in a South African City.)

53. Millar, C. J., *The Educational Significance of the Boy Scout System*, Bachelor of Education Paper, University of Cape Town, South Africa, 1958.

54. Muller, Shulsmith, "Juvenile Delinquency and the Colour Bar," *Africa South*, III, 3 (1959), 35-41.

An attack on the color bar in South Africa and its affect on the rate of juvenile delinquency. The author notes that the colored people do not go to the police for protection or justice. Poverty, the lack of family security, the lack of parental control, the changing mores of law breaking, and the lack of opportunities for work and constructive activities are all contributing to the rise of delinquent behavior. The author concludes that as long as there is a color bar in South Africa no government action can eliminate or reduce the incidence of juvenile delinquency.

55. Nel, B. B., "A Phenomenological Approach to the Problems of Youth, Work and Community for the Advancement of Pedagogy as a Science," Faculty of Education, *Educational Studies*, VIII, 27 (1960), University of Pretoria.

56. Nzimende, A., *A Comparative Study of the Concept and Use of Time in Groups of African and European Children,* Unpublished Master's Thesis, University of South Africa, 1952.

57. O'Neara, J. J., *A Comparative Study of the Personality and Motives of Students Who Enter the Teaching Profession,* Unpublished Master's Thesis, University of Witwatersrand, 1947.

58. Pettigrew, Thomas F., "Social Distance and Attitudes of South African Students," *Social Forces,* XXXVIII (1960), 246-253.

An investigation of the social distance attitudes in South African students; 627 white South African college students were questioned in 1956 by use of an ethnic attitude questionnaire which contained a social distance scale, three Likert scales to measure authoritarianism, items on social conformity, anti-African prejudice, and a variety of personal information items.

The results were strikingly similar to American fiindings. (1) ethnic membership was an important correlate of social distance, (2) Afrikaner subjects tended to be the most intolerant of nonwhites, and Jewish subjects tended to be the most tolerant of nonwhites, (3) authoritarianism social conformity, and anti-African prejudice were all positively related to the attitudes of the English toward outgroups, (4) students from the working class were more hostile toward nonwhites yet willing to marry Jews than students from nonmanual families.

The author notes in conclusion, "The close parallel between these data and American data strongly suggests that racial, religious, and ethnic prejudices operate in similar ways in various Western societies."

59. Pienaar, P. M., *'n Sosiaal-Paigologiese Ontleding van die aanpassingsklas aan n Hoerskool met Behulp van die Sosoigram* (*A Sociological-Psychological Analysis of an Adjustment Class in a High School with the Aid of a Sociogram*), Master's of Education Thesis, University of Pretoria, 1957.

60. Pieterse, J. C., "Jeugmisdaad onder die Stedelike Bantoe" (Juvenile Delinquency among the Urban Bantu), *Bantu/Bantoe,* 11 (November, 1957).

61. Prins, J. M. G., *Aspekte van die Lewe van die Stedelike Bantoejeug en Hulle Sendingbenadering* (*Some Aspects of the Life of the Urban Bantu Youth and Mission Work among Them*), B. D. Thesis, University of Stellenbosch, 1961.

62. Roberts, G. C., *The Reading of Comics by Pupils Attending High Schools in the Cape Peninsula,* B. Education Paper, University of Cape Town, 1955.

63. Scheepers, D. J., *Factors Influencing Secondary School Pupils in Their Choice of a Career*, Master's of Education Thesis, University of Witwatersrand, 1959.

64. Smuts, Adriaan Josias, *The Education of Adolescents in South Africa*, Ph.D. Dissertation, Columbia University, 1938.

65. Steinberg, S., *A Study of Feelings of Inferiority amongst First-Year Students at the U. C. T. (University of Cape Town)*, Unpublished Master's Thesis, 1946, University of Cape Town, South Africa.

66. Stone, W. M., *An Investigation into the Reading Interests of 12-15 Year Old English-Speaking Pupils in the Cape Peninsula and Suggestions for the Improvement of Reading Materials for this Age Group*, Unpublished Ph.D. Dissertation, University of Cape Town, 1953.

67. Strating, H. H., *Wangedrag van Dogters* (Juvenile Delinquency among Girls) (H.A.U.M., University of Pretoria, 1961).

68. Venter, H. J., *Youth at the Crossroads* (Cape Town: H.A.U.N.) (Publication of the Department of Sociology, Criminology and Applied Sociology at the University of Pretoria), 3, 1959.

69. Venter, H. J. and G. M. Retief, *Bantoejeugmisdaad. 'n Krimineel-Sociologiese Ondersoek van 'n Groep Naturele-jeugoortreders in die Boksburgse Landdrosdistrik* (*Bantu Juvenile Delinquency. A Criminal Sociological Study of a Group of Non-White Juvenile Delinquents in the Magistrate District of Boksburg*) (Cape Town: H.A.U.M., University of Pretoria, 1960).

70. Venter, H. J. and G. M. Retief, *Bantoe-Jeugmisdaad* (Juvenile Delinquency among Bantu) (Cape Town: H.A.U.N., University of Pretoria, 1960).

71. Wilson, Monica, "South Africa," *UNESCO International Social Science Journal*, XIII, 2 (1961), 225-245.

72. Young, G., *War on the Home Front: An Approach to the Problem of Juvenile Delinquency in South Africa* (Cape Town: Methodist Publishing House, 1957).

SOUTHERN RHODESIA

1. Frantz, C., "Southern Rhodesia," *UNESCO International Science Journal*, XIII, 2 (1961), 215-225.

2. Ibbotson, P., *Report on a Survey of Juvenile Delinquency in Southern Rhodesia* (Bulawayo: Federation of Native Welfare Societies, 1945).

3. Parker, Franklin, "Education of Africans in Southern Rhodesia," *Comparative Education Review*, II (October, 1959), 27-30.

The growth of African education in Southern Rhodesia has seen several stages. Initially, from 1899 to 1927 we see "The Path of Salvation," when Christianity industrial education bias, and benevolent paternalism were pressures used to shake indifferent Africans out of their apathy.

Following this period, from 1927 to 1935 we have the "Adaptation to Environment," an experiment that failed as advancing Africans became stirred by Western incentives and embraced education as the path to progress.

Finally, from 1935 to 1960 comes the period of "The Awakened African," who accepted Western schooling and even demanded it with passion while he outwardly showed a growing antipathy to white dominance and missionary guidance.

SUDAN

1. Forrest, Ronald, "Sudan's Secondary Schools: Two Cultures in the Classroom," *Guardian* (July 15, 1960).
2. Lister, C., "War of Nerves" (Englishmen Teaching in Sudanese Secondary Boarding Schools), *Spectator*, CC (March 14, 1958), 321.
3. "Sudan Struggles to Learn," *The Arab World*, VIII (September/October, 1962), 8-15.

TANGANYIKA

1. Beidelman, T. O., "Beer Drinking and Cattle Theft in Ubagura: Intertribal Relations in a Tanganyika Chiefdom," *American Anthropologist*, LXIIII (June, 1961), 534-549. (Bibliography)
2. Fosbrooke, H. A., "An Administrative Survey of the Masai," *Tanganyika Notes and Records*, XXVI (1948), 1-50.
3. "New National Costume Proposed for Tanganyikan Women," *Illustrated London News*, CCXXXVII (December 15, 1960), 644.
4. Raum, O. F., *Chagga Childhood* (London: Oxford University Press, 1940).

A detailed study of child-training patterns among the Chagga of Northern Tanganyika.

5. Stewart, J. C., "Problems in Southern Tanganyika," *Oversea Education*, XXVIII (1957), 157-162.

The author reviews some of the educational problems in the

southern Province of Ranganyika. He is quick to point out that this province is not necessarily representative of Tanganyika as a whole, yet its problems are a good illustration of the problems faced by Africa. Some of these problems are:

1. Many smaller villages which need a school are not large enough to support a school.

2. In numerous instances schools open with enthusiastic enrollments, but by the third or fourth year the school must close because of poor attendance. Some causes for this are: (a) concealed opposition from Muslim teachers, (b) lack of grass roots support, (c) a department requirement that one-third of the school population be girls, and (d) a lack of interest by local native education councils.

6. Wilson, Gordon, "The Tatoga of Tanganyika," (Part II), *Tanganyika Notes and Records,* XXXIV (1953), 35-56.

UGANDA

1. Musgrove, F., "A Uganda Secondary School As a Field of Cultural Change," *Africa,* XXII (1952), 234-238.

   A discussion of a secondary school as an institution in cultural contact. The author, the principal of the school, sampled 100 boys between the ages of 12 and 18 from eleven tribes of Uganda. It is noted that the behavior patterns associated with the school situation, classes, etc., are common to groups everywhere. The job of the school is to compensate for the inability of the family to orient the children toward modern demands. The author feels that it is the contradiction between the West's science and religion that causes more troubles for the student than does the conflict between traditional and European customs.

2. Page, A., "Student Self-Government at Busubizi College, Uganda," *Oversea Education,* XXXII (1960), 2-19.

   This is a report on an experiment in student self-government in a teacher's college in Uganda. The mechanics and responsibility of the 27-member Student Council are enumerated. Perhaps the most important aspect of this experiment is the assumption that those students who refused to cooperate with the student government and took a hostile attitude toward its decisions would not become good teachers. For many students, the art of cooperation was learned, thus giving them invaluable training for the future. The responsibility for various functions of the college tended to produce real leaders who might otherwise have gone undiscovered.

3. Swinbanks, W. F., "Rural Trade Schools in Uganda," *Oversea Education* XXXII, (1961), 164-170.

The aim of the Rural Trade School is to supply the growing needs of various types of industry with trained personnel. Usually students entering these rural trade schools have completed six years of primary schooling.

Uganda will probably remain a country of peasant farmers for a long time, and so while some students are trained in such arts as mechanics, carpentry, and bricklaying, the majority are being trained in farming methods and hence raise their standard of living. The curriculum embraces those things in traditional methods which are of value and introduces modern techniques and standards as well. An example of this may be seen in the building of houses. Traditional education taught students how to build weatherproof, well-ventilated houses.

Every effort is made in preparing the curriculum to keep a balance between what is needed and what is wanted.

GENERAL

1. Adegbite, Joseph Adejunmobic, "Youth Organizations in Africa," *Journal of Human Relations,* VIII (Spring/Summer, 1960), 718-729.

In the past it has been the family which has taken care of the training of the youth. They usually had satisfactory results in preparing the youth. Today (1960) various groups, state, Islamic, and church, have provided new avenues of development for the young people. In Nigeria there are the Scouts, the Guides, YMCA, YWCA, 4H, and the Federation of Boys and Girls Clubs. In Lagos there is the Standing Conference of Voluntary Youth Organization. All of the organizations are devoted to the preparation of good citizens and effective young people, people who are equipped to handle the problems of modern living.

2. *African Juvenile Unemployment in Duncan Village, East London,* being the report of the Mayor's Committee, East London, East London Society for the Protection of Child Life, 1954.

3. "Africans Want to Be Clerks: Colonial Education and Its Products," *Roundtable,* XL (December, 1949), 48-53.

4. Allport, Gordon W. and Thomas F. Pettigrew, "Cultural Influence on the Perception of Movement: the Trapezoidal Illusion among Zulus," *Journal of Abnormal and Social Psychology,* LV (1957), 104-113.

Purpose was to test the following hypothesis: "Zulu children, provided they are unacculturated (amabinca) will report the illusions of sway in the trapezoidal window less often than will urbanized acculturated Zulu children (amabunguka) or than white (European) children." Four groups of 20 boys each (10 to 14 years of age) were used in the major experiment. Two groups were unacculturated (Polela Rural Africans and Nongoma Rural Africans), and Ss "who had lived all or most of . . . their lives in western culture . . ." constituted the other two groups, (Urban European and Urban African boys). Two factors, monocular vs. binocular viewing and distance from the stimulus object (10 and 20 feet) were varied experimentally. The Ss responded, in terms of the presence or absence of an illusion, to revolving rectangular and trapezoidal windows under various treatment combinations of the two factors given above. Considering the experimental treatment conditions as a whole, there was statistically significant evidence that the urban groups reported the illusion more frequently than the rural groups. The authors conducted a control experiment involving new Ss "to determine whether unwanted suggestive affects, caused by our order of presentation were influencing the results. . . ." The findings were "Practically identical" with those reported in the major experiment.

5. Banton, Michael, "Africa South of the Sahara," *UNESCO International Social Science Journal*, XIII, 2 (1961), 197-214.

   This discussion of race relations in Africa south of the Sahara has one note on the youth namely, "Essays written by African schoolchildren frequently reveal an ambivalence between emulation of the white man in certain specific connections and a violent rejection of anything seeming to imply political subordination."

6. Barnard, G. L., "Gold Coast Children Out of School," *Oversea Education*, XXVIII (1957), 163-172.

   A study noted that teachers in the Gold Coast are unaware of the personality dynamics of their pupils. Also the teachers failed in many instances to structure lessons in order to be meaningful to the child. These factors have a great deal to do with the problem of school leavers in the Gold Coast.

   This study conducted by the University College of the Gold Coast was an attempt to find out on a limited scale what were the ambitions and interests of middle-school children. The object was to provide information for teachers which would assist them in teaching in a meaningful way. The data for this study are listed.

7. Bascom, William and J. Herskovits (eds.), *Continuity and Change in African Cultures* (Chicago: University of Chicago Press, 1959).

8. Batten, T. R., *Communities and Their Development* (London: Oxford University Press, 1960).

Batten's book is an introductory study to the subject of community development. He makes special references to various agencies involved in community development.

He devotes one chapter to the school as an agent in the community. In it he notes that with few exceptions the school has not been very effective in helping small communities adapt themselves constructively to change. The reason for this is thought to be that the school is essentially a foreign institution with little direct relevance to community life. Batten cites heavy drop outs and poor attendance figures as symptoms that the school has only a negligible effect on community life.

9. Beidelman, Thomas O., "Hyena and Rabbit: A Kaguru Representation of Matrilineal Relations," *Africa,* XXXI (1961), 61-74.

10. Blanguernon, Claude, "The Schools for Nomads in the Hoggar," *Fundamental and Adult Education,* VI (1954), 8-12.

A discussion of the difficulties involved in offering education to nomadic peoples. The article focuses on Hoggar, a mountainous section in the central Sahara. The author suggests that the educational system should not interfere with local customs or religious beliefs. Education should not be rushed too fast, but allow the people to become accustomed to it. It is also suggested that the area be protected from the encroachment of outside interference, and be allowed to develop its own system in accordance with its needs and desires.

11. Bohannan, Paul (ed.), *African Homicide and Suicide* (Princeton, N. J.: Princeton University Press, 1960),

12. Brady, Thomas F., "Gold Coast: Laughter, Wealth, Freedom," *New York Times Magazine* (October 7, 1956), 14-18.

13. Brembeck, Cole S. and John B. Keith, *Education in Emerging Africa: A Select and Annotated Bibliography,* Michigan State University Education in Africa Series 1, College of Education.

14. Buitendag, F. W. C., "The Emergence of the Urban African," *Race Relations Journal,* XVIII, 3 (1951), 205-211.

15. Chaplin, B. H. G., "School Attitudes to Agriculture," *West African Journal of Education,* V (1961), 94-96.

This article reports on an investigation which attempted to conduct an exploration of two areas of contact between formal education and agriculture: (1) the relationship between pre-secondary schools and local farmers and farming; (2) factors affecting the university students' choice of an agricultural career.

The following results were noted:

1. Very few farming parents wish their children to become farmers.
2. Farming is largely associated with illiteracy.
3. In most schools the manner in which rural science is taught tends to reinforce the views expressed in 1 and 2.
4. There are many school gardens and farms which are unsatisfactory from both an agricultural and educational point of view.
5. In the majority of cases there is little relationship between classroom teaching, the school garden and/or the local farming practice.

16. Cole, Robert W. *Kossoh Town Boy* (London: Cambridge University Press, 1960).

17. Comhaire, J. L. L., "Urban Segregation and Racial Legislation in Africa," *American Sociological Review*, XV, 3 (June, 1950), 392-397.

18. Counseil International des Sciences Sociales, Bureau International de Recherche Sur Les Implications Sociales Du Progres Technique, *Consequences Sociales de L'Industrialization et problemes Urbains en Afrique* (September/October, 1954).

19. Cory, Hans, *African Figurines, etc.* (Puberty Rites) (London: Faber & Faber, Ltd., 1956).

20. Creighton, T. R. M., "Education and Society in East Africa," *Overseas Quarterly* (December, 1958), 104-106.

21. Davis, J. M. (ed.), *Modern Industry and the African* (London: International Missionary Council, Department of Social and Industrial Research, The Macmillan Company, 1933).

22. Davie, James, et al., *IIE Survey of the African Student: His Achievements and His Problems*, Institute of International Education (November, 1961), Library of Congress No. 61-18847.

A study of the African student in the United States. While it reveals little of interest about the adolescent period in the home situation it is of great interest for a picture of the social, economic, and academic situation of a cultural group in the United States.

23. Delius, Anthony, "Travels in Tribalism," *Africa South,* IV (January/March, 1960), 27-36.

24. Dickson, A. G., "Mass Education in Togoland," *African Affairs,* XLIX, 49, 195 (April, 1950), 136-150.

25. Dooley, C. T., "Child Training among the Wanguru," *Primitive Man,* VII (1934), 22-31; VIII (1935), 73-80; IX (1936), 1-12.

26. *Education in Africa,* World Confederation of Organizations of the Teaching Professions Reprint, I, 4 (Winter, 1959).

27. Eells, Walter Crosby, *Communism in Education in Asia, Africa, and the Far East* (Washington: American Council on Education, 1954).

28. Ehrenfels, U. R., "The African Woman: between Apartheid and the Bride Price," *United Asia,* XIII (1961), 129-133.

In this article the author is attempting to discourage the seemingly imminent discontinuance of a traditional African practice—that of bride selling. Historically, attitudes toward the practice have gone from one polar extreme to the other. The early Christian missionaries abhorred it because it seemed much like the buying and selling of commodities. Later, anthropologists noting that it was not merely a matter of an irrevocable sale to the highest bidder (there were other factors in selection or conditions that must be met), discovered certain positive aspects. It was the vehicle of many useful and varied social functions. Many then favored it. In the more recent past, the practice has diffused among tribes not originally subscribing to it, and industrialization and the emergence of a money economy have caused some shaking abuses, e.g., trading daughters for jeeps, husband's reselling brides in Arabia, etc. At the present time the modern generation favors completely abolishing it. The author feels that the practice could be modified without losing many cultural and traditional wealths. However, the younger generation seems about to prevail, and throw the baby out with the wash.

29. Elias, Olawale, T., "British West Africa, Past and Present," *Africa South,* III (January/March, 1959), 85-93.

30. Evans-Pritchard, Edward E., *Kinship and Marriage Among the Nuer* (London: Oxford University Press, 1953).

31. Evans-Pritchard, Edward E., *The Nuer* (London: Oxford University Press, 1940).

32. Ford, Eric, "A New Deal for the Women of Africa," *African World* (August, 1962), 7-8.

33. Fortes, Meyer, "Time and Social Structure: An Ashanti Case Study," in Meyer Fortes (ed.), *Social Structure: Studies Presented to A. R. Radcliffe-Brown* (London: Oxford University Press, 1949).

34. Fradier, G., "New Schools for Africa," *UNESCO Courier*, XIV (February, 1961), 21-23, 27.

35. Gussmann, B. W., *African Life in an Urban Area* (Bulawayo: 1952).

36. Hey, P. D., "African Aspirations for Education in Rural Natal," *Comparative Education Review*, V (1961), 112-117.

"Education is like a field which gives you a good return."—M. Zuma, Pholela Induna (chief).

This interesting article is an attempt to find out what African aspirations for education are in Natal. The method used in finding some of these aspirations was the questionnaire. Some of the results were:

1. African children are staying in school for longer periods than their parents, 2.8 years longer than their fathers and 3.6 years longer than their mothers.
2. The majority of girls wanted educations so as to become nurses. This profession is preferred over that of teaching.
3. The majority of boys wanted to be clerks, as this job did not entail heavy manual labor.
4. Children's desires for careers reflected their parents wishes for them.
5. Their hopes and fears for education were that schools would be advanced and that they would pass in order to get good jobs.
6. Subjects most desirable were English, arithmetic, and Afrikaans. The most difficult are arithmetic, geography, Afrikaans, and history.

37. Hilliard, F. H., *A Short History of Education in British West Africa* (London: Nelson, 1957).

38. Hodgkin, R. A., *Education and Change: a Book Mainly for Those Who Work in Countries Where Education is Part of a Process of Rapid Social Change* (London: Oxford University Press, 1957).

This description of educational processes in Africa is a general approach to the "how" and "why" of education in a changing society. Only generally does it deal with the adolescent. It is noted that the attitudes of the youth in a changing society are expected to change. In this situation the youth may reject the traditional religion as well as traditional secular values and customs. The emotional and psychological insecurity of even the educated African is discussed.

39. Howard University (Washington D.C.), Library, Moorland Foundation, A *Catalogue of the African Collection,* Published by Howard University Press for the Moorland Foundation, 1958.

40. Hunter, Guy, "Emerging Africans," *Adult Education,* XXXII (1960), 101-107.

The author deals with the perennial problems of school dropouts and women's education. His third point deals primarily with the problem of the isolation of educated Africans. The isolated group of educated Africans is comprised of the group of scholars who have completed a minimum of 10-12 years of schooling. They may be teachers, vocational and agricultural instructors, medical assistants, etc. By the day this force works in European settings, with European supervisors. They are well dressed and fluent in English. Their problem arises after office hours. They go back to a bed space in the African township, or a box-like brick house in an endless row of boxes, to a wife almost certainly far less educated, without books, electricity, or other modern conveniences.

These educated Africans find themselves, in after-work hours, isolated from both European and traditional African contacts and fellowships.

41. *Industrialization in Africa, Part I. Digest of Information Concerning Industrialization in Africa, Part II, Survey of Recent Field Studies on Urbanization in Africa* (London: International African Institute, 1954).

42. Jahoda, Gustav, "Assessment of Abstract Behavior in a Non-Western Culture," *Journal of Abnormal and Social Psychology,* LIII (1956), 237-243.

A report on an investigation concerning the validity and applicability of tests of abstract behavior, such as the Goldstein-Schurer Cube Test in a non-Western setting. The subjects consisted of 27 adolescent boys from schools in or near Accra, on the Gold Coast of Africa. The modal age was 15.

It was found that, "Tests of abstract ability are no more 'culture-free' than tests of intelligence." It was also noted that, "Boys from literate homes performed significantly better than those from illiterate ones, evidence that cube test results are not unaffected by environmental influences."

43. Jahoda, Gustav, "Love, Marriage, and Social Change: Letters to

the Advice Column of a West African Newspaper," *Africa*, XXIX, 2 (April, 1959).

44. Jahoda, Gustav, "The Social Background of a West African Student Population," *British Journal of Sociology*, V, 4 (December, 1954), 355-365; VI, 1 (March, 1955), 71-79.

The purpose of this study is to show the transformation that has taken place in educational level in some sections of Gold Coast society by comparison with preceding generations, to study occupational aspirations, and to study adjustment to home after college. Two hundred and thirty-eight West African students were interviewed for this study. Fifty per cent of these students have only one literate ancestor.

With regard to occupational aims, 40 per cent of the Arts and 63 per cent of Science students intended to stay in the same occupational group. Twenty-five per cent wanted to stay in the field of education. For the science students medicine was very popular. The author felt that there was reflected in the sample an excessive emphasis on a small number of high prestige and reward occupations.

The adjustment to home life was a serious problem for only 35 per cent of the students questioned. Forty-five per cent found the transition easy, and 20 per cent reported a difficult period of adjustment but no serious consequences.

45. Joy, Charles R., *Young People of West Africa* (New York: Duell, Sloan & Pearce, Inc., 1961).

A collection of first-person essays written as children's introductions to various countries of West Africa. The collection includes selections written by teen-agers from Canary Islands, Dahomy Mauritania, Gambia, Portuguese Guinea, Republic of Mali, Republic of Guinea, Sierra Leone, Liberia, Ghana, Nigeria, Gabon, the Cameroons, Angola, and the Republic of the Congo.

46. Kahl, J. A., "Some Social Concomitants of Industrialization and Urbanization," *Human Organization*, XVIII (Summer, 1959), 65-67.

A short discussion of the social effects of urbanization and industrialization. In the rural domestic unit are found more than one nuclear family. This changes with the shift to the urban form.

The kinship system affects the transitional period from rural to urban life by slowing down the emergence of class differences.

Since the wage job is individualistic and the members of the group no longer live in close association, the extended family is further diluted by industrialization and urbanization. The urban woman demands and receives more independence from her husband's authority. The control of the parents over the adolescent children weakens as the urbanization process continues.

47. Keehn, J. D. and E. T. Prothro, "National Preferences of University Students from 23 Nations," *Journal of Psychology*, XLII (1954), 283-294.

48. Larby, Norman, "A Case Study in East African Higher Education—Makerere," *Higher Education—The Yearbook of Education*, 1959 (New York: Harcourt, Brace & World, Inc., 1959). 1959).

49. Lindblom, Gerhard, "The Akamba, Upsala," *Archives D'Etudes Orientales* (1920).

50. Little, K., "Some Urban Patterns of Marriage and Domesticity in West Africa," *Social Research*, VII (June, 1959), 65-82. (Bibliography)

51. Lloyd, F. and D. A. Pidgeon, "An Investigation into the Effects of Coaching on Nonverbal Test Material with European, Indian, and African Children," *British Journal of Educational Psychology*, XXXI (1961), 145-151.

Samples of children of European, Indian, and African background were tested to compare their results on standardized tests. After the initial testing, half of each sample were coached on the material and then retested. While the initial scores of the European children were much higher than the others the results of the coaching revealed that the African children improved twice as much as the Europeans. The Indians showed no improvement with coaching. The author concludes that the scores on standardization tests applied to children from different cultural backgrounds cannot be considered comparable.

52. Lorimer, Frank, *Culture and Human Fertility: A Study of the Relation of Cultural Conditions to Non-Industrial and Transitional Societies* (New York: UNESCO, 1955).

53. MacQuarrie, J., "The New Order in Bantu Education," *Africa South*, I (October/December, 1956), 32-42.

54. Mair, L. P., *An African People in the Twentieth Century* (London: Routledge, 1934).

A study of social and cultural change in Buganda after forty years of British rule, using Roscoe's *The Buganda* as an ethnographic base line. Some consideration of applied anthropology.

54. Malinowski, Bronislaw, "The Pan African Problem of Culture Contact," *American Journal of Sociology* (May, 1943), 649-666.

55. Marris, P., "Family and Social Change in an African City," *New Statesmen, Weekend Review*, LXIII (February 23, 1962), 269-270.

56. Mason, R. J., *British Education in Africa* (London: Oxford University Press, 1959).

57. Mathew, Gervase, "The East Coast Culturers," *Africa South*, II (January/March, 1958), 59-63.

58. Matthews, Z. K., "Ethnic Universities," *Africa South*, I (July/September, 1957), 40-49.

59. McCall, Daniel, "Dynamics of Urbanization of Africa," in Phoebe Ottenberg, *Cultures and Societies of Africa* (New York: Random House, Inc., 1960).

60. McFie, J., "The Effect of Education in African Performance on a Group of Intellectual Tests," *British Journal of Educational Psychology*, XXXI (1961), 232-240.

A test-retest examination of a group of 26 African adolescents who were entering technical school. The tests included verbal, nonverbal, numerical, pictorial, and constructional material. The only differences between these subjects and English subjects were in the areas of the nonlanguage tests in which they were slower. At the time of the retest, two years later, it was found that the results of the nonlanguage tests had increased appreciably. The results suggested to the author that the ability to see visual material as a whole (Gestalt perception) may be one area where educational association may overcome cultural background.

61. Musgrove, F., "Carrying Conviction in Africa," *Overseas Education*, XXVII (1955), 26-27.

The author suggests that English teachers become frustrated when African children fail to comprehend obvious truths. He suggests that these truths appear obvious only because of the teachers' unconscious cultural background.

Musgrove suggests that the best way to make Africans aware of the advances in another culture is to have schools in two culture exchange surveys, e.g., English school boys could survey the traffic counts in their towns and Africans survey their transportation system. "The contrast . . . would usually be sufficiently startling to be memorable and instructive."

By such a learning experience, students would gain "a new consciousness of the quality and limitations of their own culture, and deep insight into another." Such a learning system would tend to give the African student a positive feeling of personal exploration rather than the negative fears of cultural exploitation.

62. Nissen, H. W., et al., "A Study of Performance Tests Given to a Group of Native African Negro Children," *British Journal of Psychology*, XXV (1935), 308-355.

The results of the performances of 50 West African Negro children, ages 5-14 years, who were given 12 different performance tests indicate that the subjects performed poorly on tests which required experience common to a particular cultural environment. The subjects had little trouble with the tests which were based on materials which were common to all races in all environments. Thus, as cultural and environmental influences are increased in a given test the subject from a cultural background different to that of the subject culture will do progressively poorer.

63. Ntantla, Phyllis, "The Abyss in Bantu Education," *Africa South*, IV (January/March, 1960), 42-48.

64. Olouch, Justus, "Educating African Peasants in Nyanza," *African World* (April, 1961), 10-11.

65. Ottenberg, Simon and Phoebe (eds.), *Cultures and Societies of Africa* (New York: Random House, Inc., 1960).

66. Paye, Lucien, "France's Hopes for the Instruction and Education of the African Citizen," *Phi Delta Kappan*, XLI (January, 1960), 186-190.

The African family exerts a powerful influence on the child. It instills in him a profound sense of natural forces, in particular that of the relations existing between man and those forces which surround him. The ritualistic initiating demanded by the adult keeps the child closely bound to the primitive society of which he is a member.

In order to bring progress to these cultures, it is obviously necessary that such unitive and disciplinary forces, now serving traditional ways of life which have retained much of their vitality, be utilized for goals higher than those of the individual or of the basic unit of society.

67. Phillips, Arthur, *Survey of African Marriage and Family Life*, Published for International African Institute (London: Oxford University Press, 1953).

68. Pope, Maurice, "Universities in Ethnasia," *Africa South*, IV (October/December, 1959), 41-50.

69. Price, Thomas, *African Marriage* (London: SCM Press, 1954).

70. Read, Margaret, *Africans and Their Schools* (London: Longmans, Green and Company, 1953).

Modern education in Africa must prepare pupils for the following responsibilities:

1. Help boys and girls to grow up and develop into mature persons who can be relied on to play their part in their society. Education must do this now in a world of great complexity with cross currents from the old and the new affecting persons and determining the foundations of their life. There is no secure safe life for young Africans today, and their schools must help them make adjustments to whatever is in store for them.

2. Help them to create a modern sense of citizenship. This can be related to tribal loyalties but it must go beyond them, and give young Africans an understanding of citizenship in their own territory and the world at large.

3. Train students how to produce goods as well as services. Unless they are trained to achieve this, the pace of progress is to be greatly slowed down.

4. Teach students the meaning of good government, including law and order. Colonial systems of the past removed this responsibility to a large extent and as the emergent countries near their political freedom the responsibility becomes theirs. Teachers and parents alike must always be aware that the schools are the spearhead of modern ideas and ways of living, but at the same time they must help to preserve that social continuity and stability without which no community or country can exist.

71. Read, Margaret, *Education and Social Change in Tropical Areas* (London: Thomas Nelson and Sons, Ltd., 1956).

The problems posed for the educationalist cannot be solved without the help of the anthropologist. Few educationalists would like to think that they were destroying, deliberately, these separate cultural groups. They, with other alien influences may be undermining the foundation of these groups; many would like to cushion the shocks of cultural change—but how, without the anthropologist?

Major dilemmas in the cultural range of education are:

1. After having given the tools of writing and reading it has to be decided whether education is to be based on local or other cultures in Africa how do you build a modern society on a preliterate culture?

2. The urgency of the political situations in Africa forbid the following of a "gradual education system." Two methods for speed-up are (a) utilize fully existing financial and personnel resources and (b) advance adult education.

3. Has education based on foreign culture had any real contributions to the peoples of Africa?

The anthropologist might be in a position to determine the effects on cultural change. Anthropologists could contribute to the assessment of sociological and economic changes resulting from increased literacy if they would include this phenomenon in their survey of social change.

72. Read, Margaret, "Migrant Labour in Africa and Its Effects on Tribal Life," *International Labour Review*, XLV, 6 (1942), 605-631.

73. Read, Margaret, *Studies in Education*, II (London: University of London Institute of Education, 1950).

The field of education and cultural tradition covers the fields of: (1) social relations, (2) the conceptions and allegiances to political entities, (3) the accumulated knowledge of the people, and (4) religious beliefs and practice, their value systems and their philosophical outlooks.

Major problems faced by the field of education are:

1. The failure to integrate the local cultural tradition and thought with a Western form of school and college education.

2. The need for full histories on education in each area, in order to determine ideological intentions of those promoting education so as to assess effects on local education.

3. Information from social anthropological studies and personality and culture studies are needed before the relationship of the school and the community can be assessed.

74. Rheinnalt, Jones J. D., "The Effects of Urbanization in South and Central Africa," *African Affairs*, III (January, 1953), 37-44.

This is primarily a discussion of labor conditions in South and Central Africa. The author notes that the growth of the family in the towns creates a large population of adolescents who, while their parents attempt to send them back to the rural areas, desire to remain in the urban areas. These young people remain in the city as members of the labor force, but since there is no special wage law for youth, they remain largely unemployed and unemployable.

75. Richards, Audrey I. (ed.), *Economic Development and Tribal Change: A Study of Immigrant Labour in Buganda* (Cambridge: W. Hoffer, 1954).

76. Roucek, Joseph, "Education in Africa South of the Sahara," *Journal of Human Relations,* VIII (1960), 810-818.

One of the most dynamic elements of African nationalism has been the desire to achieve "moral status" first in the homeland and then in the world. In that respect this has aroused the desire for learning—so intense, in fact, that in many parts of Africa schools flourish like mushrooms, including open-air schools held under tropical trees. And, they are not missionary or government schools, they are African, owned and operated.

For the first time African history has come to be an item in the school curriculum. Parallel with this change is the way in which newspapers have begun to invade rural countryside. Since young politicians have to appeal to the masses, African symbols and institutions are used in place of language and ideas of Western liberalism.

Educational problems in Africa are concerned with agricultural and technical education and the planning of community life, a type of education which would not limit the graduates to white-collar jobs.

From the very beginning, Western education tended to educate an elite. In turn, this elite separated themselves from the masses with the result that a division grew between the educated elite and the traditional elite. The educated elite must somehow communicate with the masses and give to them in a general way the education the country needs in this stage of its development, namely: agricultural, vocational, and technical education.

77. Scanlon, David G., "The Bush School," *Phi Delta Kappan,* XLI (January, 1960), 148-150.

In West Africa the bush school reached a high level of development. Basically, the bush school was an attempt to introduce to young men all the aspects of social, religious, economic, and political forces of the tribe. During the three years of training in the bush school the boys learned the best techniques of farming and the trades necessary for survival and well being. They had to build their own huts. Beyond the practical, they were taught the theoretical basis on which society existed, e.g., theological, political, and legal patterns of the village organization. European schools have contributed to the disintegration of the bush school.

78. Schapera, I., *Select Bibliography of South African Native Life and Problems,* Compiled for the Inter-University Committee for African Studies under the direction of I. Schapera (London: Oxford University Press, 1941).

79. Segall, M. H., "Psychological View of Changing Africa," *Antioch Review,* XXI (Fall, 1961), 270-280.

80. Sihlai, Leo L., "Bantu Education and the African Teacher," *Africa South,* I (October/December, 1956), 42-51.

81. "Social Research in Central Africa," *Nyasaland Journal,* XI (July, 1958), 29-34.

82. South African Government, "The Progress of the Bantu Peoples Towards Nationhood," *South Africa Government Information Services,* II.

Since the Bantu Education Act of 1953, which initiated a new deal in education, Bantu school enrollment has increased more than 60 per cent. Great progress had been made since full status was given to the education of the Bantu with the establishment of a Department of Bantu Education under its own Cabinet Minister.

At the present rate of increased enrollment in the schools, illiteracy will be abolished in the next two or three decades.

83. "Problems of Appreciation," *The Times Educational Supplement,* MCMXXXV (June 30, 1950), 517.

The reporting correspondent gave an account of the findings by Dr. Gurrey, Head of the English Department of the Gold Coast University College. Dr. Gurrey was interested (1) in assessing the quality of undergraduates' command of English, (2) in testing their appreciation of literature, and (3) in knowing if appreciation led on to some kind of evaluation.

Some of Dr. Gurrey's findings were:

1. African students had problems of comprehension, not just the dictionary meaning of some of the words, but of the full content of the sentences, phrases, or verses.

2. Figuratively, language caused problems.

3. A third problem concerned rhythm and word sounds. The majority of students failed to distinguish the different rhythms with any precision.

4. A more serious problem was that some students were unable to control the emotional response to poetry.

84. "Spread of Western Knowledge," *The Times Educational Supplement*, MDCCCXIII (January 27, 1950), 57.

The correspondent begins by noting the hunger for education throughout Africa. He states that it is not unusual in West Africa to find a group of children waiting patiently all day in hope that one of the lucky children inside might be taken ill or otherwise have to leave school. Such a vacated place would be quickly filled.

The correspondent challenges the validity of two popular beliefs, namely:

1. That African pupils want to become clerks when they leave school.
2. That African education is too academic and unrelated to everyday life.

The author finally suggests that due to the rapid and sweeping changes in Africa, education should be related not to the present but to the future, 20 or 50 years hence.

85. Tooth, G., *Survey of the Juvenile Delinquency in the Gold Coast* (ms.).

86. Turnbull, Colin M., *The Lonely African* (New York: Simon & Schuster, 1962).

87. UNESCO, "Draft Resolutions Submitted by the Delegation of France" (On assistance to youth movements in Africa, South of the Sahara) (November 14, 1960), 1.

88. UNESCO and the International African Institute, London: *Social Implications of Industrialization and Urbanization in Africa South of the Sahara* (Paris: The Organization, 1956).

This study relates to social changes resulting from the growth of urban areas in Africa south of the Sahara. Pages 319-344 treat organization and problems of education in the Belgian Congo.

89. UNESCO, *International Social Science Bulletin*, VIII (1956), Entire issue on "Elites."

The entire issue of the journal is devoted to discussions of various elites in Africa. The effect of changing social composition has considerably changed the structure of the elite groups.

90. UNESCO, *World Survey of Education* (Paris: UNESCO, 1955).

Ethiopia. In an effort to give all school-age children an opportunity to get an education, the one-room school system is being studied seriously and will be given a trial. A further problem is how to keep well-trained young men in the teaching profession when there is a dearth of manpower in other fields requiring their intellectual and clerical services.

Gold Coast (Ghana). Serious educational problems are:

1. The conflicting demands of quality vs. quantity at the primary level.

2. The need for more trained teachers and an adequate salary structure.

3. Language policy in schools is also difficult to settle. In the Colony and Ashanti well-established languages such as Twi have an adequate literature for school purposes, but this is not the case with the vernaculars of the northern territories.

4. Finally the differing rate of educational development between northern territories and the Colony and Ashanti, is a general question affecting all levels of educational administration.

Kenya. As may be expected in an educational system that is expanding rapidly, Kenya faces problems of shortages in buildings, trained teachers, and finances. For African education, the policy is to develop facilities at all levels, but particularly at that of the intermediate school where training can be given in agriculture and technology.

Liberia. The major problems confronting the Liberian Education Department are: (1) The need for trained teachers, and (2) The need for adequate buildings and equipment. The principle trend in education in Liberia is the organization and operation of vocational and technical schools.

Libya. The major problem in Libya is the limitation in the budget and, indeed, in the national capacity to pay for educational needs. An allied problem is that of the lack of educated leadership. Future trends will be to develop primary schooling and to expand vocational and teacher training at the intermediate level.

The special problem of the backwardness of girl's education is being dealt with progressively by the government.

Nigeria. The special needs of the Nigerian educational system are:

1. The need to establish equal standards throughout a school system which is essentially decentralized.

2. The phenomenal growth of primary education systems has revealed a shortage of teachers and school facilities.

3. The problem of retardation and of wastage in the school population is ever-present.

4. Too few teachers are qualified or certificated. (About one-fourth in 1950-51.)

Northern Rhodesia. The problems of a rapidly expanding system of education are numerous: finance, staff, and bulidings. Particular mention may be made of wastage in the primary school and of difficulties in the way of decentralizing school control. The readjustment plan for African education stresses this latter point, and provides effective local education authorities which will represent the central government, missionary societies, native authorities, and recognized African bodies.

Nyasaland. The first five-year plan for education in Nyasaland aimed primarily at an expansion of the numbers of schools in all classes. Many of the objectives of the plan were achieved, but progress was hampered by the fact that the portion of Africans remaining long enough at school to benefit from the course was too low.

The second five-year plan began with a survey of all assisted and unassisted schools in the Protectorate. The keynote of the second planning period is qualitative rather than quantitative. The result has been an improvement of standards of education and a great increase in the number of pupils completing the full primary course at the right age. This has also led to a steady increase for candidates for entry into secondary school. Universal education up to Standard III is aimed at but will not be attainable in this five-year period.

Southern Rhodesia. During the past decade (1945-1955) school enrollment had more than doubled and the public demand for education continues to grow. The principal problem facing the Department is the shortage of buildings and teachers. While the majority of pupils are to be found in lower classes, there is a tendency for children to stay at school longer with a corresponding demand for central primary schools and various forms of post-primary education.

Swaziland. The number of African children attending school has risen by 50 per cent over four years: from 10,800 in 1948 to 15,000 in 1952. Over the same period the number of teachers employed in African schools rose from 227 to 447.

Secondary school enrollment has shown a steady increase and to meet the demand two schools have recently been developed to high school status. A teacher-training college has been built: approximately 35 primary school teachers will be trained each year.

Uganda. The whole problem of African education has been under consideration by a committee. The recommendations of the committee have been: the reorganization of the primary system into one eight-year period and four years primary rather than the old division of six years primary, three years junior secondary, and three years secondary.

One of the main difficulties is to get Africans to take the initiative in expanding education and in insisting on high standards in their schools instead of looking to the government to arrange everything for them. The greatest and most important development today is the vast expansion of technical training on which the government is laying great emphasis. Every effort will be made to insure that women's education becomes more popular.

91. U.S. Library of Congress, Africa South of the Sahara, A selected annotated list of writings compiled by Helen F. Conover (Washington, D.C.: The Library of Congress Press, 1951-1956).

92. Watkins, Mark H., "The West African 'Bush' School," *American Journal of Sociology*, XLVIII, 6 (May, 1943), 666-675.

93. Williams, P. Morton, "The Social Consequences of Industrialism among the S. W. Yoruba: with Comparison from Hausa Society," *West African Institute of Social and Economic Research*, Annual Conference, Sociology Section, University College of Ibadan (March, 1953), 21-37.

LATIN AMERICA

The countries included in the Latin America section are:

Argentina
Brazil
Chile
Colombia
Costa Rica
Cuba
El Salvador
Guatemala
Haiti
Jamaica
Mexico
Panama
Peru
Puerto Rico
Uruguay
Venezuela
General

Most research on adolescence emanating from Latin America concerns those countries which are now coming to grips with industrialization, such as Mexico, Puerto Rico, Colombia, Brazil, and Argentina.

Many articles are a result of the great and growing concern with the apparent deterioration of the family, with juvenile delinquency, and with other evidences of the beginnings of an adolescent subculture.

Socialization of children and adolescents is a problem increasingly less solvable within the family. Formal institutions are required to transmit specialized skills for success in an industrializing society. Cultures vary, as Nash (Guatemala—4) has suggested, in their ability to absorb change. Ability to adjust is related to feelings of control over the social situation. In Argentina (Argentina—1) it has been necessary to enact legislation in order to provide opportunities for the youth, as the older members of society do not spontaneously pave the way for adolescents to move beyond them. Control of youth employment and apprenticeship is under state control and regulation. This comprehensive program even attempts to deal with the cultural, moral, and civil development of adolescents. In Mexico (Mexico—23), the situation is quite different. Socialization still belongs to the parents, and peer-group cohesions are weak. Delinquency is rarely found in a primitive or traditional (static) society (see Smith, Panama—4).

As adolescents move out of the family circle for education, they begin to change their values and become oriented to a larger community. They see themselves as citizens of a country in relation to a world instead of as a part of a village or tribe (General—4, Panama—5). As perspectives change, so do values. Youths seek approval and goals from peers instead of parents, as parents are no longer the only significant referents. (Panama—4, Brazil—5). The total adjustment of adolescents in the transition to modernity has created serious personality adjustment problems. In such a situation, we can expect to find delinquent behavior that is essentially antisocial, rather than integrated peer activity. Perez (Colombia) supports this notion, noting that the most frequent form of delinquency is destruction of property, which is clearly antisocial. In transition, there is a breakdown of many traditional values and social structures, which are no longer expedient.

There is, in South America, as in other culture areas of the world, an effort to smooth the transition to modernity, to approach change with methods adaptable to the specific culture. Allen (Brazil—1) found this process in Brazilian professional training. Rosen (Brazil—14) found that to the extent that the father is authoritarian, the son will be frustrated in his attempt to realize self-reliance. Willems (Brazil—17) found a close resemblance between the Brazilian family structure and the family structure of other Latin American nations. Hence, the above statements are extensile to most of the culture area.

The breakdown of traditional values and behavior comes more quickly among boys than girls. When the parents remain adequate referents, as in nonindustrial villages, this pattern does not exist. Boys are schooled in the trades of their fathers, and very early in life begin to work side by side with them. In such societies (Guatemala—7, Mexico

—22, Panama—4) there are no apparent adolescent subcultures. A smooth transition is made from childhood to adulthood and most traditional values and patterns remain intact.

It is when socialization shifts outside of the family that the institutional framework develops that can support an adolescent subculture. Youths look forward to a future quite different from the world of their parents, and seek help from those referents who can help them attain skills necessary for success. When awareness of the new industrial order occurs to adolescents, to whom referents are not available, or to whom opportunities are unavailable, alienation and delinquency seem to emerge (Mexico—15, Mexico—57, Peru—2). In Jamaica (Jamaica—7) the youths have been exposed to industrial society, but do not have adequate opportunity to realize their aspirations. The result is frustration and eventual alienation from society. Avenia (Brazil—3) found that changes in the family structure and other institutions reflect personality disorganization and social maladjustment, with the consequence of a growth in juvenile delinquency.

Candido (Brazil—5) found that the family has undergone several structural changes. The father is no longer the economic task leader, but has gained in the expressive role. The entire family system is seen as increasing in affective relationships. At the same time, he says there is a weakening of kinship bonds and a loss of parental control over children. A cross-cultural experiment by Levy (Guatemala—3) found that Argentine and Guatemalan children, in a play situation, demonstrated feelings of jealousy, hostility, regression, self-punishment, and guilt to members of their families. The results from the two societies are similar. The personality adjustment of adolescents is an important criterion of their educability in formal educational settings. Anderson (Mexico—1) found that children with authoritarian fathers react significantly different than children from more permissive family environments.

In Mexico (Mexico—15) the preponderance of delinquency is in the outer fringe areas of cities. These fringes are filled with peasants trying to make the transition to an industrial society. The atmosphere is that of the inner city slum. Here the adolescents see what industrial society offers to some, but they are unable to perceive themselves as in a position to succeed. They lack referents who can help them to develop the correct skills, and they react with aggression toward those whom they see as withholding opportunities for mobility.

Much delinquency is centered around destruction of property (Colombia—2). This is an expression of aggression toward society rather than the individual. Property is a symbol of success; it is a traditional index of social class.

In delinquent adolescents, as in those who are successfully making the transition, males are in the foreground (Colombia—2). Females are slower to abandon traditional values (Puerto Rico—1). This is explainable, as the female role is not affected as dramatically by industrialization. Changes in the role of the female if made at all are more gradual (Mexico—15). She can still find referents within the family for many unchanging female roles such as child-rearing, cooking, and homemaking. As the family can provide referents for the learning of these skills, the female adolescent remains more allied to the family, and is more likely to retain traditional values (Puerto Rico—1). It is interesting to note that as the male adjusts his values to social change, the traditional values he relinquishes least readily are those concerning females (Puerto Rico—7). The male has been particularly reluctant to devalue female virginity at marriage in Latin America. He has also been somewhat hesitant in admitting equal rights and status to women, and the patriarchal family is still the ideal in many Latin American countries (see, for example, Brazil—14 and Mexico—10).

ARGENTINA

1. "Apprenticeship and Employment of Young Persons in Argentina," *International Labour Review,* L (November, 1944), 654-655.

    A short article discussing the Argentine Decree, number 14538 of 1944, which introduced regulations concerning apprenticeship and changed the existing regulations concerning the employment of young people.

    With regard to apprenticeship (any form of employment which gives the person concerned effective training for an occupation, including theoretical and practical experience and subjects needed for the cultural, moral, and civil development of the youth) the degree, in effect, established state supervision and control of the employment and apprenticeship of young persons between 14 and 18 years of age.

    One interesting comment concerned the directive that all employers, with the exception of those claiming exemption, were required to employ a specified number of young people, usually between 5 and 15 per cent of the skilled workers employed.

    The article specifies the working conditions and allowable hours of work for various age groups.

2. Henry, Jules, "Doll Play of Pilaga Indian Children," in Clyde Kluckhohn and Henry A. Murray (eds.), *Personality in Nature, Society and Culture,* 2nd ed. (New York: Alfred A. Knopf, Inc., 1953), 293-307.

3. Henry, Jules, "The Social Function of Child Sexuality in Pilaga Indian Culture," in Paul Hoch and Joseph Zubin (eds.), *Psychosexual Development in Health and Disease* (New York: Grune & Stratton, Inc., 1949).

4. Henry, Jules, "Some Cultural Determinants of Hostility in Pilaga Indian Children," *American Journal of Orthopsychiatry,* X (1939), 111-121.
5. Hilger, M. Inez, *Araucanian Child Life and Its Cultural Background* (Washington, D.C.: Smithsonian Institution, 1957).
6. Stocker, C., *Los Jovenes del signo XX frente al mundo* (Youth of the Twentieth Century Facing the World) (Buenos Aires: Editorial Victor Hugo, 1955).
7. Taylor, C. C., "Rural Locality Groups in Argentina," *American Sociological Review,* IX, 2 (April, 1944), 162-170.

BRAZIL

1. Allen, W. H., "Problems Encountered in Teaching Brazilian Students," *Human Organization,* X, 4 (1951), 21-25.

   A short article which emphasizes the necessity for awareness of cultural differences in professional training. It describes the problems encountered by American instructors attempting to teach weather observation and meteorology to Brazilian students at the Escola Technica de Aviacao. The results of the observation of students in the class leads the author to the conclusion that the instructors should modify their teaching methods to better approach the Brazilian culture.

2. Assis Dias, A., "Aspectos atuais da juventude" (Present Aspects of Youth), *Vozes,* LIV, 1 (January, 1960), 26-34.
3. Avenia, Maria N., "Desorganizacaoda Familia e Desajustamente Juvenil" (Family Disorganization and Juvenile Maladjustment), *Boletin do Servico Social dos Menores,* XI (1952), 25-32.

   One thousand Brazilian young people were examined in this attempt to test the hypothesis that the changes in family structure which occur with family disorganization are reflected in the disorganization of the personality and its components. The author related deviant behavior to the moral and social training within the home and presented tables on crime, alcoholism, etc. The study suggests that delinquent behavior results from various social, economic, and psychological factors. The author asserts that the disorganization of the family presents a favorable condition for the development of personal and social maladjustment and supports the growth of juvenile delinquency.

4. Azevedo, Fernando De, *Brazilian Culture: an Introduction to the Study of Cultural in Brazil,* translated by William R. Crawford (New York: The Macmillan Company, 1950).

A still timely translation of a 1943 work by F. D. Azevedo, an outstanding Brazilian sociologist and historian. The survey covers many aspects of life in Brazil.

5. Candido, A., "The Brazilian Family," in T. L. Smith and A. Marchant (eds.), *Brazil: Portrait of Half a Continent* (New York: The Dryden Press, Inc., 1956), 291-312.

The author discusses the structure and the relationships of the family in Brazil. The impact of changing economic functions, of cultural participation, and of domination and subordination on the family considered. The problem is approached from three sides: structural, functional, and the moral aspects.

Data and examples quoted refer primarily to the central and southern parts of the country. This section contains about one-half of the population of Brazil and is where the strongest effects of urbanization and industrialization are being felt.

In a discussion of the historical structure and function of the family in Brazil the author notes that paternal authority was exceptionally strong and the older children had authority over the younger. Marriage was usually contracted on the basis of a rational policy of strengthening the paternal group. "Family" included household servants, slaves, illegitimate children, mistresses, etc. He concludes that the Brazilian family of colonial times served primarily economic and political functions and was not primarily an affectionate, sexual system.

". . . The change in the general structure of society . . . consists essentially of an uninterrupted series of restrictions upon the economic and political functions and the concentration upon the more specific functions of the family—procreation and the disciplining of the sex impulses." The most significant feature of the structural change is the extinction of the father as a group leader due primarily to the division of social labor. The author notes that urbanization is the prime and decisive factor in the evolution of the Brazilian family.

Among the emerging traits in the familial structure are noted: (1) greater equality of status on the part of men and women, (2) greater participation of women in gainful activities, (3) increase of birth-control measures, (4) decrease of parental authority and lessening of social distance in the family, (5) a weakening of kinship bonds and a change from the extended to the conjugal family.

Among the traits preserved in the contemporary family are: (1) tolerance for indiscreet adultery on the part of the husband, (2) intolerance for female adultery, (3) taboo against loss of female virginity, (4) prostitution as a fully accepted phenomenon with institutionalized structure, (5) a developing sense of proprietorship of the Brazilian man in relation to his wife.

6. Frazier, E. F., "The Negro Family in Bahia, Brazil," *American Sociological Review*, VII, 4 (August, 1942), 465-478.

While this article does not deal directly with adolescents in Bahia, it does present some background information on the cultural setting of the adolescent in this particular setting. The purpose of the article was to investigate the Negro families in Bahia to see if any African culture traits were still present in the population.

Data were gathered from interviews with over fifty families in the area. The author includes details of Bahia's history. Most of the Negro population lives outside the city in thatched huts (semirural area). A high degree of racial mixture is present with the families referring to themselves as Brazilians rather than as Negroes. Children in these families are treated indulgently by both parents and are usually very welcome in the family. In general, the traditional African patterns of life have disappeared.

7. Ginsberg, Aniela M., "Comparacao entre os resultandos de um teste de nivel mental aplicado en diferentes grupos etnicos e sociais" (Comparison of the results of a test of mental level administered in different ethnic and social groups), *Arquivos Brasileiros de Psicotecnia,* III, 4 (1951), 27-44.

This article reports a Brazilian application of the Terman Groups Test of Intelligence. The test was adapted for use in Brazil prior to its application. The sample consisted of 4,160 students in the secondary schools of five Brazilian cities. 500 students were drawn from each city. The author found significant differences between the students from higher, middle, and lower socio-economic levels. In general, the males score higher than the females and the whites scored better than the non-whites or Indians.

8. Hutchinson, Bertram, "Origem socio-economica dose studentes universitarios de Sao Paulo" (The Socio-Economic Origin of Sao Paulo University Students), *Educacao e ciencias sociais,* Rio De Janeiro, I, 3 (December, 1956), 91-107.

9. Hutchinson, Bertram, "The Social Grading of Occupations in Brazil," *British Journal of Sociology,* VIII (1957), 176-189.

This article reported in a British journal, revealed similarities between occupational ratings in Brazil and Britain. The sample was drawn from upper-middle class undergraduates at the University of Sao Paulo, Brazil. It was found that occupations demanding a high educational level, great social responsibilities, and offering high income had the greatest prestige and the highest ranking. Those winning the lowest ratings and the least prestige were occupations with traits opposite to those above.

10. Lourenco, Filho, Manoel B., *Education in Brazil.* Translated by John Knox (Rio de Janeiro: Ministry of Foreign Relations, 1951).

11. Pierson, D., "The Negro in Bahia, Brazil," *American Sociological Review,* IV, 4 (August, 1939), 524-533.

The Frazier article noted above illustrates the absence of African culture in the population of Bahia, Brazil. This article (1939) is more concerned with the historical process of slavery in Brazil and deals with the circumstances and conditions under which migration and settlement occurred. He also deals with the absorption of the Negro and the early survival of traditional cultural traits.

The author notes that the importation of Africans into Brazil probably exceeded that of any other country. In spite of that he notes that the Negro as a racial unit seems to be gradually disappearing.

One reason for the maintenance of tribal customs was the fact that, in Brazil, the tribal unit was not broken up as it was in other areas. In spite of the potential present for the continuation of tribal customs and continuity of socialization of the young, the social attitude of Brazil, with its lack of segregation and its relatively open class structure is leading gradually to the absorption of the Negro as a racial unit.

12. Pinheiro, Z. B., "Os universitarios bahianos e a Constituicai" (Bahia University Students and the Constitution), *Revista brasileira de estudos politicos,* II, 3 (Belo Horizonte: January, 1958), 233-251.

13. Ribeiro, R., "On the Amaziado Relationship and Other Aspects of the Family in Recife, Brazil," *American Sociological Review,* X, 1 (February, 1945), 44-51.

The author discusses the differences between the amaziado and the maritalmente relationships in Brazil and, through 200 street interviews, concludes that, in Recife, there is little distinction drawn between the two. The amaziado relationship is typically a "free love" type of alliance, while the maritalmente relationship is more like common-law marriage. In Recife the amaziado relationship is not entered as a passing sexual liaison but implies a more durable relationship not unlike maritalmente.

14. Rosen, Bernard C., "Socialization and Achievement Motivation in Brazil," *American Sociological Review,* XXVII (October, 1962), 612-624.

The author examines the relationship of the family structure to the socialization process and achievement motivation in Brazil. The main points of focus are (1) How prevalent are independence training and achievement training in Brazil? (2) What is the relationship of these child-rearing practices to family structure? (3) What effect does this structure have on the development of achievement motivation?

A stratified sample was utilized including two Brazilian and two American samples. In the Brazilian samples, the first included 212 boys (age 9-11) and many of their mothers and was drawn from a large city. The second included 134 boys (age 9-11) and mothers from a small city. The United States samples included 427 and 367 boys and their mothers. Data were gathered by means of interviews, questionnaires, and the application of the Thematic Apperception Test.

It was found that the authoritarian, father-dominated family was more often employed in Brazil than in America. In this setting the boys receive little training in the development of achievement motivation and independence. The father acted more as a frustration to the son's attempts at self-reliance and autonomy. The combination of authoritarianism, protectiveness, and early indulgence which was found in the Brazilian authoritarian, father-dominated family, was felt by the author to be partly responsible for the finding that the Brazilian boys, on the whole, had lower achievement motivation than did the boys examined in the American sample.

15. Smith, T. Lynn, *Brazil: People and Institutions,* rev. ed. (Baton Rouge: Louisiana State University Press, 1954).

A compilation of a great deal of important material on Brazil. It deals with a wide range of topics related to social matters in Brazil. Includes a section of education in Brazil. An extensive bibliography is also included.

16. Wagley, C. (ed.), *Race and Class in Rural Brazil* (Paris: UNESCO, 1962).

17. Willems, E., "Structure of the Brazilian Family," *Social Forces,* XXXI (May, 1953), 339-345.

This is a preliminary study and description of the Brazilian family. Data were gathered over a 19-year period during which the author was a resident of Brazil. Topics discussed include marriage and chastity patterns, class differentials in family structures, male and female roles. The author concludes that there is a close resemblance between the Brazilian and the Portuguese family structures as well as similarities between Brazilian family structure and the family structure of other Latin American countries.

CHILE

1. Campbell, Margaret V., "Education in Chile, 1810-1842," *Journal of Inter-American Studies,* I, 3 (July, 1959), 353-375.
2. Hilger, M. Inez, *Araucanian Child Life and Its Cultural Background* (Washington, D.C.: Smithsonian Institution, 1957).
3. Samper, A., *A Case Study of Cooperation in Secondary Education in Chile* (Washington, D.C.: National Planning Association, 1957).

COLOMBIA

1. Calderon, Luis, et al., *Problemas de Urbanizacion en America Latina,* Los Grupos Sociales, Las Barriadas Marginales, La Accion Religiosa (Bogota, Colombia: Centro de Investigaciones Sociales).
2. Perez, L. C., "Delinquency among Yiung People in Colombia" (abstract), *Nature,* CLVIII (December 28, 1946), 941.

   A statement on the factors responsible for crime in Colombia, particularly youth crime. He notes that the most typical offenses are property offenses with offenses against the person and vagrancy following far behind. The recividism rate is high. Male offenders outnumber female offenders. He discussed other problems such as the criminality of women, the problem of crime among the Indians, and the relationship of the law to the Indian in Colombia.

COSTA RICA

1. Biesanz, John and Mavis Biesanz, "Costa Rican Education and the National Culture," *Education,* LXVII, 1 (September, 1946), 57-62.

   A general discussion of education in Costa Rica. The authors note that Costa Ricans credit their schools with great contributions to the national life. While there is a great lack of vocational and adult education, many gains are being made. Some of the hindrances to educational advancement include, political considerations, poverty, centralized control, and the strong hold of tradition.

2. Dobles, Margarita, *Identification of Youth Problems in Costa Rica,* Ph.D. Thesis, Stanford (1958).

CUBA

1. "Ready for Victory" (Youth and Sports in Cuba), *Cuba* (January, 1962), 36-45.
2. "Onward, Youths of Cuba, to Fulfill New Tasks," *Cuba* (January, 1962), 57.

EL SALVADOR

1. Fernandez, J. F., *Patria y juventud en el mundo de hoy* (Fatherland and Youth in the World of Today) (San Salvador: Ministerio de Cultura Departamento Editorial, 1956).

GUATEMALA

1. Billig, O., et al., "Aspects of Personality and Culture in a Guatemalan Community," *Journal of Personality,* XVI (1947), 153-158; (1948), 326-368.

An examination of the interrelations of culture and personality in San Luis, Guatemala. It is shown that the population contains two caste-like elements which are in a ranked relation to each other. Each of these systems has its own system of social organization which reflects different total configurations, goals, and values.

2. Lanning, John Tate, *The University in the Kingdom of Guatemala* (Ithaca: Cornell, 1955).

Basically a history of a colonial Latin American university. The sections concerning the social and intellectual life of the university are particularly pertinent. Bibliographical footnotes are included.

3. Levy, D. M., "Sibling Rivalry Studies in Primitive Groups," *American Journal of Orthopsychiatry,* IX (1938), 205-214.

Argentina and Guatemala provide the setting for this investigation of the child's response to the problem of family adjustment. The article discusses two cases from the study in which a play situation—dolls representing members of the family—was used. From the responses of the child to the doll situation, feelings of jealousy, hostility, regression, self-punishment, and guilt could be gauged and compared cross-culturally.

It was found that feelings of jealousy, hostility, etc., were displayed in quite similar fashion in the two examined cultures.

4. Nash, Manning, *Machine Age Maya: The Industrialization of a Guatemalan Community* (New York: The Free Press, 1958).

In the discussion of the family the author of this book on the industrialization of a Guatemalan community (Cantel) notes that the family is much like it was prior to the coming of the textile factory. It is his conclusion that factories may be introduced into peasant societies without drastic changes in the social, cultural, and psychological structure of the community. It is also held that a peoples' ability to adjust to new cultural forms is related to their feelings of control over the social situation. Some societies, then, may be able to accommodate industrialization with relative smoothness.

5. Paul, Benjamin D., "Symbolic Sibling Rivalry in a Guatemalan Indian Village," *American Anthropology*, LII (1950), 205-218.

Another article on symbolic sibling rivalry in Guatemala. The author deals with the San Pedro chicken-eating ritual which is believed to "cure" an older child of his aggressions toward the younger child by "eating" his soul and spirit. Dr. Paul discusses the context of socialization in which sibling attitudes are formed, the circumstances evoking the ritual, and the cultural beliefs and dispositions underlying the ritual.

The chicken-eating ritual is seen as an institutional means of relieving pressure and a symbolic expression of repressed antisocial sentiments.

6. Tumin, M., "Reciprocity and Stability of Caste in Guatemala," *American Sociological Review*, XIV, 1 (February, 1949), 17-25.

7. Wagley, Chas., "The Social and Religious Life of a Guatemalan Village," *American Anthropologist*, LI, 4, Pt. 2 (October, 1949).

A supplement to the *American Anthropologist* which discusses the social and religious life of Chimaltenango, a village in Guatemala. Applicable sections include those on Kinship and Family Groups and The Life Cycle—Childhood.

Within the village families are exogamous and patrilocal. Kinship seems to be extended on both paternal and maternal sides. The domination of the father over his son is based essentially on economic control—a son is dependent on his father for a wife and later for a home.

While the child at six or seven is located in the school

system, family pressure is usually such that he or she receives only minimal education. At about ten years of age, the boy becomes his father's constant companion. He learns the different occupations of a man and works hours as long as a man's. Girls learn different techniques but the method of teaching is the same. Marriage often occurs for girls at the age of 13 or 14. For about ten years the lives of both boys and girls are not essentially different from the lives of adults. There is no sudden transition from childhood to adult life and hence there are no ceremonies which indicate the period of adolescence.

HAITI

1. Herskovits, Melville J., *Life in a Haitian Valley* (New York: Alfred A. Knopf, Inc., 1937).
2. Leyburn, J. C., *The Haitian People* (New Haven: Yale University Press, 1941).
3. Simpson, G. E., "Haiti's Social Structure," *American Sociological Review,* VI, 5 (October, 1941), 640-649.

   A descriptive and historical analysis of the social structure of Haiti in 1941. The data was gathered on a field expedition in Haiti and the observations were combined with existing secondary sources for the article.

   Observations on education include the note that while the children of the elite class receive extensive education only 20 per cent of all children in Haiti are in school. The elite send their children to private schools while the bulk of the peasant children who go to school are enrolled in rural public schools.
4. Underwood, F. W., "Peasant Child Rearing in Rural Southwestern Haiti," *American Anthropologist,* XLIX (October, 1947), 565-574.

JAMAICA

1. Clarke, Edith, *My Mother Who Fathered Me; A Study of the Family in Three Selected Communities in Jamaica* (New York: Humanities Press, 1958).

   "This account of the family in rural Jamaica consists of a comparative study of three communities which reflect the different ways in which the rural population is organized, and attempts to show how these different ways of life affect patterns of family life, the relationship between the members of the family, and the composition of the household."

   The material directly pertaining to adolescence is rather

brief but the book as a whole presents an interesting picture of the forces shaping the life and culture of the rural Jamaican.

It is noted that there is a definite lack of parental instruction or guidance at the age of puberty. In the transition from youth to adolescence, the child is unprepared and inadequately equipped to deal with the life he must face. They possess only the basic rudiments of education.

2. Cohen, Y. A., "A Contribution to the Study of Adolescence: 'Adolescent Conflict' in a Jamaican Community," *Samiska,* IX (1955), 139-172.

3. Cohen, Y. A., "Structure and Function: Family Organization and Socialization in a Jamaican Community," *American Anthropologist,* LVIII (August, 1956), 664-686.

The author undertakes to demonstrate that personality processes are historically determined and that these processes must be taken into account in the analysis of relationships between cultural forms and their historical precedents. It is felt that the socialization processes leading to an emphasis on economic wealth, lack of community solidarity, individual rather than intrafamily competition, loose kinship ties, and the lack of authoritarianism in a Jamaican community are ". . . functions of its historically determined structure of family organization."

With reference to parent-child relations, it was noted that maternal discipline is very strict and the child becomes emotionally dependent upon the mother. The child has few connections with persons outside the family and a great deal of sibling rivalry within the family. The father plays a passive role in the socialization of the children but he does instruct the male children in work methods. The economic independence of male children is stressed while the female children are confined at home and watched by the mother. Boys have great freedom, girls have little.

Upon reaching adolescence the boys are given plots of land to work and are expected to provide for themselves from the produce of this land. They spend little time at home. It is in the question of the distribution of land where much sibling rivalry is expressed. The father, however, maintains control of the land and his will is never contested. With the lack of emotional attachment of the children to the father it is often seen that the family has difficulty in perpetuating itself as a working whole from generation to generation.

4. Henriques, F., "West Indian Family Organization," *American Journal of Sociology,* LV (1949), 30-37.

The author discusses the West Indian family organization and the effect of plantation slavery. He takes the island of Jamaica as typical of society in the Caribbean.

It is noted that there are four types of families in Jamaica: the Christian family, faithful concubinage, maternal or grandmother family, and keeper family. These familial forms exhibit a high degree of stability, but as a whole they can be regarded as indicative of the disequilibrium inherent in the society.

During the period of adolescence of the children disputes within the family are frequent. They arise usually over choice of work for the sons or the daughter's excessive associations with boys.

5. Mischel, Walter, "Preference for Delayed Reinforcement: An Experimental Study of a Cultural Observation," *Journal of Abnormal and Social Psychology*, LVI (1958), 57-61.

This experiment utilized subjects from the East Indian and Negro populations of Trinidad, British West Indies. The area of focus was personality differences and delayed reinforcement.

It was noted that primary results indicated significant differences between immediate, smaller versus delayed, larger reinforcement and the absence of the father in the home. Age was also a significant factor of difference.

6. Seaga, E. P. G., "Parent-Teacher Relationships in a Jamaican Village," *Social Economic Studies*, IV, 3 (September, 1955), 289-302.

In this situation the parents desired the retention of old British colonial culture. They objected to the introduction of readers in the school situation. The objection was based on the fact that the readers utilized local folklore as opposed to the more traditional subject matter. The parents also objected, on purely superstitious grounds, to a scheduled visit by the school children to a local power plant.

The article generally deals with parental misunderstanding, mistrust, and dissatisfaction with the curriculum content; the goals of the educational system; and the personal conduct of teachers—both in school and out. Recommendations are offered for the resolution of the conflicts.

7. Smith, M. G., "Education and Occupational Choice in Rural Jamaica," *Social and Economic Studies*, IX, (1960), 332-354.

This article discusses the patterns of occupational desires in rural Jamaica. The author utilizes data from several independent studies. He notes the correspondence of career choices among peasant adults and children and explores the relationship of the desires to local opportunities. One of the studies deals with elementary school children (2,050 boys and 2,850 girls). He also utilizes the results of a 1955 survey by Smith in the 15-24 age range.

The results of the analysis reveal a gap between reality and desire in the area of occupational desires. It appears that rural conditions are such that parents want their children to escape them by occupational means. The school gives the children a notion of alternative ways of life and disvalues the peasant mode of existence. As a result the children acquire unrealistic aspirations. The data reveal a period of disillusionment after the children leave the school atmosphere. The data also reveal a disparity between the occupational choices of rural adults and children.

A great deal of frustration and anomie are the results of the inconsistencies of the social system in its reinforcing aspirations that will inevitably be frustrated.

8. Smith, M. G., "Plural Framework of a Jamaican Society," *British Journal of Sociology*, XII (September, 1961), 249-262.

MEXICO

1. Anderson, H. H., et al., "Image of the Teacher by Adolescent Children in Four Countries: Germany, England, Mexico and the United States," *Journal of Social Psychology*, L (1959), 47-55.

Problem: ". . . to develop and test an instrument that would be sensitive to cross-national similarities and differences, and to examine children's responses in the light of certain hypotheses." "The hypotheses tested were that responses from children in a more dominating authoritarian culture will be different from those of children in a more integrative or more democratic culture. Specifically, that in more dominating cultures there will be relatively higher frequencies of the teacher's initiating contact with the child, of the child's telling a lie, of the teacher's disbelieving the child, of the teacher's punishing the child."

The study was conducted using as subjects over 3,178 fourth- and seventh-grade children in the four countries of Germany, England, Mexico, and continental United States, during the period from 1952 to 1957. Researchers used an incomplete short story, "The Lost Composition" of the *Anderson Incomplete Stories*, which the children were asked to complete.

"It is concluded that the *Anderson Incomplete Stories* is an instrument sensitive to cross-national similarities and differences, and that children reared in allegedly more authoritarian and dominating cultures hold images of the teacher that are significantly different from those held by children in less dominating, that is, more integrative or democratic cultures."

2. Ballesteros, Usano A., "Suicides in Adolescence," *Proceedings of the International Congress of Mental Health* (1951), 281-289.

   This article discusses the frequency, age range, and methods employed by adolescent suicides in the Federal district of Mexico. Proposals are made concerning the control of the problem.

3. Beals, Ralph L., "The Mexican Student Views the United States," *Annals of the American Academy of Political and Social Science*, CCXCV (1954), 108-115.

   The article considers the results of study in the United States on the attitudes of Mexican students toward the United States. Data were gathered from intensive guided interviews with 10 students at the University of California at Los Angeles. Confirmatory evidence is provided by background information, a simple projective test, and an ideological test from over 40 additional students from seven other universities and colleges. The subjects were mostly graduates and came from the upper and middle classes.

   Among the findings it was noted that ". . . The discovery that the dichotomy between materialistic and spiritual goals is less sharp than expected seems to pose a severe threat to the self-esteem of the Mexican student. Only students with an objective sense of cultural relativism seem undisturbed. Others seem either ripe for alienation from their own culture or take refuge in an iteration of moral superiority."

   Many of the students held diverse views of the "mass culture" and the independence of children and women. They also felt that Americans do not make real friendships, although they are friendly and courteous. While they appreciated the informal methods of professors, they objected to the competitive grading system encountered. Many were shocked by the reality of the discrimination against Negroes, but they interpreted the feeling toward Mexicans as a class feeling rather than a racial feeling.

   It was generally concluded that the student view of the United States will depend upon the length of his stay, the closeness of his contacts, and the interest he has.

4. Beals, Ralph L. and Norman D. Humphrey, *No Frontier to Learning: the Mexican Student in the United States* (Minneapolis: University of Minnesota Press, 1957).

5. Beard, B. B., "Mexico's Way with Children," *Journal of the American Association of University Women*, XXXVIII (1944), 15-18.

The author asks the question, why does Mexico have a lower rate of juvenile delinquency than the United States? Discussion is based on a two-month study in Mexico, during which causes, extent, and treatment of juvenile delinquents were examined. Visits were made to all types of social agencies and institutions dealing with delinquency.

The general conclusions include the following: there are no juvenile gangs in Mexico; a common offense for boys is larceny, for girls, prostitution; Mexico has been slow to use foster home care, especially for delinquent children; punishment of offenders is generally handled by the parents and/or the priest (this is offered as a partial explanation of the disparity in rates of delinquency between the United States and Mexico).

6. Calderon De La Barca, Frances Erskine (Inglis), *Life in Mexico* (New York: Dutton, 1954).

7. Cervantes De Salazar, Francisco, *Life in the Imperial and Loyal City of Mexico in New Spain, and the Royal and Pontifical University of Mexico* (Austin: University of Texas, 1954).

8. "Delinquents in Mexico: Religious Education," *Ave Maria*, LXXXVI (December 8, 1957), 18.

9. Ellis, Christine Evangeline, *The Relation of Socio-Economic Status to the Intelligence and School Success of Mexican Children*, M. A. Thesis, University of Texas (1932).

10. Fernandez-Marina, et al., "Three Basic Themes in Mexican and Puerto Rican Family Values," *Journal of Social Psychology*, XLVIII (November, 1958) 167-181.

In an earlier study Diaz Guerro reported on a study of Mexican families which revealed that: (1) the mother is a strong figure of affection, so much so that it may interfere later in the marital situation, (2) emphasis in the Mexican family is on the child's learning submission and obedience to the father and other authority figures, (3) boys have a higher status than girls in life. The authors of the present article take these results as a basis for their investigation of family life in Puerto Rico. Specifically, they are interested in the extent to which the values of the Puerto Rican family have changed from the typical Latin American values described above to more American values. They hypothesized that the Puerto Rican values would be more like the Latin American than the American values despite 60 years of direct American influence.

A questionnaire was administered to 496 teen-age students, freshmen at the University of Puerto Rico. The results of the analysis indicated that: (1) the concept of male dominance and superiority in the family is still prevalent, (2) the mother is held in higher affectional regard than the father, (3) the male child is accorded greater status than the female, (4) the values of the middle-class Puerto Rican family are more similar to those of the Mexican than to those of mainland America, (5) the hypothesis was substantially upheld.

11. Foster, George M., *Empire's Children: The People of Tzintzuntzan* (Mexico: Imprinta Nuevo Mundo, 1948).

12. Gillespie, J. M. and G. W. Allport, *Youth's Outlook on the Future* (Garden City, New York: Doubleday and Company, Inc., 1955).

A successful pilot study, covering 1,819 case studies from 10 countries, the object of which was to examine the attitudes of college students in ten countries toward their individual and collective futures; no hypotheses were tested. At least partial answers were sought to three questions: (1) How do youth in various countries view the future? (2) Do young people in different countries view their futures in essentially the same way? (3) Is international social research at the present time practicable and beneficial? A cross-cultural analysis of attitudes, aspirations, and moral values among students from the United States, New Zealand, Egypt, Mexico, France, Italy, Germany, Japan, Israel, and South Africa was attempted by administering a questionnaire—including both multiple-choice and open-ended questions—to 100 males and 100 females from each country. (This was the goal; the attempts occasionally fell short.) In addition an essay entitled "Autobiography: from Now to 2000 A.D.," was required from each respondent. Some of the similarities discovered were: "Familism is a universal foundation for individual and group life." "Basic moral values and ethical codes of conduct are everywhere prized." "Most students (Africaners excepted) . . . desire to see greater equality between white and colored races." "Most youth regard war as needless and preventable . . . [but are] . . . pessimistic as to the possibility of avoiding a third world conflict." There were, of course, a great number of national differences, but the authors conclude that ". . . it is a wholesome corrective to note that these differences may be dramatic figures etched upon a ground of basic resemblance."

13. Gonzales, Aurora Marjorie, *A Study of the Intelligence of Mexican*

Children in Relation to Their Socio-Economic Status, M.A. Thesis, University of Texas (1932).

14. Hayner, N. S., "Mexicans at Play—a Revolution," *Sociology and Social Research,* XXXVIII (November, 1953), 80-83.

Discusses the growth of recreation and sports in Mexico. The author notes the acceptance of baseball, handball, soccer. The biggest professional sports are bullfighting, soccer, wrestling, and baseball. The recent trend in amateur sports (1953) has been the reduction of participation in private clubs in favor of large-scale participation under public sponsorship.

15. Hayner, N. S., "Notes on the Changing Mexican Family," *American Sociological Review,* VII (1942), 489-497.

In this article on the changing Mexican family we note the following items on youth: (1) few girls have more than a sixth-grade education (formal), (2) in rural areas about half of the males are married before they are 20, about half the girls before they are 15, (3) there is a high rate of juvenile delinquency in the "zone in transition" surrounding Mexico City, (4) the changes occurring in the relationships of youth (as well as effects to the society as a whole) include industrialization, the opening of new paved highways, and the popularity of American-made movies.

16. Humphrey, N. D., "Family Patterns in a Mexican Middletown," (Tecolotlan Jalisco), *Social Service Review,* XXVI (June, 1952), 195-201.

In this discussion of family life in Tecolotlan, Jalisco, the author notes that there is little aspiration on the part of the children toward the goal of preparing themselves for different lives or a changed community. It is expected that they will live in much the same manner as do their parents.

17. Iturrioz, J., "Nuestra juventud" (Our Young People), *Razon y Fe,* CLIX, 736 (May, 1959), 453-464.

18. Johnson, Granville B., Jr., "The Origin and Development of the Spanish Attitude toward the Anglo and the Anglo Attitude toward the Spanish," *Journal of Education and Psychology,* XLI (1950), 428-439.

An article discussing the development of prejudicial attitudes in Spanish and Anglo children. The focus is on the childhood, preadolescent attitude development.

19. Lavalle, Urbina, Maria, "Delincuencia Infantil" (Juvenile Delinquency), *Criminalia Mexico*, XV (1949), 134-146.

    The author discusses the causes of juvenile delinquency. She discusses both external and internal causes which she refers to as social and individual respectively. Heredity, physiology, childhood environment, and family and social conditions in Mexico are considered in relation to delinquency.

20. Leslie, Charles, *The Children of Sanchez: Autobiography of a Mexican Family* (New York: Random House, Inc., 1961).

21. Lewis, Oscar and Ruth Lewis, "A Day in the Life of a Mexican Peasant Family," *Marriage and Family Living,* XVIII (February, 1956), 3-13.

22. Lewis, Oscar, *Life in a Mexican Village: Tepoztlan Restudied* (Urbana, Illinois: University of Illinois Press, 1951).

    This well-known study of Tepoztlan contains some reference to the youth of the area. Specifically, it is noted that, since 1910, girls tend to marry at a later age and boys at an earlier age. This tends to shorten the period of adolescence. In Tepoztlan the adolescent usually works for the parents rather than attending school. "The strongly authoritarian family and other factors have tended to produce passive, dependent youth rather than youths noted for initiative ambition, drive, and independence." The author notes a notable absence of open revolt against the parents or against the local traditions. The only rebels are those youths educated outside the village.

    In the twenty years prior to 1951 the principal changes in the culture occurred in areas such as increased population, rising standard of living, division of labor, rise in literacy, and a greater incorporation of the village in the main stream of national life.

23. Maslow, A. H. and R. Diaz-Guerrero, "Delinquency as a Value Disturbance," in J. G. Peatman and E. L. Hartley (eds.), *Festschrift for Gardner Murphy* (New York: Harper & Row, Publishers, 1960), 228-240.

    This article discusses the differences in behavior between Mexican children and American children. The authors utilize existing secondary sources and personal experience in their analysis and discussion. The differences in the behavior of Mexican and American children, particularly in the area of antisocial behavior, are seen as the results of various cultural differences.

    It is noted that the Mexican child is generally better behaved than the American child. There seems to be little or no sibling rivalry. Mexican parents, the authors note, seem to have less trouble with their children than do parents in the United States. Mexican children seem to resent authority less, to demand less, to be less whining and complaining, to be less of a nuisance, and to cry less often."

Perhaps the most significant comments are found in the discussion of the limits set by the Mexican parents. In Mexico both the parents and the culture have set limits and values of childrearing. As a result a child will always know, at any given instant, exactly where he stands with his parents. The roles of the father and the mother are very distinct and the masculine and feminine roles are taught in early childhood. Thus we see the Mexican child living more in the family than in the peer group. The authors note, ". . . the Mexican child is confronted by a more stable, widely agreed upon set of adult values with respect to child rearing." "The Mexican child is much more likely to be brought up exclusively in the bosom of the family than is the American child."

What this article illustrates in part is the formation, or lack of formation, of peer-group values and norms as a result of the operation of a well-integrated and cohesive family and cultural structure with regard to the child.

24. Mendieta y Nunez, L., "La organizacion de la juventud como problema de educacion social" (The Organization of Youth as a Problem of Social Education), *Estudio Sociologicos* (Mexico: UNAM, 1953), 117-124.

25. Qureshi, I. H., "Education in Mexico," *Pakistan Horizon,* VI, 4 (December, 1953), 135-139.

26. Ramirez, Santiago and Ramon Parres, "Some Dynamic Patterns in the Organization of the Mexican Family," *International Journal of Social Psychiatry,* III (1957), 18-21.

A psychoanalytical discussion of the family dynamics in Mexico. The sample consisted of 500 families from the Children's Hospital in Mexico City and from 135 families from the Centers for Mental Hygiene. The authors discuss the mother-child relationship, the relationship of the relatives to the family and the actions of the father in the family situation. Three basic dynamic tendencies are discussed: (1) intense mother-child relationship during the first year of life; (2) dilution of the father-child relationship; and (3) the traumatic rupture of the mother-child relationship at the birth of the next child.

27. Simpson, Leslie Byrd, *Many Mexicos* (Berkeley: University of California Press, 1959).

28. Villa Rajar, Alfonso, "Kinship and Nagualism in a Tzeltal Community, Southeastern Mexico," *American Anthropologist,* XLIX, 4 (October/December, 1947), 578-586.

PANAMA

1. Biesanz, John B. and Mavis Biesanz, *The People of Panama* (New York: Columbia University Press, 1955).
2. Goldrich, Daniel, *Radical Nationalism The Political Orientations of Panamanian Law Students,* Bureau of Social and Political Research, College of Business and Public Service, M.S.U., E. Lansing (1962).

A pamphlet by a political scientist at Michigan State University which discusses the political orientations of 83 law students in Panama during 1960. According to the author, "This study represents an attempt to assess the degree of radical nationalism in a significant sector of a society moving toward basic social change, as well as their orientation toward the existing political system, social change, and contemporary revolutionary events throughout the world, and to estimate crudely the probably impact of the group on future national and international politics."

3. Goldrich, D. and E. Scott, "Developing Political Orientations of Panamanian Students," *Journal of Politics,* XXIII (February, 1961), 84-107.

This article discusses the political orientation of two groups of Panamanian students. These orientations are seen as a result of socio-economic factors, the political system, and the process of acquiring the adult social role. The political orientations developed in the school setting are investigated, stability and saliency.

Questionnaires were applied to a sample of 91 eleventh-grade students. One group were private school students (upper class), and the other group was from the public school (middle and lower class).

The results indicated that: (1) the upper-class students were much more liberal than expected; (2) the middle- and lower-class students expressed more reform and liberal orientations; (3) "Dissatisfaction with the existing allocation of values has been a common characteristic of students and intellectuals in colonial and modernizing areas." Students in Panama both past and present share this dissatisfaction. The strength of the response or orientation varies with socio-economic status and its stability is a function of the relationships between career expectations and their fulfillment and nationalistic movements.

4. Smith, Carol Cordes, "The San Blas Sans Juvenile Delinquency," *Journal of Educational Sociology*, XXIX (1956), 259-263.

 The problem here is to determine whether the Cuna Indians, a "primitive" tribe, had a juvenile-delinquency problem. The author notes an absence of delinquency in the group and attributes this to the adults presenting "nondelinquent" behavior patterns which the children emulate. He finds strong tribal mores, social control, sanctions, all of which hold down the incidence of delinquency.

PERU

1. Gillin, John, "Approaches to Marriage on the North Peruvian Coast," *Marriage Hygiene*, I (1948), 160-164.

 The author notes that in Moche, Peru, social organization is based on kinship by blood, affinity, or ceremony. When a couple decide to play house, the permission of the girl's parents is usually sought. While engagement and marriage ceremony is desired, in many cases both are forgotten. Premarital intercourse is taken for granted, but not officially condoned. Prostitution is not widespread. Female virginity is highly prized, but many young people do not abide by the norm.

2. Guerra, Luis A. and Bernardino H. Jines, "Aparte al Estudio del Mentor en Estado Peligroso en Lima," (An Approach to the Study of the Juvenile Delinquent in Lima), *Revista de Neuro-Psiquiatria*, IX (Lima: 1946), 242-278.

 An examination of Juvenile Delinquency in Peru. The author selected cases from three state institutions and analyzed them with the assumption that juvenile delinquency is a product of both sociological and individual factors. Social factors include the influence of the home, the school, and the street. The individual factors examined include intelligence, personality, world view, and education.

3. Hammel, E. A., "Family Cycle in a Coastal Peruvian Slum and Village," *American Anthropologist*, LXIII (October, 1961), 989-1005.

4. Pisculish, R. E., *Estudio Psico-Social de 100 Menores Delinquents* (*Psycho-Social Study of 100 Delinquent Minors*) (Lima: Imprenta Gil, 1946).

A study based on the investigation of 100 cases of juvenile deviants. The ages ranged from 7 to 20. Areas of focus for the analysis include home and school relationships, delinquent activities, mental deficiency, and normality of personality. It was found that the economic factor was a great determinate of the predelinquent state. Vagrancy and truancy were among the most popular juvenile offenses. The cases examined revealed no significantly higher degree of psychological abnormality than the population in general. It was noted that the government could possibly effect better control of the delinquency situation than it does.

PUERTO RICO

1. Back, K.W., "Change-prone Person in Puerto Rico," *Public Opinion Quarterly*, XXII (Fall, 1958), 330-340.

The problem posed here concerns the types of persons who are most ready to accept and embrace social change in places and during periods of rapid change. The investigation centered on the government housing developments and their impact on the people affected. The sample was drawn from 5 slum areas for which no clearance had been planned, 5 slum areas which had been surveyed for clearance and relocation, 5 slum areas already partially cleared, and 5 housing projects. Families who had not moved when they were qualified and families who had moved out of the government projects were also questioned. The final sample contained 405 respondents—173 men and 232 women. The instruments utilized included: structured questionnaires, role-playing scenes adapted from the Stanton-Litwak battery for interpersonal competence, and the projective Albizu-Tumin Sentence Completion Test.

It was found that those who accepted change were more likely to be men, a little younger and generally better educated. The families who were most receptive to change were those in which the breadwinner was in a high status job or a highly skilled job useful in the process of industrialization. Opposition to change was found in the families of service workers, laborers, and farm workers. The author notes, "The total picture of changeability points to persons with an opportunity for social mobility; who are young enough to look to the future, and who fit into government programs for education and economic change. . . . The key ingredient in modernization is orientation toward the future. Among the personality traits on which this attitude could be based, modifiability of response proved to be most important."

2. Batista Martinez, Christina (University of Puerto Rico), "Estudio de Actitudes Hacia los Estados Unidos de un Grupo de Estudiantes Latinoamericanos en al Universitad de Texas" (A Study of the Attitudes toward the United States of a Group of Latin American Students at the University of Texas), *Pedagogia, Rio Piedras,* V, 2 (1957), 35-48.

An examination of attitudes of a group of Latin American students at the University of Texas. A questionnaire was applied to a sample of 29 students in order to obtain their opinions on American family life, social life, community life, and the educational system. The subjects came from 12 different South American nations. Because the number in the sample is so small, the total results are not as accurate or as interesting as the individual opinions expressed.

3. Brameld, Theodore, "Explicit and Implicit Culture in Puerto Rico: A Case Study in Educational Anthropology," *Harvard Educational Review,* XXVIII, 3 (Summer, 1958), 197-213.

4. Brameld, Theodore, *The Remaking of a Culture: Life and Education in Puerto Rico* (New York: Harper & Brothers, 1959).

One chapter in this publication deals with value problems of Puerto Rican youth. Data for this chapter as well as the rest of the publication were gathered over a period of three years in Puerto Rico. Many interviews were held with Puerto Rican youth and their families.

Among the comments made we find under Norms of Adolescents: (1) youth seek to win the approval of their peers rather than their elders, (2) there is an urge to revolt from the authoritarian family patterns, (3) the younger people are self-centered, pleasure seeking, and disrespectful to parents who pay little attention to them, (4) one change is noted in the emphasis on vocational guidance at the levels of junior and senior high school.

Concerning sex values we note: (1) it was generally held that adolescent attitudes toward sex were more healthy than in previous years, (2) proposals are offered for the content of sex education courses.

Concerning the world situation we note: (1) while Puerto Rican youth are world-minded, they are not especially sensitive to the values of other cultures, (2) most of the student leaders were of the opinion that the world today is in a period of crisis, (3) some insecurity was seen as a result of the high probability of military service for the youth, a period of service which precluded definite plans for the future.

The author notes a strong conformity in the value orientation of Puerto Rican youth.

5. Casanova, T., *Educational Psychology and Some Aspects of Education in Latin America* (San Juan, Puerto Rico: Imprinta Venezuela, 1934).

6. Hansen, M., "The Family in Puerto Rico Research Projects," in *Approaches to Problems of High Fertility in Agrarian Societies* (New York: Milbank Memorial Fund), 50-61.

7. Hill, Reuben, "Courtship in Puerto Rico: an Institution in Transition," *Marriage and Family Living*, XVII (1955), 26-35.

   An examination of the courtship system in Puerto Rico to answer such questions as: (1) what occurs when the Spanish and American cultures clash; (2) which American practices, if any, have been adopted; (3) what traditional beliefs have survived. The author's observations are based on two years of intermittent visits to Puerto Rico and 13 months' continuous residence. Some of the data is based on observation, some on a survey of 275 university students and some is based on a previous study conducted in 1951-1953.

   It was noted that the courtship patterns in Puerto Rico were still more Spanish oriented than American oriented. The two systems have merged in some areas with the American ideal of free mate choice being tempered with the distinct possibility of parental veto. There is, in effect, little latitude of choice. In the university setting stag parties and open-field dating is virtually unknown. The ideal for the girls is to get a steady boyfriend and to marry early while at the same time keeping her virginity intact. The engagement period is not a period of trial marriage but rather a promise to marry. The author notes, "The system is ideologically oriented increasingly toward the beliefs of North America but its forms and practices remain predominantly those of the hispanic-catholic world."

8. Hill, Reuben, "Obstacles in the Freedom of Selecting a Mate in Puerto Rico," *Rev. Asoc.*, XIII (Maestros, Puerto Rico: 1954), 120-121, 134.

9. Landy, David, *Tropical Childhood: Cultural Transmission and Learning in a Rural Puerto Rican Villlage* (Chapel Hill: University of North Carolina Press, 1959).

   The goals of this research were an exploratory descriptive ethnographic study of socialization, or cultural transmission and learning and a systematic comparison of child training and behavior between the rural families and those of an urban New England community. Interviews, doll-play situations and observation, were utilized from 18 lower-class families in a rural Puerto Rican village.

While the emphasis here is on the Freudian interpretation of the preadolescent period there is some discussion of the adolescent period and the effect of early environment and training on the development and behavior of the adolesecnt.

10. Mellado, R. A., *Culture and Education in Puerto Rico*. Educational Monography Bureau of Publications, Puerto Rico Teachers Association.

11. Ramsey, Charles E. and Jenario Collazo, "Some Problems of Cross-Cultural Measurement," *Rural Sociology*, XXV (1960), 91-107.

    An article discussing the problems involved in the cross-cultural application of an instrument to measure the standard of living.

12. Sanchez Hildalgo Efrain, "Possible Effects of Rapid Industrialization on the Puerto Rican Family," *Pedagogia*, II, 1 (Rio Piedras: 1954), 117-128.

13. Steward, Julian H., et al. (eds.), *The People of Puerto Rico: A Study in Social Anthropology* (Urbana: University of Illinois Press, 1956).

14. Tumin, M. M. and A. S. Feldman, "Status, Perspective and Achievement: Education and Class Structure in Puerto Rico," *American Sociological Review*, XXI (August, 1956), 464-472.

15. Wolf, K. L., "Growing Up and Its Price in Three Puerto Rican Subcultures," *Psychiatry*, XV, 401-433.

    This study is specifically concerned with the norms of adult behavior and child behavior. The author attempts to demonstrate the different psychological dynamics found in three subcultures on the island of Puerto Rico. She holds that there is no one Puerto Rican personality type.

    Subjects for this study were drawn from three areas: the small farmers of the Barrio Manicaboa; the landless sugar-workers of the Barrio Royal; and the middle-class population of San Jose.

    Among the small farmers of Manicaboa the maintenance of the family is a principal aim. The father is the head of the family and the women and children must repress their aggressive impulses. The maintenance of the family is primary. The result is atrophy of the sense of individual autonomy and ego development is severely limited.

    The sugar workers of Royal train a sense of work-group

loyalty into their children. In this case the work group is the community. There is little stress on the individual and little competition between individuals. A young man can easily become his father's equal. Aggression is released against an out group.

The middle class of San Jose aims primarily at improving its standard of living and social status. There is little sense of group identity and much competition between individuals. Most men feel insecure in their role. The author notes ". . . a decline of male dominance and an increase of female autonomy."

The author concludes, "Each group carries certain ideal norms for male and female behavior, and in each group children must be raised to approximate these ideals. The ideal behavior can never be duplicated in reality. . . . In each case, the people involved must pay a psychological price for the predominance of the cultural ideal over the psychological forces which threaten its stability. . . . Each of the class groups discussed shows a balance of achievement and its cost."

URUGUAY

1. Amezaga, J. J., "To Youth," *Free World,* IX (March, 1945), 77.

   A speech delivered by President Amezaga of Uruguay on December 31, 1944 at a session organized by the Uruguayan Free World.

VENEZUELA

1. Prieto, F. L. B., "Las Asociones Juveniles y su Influencia Moral en el Desarrollo de la Personidad: Organizacion y Direccion" (Youth Groups and Their Moral Effect on the Development of the Personality: Organization and Management), XVII (1943), 474-483.

   A report on the attempt by the government of Venezuela to establish a system of youth groups to help meet the developmental personal needs of adolescents. Democratic organization from below is stressed with adult supervision being of an advisory nature. It is noted that the functioning of such groups should always be related to the facts and conditions of psychological development of the adolescent.

2. Vegas, R.. *Contribucion al estudio de la situacion economico-social del alumno caraqueno* (A Contribution to the Study of the Socio-Economic Situation of School Children in Caracas) (Caracas: Escuela de Educacion, Facultad de Humanidades y Educacion, Universidad Central de Venezuela, 1956).

GENERAL

1. Adams, Richard N., "An Inquiry into the Nature of the Family," in Gertrude E. Dole and Robert L. Carneiro (eds.), *Essays in the Science of Culture in Honor of Leslie A. White* (New York: Thomas Y. Crowell Company, 1960), 30-49.

2. Dardis, Panos D., "Attitudes toward Dating among Foreign Students in America," *Marriage and Family Living.* XVIII (1956), 339-344.

3. Bonilla, Frank, *Students in Politics: Three Generations of Political Action in a Latin American University*, Ph.D. Thesis, Harvard (1959).

4. Chavez Reyes, Mario, "Latin America: The Student Citizen," *IIE News Bulletin,* XXXIV, 5 (January, 1959), 18-22.

An article which gives some insight as to why Latin American students have been paying so much attention to the economic, political, and social problems of their countries.

During the colonial period, education was a privilege accorded only to the highest classes. The lower classes lived in poverty. With the coming of the republican era educational restrictions were removed but progress was slow. During the revolutions the students played an important part and the universities came to be the gathering point for all the revolutionary ideas. It was from the universities that the reform movements started. The schools made their graduates aware of the social and also aware that if the youth did not act there would be little hope of the reforms ever being accomplished. The student studies the social, economic, and political problems of the day. The students see themselves as carrying the burden of future reform and hence, the future of their respective countries.

5. Childs, James B., "Latin American Current National Bibliographies," *The Library Quarterly,* XI (1941), 360-364.

6. Comas, Juan, "Latin America," *UNESCO International Social Science Journal* XIII, 2 (1961), 271-303.

7. Davis, Thomas, "A Survey of Elementary and Secondary Education in Latin America," *Journal of Inter-American Studies,* III (January, 1961), 97-120.

A discussion of the structure and progress of the educational system in Latin America as a whole. The author notes, "Latin American educational legislation bears but faint relationship to the facts, and from each of the countries comes the standard explanation: 'Because of the lack of buildings, trained teachers, and sufficient funds, the national ideal of education for all has not been realized.' "

The author notes that the elementary education of Latin Americans is, in some ways, superior to that of the United States, but generally the educational system has a long way to go to provide adequate education to the general population, a desire of all the progressive Latin American nations.

8. Davis, Kingsley and Ana Casis, "Urbanization in Latin America," *Milbank Memorial Fund Quarterly*, XXIV, 243 (April/June, 1946), 1-45.

9. Enochs, Elisabeth S., "The Children of Latin America in an Age of Anxiety," *Journal of Educational Sociology*, XXVIII (March, 1955), 299-307.

This article discusses the issues and obstacles facing Latin American youth. It includes an overall country-by-country inventory. Among the problems noted by the author are: the development of social services, abandoned children, the regulation of child labor. The general conclusion is reached that the problem of youth is primarily an economic one and not a problem of social and special services.

10. Frank, Waldo, "To the Youth of Latin America," *The Nation*, CLXVIII, 12 (March, 1949), 343-345.

An open letter to the youth of Latin America regarding the Venezuelan counter-revolution by the military forces. The author states his general distaste for such action and says that all society must collaborate to be on guard against such further actions by the military. He claims that there is no need for further violence. Meetings and demonstrations are acceptable, but violence should be put aside.

11. Gillin, J. P., *The Emerging Middle Class of Latin America* (London: The King's Crown Press, 1957).

12. Gillin, J. P., "Modern Latin America Culture," *Social Forces*, XXV, 243-248.

13. Hulbert, Winifred, "Social Movements among Workers and Students," *Latin American Backgrounds* (New York: Friendship Press, 1935) 158-160.

14. Goldrich, Daniel, "Toward an Estimate of the Probability of Social Revolutions in Latin America: Some Orienting Concepts and a Case Study," *The Centennial Review*, VI, 3 (Summer, 1962), 394-408.

An assessment of the revolutionary potentials among the students of Panama. Data were gathered by means of a questionnaire applied to four groups of secondary-school students in Panama City during the summer of 1961. The total sample of 1,000 was divided between an upper-class sample from the two private schools having the highest prestige in the city, a middle-class sample from a private secular school, and a working-class sample from a public mechanical vocational arts school.

The findings reveal that the upper class (uc) and the middle working class (mwc) students discuss politics more frequently than the working (wc) students. With regard to the Cuban revolution no group wholly supported it but the mwc students were the most favorable (30 per cent) and the wc students were the most critical (60 per cent). The wc student on the whole feels that it makes little difference who wins the elections in Panama. Many lack any intention to vote and some feel that political parties should be dissolved. Most of those critical toward politics and the government are found in the wc students.

In summary, it was felt that the wc student does not look to government for improvement of opportunities and living conditions, the wc student is least involved in active politics and is most dissatisfied with the government. Thus the author feels that it is the minority in the student body that organizes the leadership for today and the future.

15. Goode, W. H., "Illegitimacy in the Caribbean Social Structure," *American Sociological Review*, XXV, 1 (February, 1960), 21-30.

A study of the variations in norms and practices related to legitimacy in Caribbean society. In the Caribbean area, illegitimacy rates are often over 50 per cent. Various writers have spoken of a "matrifocal family," and have raised doubts as to whether a sociological father exists. Following are the factors of importance in the decision to marry or to enter a consensual union:

1. Only middle- and upper-class individuals marry, and also may have mistresses whom they do not marry. Lower-class people also marry eventually. In communities with higher social standing a substantial majority of all marital unions are legal.

2. When marriage does occur, the man and the woman are equals in rank.

3. The girl's parents or relatives are seldom punished if they make or fail to make her behavior conform to ideal norms.

4. The average girl has little chance at marriage unless she

is willing to gamble that a more permanent union will grow from one relationship or another.

5. In the Caribbean, there is no "free" adolescent courtship system. Most of the men a girl first meets are ineligible for marriage because of the high cost of a wedding. As a result the girl's first love and sex contacts occur away from home and without the knowledge of the family.

16. Keehn, J. D. and E. T. Prothro, "National Preferences of University Students from 23 Nations," *Journal of Psychology,* XLII (1956), 283-294.

17. Martin, R. P., *The Adjustment of Latin-American Male Students in Selected Private Secondary Schools in the United States* (Ann Arbor: University microfilm, 1954).

18. Mead, Margaret, "Energy Changes under Conditions of Cultural Change, *Sociometry,* XVIII, 4 (1955), 457-467.

19. Mendieta y Nunez, Lucio, "Racial and Cultural Tensions in Latin America," *International Social Science Bulletin,* IV, 3 (1952), 442-451.

20. Numez de Bunker, Celia, "El Adolescents en la Familia" (The Adolescent in the Family), *Pedagogia,* IV, 2 (1956), 23-32.

A general article discussing the adolescent and the family with respect to psychological weaning, family problems, adult behavior, vocational guidance for the adolescet, sexual relations, and the adolescent as a person.

21. Stycos, J. Mayone, "Further Observations on the Recruitment and Trainings of Interviewers in Other Cultures," *Public Opinion Quarterly,* XIX, 1 (Spring, 1955), 68-78.

22. White, Langdon C. and Donald Alderson, "Industrialization: Panacea for Latin America?" *Journal of Geography,* LVI, 7 (October, 1957), 325-332.

23. Wilgus, A. Curtis (ed.), *The Caribbean: Its Culture* (Gainesville: University of Florida Press, 1956).

24. UNESCO, "Report by the Director-General on the Joint United Nations/UNESCO Seminar on Urbanization in Latin America," Santiago, Chile, (July 6-18, 1959) (February 26, 1960).

25. UNESCO, "Report on the Study and Information Seminar for Leaders of Youth Movements in Latin America," Ceibe del Agua, Havana, Cuba (October 5-26, 1954), Paris (February 14, 1955).

AUSTRALIA, NEW GUINEA, AND NEW ZEALAND

AUSTRALIA

1. Anderson, A. W., "Personality Traits of Western Australian University Entrants," *Australian Journal of Psychology,* XII (1960), 4-9.

   To describe the personality traits of western Australian University entrants. the Sixteen Personality Factor Questionnaire (Form A) was administered to students entering the University of Western Australia in 1958 and 1959. The article includes the raw scores obtained by these entering students on the sub scales of the 16PF test. These raw scores are compared by the author in relation to sex and course. A less detailed comparison was done in regard to age.

2. Anderson, A. W., "Personality Traits of Western Australian University Freshmen," *Journal of Social Psychology,* LI (February, 1960), 87-91.

   To compare the personality traits of Australian students with those of American students the Sixteen Personality Factor Questionnaire was administered to 290 male and 138 female entering students, at the University of Western Australia in 1958. The scores were compared with those obtained by comparable American groups on the 16PF Tabular Supplement, and a provisional age correction was given. The significant differences were found on factors A, B, G, H, L, M, N, and Q2 for the males and on factors A, B, F, H, I, L, N, O, and Q2 for the females. The findings suggest that there are real differences between the American freshmen and the Western Australian freshmen in that the American freshmen are more outgoing, sociable, relaxed, and group dependent; the American females are less effeminate and more practical than are the Western Australian females. Similar sex differences are manifested in the American and Australian groups. In regard to such factors as dominance, ego strength, radicalism, self-sentiment formation, and ergic tension no significant differences appeared.

3. Barcan, A., "The Australian Student," *Meanjin,* 2 (University of Melbourne, 1961) 194-207.

   Since 1945 there have been some rather extensive changes in Australian higher education mainly in regard to the growth in size and numbers of institutions and in regard to their transformation in character. Relying upon facts and figures from surveys made by the Committee on Australian Universities and upon data supplied by the schools themselves, the author has concluded that an expanding white-collar group is currently being trained by the universities. The large proportion of students traditionally enrolled in liberal arts curriculums is decreasing, whereas the more specialized fields of science, engineering, and commerce are growing. Universities are recruiting from a broader social base, and the failure rate (traditionally high) is remaining high. Apathy, conformity, and a concern with personal adjustment rather than an interest in politics, heightened activity, and intellectual commitment have become the hallmarks of the typical student.

4. Barrett, J., "Youth Welfare in Australia," *Nature*, CXLVI (May, 1941), 671.

5. Campbell, W. J. and Jan Cochrane, "Citizenship Expectations in a Rural Community," *Australian Journal of Education*, III (1959), 90-96.

   In an attempt to discover the prerequisites for good citizenship in the rural Australian community of Karribee (pop. 500), a poll was taken of all the adult members of the community. The replies to a question to this effect, i.e., what must a child or adolescent do to become a good citizen?, were classified into areas of expectation and were ranked in order of relative importance as follows: (1) health and body use, (2) personal and spiritual contentment, (3) moral characteristics, (4) marriage and family life, (5) knowledge and skills, (6) getting along with others, (7) social responsibility, (8) occupational choice and performance. Women stressed the second factor significantly more than did the men. It was agreed that the home should bear the major burden of responsibility to the youth in regard to the achievement of these expectations; the school and church (in that order) were perceived as supporting agencies. Data concerning child and adolescent perceptions confirmed the suggestion that the community (as distinct from family, school, church, etc.) has little direct influence on the youth. This particular study was part of a larger community study of Karribee.

6. Connell, W. F., et al., "Growing Up in an Australian City (Melbourne, Australia; Council for Educational Research, 1957). (ACER Research Series N. 72)

   To study the process of how adolescents arrive at an acceptable normative standard in a society whose normative order is unclear, a sample of 10,000 children between the ages of 13 and 18 was taken. The sample was representative in regard to age, sex, living area, and school or occupational group for the universe of 100,000 adolescents, living in Sydney. The instruments used were questionnaires, interviews, diary records, and written memoirs of college students. It was found that younger adolescents are heavily influenced by parents, teachers, and other adults. As they grow older the peer group becomes increasingly more important; a majority drop out of school at age 15. The importance of social skills and personality factors was shown, especially in regard to friendship formation. The urban Australian adolescent experiences three crucial periods or reorientation: (1) at puberty, (2) upon entering secondary school, and (3) at public examination time when a vocational choice is imminent. The typical Western adult-child role conflict is prominent and is increasing. Rather conservative behavior is expected of the older adolescent and young adults in Sydney. Somewhat detailed information concerning the adolescent's life style is also included in the article, e.g., his reading habits, intellectual interests, and entertainment preferences.

7. Crane, R. R., "A Note on Pre-Adolescent Gangs." *Australian Journal of Psychology*, III (1951), 43-46.

It was suggested that, contrary to a widely held view, pre-adolescent gangs are not exclusively the product of subnormal environments. A questionnaire was given to 90 men at the Armedale Teachers' College and it was found that 71 of these students had been members of 66 different gangs. The gangs had an average membership of 7, ranging in age from 9-13 years. "The essence of the behavior of boys' gangs is a testing of the restrictions placed by adult mores upon the behavior of the boys (e.g., against swearing, stealing, fighting, etc.)" The gangs are predatory and are typified by systems of mores that tend to produce in-group identification and cohesiveness. The author feels that the socially unacceptable behavior patterns of the gang will not necessarily persist into adulthood, and that gang membership may contribute significantly to a member's socialization.

8. Cunningham, K. S. (ed.), *The Adjustment of Youth* (Victoria: Melbourne University Press, 1951).

To "investigate the agencies and instrumentalities operating in the United Kingdom and North America to assist young people to realize to the utmost their potentialities for physical, mental and moral development while preparing themselves to fill worthy places as adult members of society" was the object of this study by four Australian investigators who were attempting to gain insight that would assist those in Australia concerned with the problems of youth. The four investigators each spent from five to seven months in North America and England. They utilized existing research and historical accounts of education, recreation, welfare, vocational guidance, and employment policies. In addition they interviewed and observed in the field. Their primary concern was the 15-19 age group. Each investigator represented a general area of competence and experience: (1) education, (2) health and physical recreation, (3) vocational guidance and youth employment. Among the conclusions reached were, that although more attention should be given to those youth unfit for apprenticeship programs, the English system of apprenticeship, whereby a young employee continues his schooling (often at the request of the employer) on a part-time basis while working, has a definite value. The two-class system of English education was judged as having a tendency to divide the community in an unhealthy manner; the American system was preferred. It was suggested that social case work is beginning to supply insights into the process of influencing youth, whereas the authority of parents, the school, the church, and employers has become increasingly weaker. Finally, it was concluded that, "Work in the youth field cannot, or should not, be monopolized by public servants however free from the bureaucratic spirit." "Government machinery should be established only when voluntary action cannot cope with procedures agreed upon as desirable for all."

9. Earle, Margaret J., "Rakau Children," *Victoria University of Wellington Publications in Psychology*, 11 (1958).
10. Flanagan, E. J., *Report on Austrian Youth Activities* (Washington 25, D.C.: Operations Branch, Office of the Adjutant General, U.S. Department of the Army, 1948).
11. Harwood, E., "Social Development in the Queensland Adolescent," *Australian Journal of Education* (July, 1959), 77-87.
12. Mulligan, D. G., "Maori Adolescence in Rakau," *Victoria University College Publications in Psychology*, 9 (1957).
13. National Fitness Council of South Australia, Associated Youth Commission, *The Youth Book*, 1946.
14. The National Fitness Council of Victoria, *Youth Leadership Training*, A Survey of Selected Voluntary Youth Leadership Training Courses Held by the National Fitness Council of Victoria During 1956 (Melbourne: 1961).
15. Oddie, N. M. and D. Spearritt, *Some Activities of Australian*

Adolescents V. I, Educational Activities of Victorian Adolescents (Melbourne: Australian Council for Educational Research, 1958).

16. Oddie, N. M. and D. Spearritt, *Some Activities of Australian Adolescents,* V. II (The Occupational Activities of Victorian Adolescents (Melbourne: Australian Council for Educational Research, 1958).
17. Oddie, N. M. and D. Spearritt, *Some Activities of Australian Adolescents,* V. III, "Some Occupational Characteristics of Victorian Male Adolescents" (Melbourne: Australian Council for Educational Research, 1959).
18. Scott, W. J., *Reading, Film and Radio Tastes of High School Boys and Girls* (Australian Council for Educational Research, 1947).
19. "A Sudden Surge" (In the Numbers of Young People between the Ages of 15 and 24; Australia), *IPA Review,* XIII (October/December, 1959), 117-122.
20. "Sydney Boom in Youth Work: Teenage Cabaret Fills Need in Modern Life," *Inter-Church News,* VI (August, 1961), 5.
21. Taft, Ronald, "The Social Grading of Occupations in Australia," *British Journal of Sociology,* IV (1953), 181-188.

To study the social grading of occupations in Australia, a self-administering questionnaire was distributed. The questionnaire required that the subject rate each of 20 occupations on a five-point scale. A strong hierarchy of occupations was found to be common in the minds of the individuals included in the sample. The sample included individuals from widely separated areas with varying ages and occupational backgrounds. The findings were compared with American and English studies, but no consistent direction was found in the differences. However, farmers were given higher status, whereas commercial travelers were given lower status in both Australia and England as compared with America.

22. Taft, Ronald, "Some Sub-Cultural Variables in Family Structure in Australia," *Australian Journal of Psychology,* IX (1957), 69-90.

This paper is mainly an elaboration of the Melbourne UNESCO studies in which family organization was studied especially in regard to sex, socio-economic class, type of school attended, religion, and geographical area. "The questionnaire consists of 31 household activities grouped in terms of their manifest content: wife's household area, husband's household area, child care and control, social activities and economic activities. . . . For each activity the subjects were asked to indicate:

whose job it is, who helps with it, who wouldn't ever do it, who decided when or how it is to be done, and whether the parents disagree regarding when and how it is done." The sample was 80 sixth-grade children in two state schools, and the data was collected in 1949. It was found that more tension existed in each area except husband's and common household duties for private school families than for state school families. Catholics were higher than Protestants on "both decide and both act" and on "wife decides" and "wife acts." Girls reported the wife more autonomous, whereas boys found the father more dominant. Working-class families were reported to be wife autonomous and wife dominant while middle-class families were reported to be syncratic. In comparison with a sample taken in Perth, the Malbourne family was typified by syncratic cooperation and wife autonomy, whereas the husband dominant structure was more prevalent.

23. "Teaching the Australian Aboriginals to Live in a Modern World," *Illustrated London News*, CCXXXVII (August, 1960), 301.

24. Warner, W. L., "The Family and Principles of Kinship Structure in Australia," *American Sociological Review*, II, 1 (February, 1937), 43-54.

25. Wheeler, D. K., "Popularity among Adolescents in Western Australia and in the United States of America," *The School Review*, LXIX (Spring, 1961), 67-81.

The object of this study was to compare factors contributing to the adolescent's popularity (e.g., personality traits, physical skills, and physical characteristics in America and Western Australia. The American data were drawn from Tyron (*Evaluations of Adolescent Personality by Adolescents*. Monograph of the Society for Research in Child Development, IV, 4, Washington: National Research Council, 1939) and Kuhlen and Lee ("Personality Characteristics and Social Acceptability in Adolescence," *Journal of Educational Psychology*, XXXIV, 1943, 321-340). For Western Australia Wheeler chose a sample of 800 adolescents from a variety of secondary schools. Beginning at the sixth-grade age bracket for the boys, the major difference between the two groups is found. Although looks, build, sporting abilities, and enthusiasm were mentioned by both groups, the Australian sample placed a relatively greater emphasis on cognitive abilities and kind, generous, helpful, and sympathetic traits. The same general pattern is followed through the other age brackets with the American group eventually stressing interest in the opposite sex as a popularity trait. For girls, popularity traits were found to be quite similar in both cultures. The younger girls in both groups cited friendliness, enthusiasm, looks, and cognitive abilities. Unlike the boys whose preferences tended to persist over time, the girls eventually began to devalue sporting abilities. It was assumed that, although they were infrequently mentioned, the traits of neatness and tidiness were substituted. (They were probably taken for granted and, therefore, were not mentioned.)

26. Wheeler, D. K., "Development of the Ideal Self in Western Australian Youth," *Journal of Educational Research*, LIV (1961), 163-167.

27. Whiting, J. W. M., *Becoming a Kwoma* (New Haven: Yale University Press, 1941).

NEW GUINEA

1. Mead, Margaret, *Growing Up in New Guinea* (New York: New American Library, 1930).

This book was part of an effort to investigate the "original nature of the child." With special emphasis on education and personality development the author has written an account of her experiences among the Manus, a closely knit, patriarchal, and primitive society in New Guinea. The child's world is quite isolated from the world of adults. Although the boys are given somewhat casual instruction in swimming, canoeing, and fishing they are left pretty much to themselves. The child's world is one of the supernatural, other children, and usually unprescribed activity. At puberty the sexes are separated. The boys continue to exist together and enjoy a wide range of activities, but the girls, after the puberty ceremony, are relegated to an even more severe form of isolation until they marry. The boy at this time is more or less systematically taught how to be a member of a boat's crew, to be a "police boy," or a child's nurse. The adult who fosters a child in Manus usually attempts to instill his attitudinal biases and predilections within the child. The foster father plays a significant role here, and the relationship is characterized by tenderness and by the absence of excessive domineering. A cause of confusion among the girls is the break-up of this relationship when they reach the age of eight. Another cause of confusion and/or disorganization among both sexes is that there are no religious leaders or historical and mythical personalities; there are few great differences in rank among the members of the Manus society. Eventually the child becomes an adult, participating member of the society, and ". . . The Manus baby, born into the world without motor habits, without speech, without any definite forms of behavior, with neither beliefs nor enthusiasms, has become the Manus adult in every particular. No cultural item has slipped out of the stream of tradition which the elders transmit in this irregular unorganized fashion to their children, so unpremeditated, so often definitely hostile to its ultimate ends."

NEW ZEALAND AND OCEANIA

1. Adcock, Cyril J., et al., "An Analysis of Maori Scores on the Wechsler Bellevue," *Australian Journal of Psychology,* V (June, 1954), 16-29.
2. Ausubel, David P., A *Comparative Study of Aspirational Traits among Maori and European Adolescents in New Zealand* (Wellington, New Zealand: Victoria University, Department of Psychology, 1957).
3. Ausubel, David P., *Maori Youth* (Wellington, Prince Milburn: Victoria University of Wellington Publications in Psychology, N. 14, 1961).
4. Ausubel, David P., *Peer Group and Adolescent Conformity in the New Zealand Cultural Setting* (Wellington Lectures, Association for the Study of Childhood, 1958).
5. Ausubel, David P., "Race Relations in New Zealand," *Landfall,* XII (1958), 233-246.
6. Ausubel, David P., "Acculturative Stress in Modern Maori Adolescence," *Child Development,* XXXI, 4 (December, 1960), 617-631.

To study the psychological mechanisms operating within the Maori adolescent as he experiences acculturation and its accompanying stresses, a sample of 50 Maori male adolescents was compared with a sample of 50 Pakeha * male adolescents; both samples included individuals from rural and urban areas. A variety of instruments were used: structured academic and vocational interviews, a test of occupational prestige needs, the Achievement Imagery Test, the Vocational Tenacity Test, and the Responsiveness to Prestige Incentive Test; teachers' ratings of motivational and aspirational traits and participant observations at community functions were also employed. "The major finding of this study was the much greater similarity between Maori and Pakeha pupils with respect to their expressed educational and vocational aspirations than with respect to those factors necessary for the internalization and implementation of these aspirations, namely, underlying needs and motivations for achievement, supportive traits, and perceived pressures and opportunities for academic and occupational success." Due to exposure to, and observation of, the Pakeha culture, the differences between rural and urban Maori are increasing, whereas the Maori-Pakeha differences are becoming smaller.

* *Pakeha* is the Maori word for "white man."

7. Ball, Douglas E., "Education of the Maori," *Educational Leadership*, X (Washington: October, 1952), 53, 55, 57.

During the period from 1844 to 1931 the British policy concerning the education of the Maori was to make available a European education. A survey revealed that the Maori were not assimilating the European habits and usages as planned, and a new policy was begun. If education was to assist the Maori, it ". . . should both give attention to the cultural inheritance of the Maori and understand his present predicament and help him to meet the needs arising therefrom." The results of this 1931 policy may be summarized as follows: (1) There was an increase in vitality and working spirit. (2) More Maori students are seeking education beyond the elementary level with increasing number attending Teachers Training Colleges. (3) Maori girls are also seeking higher education with more entering the nursing and dental professions. (4) There has been a rural to urban movement among the youth.

8. Beaglehole, Ernest, "The Maori in New Zealand," *International Labour Review*, LXXVI, 2 (1957), 103-123.
9. Beaglehole, Ernest and P. Beaglehole, *Some Modern Maoris* (Wellington: New Zealand Council of Educational Research, Series N. 25, 1946).
10. Beaglehole, Ernest and James Ritchie, "The Rakau Maori Studies," *Journal of Polynesian Society*, LXVII (1958), 132-154.
11. Best, Elsdon, *The Maori As He Was* (Wellington: Government Printer, 1952).
12. Biggs, Bruce, *Maori Marriage* (Polynesian Society Monography, N. 1: 1960).
13. Biggs, Bruce, "The Structure of New Zealand Maori," *Anthropological Linguistics* (Indiana University), III, 3 (March, 1961), 55.
14. Booth, John, "The Maori in Town and Country," *Pacific Viewpoint*, I, 1 (1960), 111-114.
15. Booth, John, "A Modern Maori Community," in Freman, J. P. and W. R. Geddes, *Anthropology in the South Seas* (New Plymouth, New Zealand: 1959).

16. Borne, W. D., "Some Economic and Social Implications of Maori Population Growth in New Zealand," *Journal of Polynesian Society*, LXX, 4 (December, 1961), 410-418.

17. *Boy's Brigade* (NZ), "All About the Life Boys" (Wellington: 1962).

18. Brown, L. B., "The 'Day at Home' in Wellington, New Zealand," *Journal of Social Psychology*, L (1959), 189-206.

19. Buck, P. H., *The Coming of the Maori* (Wellington: Whitcombes and Tombs, 1949).

20. Buck, P. H., *Vikings of the Sunrise* (Now republished as *Vikings of the Pacific*) (University of Chicago, paperback series [Phoenix Books], 1960).

21. "Confessions of a Bodgie," *New Zealand Parent and Child*, VI, 3 (May/June, 1958), 18-19.

22. Conglaton, A. A., "Social Class Consciousness in Adolescents," *Victoria University College Publications in Psychology*, 3 (1952), 107.

To study this phenomenon of class consciousness a 35-item questionnaire was administered to 100 male New Zealand secondary school pupils. Analysis of the responses revealed that a well-defined social class consciousness existed among these students. However, the classes themselves were not able to be explicitly defined. The criteria used by the students to indicate class membership were, in general, the following (ranked in order of decreasing importance): (1) wealth (e.g., money, property, and income), (2) occupation, (3) title, and (4) residential area.

23. Cross, I. R., *The God Boy; A Novel* (New York: Harcourt, Brace and Company, Inc., 1957.

24. Culliford, S. G., *New Zealand Scouting; the First Fifty Years*, 1908-1958 (Wellington: Boy Scouts Association of New Zealand, 1958).

25. Currie, Sir George (chairman), "Maori Education," *Report of the Commission on Education in New Zealand* (Government printed, 1962), 401-437.

26. Dale, William Sydney John, *The Maori of New Zealand, or Whither the Maori*. Ph.D. Thesis, Yale, 1936.

27. Dale, William Sydney John, *The Missionary Impact—Its Educational Effects on the Maori*, M.A. Thesis, Yale, 1934.

28. Davies, F. R. J., "Problems in Pacific Islands Education," *Overseas Education,* XXXI (July, 1959), 69-76.

Describes educational administration of the Pacific Islands under New Zealand jurisdiction, discussing common problems of financial resources, adaptation of education to needs of the people, schooling in the vernacular, and the shortage of textbooks and reading materials.

29. Douglas, R. and J. M. Stavely, "Blood Groups in Maoris," *Journal of Polynesian Society,* LXIX, 1 (March, 1960).

30. Earle, Margaret J., *Rakau Children from Six to Thirteen Years, Publications in Psychology* N. 11, (Wellington: Victoria University of Wellington, 1958).

31. "Education and Child Labour in New Zealand," *International Labour Review,* I (October, 1944), 526-528.

32. Firth, Raymond, *Economics of the New Zealand Maori* (Wellington.: Government printed, 1959) (first published 1929).

33. Fitt, A. B., "An Experimental Study of Children's Attitude to School in Auckland, New Zealand," *British Journal of Educational Psychology,* XXVI (1956), 25-30.

34. Gillespie, J. M. and G. W. Allport, *Youth's Outlook on the Future* (Garden City, New York: Doubleday and Company, Inc., 1955). (1,819 case studies from 10 countries)

This was a successful pilot study the object of which was to examine the attitudes of college students in ten countries toward their individual and collective futures; no hypotheses were tested. At least partial answers were sought to three questions: (1) "How do youth in various countries view the future?" (2) "Do young people in different countries view their futures in essentially the same way?" and (3) "Is international social research at the present time practicable and beneficial?" A cross--cultural analysis of attitudes, aspirations, and moral values among students from the United States, New Zealand, Egypt, Mexico, France, Italy, Germany, Japan, Israel, and South Africa was attempted by administering a questionnaire—including both multiple-choice and open-ended questions—to 100 males and 100 females from each country. (This was the goal; the attempts occasionally fell short.) In addition an essay entitled "Autobiography: From Now to 2000 A.D." was required from respondent. Some of the similarities discovered were: "Familism is a universal foundation for individual and group life." "Basic moral values and ethical codes of conduct are everywhere prized." "Most students (Africaners excepted) . . . desire to see greater quality between white and colored races." "Most youth regard war as needless and preventable . . . [but are] . . . pessimistic as to the possibility of avoiding a third world conflict." There were, of course, a great number of national differences, but the authors conclude that, ". . . it is a wholesome corrective to note that these differences may be dramatic figures etched upon a ground of basic resemblance."

35. Havighurst, Robert J. and Donald V. MacDonald, "Development of the Ideal Self in New Zealand and American Children," *Journal of Educational Research*, XLIX (1955), 263-273.

36. Hawthorn, Harry Bertram, *The Maori; A Study in Acculturation*, Memoir. N. 64 (Menasha, Wisconsin: American Anthropological Association, 1944).

37. Holst, Halvor, "The Maori Child's First Year at Post-Primary School," *Education*, VI (Wellington: November, 1957), 45-48.

38. Holst, Halvor, "The Maori Schools in Rural Education: A Historical Survey," *Education*, VII (Wellington: March, 1958), 53-59.

39. Hunn, J. K., *Report on the Department of Maori Affairs* (Usually referred to as the *Hunn Report*) (Wellington: Government printed, 1961).

40. Jackson, Patrick M. (ed.), *Maori and Education; or the Education of the Natives of New Zealand and Its Dependencies* (Wellington, 1931), 481.

41. Keehn, J. D. and E. T. Prothro, "National Preferences of University Students from 23 Nations," *Journal of Psychology*, XLII (1956), 283-294.

". . . To demonstrate the feasibility of cross-national research on international attitudes," questionnaires were given to college or university students aged from 16 to 25 from 30 countries. The 30 national groups were listed on the questionnaire, and questions involving a preference among the countries were asked. In general, and in agreement with other research, the British, Swiss, and Americans were most preferred. The Swiss seemed to enjoy the most general popularity. English-speaking countries tended to prefer Britain, Canada, New Zealand, Australia, and America; the Japanese, Egyptians, Israelis, and Turks were rejected. Students from the Arab-Mediterranean area preferred the Egyptians, Syrians, Germans, and Swiss; they rejected the Turks and Israelis. Western Europeans preferred the Dutch, Finns, Swiss, and Germans, rejecting Middle-Easterners.

42. Keesing, Felix M., "Aftermath of Renaissance: Restudy of a Maori Tribe," *Human Organization*, XXI (Spring, 1962), 3-9.

This article is a description of the effects of a renaissance or revolution on a geographically marginal group—the Ngati-porou, a Maori tribe inhabiting the east coast of New Zealand. Relying upon his observations and written documents, the author notes that the general tendency has been for the tide of events to sweep past them, but a minimal amount of solidarity has been maintained, largely through the efforts of their leader, a university-educated Maori who modeled his role on that of a tribal war leader. Although Maori schools were provided which reinforced traditional Maori values and the leader instituted intertribal sports competitions, the period from 1939 to 1950 was characterized by an out-migration among the youth; the population has become increasingly comprised of preadults and older adults.

43. Keesing, Felix M., *The Changing Maori* (New Plymouth, New Zealand: 1928).

44. Lee, J. A., "Children of the Not-So-Poor," *New Zealand Listener*, XLIII, 1099:4 (September, 1960), 4.

45. Lovell-Smith, H. K., *The Story of the Christchurch Young Women's Christian Association; a Venture With Youth From 1883-1894—1901-1960* (Christchurch: Christchurch Y.W.C.A., 1961).

46. Manning, Arthur E., "Auckland Psychologist Examines the 'Bodgie' Problem," *New Zealand Parent and Child*, VI, 5 (September/October, 1958), 18-19.

47. Manning, Arthur E., *The Bodgie, A Study in Abnormal Psychology* (Wellington: A. H. and A. W. Reed, 1958).

Also, *The Bodgie: A Study in Polynesian Abnormality* (Sydney: Angus and Robertson, 1958).

48. Maxwell, Gabrielle M., "Some Demographic Indications of Population Movement among New Zealand Maoris," *Journal of Polynesian Society*, LXX, 1 (March, 1961), 31-42.

49. Meek, Ronald L., *Maori Problems Today* (Wellington: 1944).

50. Metge, Joan, "Marriage in Modern Maori Society," *Man*, LXII, Article 212.

51. Metge, Joan, "The Urban Maori," Department of Anthropology, University of Auckland, 1953.

52. Metge, Joan and D. Campbell, "The Rakau Maori Studies,"

Journal of the Polynesian Society, LXVII (December, 1953), 353-386.

53. McQueen, H. C., *Vocations for Maori Youth* (Wellington: New Zealand Council for Educational Research, 1945).
54. Mulligan, D. G., *Maori Adolescence in Rakau* (Wellington: Department of Psychology, Victoria University of Wellington, 1957).
55. New Zealand Department of Justice, *Absconders from Penal Institutions* (Wellington: 1961).
56. Ngata, Sir Apirana Turupa, *The Price of Citizenship* (Wellington: 1943).
57. Parsonage, William, "The Education of Maoris in New Zealand," *Journal of the Polynesian Society,* LXV (March, 1956), 5-11.
58. Patrick, M., "Modern Maori Education," *Canadian Geographical Journal,* XXXV (November, 1947), 242-245.

    Attempts have been made to educate the Maori in European ways so that they can understand and appreciate the European elements in their setting. Simultaneously, efforts have been made to help the Maori retain his unique culture and traditions. Relying upon his own observations and a knowledge of the situation's history, the author concludes that both efforts are meeting with success.

59. Pearson, W. H., "Attitudes to the Maori in some Pakeha Fiction," *Journal of Polynesia Society,* LXVII, 3 (September, 1958).
60. Philip, Eileen, *Juvenile Delinquency in New Zealand* (New Zealand Council for Educational Research, 1946).
61. Piddington, Ralph, "Maori Child Welfare: The Cultural Background," *The New Zealand Child Welfare Workers' Bulletin* (October, 1952).
62. Pool, Ian, "Maoris in Auckland," *Journal of the Polynesian Society,* LXX, 1 (March, 1961), 43-66.
63. Riske, M., "Let's Look at Teenagers," *New Zealand Parent and Child,* V, 4 (June, 1957), 4-6.
64. Ritchie, J. E., *The Effect of Technological Change on Four New Zealand Maori Communities* (Research Reports N. 1 and 2) Wellington, 1954-55).
65. Ritchie, J. E., "Human Problems and Educational Change in a Maori Community," *Journal of the Polynesian Society,* LXV, 1 (March, 1956), 13ff.
66. Ritchie, J. E., "Together or Apart: A Note on Urban Maori Resi-

dential References," *Journal of the Polynesian Society*, LXX, 2 (June, 1961)., 194-199.

67. Roe, Noel M., "The Young Maori Beginning His Career," *Education*, VII (Wellington: August, 1961), 195-201.
68. Scott, K. J. (ed.), *Welfare in New Zealand* (Wellington: New Zealand Institute of Public Administration, 1955).
69. Shadbolt, M. F. R., *The New Zealanders; A Sequence of Stories* (Christchurch: Whitecombes and Tombs, 1959).
70. Simpson, S., "Seventeen," *New Zealand Parent and Child*, V, 1 (January/February, 1957), 4.
71. Sutherland, I. L. E., *The Maori People Today* (Wellington: 1940).
72. Sutton-Smith, B., *The Games of New Zealand Children* (Berkeley, Calif.: University of California Press, 1959). (University of California Publications, Folklore Studies, 12)
73. Sutton-Smith, B., *Our Street* (Wellington: Reed, 1950).

    Includes notes on social implications of the story.
74. "Time on Their Hands," *New Zealand Listener*, XXXVI, 908 (January, 1957).
75. Walters, Richard H., "The Intelligence Test Performance of Maori Children: A Cross-Cultural Study," *Journal of Abnormal and Social Psychology*, LVII (1958), 107-14.
76. Wiggs, C. T., "Social Phenomena of the Teenager," *Management* (New Zealand Institute of Management), VI, 8 (November, 1960), 31-33.
77. Williams, John S., *Maori Achievement Motivation* (Wellington: Victoria University Publications in Psychology, N. 13, 1960).
78. Winterbourn, R., "Vocational Guidance in New Zealand," *Occupational Psychology, London*, XIV (1940), 162-174.
79. "Youth Without Purpose," *New Zealand Listener*, XXXIX, 990 (August, 1958), 5.
80. Austen, Leo, "Cultural Changes in Kiriwina," *Oceania*, XVI (September, 1945-June, 1946), 15-60.
81. Geddes, W. R., "Acceleration of Social Change in a Fijian Community," *Oceania*, XVI (September, 1945-June, 1946), 1-14.
82. Guiart, Jean, "Forerunners of Melanesian Nationalism," *Oceania*, XXII (December, 1951), 81-90.
83. Niles, John, "The Kuman People: . . . ," *Oceania*, XXIV, 1-27 and 199.

U.S.S.R. AND SATELLITE NATIONS

ALBANIA

1. Kopalin, I. P., V *strane gornyh orlov: ocerki o molodezi Narodnoj Respubliki Albanii* (*In the Country of Mountain Eagles: Essays on the Youth of the Albanian People's Republic*) (Moskva: Molodaja Gvardija, 1954).

BULGARIA

1. Sanders, I. T., "Communist Dominated Education in Bulgaria: A Study in Social Relationships," *American Slavic and East European Review,* XV (October, 1956), 364-381.

An analysis and discussion of the changes in the educational system of Bulgaria as introduced by the socialist transformation. The comments are based on newspaper accounts, interviews with refugees, and the reports of Radio Free Europe. The traditional Bulgarian school was urban oriented with little emphasis and concern for village affairs. Under the Communists, the school has been oriented toward village affairs and life. The present emphasis is on present achievements and goals rather than past accomplishments.

The conflict between the traditional and the Communist value systems is illustrated in the area of teacher-pupil relations. Under the traditional system the teacher had an undeniably higher status than the student. The present situation does not specify the authority-power relationships. There is particular illustration of this in the cases where non-Communist teachers hold positions of lower status than do their Communist students. Dominant-subordinate pupil-teacher relationships vary with party membership. The pupil is subordinate when both the teacher and the pupil are party members, when the teacher is a member and the student is not, and when both are not members. The pupil is dominant in many cases other than the above, depending on role. Both Communist teachers and students play a greater role in community affairs than those who are not members of the party. In spite of the restrictions imposed on the non-Communist teacher the report indicates that the non-political teacher is better liked, and held to be a better teacher.

In the matter of discipline the pupils tend toward argumentation and the flagrant violation of regulations. This does not apply to the students in the Gymnasia. Activity in political organizations is a necessity of a student contemplating a professional career.

The author notes that non-Communist students have a tendency to establish informal rules and methods for dealing with students suspected of being Communist informers. However in many cases the Communist students have succeeded in overcoming the literate opposition. They have successfully instilled the notion of social isolation to the point where the individual cannot trust his peers. In this position the individual is more easily led into the Communist camp.

2. Simitrov, Georgi, *For Youth* (Sofia: Foreign Languages Press, 1959).

CZECHOSLOVAKIA

1. Davies, Bob, "Pioneer Movement in Czechoslavakia: Social and Economic Conditions of Young People," *North Central European Observer*, II (November 26–December 10, 1949), 290, 302.

2. Dudek, E. E., "A Factor Analysis of a Questionnaire on Political Attitudes of Czechoslovak Students," *Psychological Bulletin*, XXXVI (1939), 637.

A factor analysis of 300 students' scores (based on scale values) resulting from a questionnaire survey of Czechoslovak student political attitudes revealed four factors: Democratic, Nationalistic, Anarchistic, and Tolerance. A second analysis based upon tetrachoric r's between selected items in the same questionnaire failed to show the same factors.

3. A Group of Czech Refugee Students, "The Present Situation in the Universities of Czechoslovakia," *Harvard Educational Review*, XX, 2 (Spring, 1950), 83-90.

This article is a description of how and to what extent the Czechoslovakian academic community has changed since—and as a result of—the Communist takeover in February, 1948. Through so-called "Action Committees" and other arbitrary measures "purification" was attempted: professors were replaced (often by intellectual inferiors), curriculums were altered, students were expelled, and new admission standards were created in order to enhance the Communist position and to discourage resistance. Many former students were relocated in forced labor camps, and the new academic standards reflected a strong political bias, thus making the Communist student's position a secure one. Although at the time of the writing the Communists had not been completely successful, it was estimated that these measures would eventually "take care of" 60 per cent of all of the students in the universities at this time (1950).

4. "International Cooperative Youth Conference" (Prague, Czechoslovakia), *Review of International Cooperation,* XLI (November, 1948), 244-247.

5. Kubat, Daniel, "Social Mobility in Czechoslovakia," *American Sociological Review,* XXVIII (April, 1963), 203-212.

   Utilizing data drawn from demographic and labor statistics and information found in Czechoslovakian publications as well as other secondary sources the author discusses the mobility situation in Czechoslovakia. It is noted that the rate of social change has slowed down within the last decade. This is attributed to intrinsic factors operative in a command economy. Thus, the ideology of Marxism does not favor a mobility ethos but does favor the reduction of status differences between occupations. Of the traditional avenues of mobility only one remains open. This one, education, is also hedged by restrictions which preclude effective mobility channels. The educational system theoretically is open to all, but in effect, the proportion of college students claiming worker parents is only 30 per cent. The financial factor also influences the college career. Thirdly, educational careers are closely linked with formalized ideological identification, a position which workers find difficult to assume. The educational process is also noted as containing, for Czechoslovakian youth, the same dangers and difficulties that youth in all industrialized societies.

6. "O zi vote mladeze u nas a v kapitalistckych zemich" (The Life of Youth in Our Country and in Capitalist Countries), *Odborar,* XI, 9 (May, 1958), 488-592.

7. World Trade Union Conferences of Young Workers, "A Youth Conference Worthy of the International Working Class Movement" (Prague, Czechoslovakia, July 14-20, 1958) (1958), WFTU publication.

EAST GERMANY

1. Dubel, S., "Die Situation der Jugend im kommunistischen Herrschaftssytem der sowjetischen Besatzungszone Deutschlands (The Situation of Youth in the Communist System of Government of the Soviet Occupied Zone of Germany) (Bonn Bundesministerium fur Gesamtdeutsche Fragen, 1957).

2. London, Ivan D., "The Young East German and Soviet Defector:

A Report on Similarities," *Journal of Psychology,* XLIII (1957), 103-109.

3. "Some Student Problems in East German Universities," *World Today,* XIII, 11 (London: November, 1957), 481-489.
4. Suri, S., "Education in Eastern Germany," *Contemporary Review,* CXCII (August, 1957), 96-98.
5. UNESCO, "East Germany's Communist Youth," *Social Justice Review,* LI (January, 1959), 309.
6. Wagner, H. R., "Cultural Sovietization of East Germany," *Social Research,* XXIV (Winter, 1957), 395-426.
7. "Young East-Zone Skeptics: Resume of Public Opinion Survey," *United States High Commander, Germany, Information Bulletin* March, 1952), 7-9.

    Complaints of youth living in the Russian zone of Berlin on the political emphasis in their education.

HUNGARY

1. Arnstein, George E., "Hungarian Dilemma," *NEA Journal,* XLVI (February, 1957) 93-95.

    The author conducted interviews with refugee Hungarian teachers at Camp Kilmer in an attempt to gain perspective on educational conditions behind the Iron Curtain. He reports his findings.

2. "Communist Youth Union of Hungary, Hungarian Youth Movement" (Budapest, Hungary: 1957). Cover Subtitle: 1919-1957 KISZ.
3. Faludy, S., "Hungary: Double Faced Youth," *20th Century,* CLXII (August, 1957), 123-130.
4. Glutman, Henry, "Youth in Revolt: The Failure of Communist Indoctrination in Hungary" (1957) (Studies in Contemporary Communism 2), Free Europe Press.
5. Kobol, J., "A dolgozo Ifjusag Svovetsege munkajanak nehany problemeja" (Some Problems in the Work of the Union of Labor Youth), *Tarsadalmi Szemle,* X, 7-8 (July-August, 1955), 46-61.
6. Pfeiffer, Ede, *Child of Communism* (London: Weidenfeld and Nicolson, 1958).

POLAND

1. Benedict, Ruty, "Child Rearing in Certain European Countries," *American Journal of Orthopsychiatry*, XIX (1949), 342-350.

2. Boroff, David, "Youth League in Central Europe: Old and New Problems of Control," *World Today*, XI (1955), 380-390.

    The Youth Leagues in Czechoslovakia, Poland, and Hungary, supposedly leaders in work and inculcators of patriotism; organized along military lines, are experiencing a decrease of membership (1955) and a general lack of enthusiasm for them by the youth of these nations. Though under direct Party control and though stressing national defense by participation in activities, both military and productive, deemed necessary to national defense the Leagues have not been able to hold youth on the collective farms or keep them in agricultural occupations even while a great need for labor exists in these areas. Despite efforts by the governments and by the leagues to keep youth on the farms youth are becoming dissatisfied with the restrictions of rural life. Many have left agriculture for jobs in industry and cannot be induced to return to the farms voluntarily. The weakness of the Youth Leagues is seen as the greatest contributary factor to this problem.

    ". . . [T]he merciless monotony of work, the endless talk of planning and rigid regimentation," are seen as some of the reasons for the failure of the Leagues to promote a greater enthusiasm for themselves, for the programs which they participate in and for the failure to hold their membership and increase in numbers.

    A lack of romanticism, constant preaching, unfriendly climate, and the drabness of the movement has lead to indifference by many members and to unlawful behavior in many instances.

    A solution to the problems experienced by the Youth Leagues would be: greater enforcement of interest in intellectual affairs, the more realistic presentation of present conditions, more extensive political indoctrination to induce goal-directed behavior and the greater improvement of material benefits.

3. Brzezinska, Zogia, "Dzisiejsza Postawa Zyciowa (Spoleczna) Mlodziezy w Swietle Jej Wlasnych Opinii" (The Attitude of Today's Youth Toward Life), *Psychologia Wychowawcza,* III (1960), 150-166.

4. "Ende der Staatsjugend in Polen (Das)" (The End of the State Youth in Poland), *Ost-Probleme* (Bad Godesberg), IX, 3 (January, 1957), 92-98.

5. Glaj, D., "O sytuacji i perspektywach mlodziezy wiejskiej" (The Situation and Future of Rural Youth), *Nowe Drogi,* IX, 11 (November, 1955), 75-93.

6. "He and She: The Manners and Morals of Poland's Youth," *East Europe,* IX (November, 1960), 26-32.

7. Hiscocks, Richard, "Education in Poland," *International Journal,* XIV, 4 (Autumn, 1959), 259-271.

8. Jordan, Z., "Kluby mlodej inteligencji w Polsce" (Young Intellectuals' Clubs in Poland), *Kultura,* 4 (Paris: April, 1957), 81-88.

9. Jozefowicz, Z., et al., "Studenci: mity i rzeczywistosc" (Students: Myths and Reality), *Przeglad Kulturalny* 29 (Warszawa: 1958), 1, 3.

10. Kaplinski, J., "Wiecej uwagi mlodziezy" (More Attention to Youth), *Nowe Drogi* (New Paths), III (Warsaw: March, 1951), 77-78.

11. Karpinski, R., "Gdy biora nas za slowo (wyniki badan sociologicznych wsrod studentow)" (When We Are Taken Literally [The Results of Sociological Research Among Students]), *Odra,* 40 (1958), 1, 12.

12. Klimowicz, Tadeusz, *Psychologia dziecka wiejskiey na tle ogolnej psychologii rozwoju dzieci i mladziezy* (The Psychology of the Country Child on the Background of the Developmental Psychology of Children and Youth) (Warsawa: Spoldzielnia wydownicza, "Chlopski Swiat," 1948).

13. Kowal, Czestow, "O Pogladach spoleczno-moralugch mlodziezy licealnej" (About the Social and Moral Opinions of Graduates of Secondary Schools), *Psychologia Wychowawcza,* II (1959), 34-50.

The author presents the results of polls regarding the opinions of graduates of two secondary schools (83 people) on the subject of certain social and moral problems. The purpose of the poll was to find out whether opinions—voiced during the last years in the Polish daily press and in periodicals to the effect that contemporary youth is demoralized, without any ideals, indifferent toward social matters and deprived of any valuable ambitions—are correct. The author of the article gave the above-mentioned accusations in the form of general statements, expressing a negative attitude toward a number of moral and social values and submitted them to the graduates of secondary schools, asking them to present arguments justifying their correctness or incorrectness. These statements were as follows: "In our times it is not worth while to try to be decent and honest." "A man lives to enjoy life and not in order to live a sensible life and to accomplish something useful." "In no circumstances and for nothing is it worth while to risk one's life." "It is no use to be interested in politics." "It is no use to be concerned about matters that keenly interest society." "Socialism is a less perfect social and political system than capitalism." The overwhelming majority of those investigated rejected the life principles suggested by these statements, supplying convincing arguments for their attitude of a moral and a social nature. From an analysis of the material it results that a negative attitude to the above-mentioned statements was voiced by a considerably larger percentage of girls than boys and by a relatively larger percentage of youth of worker and peasant origin than of those from the intelligentsia.

14. Kowalski, W., *Mlodziez polska w walce o nowa wies* (*Polish Youth in the Struggle of the New Village*) (Warszawa: Iskry, 1955).

15. Kapkowska, S., "The Influence of Co-Education on Erotic Interests of Adolescent Boys," *Psychologia Wychowawcza,* 4 (1960), 419-431.

The purpose of this study was to investigate the influence of coeducation on erotic interests of adolescent boys. Subjects consisted of 100 boys who were enrolled at a coeducational school and 100 boys who attended a boys' school. The subjects were well matched with respect to such variables as age and socioeconomic background. In order to obtain information about their erotic interests, the boys were instructed to write essays on the following problems: (1) an attempt at a personal characteristic; (2) my ideas of my life in 3 to 5 years time; (3) experiences I shall not forget. To ensure the absolute spontaneity of any erotic associations, the problems were phrased deliberately in a neutral way. The findings were that interest in sex is much greater at a boys' school than at a coeducational school. At the boys' school reference to sex was found in 75 per cent of the essays written on the first subject, 78 per cent in the essays on subject 2, and 85 per cent in those on subject 3. On the other hand, at the coeducational school the corresponding figures were 32, 26, and 34 per cent. Also, the study revealed that 8 per cent of the students at the boys' school mentioned sexual intercourse, while only 3 per cent of those attending the coeducational school made this reference.

16. "The Manners and Morals of Poland's Youth," *East Europe,* IX (November, 1960), 26-32.

In this discussion of youth in Poland it is noted that the

prevalence of changing values of sex and other social attitudes may not be as drastic as has been noted. The church still exerts a great influence among the youth. The attitudes toward sex are noted as based on traditional fear rather than traditional morality.

17. Mazur, F., "Opracy partii usrod mlodziezy" (Party Work With the Youth), *Zycie Partii* (*Party Life*), IX (Warsaw: September, 1950), 9.

18. Mekarski, S., "The Young Generation in Present-Day Poland," *Polish R.*, I, 2-3 (April-September, 1956), 22-40.

19. Nagurska-Rosenthal, "O Ludyzmie Mlodyiezy" (On the Extra-Curricular Activities of Youth), *Zdrowie Psych*, II (2-4), (1947), 120-122.

20. Nowak, Irena and Stefan, "Poland: Meeting on a Middle Ground," *The Student in Society. News Bulletin*, XXXIV, 38-41. (New York: Institute of International Education, Jan., 1959).

The authors conducted a survey among 836 Warsaw students (representing all branches of higher education) asking such questions as: "In your opinion in which areas of economic activity should private initiative be allowed without restriction?" "Would you want the world to move toward some form of Socialism?" and inquiring about students' religious beliefs and life goals.

21. Nowak, S., "Egalitarian Attitudes of Warsaw Students," *American Sociological Review*, XXV (April, 1960), 219-231.

Nowak tests the hypothesis that responses to questions concerning economic equality are correlated with self-interest of the responding person. He attempts to show the relation of the students' self-interest to the socio-professional standing of the students' parents, family income, and his own income expectations.

The sample is taken from students at the University of Warsaw, Polytechnical School, and other institutions. 836 persons were selected with 732 participating. The questionnaire stressed anonymity.

The original hypothesis concerning the correlation of self-interest and egalitarian attitudes was supported when self-interest was measured by occupational or income stratification of the students' parents as well as when measured by the income expectations of the students themselves. The results were elaborated by the introduction of several test variables. It was then found that: (1) attitudes change over time—the role of family background decreases and the role of income expectation increases over time; (2) the character of the relationship between family background and egalitarianism is influenced by the type of personal contact and the degree of the students' communication with his family; (3) constancy of egalitarian attitudes is dependent on the socio-occupational group of the respondent and is higher for the higher status groups.

22. Pilicz, S. and E. Wasilewski, "Niektore zagadnienia socjalne i-kulturalne z zycia studentow Politechniki Warszawskiej" (Some Social and Cultural Problems in the Life of the Students of the Warsaw Polytechnical Institute), *Zycie Szkoly Wyzszej*, 2 (1958), 121-127.

23. Praga, Rafal (ed.), *People's Poland and Her Youth* (Warsaw, Poland: Ksiazka i Wiedza Ag, 1951).

    Published on the occasion of the Third World Youth Festival, Berlin. Pictorial record of life in Poland today with special reference to the youth of the country and the Union of Polish youth.

24. Scheidlinger, S., "Comparative Study of the Boy Scout Movement in Different National and Social Groups," *American Sociological Review*, XIII (December, 1948), 739-750.

    In this 1948 discussion Scheidlinger attempts to show how the institution of scouting has become a tool for indoctrination of the youth into desirable behavior patterns of the particular nation. The methods and objectives of the international Boy Scout movement are influenced by the national and cultural interests of the particular nation. The author notes the ways the scout program has been utilized and examines the Boy Scout Alliance of Poland (prior to 1939) and the Boys Scouts of America. In addition he notes the Jewish Scout movements of Poland and the Polish Scout organizations in the United States.

    He notes that since 1922 the emphasis on brotherhood and international good will has been offset by a tendency to glorify one's own country within the scout movement. It is noted further, that, within the United States, the absence of a national religion has been offset by the major denominations' support of the movement, a support which, in itself, has attempted to infuse scouting with religious education. In Poland the relations between church and state have been such that religious and ethnic minorities have been excluded from the scouting program. Scouting in Poland is directly related to and supervised by the government. The Polish Scout organizations in the United States have been used to maintain the ties between Poland

and second generation Poles while still retaining loyalty to the United States. In Poland, however, the Zionist Scout movement is seen as "outposts of passive resistance against the regime."

25. Sherman, George, "Poland's Angry and Un-angry Young Men," *Problems of Communism,* VII (May/June, 1958), 30-38.

26. Staar, R. F., "Regimentation of Youth in Satellite Poland," *Southwestern Social Science Quarterly,* XXXVII (June, 1956), 7-19.

    A discussion of Communist youth organizations in Poland. It is noted that about 38 per cent of the total population are targets of Communist youth policies. Voluntary organizations are available to the youth from the age of five to twenty-five. All youth between the ages of 16 and 20 are required to belong to an organization, namely the Service to Poland organization. It is noted that after the liberation of Poland the Scout movement was infiltrated with Communists and assumed the name Union of Polish Pioneers. The functions of these groups is service to the country, but political indoctrination is very prevalent and pervasive.

27. Szczepanski, J., "Mlodziez we wspolczesnym swiecie" (Youth in the Modern World). *Nowa Szkola,* 9 (1958), 1-11.

28. Wojciechowski, K., "Zainteresowania umyslowe mlodziezy pracujacej w miescie i na wsi" (Intellectual Material Interest of Young Workers in the City and in the Country), *Kultura i spoleczenstwo,* 3 (Warszawa: July-September, 1960), 141-161.

29. Wojtas, S., *Wsrod uczniow: o pracy organizacji AMP w szkolach* (Among Fellow-students: The Work of the Union of Polish Youth in the Schools) (Warszawa: Iskrv, 1954).

30. "Youth in Ferment: A Survey of Current Problems in Poland, Czechoslovakia and Hungary," *News of the Iron Curtain* (October, 1956), 16-26 (November, 1956), 19-27; *East Europe,* XXVI (January, 1957).

31. "Youth Leagues in Central Europe: Old and New Problems of Control" (By the Communist Parties in Czechoslovakia, Hungary and Poland), *World Today,* XI (September, 1955), 280-290.

32. Zebrowska, Maria, "Wplyw Wojny na Przestepcyosc Nieletnich" (The Influence of War on Juvenile Delinquency), *Psychologia Wychowawcza,* XII, 4 (1947), 12-26.

    Report on the Geneva conference on juvenile delinquency organized in 1947 by the International Union of Care for Children.

The findings are that there was a 100 per cent to 200 per cent increase in delinquency during the war years. Reasons and remedies are given.

ROMANIA

1. Marinescu, Ion, "Steeling a New Youth in Romania," *Rumanian Review*, N. 7, 8 (1948), 80-84.
2. Mot, G., et al., *Contributii la istoria organizatiei marxisteleniniste de tineret din Romania* (Contributions toward the History of the Marxist-Leninist Youth Organization in Rumania) (Bucuresti: Editura tineretului, 1959).

U.S.S.R.

1. Ahl, Frances N., "The Youth Movement in Soviet Russia," *High School Quarterly*, XXIV (Athens, Georgia: April, 1936), 183-188.
2. Alexandrov, A. D., "Let There Be More Enthusiasts Among Students," *The Soviet Review*, III (March, 1962), 19-27.

   Though the article is mainly concerned with a plea for greater enthusiasm for scientific thought and activity among students, Alexandrov concentrates upon weaknesses existing in the University programs of a curricular nature. He feels that students are overloaded with work, that they are not sufficiently stimulated by their professors and that not enough emphasis is placed on individual study and research. Too much emphasis, he feels, is placed on merely passing exams and getting through the school experience at the lowest possible level with a minimum of work. He feels that the system of education is at fault, however, and not the individual students.

   Conclusions: ". . . [S]ometimes Komsomol activity is counterposed to study and student research; the best students shy away from the work of the Komsomol, calling its leaders 'Komsomol actives.' "

   The Komsomol seems to be more concerned with the students' recreational and social activities rather than stimulating them in their work. Often the student's specialty is considered "unromantic" and the emphasis is placed on the concept of physical and material work as being the only romantic and heroic work. The author concludes that scientific and creative work is ". . . full of inner romance," and ". . . often more difficult than the heroic exploit which calls for only brief effort of will."

3. Alexandrova, Vera, "Soviet Youth in Life and Literature," *Problems of Communism*, VIII (July/August, 1959), 30-38.

4. Alt, Herschel and Edith, *Russia's Children* (New York: Bookman Associates, 1959).

Problem: To determine how Soviet child rearing differs from that in the United States.

The authors traveled to the Soviet Union and there interviewed children and persons involved with child rearing. They also observed where possible, both institutionalized and non-institutionalized child-rearing practices where possible.

Part I of the book deals with the author's various experiences in arranging their trip to the USSR and their experiences in traveling in the USSR with their perceptions and observations of Soviet Life. Part II is concerned with "The Child and the State."

Though no section of the book is devoted specifically to adolescent behavior, adolescent behavior is included throughout the book in the discussion of the Soviet socialization process.

The main theme of Soviet education and of Soviet life is goal-directed behavior on the national level. All organized and many unorganized activities in which the child and adolescent are involved, are, in some way, correspondent to the Soviet philosophy and to the Soviet goals. The adolescent is greatly influenced by the fairly rigid restrictions placed on his behavior and on his life goals. There is little uncertainty, concerning goal-directed behavior, among Soviet adolescents and those showing deviant behavior have, according to Soviet philosophy, been neglected at some point in the education and upbringing either at home or at school.

The main conclusion reached by the authors is that more research and study has to be done of the Soviet child-rearing system for adequate understanding of it by Westerners.

5. Ambler, E., "Soviet Boarding School," *American Slavic Review*, XX (April, 1961), 237-252.

6. Anonymous Soviet Student, "Ferment among the Youth," Excerpts from a letter first published (in translation) in *The Nation* (April, 1957), 297. Reprinted in Alex Inkeles and Kent Geiger (eds.), *Soviet Society: A Book of Readings* (Boston: Houghton Mifflin Company, 1961), 238-239.

A first-person account of a student movement (informal) at Moscow State University during which the students raised significant questions concerning the Hungarian revolt, questions which could not be answered by the professor in charge. The events following the questioning led to the suspension of the course and a victory of the general student body over the Komsomol organization.

7. Arden, J., "Teddy Boys of Dniepropetrovsk," *Spectator*, CXCIII (October, 1954), 459.

8. Averbach and Bulitov, *The Act of April 7th and the Struggle with Crime among the Young* (A manuscript prepared for publication by the Institute for Criminal Research, at the Attorney-General of the RSFSR and the Supreme Court of the USSR, 1935).

9. Barkeley, R., "Effect of Soviet Propaganda," *Contemporary Review*, CXCV (February, 1959), 105-107.

10. Beier, Helen and Raymond A. Bauer, "Oleg: a Member of the Soviet 'Golden Youth,'" *Journal of Abnormal and Social Psychology*, LI (1955), 139-145.

11. Benedict, Ruth, "Child Rearing in Certain European Countries," *American Journal of Orthopsychiatry*, XIX (1949), 342-350.

12. Bereday, George F., *The Politics of Soviet Education* (New York: Frederick A. Praeger, Inc.).

13. Bereday, George F., William W. Brickman, and Gerald H. Read (eds.), *The Changing Soviet School* (Boston: Houghton Mifflin Company, 1960).

14. Bermann, Nathan, "Juvenile Delinquency, the Family, and the Court in the Soviet Union," *The American Journal of Sociology*, XLII, 5 (March, 1937), 682-692.

    Deals with official Soviet programs concerned with delinquency control.

15. Blagonadezhian, L. V., "O Formirovanii Otnosheniia Shkol'nikov k Trudu" (On the Formation of School Children's Attitude to Work), *Voprosy Psikhologii*, V, 5 (1959), 40-51.

16. Blair, K. H., "The New Generation in Russia: Seeking and Questioning," *Tablet*, CCXIV (September, 1960), 796-797, 814.

17. Blake, Patricia, "Russia: The Scientific Elite," *Reporter*, XVII (November, 1957), 17-19.

18. Blatin, A. J., *Die Freundschaft und Kameradschaft der sowjetischen Jugend* (The Friendship and Fellowship of Soviet Youth) (Berlin: Verlag Neues Leben, 1955).

19. Blos, Peter, *On Adolescence, A Psychoanalytic Interpretation* (New York: The Free Press, 1957).

    A short excerpt from Blos' book discussing the situation where the state turns the rebelliousness of youth to its own advantage.

When youth is ". . . aggrandized and given caste status by the leaders of government," as in the Soviet Union, the channels for the expression of rebellious feelings found in a democratic and capitalistic society are not needed. In this situation youth does not release its rebellious feelings against the established order, but associates with it and "these heirs of the regime will grow up to become conservative and live in rigid identification with the past order."

If the regime is defeated, however, ". . . a loss of identity (devaluation of narcissistic identification with the past order) will mobilize restitutive measures." This happened in Italy after the defeat of fascism. Youth who had been involved in the regime ". . . turned either to new, mostly radical, political ideologies, to self-deception (denial), to self-degradation, or to cynicism, delinquency, and criminality."

20. Boiter, Albert, *The Khrushchev School Reform* (New York: American Committee for Liberation, 1959). (Available from the Committee, 1657 Broadway, New York, N.Y., 10019).

Outlines the educational heritage from Tsarist Russia, the present Soviet system, and proposed features of the future educational program.

21. Boldyrev, N. I., *O moral'nom oblike sovetskogo molodezi* (Moral Features of Soviet Youth) (Moscow: Molodaja Gvardija, 1954).

22. Brown, J. E., "Training of Youth in the Soviet Union" [Efficient and tested Communist indoctrination methods; youth organizations and programs], *Catholic World*, CLXXVI (January, 1953), 256-262.

23. Brown, Rex V. (ed.), "Recreation and Social Life at Moscow University," in Alex Inkeles and Kent Geiger (eds.), *Soviet Society: A Book of Readings* (Boston: Houghton Mifflin Company, 1961), 448-453.

24. Burg, D., "Soviet Youth's Attitude to the Communist Regime," *Bulletin of the Institute for the Study of the U.S.S.R.* IV, 4 (Munich: April, 1957), 41-57.

25. Burg, D., "Soviet Youth's Opposition to the Communist Regime," *Bulletin*, IV (Munich: May, 1957), 44-50.

26. Burg, D., "The Voice of a Dissenter," *Harper's*, XXII, 1332 (May, 1961), 122.

Part of a special supplement in *Harper's* titled "The Mood of the Russian People."

27. Carlova, Jr., "Bura—A New Russian Madness," *American Mercury*, XC (January, 1960), 97-104.

A description and discussion of the evidence of and possible causes of the deviant behavior, particularly the game of "Bura" of some Russian youth.

The game of Bura, popular with some factions of Russian youth is symoblic of unrest resulting in deviant behavior in the Soviet Union. A possible cause of this behavior and unrest may be the excessive astringency of the communist state which results in a "collective hatred" for the ". . . father state of soul-deadening Communism."

In Bura, which is incorporated into games of chance, the loser agrees to place himself under the complete control of the winner and is obligated to perform any act ordered by the winner, including, if necessary, murder, or submission to homicide.

"Psychologically, the Bura craze seems to be a thrill-seeking venture, an attempt at excitement and color in what is to such a youth an unendurably drab world."

Other symptoms of dissatisfaction with the Soviet system include a passion for Western dress, dancing, etc., which is evident especially among the members of the new bureaucratic aristocracy. The government is attempting to control and eliminate these "fashion fiends" by suppressive measures and by harsh penalties for this deviant behavior.

28. Charques, Richard D., *Soviet Education: Some Aspects of Cultural Revolution* (London: The Hogarth Press, Ltd., 1932).

29. Chebysheva, V. V., O. Z. Galkina, and L. M. Ziubin, "Opodgotovke Uchashchikhsia Srednei Shkolz k Vyboru Professii" (On Readying High School Students for Choice of Vocation), *Voprosy Psikhologii*, V, 5 (1959), 29-39.

30. Chechotkina, Olga, "Soviet and American Women Meet," *Soviet Women*, 3, 1962.

31. Chikin, V. V. and B. A. Grushin, "Confessions of a Generation: Youth Opinion Poll," *The Soviet Review*, II, 11 (November, 1961), 3-24; II, 12 (December, 1961), 47-65.

To discover the nature of and the views expressed by the younger generation of Soviet citizens, and to give youth a chance to "speak for itself."

The sample consisted of 17,446 Soviet youth between the ages of 15 and 30. ". . . [W]ithout exception they represented all social groupings and professions, people who differed widely in character and outlook."

The readers of *Komsomolskaya Pravda* were asked to answer 12 questions related to attitudes and opinions held by them about themselves and their generation. Questions of a biographical nature were included and a deadline of 20 days was set for replies.

Criticism of the generation was not quantitative but was centered on a few traits which were considered ". . . uncompatible with the norms of the new society, unacceptable, unpleasant and, they hope, to be eradicated altogether." One problem discussed by many of the youth is that of excessive drinking among some elements of the population and associated "hooliganism." In addition, some persons show little liking or aptitude for participation in cultural, sport, and other activities organized by the state and made available to them. Participation in this area is increasing, however, due to increasing emphasis on these activities by official organizations. There is even a danger that new interests will outgrow existing facilities. The Komsomol has been active in increasing the interest in these activities.

One danger seen in the area of work, by the youth, is a lack of interest by certain individuals in their jobs. Youth are urged to seek employment in areas which are of interest to them and in which they can devote all their energy and creativity. It was mentioned that the school plays a very important part in the instillation of work attitudes.

THE STYLIAGA. The Styliaga are seen, by some, as youth following Western patterns of dress and fashion and as being, generally, loafers and fashion hounds. Youth are warned, however, that neither the extreme of following fads nor the extreme of conservatism of dress are good. Excessive conservatism leads to resistance to any change. It was suggested that perhaps the basis of the Styliaga movement lies in the failure of Russian industry to develop styles of its own in the modern form.

Another group views the Styliaga as those who wish to "eat but not work." It is predicted that this type of individual will not be evident for long in the USSR.

THE FUTURE. The young generation looks ahead to the time, soon to be reached, when there will be, due to the basic Communist ideology, no more negative traits evident among it.

"Probably the most characteristic single trait to emerge is singlemindedness and complete involvement." They want to work hard to avoid easy "outs" and ". . . to help eradicate everything that hinders the forward movement of our society . . ."

SOVIET. Some youth desire to help the Party and the state through work and through participation in a broad range of social activity. Others place their main goal in their work, and through their work, hope to be of maximum use to their society. Some youth hope to become specialists and experts in one field and to reach the utmost range of creativity in it. These latter are likely to become leaders in the society.

There are also youth who might be classified as dreamers. Their goals are very high and they do not realize that there are many impediments to the realization of them. These youth can end up either as malcontents, they can find their own level and make a normal contribution to the society or, with help and with accurate judgment, they can fulfill their dreams in some way.

Another type of youth can be classified as "drones." These wish only personal comfort and have little concern above that of personal aggrandizement. It is thought, however, that the socialist society itself will cause the disappearance of this type and that there will soon be a change for the better in this area.

32. Colton, E. T., "With the U.M.C.A. in Revolutionary Russia," *Russian Review,* XIV (April, 1955), 128-139.

33. "The Coming Generation in Soviet Russia," *Newsletter from behind the Iron Curtain,* II (July, 1948), 159-162.

34. "Congress of Young Communist League Maps Plans for the Future," *U.S.S.R. Information Bulletin,* IX (April, 1949), 246-247.

Moscow, March, 1949.

35. Counts, George, S., *The Soviet Challenge to America* (New York: The John Day Company, Inc., 1931).

36. Daily, K., "Recent Changes in Soviet Education," *Russian Review,* XX (January, 1961), 19-35.

37. Davis, J., "Testing the Social Attitudes of Children in the Government Schools in Russia," *American Journal of Sociology,* XXXII, 6 (May, 1927), 947-952.

Problem: To discover whether differences in education have an effect on the different status ranking of occupations by adolescents. Soviet youth are compared with American youth.

Sample: 72 children, ages 12 to 17 years, from a summer school near Moscow. Most of the children belonged to the Komsomol.

Instrument: A list of 45 occupations was shown to the participants, who were asked to rank the occupations according to their prestige positions in the society.

A similar device had been previously used on American youth.

Findings: Though in some instances the ranking given to certain occupations by Soviet and American youth did not differ greatly, in others there was a very great difference.

While Soviet youth placed the occupation of banker at the bottom of the list along with prosperous businessmen and ministers, and the occupation of peasant at the top of the list, American youth placed bankers at the top of the list, prosperous businessmen and ministers near the top, and laborers and "ditch diggers" at the bottom.

The test demonstrates that ". . . there are varying social evaluations for different professions, that such social judgments vary in different countries."

38. "The Debate on Study versus Extracurricular Activities," *The Soviet Review,* III, 4 (April, 1962), 3-15.

The article by Prof. A. D. Alexandrov, "Let There Be More Enthusiasts!" reprinted in the *Soviet Review,* March, 1962, started an animated controversy in the pages of *Komsomolskaya Pravda.* "We [*Soviet Review*] offer a cross-section sampling of readers' comments from the issues of December 4 and 28, 1961."

39. Delaney, R. F., "Youth versus the Kremlin," *Sign,* XXXVIII (September, 1958), 40.

40. Dolina, N., "Seventeen Year Olds: A Teacher's Reflections" (Encourage Independence in Pupils), *Current Digest of Soviet Russia,* XIV (February, 1962), 9-10.

41. Dostoevsky, Fedor, A *Raw Youth* (translated from Russian by Constance Garnett), (London: William Heinemann, Ltd., 1951; New York: The Macmillan Company, 1956).

42. "Educating Ivan," *Economist,* CLXXXVIII (September, 1958), 1008.

43. *Education in the USSR.* Division of International Education, International Educational Relations Branch, Bulletin 1957, N. 14 (Washington: U.S. Government Printing Office, 1957).

44. Fainsod, Merle, "The Komsomols: A Study of Youth under Dictatorship," *American Political Science Review,* XLV (March, 1951), 18-40.

A discussion of the history, training, philosophy, and problems of the Komsomol. Also found in Alex Inkeles and Kent Geiger (eds.), *Soviet Society: A Book of Readings* (Boston: Houghton Mifflin Company, 1961).

45. Fairchild, M., "The Status of the Family in the Soviet Union

Today," *American Sociological Review,* II, 5 (October, 1937), 619-629.

46. Feldmesser, Robert A., "Social Status and Access to Higher Education: a Comparison of the United States and the Soviet Union," *Harvard Educational Review,* XXVII (1957), 92-106.

    The primary thesis of this article is that status privilege in access to higher education is more pronounced in the United States than in the Soviet Union. The second part of the thesis is that the ways this difference has come about involves the violation of other values. The author begins with a statement concerning the implications of the "freedom of opportunity" proposition and proceeds to demonstrate that students coming from higher-status backgrounds are represented in greater proportion than those coming from lower-status backgrounds; in the United States the student enjoys a four-to-one advantage whereas in the Soviet Union it is a two-to-one advantage.

    Although there are differences in the overall frequency of college attendance the most important means by which status influences attendance are in the areas of administrative influence for entrance, the types of secondary education, the secondary-school record of performance, the ability to pay, and the attitude toward education. The author feels that status exerts the most influence as it influences the attitudes of the individual. Educating oneself is a patriotic duty in the Soviet Union, in the United States and motivation must come from areas other than national pride.

47. "Ferment among Soviet Youth," *Soviet Survey,* N. 12 (London: February, 1957), 16.

48. "Festival of Youth and Peace" (World Festival of Youth and Students, Moscow, Russia, August, 1957; Various Aspects and Events), *Culture and Life* (July/August, 1957), 9-22.

49. Filippov, A., "Pioneers Spend the Summer in the City," Komsomolskaya Pravda (May 27, 1949); in D. Meek, *Soviet Youth,* 125-128.

    A discussion of the facilities and organized activities for children spending the summer in the city.

    "Summer activities for children in the city are organized in conjunction with the education department. Comprehensive pioneer groups catering for children of school age are formed in schools, dwelling houses and district Houses of Pioneers."

    The Komsomol participates in the organization and direction of these summer programs. City camps have activities similar to camps in the country, sports, clubs, etc. Children in the city also tour places of cultural interest; parks, etc., in the city. The parks and cultural centers also organize programs for children.

50. Fisher, Ralph Talcott, Jr., *Pattern for Soviet Youth. A Study of the Congresses of the Komsomol, 1918-1954* (New York: Columbia University Press, 1959).

Documented and based on personal interviews, travel in the country, and original printed sources, this study investigates and analyzes the organizations and programs of the Young Communist League (Komsomol) up to 1954.

51. Floridi, U. A., "Gioventu sovietica antifonformista" (Nonconformist Soviet Youth), *Civilta Cattolica,* CVIII, 2561 (Rome: March, 1957) 478-492.

52. Frankel, J. B., "Soviet Union 25 Years from Now," *Virginia Quarterly Review,* XXXVIII (February, 1962), 269-270.

53. Furniss, Edgar S., "Soviet Youth Movement," *Current History,* XXXV (November, 1931), 303-305.

"The Communist youth movement was conceived by Lenin. The 'Communist youth' sets the age limits of its membership at 14 to 22 years. Its companion organization, the 'Youth Pioneers' is open to children at the age of 8 years with an upper age limit of 16. On International Youth Day, the official organ of the movement, 'Youth Pravda' described the status of the branches of the organization in the various countries of Europe."

54. Gaev, A., "Soviet Youth and Literature," *Bulletin,* VI (Munich: July, 1959), 46-53.

55. Geiger, K., "Changing Political Attitudes in Totalitarian Society" (A Case Study of the Role of the Family), *World Politics,* VIII (January, 1956), 187-205.

An exploration of the struggle between the parents and the state in a totalitarian society for the minds of the youth. Members of the Harvard Project on the Soviet Social System interviewed political refugees, former Soviet citizens in New York and Germany in 1950 and 1951. The interviews focused on the individuals' parents and the role they played in the development of his attitudes toward Russia and its activities.

Among the results noted were the following: (1) High incidence of parental skepticism, hostility and lack of enthusiasm for the Soviet regime; (2) The parents were often afraid of being exposed by their children. This restricted their free transmission of attitudes; (3) 71 per cent of the parents interviewed did take older children into their confidence and established free communication—19 per cent reported relative noncommunication of attitudes—10 per cent had parents who had adapted to the regime; (4) Attitudes learned in school often brought the parents into conflict with the children. Children often rejected their parents' views; (5) Many of the parents did not want to reveal their views to their children.

The author concludes that, on the whole, the family has not been effective in resisting the ideological indoctrination of their children.

56. Geiger, Kent, "Deprivation and Solidarity in the Soviet Urban Family," *American Sociological Review,* XX (January, 1955), 57-68.

57. Geiger, Kent (1956), "Winning over the Youth," in A. Inkeles and Kent Geiger (eds.), *Soviet Society: A Book of Readings* (Boston: Houghton Mifflin Company, 1961), 546-558.

Reprinted from: "Changing Political Attitudes in Totalitarian Society: A Case Study of the Role of the Family," *World Politics,* VIII (1956), 189-205.

58. Geoffrey, Gorer and John Rickman, *People of Great Russia* (London: Cressel Press, 1949).

59. Gogoberidze, G., "The 'Fashion Fiends,'" *Sovetskaya Kultura* (January 18, 1955); in D. Meek, *Soviet Youth* (London: Routledge & Kegan Paul, Ltd., 1957), 173-174.

A description of the "fashion fiends" and those who admire and emulate them.

The fashion fiends, a "worthless bunch" of youth who imitate Western bourgeois fads are a degenerate lot, characterized by their loud clothes and generally immoral conduct.

"How wretched the inner world of these people is, with its petty interests and primitive desire! Their reading matter consists of inferior pulp literature and of thrillers . . . obtained from some unknown sources. The 'art' in which they indulge consists of the shrill cacophony of jazz, the monotonous boogie-woogie, the convulsive be-bop amateurishly recorded and sold under the counter, of vulgar postcards depicting sickly beauties and foreign film stars."

Some students and young workers imitate the fashion fiends, who have their origins in ". . . poor upbringing in the home, teaching children to be irresponsible, to despise work and to admire everything foreign . . ."

Conclusion: Though there are not many fashion fiends strong measures are needed for their control. Young people must be provided with interesting leisure-time activities and should be instilled with ". . . a revulsion against the alien, ugly 'fashions' and inculcate a love for everything truly beautiful, healthy and harmonious . . ."

60. Gould, Julius, "The Komsomol (Young Communist League) and the Hitler Jugend" (Comparison of the Handbooks of the Soviet Youth Movement and of the Hitler Youth), *British Journal of Sociology*, II (December, 1951), 305-314.

61. Gregg, R. A., "Russia's Pampered Youth," *Harper's*, CCXV (August, 1957), 73-79.

62. Gregory, V., "Growing Up in Moscow 1940-1948," *Occidente*, XI, 1 (Turin: 1955), 44-57.

63. Griscom, Robert, "Report on Russian Youth," *Ladies Home Journal*, LXXIV (February, 1957), 61.

64. Gunther, John, *Inside Russia Today* (New York: Harper & Brothers, 1958).

65. Gurin, V. E., "An Individualized Approach to Upper Grade Students," *The Soviet Review*, III, 1 (January, 1962), 42-48.

Deals with an approach to classroom instruction, based on knowledge of the individual student's background, by one teacher. One case study given.

66. Halle, Fannina W., *Woman in Soviet Ruusia* (New York: The Viking Press, 1933).

67. Hamilton, G., "Communist Road Show: the Subtle Art of Poisoning," *Saturday Night*, LXVII (November 3, 1951), 11, 19.

68. Inkeles, Alex, "Social Change and Social Character: the Role of Parental Mediation," *Journal of Social Issues*, XI, 2 (1955), 12-23.

69. Inkeles, Alex, The Soviet Citizen (Cambridge: Harvard University Press, 1959).

Daily life in a totalitarian society.

70. Institute for Study U.S.S.R., "Youth in the Soviet Union: A Collection of Articles" (July, 1959) (Ser. #53).

71. "Iron Curtain Delinquency," *America*, XCVII (June 29, 1957), 356-357.

72. Isaac, Deutscher, *Russia in Transition*, XCVII (New York: Grove Press, 1960).

73. Johnson, Hewlett, *Soviet Russia Since the War* (New York: Boni & Gaer Publications, 1947).

74. Jordan, William, "Moscow's Jet Set Rides High," *New York Times Magazine*, CVI (November 4, 1956), 14.

75. Juviler, Peter H., "Communist Morality and Soviet Youth," *Problems of Communism*, X (Washington: May/June, 1961), 16-24.

An assessment of the values of Soviet urban youth against the yardstick of the major concerns of "Soviet morality." The discussion is based on observations made during three visits to the USSR between 1955 and 1960, especially a year spent at the University of Moscow (1958-1959).

Among the conclusions the author notes that devotion to Communism is tempered by various other interests and values. Among the conflicts for the urban youth are seen individual career goals, obligation to work for the common cause, the Communist Party's version of truth, the relative isolation of the USSR, and the demand for Soviet patriotism. A primary concern of the urban youth is physical security.

76. Kalb, Marvin L., "Soviet Youth: The Bewildered Generation," *New York Times Magazine*, CVI (July 28, 1957), 9.

77. Kalb, Marvin L., "Russian Youth Asks Some Questions," *New York Times Magazine*, CX (April 23, 1961), 20.

78. Kalb, Marvin L., "Russia's Bewildered Young People," *Catholic Digest*, XXII (December, 1957), 16-20.

79. Kassof, Allen, "Afflictions of the Youth League," *Problems of Communism* (Washington), VII (September/October, 1958), 17-23.

A 1958 discussion of the Komsomol which focuses on the failure of the group to gain great positive response. The author notes, "Fundamentally, the Komsomol is not a youth organization nearly as much as it is a means of preventing Soviet youth from organizing on its own, and of forestalling the explosive issues which might arise if youth could speak with its own voice and act on its own behalf." The reaction of members is seen as one of boredom and apathy. One possible cause of disinterest lies in the emphasis of the Komsomol on issues long since decided rather than dealing with the daily problems of Soviet youth. In general, the Komsomol can be seen as an instrument of control under the Communist party, an instrument which precludes the possibility that the youth will be led by "nonconformists."

80. Kassof, Allen, "The Young Generation and the Communists," (Emergence of a youth problem in Russia), *Far Eastern Economic Review*, XXIV (January 2, 1958), 3-7.

81. Kassof, Allen, "Youth vs. the Regime: Conflict in Values," *Problems of Communism,* VI (Washington: May/June, 1957), 15-23.

82. Kheroskov, I., "Reminiscences of the Moscow Students' Movement," *Russian Review,* XI (October, 1952), 223-232.

83. Khomutova, M. A., "Choosing an Occupation and Providing Employment for School Graduates," *The Soviet Review,* III, 1 (January, 1962), 57-61.

A discussion and analysis on the effect which student participation in a work program has on attitudes toward work and on psychological preparation for the future. The author examines a sample of 100 tenth-grade students in two Erevan secondary schools in 1958-1959.

The author notes in conclusion that "The analysis of the data obtained showed that the participation of pupils in productive labor in factories and their contact with workers have a beneficial effect on their attitudes toward a worker's trade and prepares them psychologically for their future work."

Among the findings are that 12 per cent decided to continue working in the trade which they had learned in school; 8 per cent decided on higher education related to the field they had experienced at school; 66 per cent decided on higher education outside of the field they had contacted in school; 86 per cent developed positive attitudes toward production as a result of their production training. Many of those who decided to attend college had, as an alternative to acceptance, a desire to work in the industrial setting.

84. King, Beatrice, *Soviet Russia Goes to School* (Delhi: People's Publishing House, Ltd., 1956).

85. Komsomolskaya Pravda (1965), "Young Men Gone Astray," in A. Inkeles and K. Geiger (eds.), *Soviet Society: A Book of Readings* (Boston: Houghton Mifflin Company, 1961), 626-629. Reprinted from *Current Digest of the Soviet Press,* VIII, 33, 8-9.

86. Kramer, R., *Practical Morality Taught to Soviet Children, As Illustrated in Four Official Soviet Periodicals, 1937-1951* (Ann Arbor: University Microfilms, 1954).

87. Kruzhin, A., "The Komsomol and the Armed Forces," *Bulletin,* VI (Munich: March, 1959), 46-53.

88. Kufaev, N. N., *Juvenile Delinquents* (Moscow: 1945).

89. Kulski, W. W., *The Soviet Regime: Communism in Practice,* 3rd ed. (Syracuse: Syracuse University Press, 1959).

90. Lamont, Corliss, "Soviet Russia in the School Curriculum," *Harvard Educational Review,* XV, 3 (May, 1945), 212-219.

91. Laqueur, W. and G. Lichtheim, *Soviet Cultural Scene* (New York: Frederick A. Praeger, Inc., 1956).

92. Lenin, V. I., *The Young Generation* (New York: International Publishers, 1940).

The drafting of 183 students into the army; organize the youth; the student movement and the present political situation; "The Youth International," a review; the tasks of the youth league.

93. Leonard, Wolfgang, *Child of the Revolution*, trans. C. M. Woodhouse (London: William Collins & Co., Ltd., 1957).

In relating personal experiences, the author gives insights into processes of thought and feeling of trained Communist Party officials. From 1934 to 1945 he was in the USSR in a German children's home, in school, in exile, and being trained in a Comintern school. Sent to East Germany, he fulfilled various Party assignments until, disillusioned by repudiation of Yugoslavia in 1949, he broke with Stalinism and fled to Belgrade.

94. Lyalin, V., "The Strength of the Community," Uchitelskava Gazeta (August 5, 1953); in D. Meek, *Soviet Youth* (London: Routledge & Kegan Paul, 1957), 73-78.

Report on and discussion of the conduct of a "problem student" and his rehabilitation in the fifth form of school in Upper Eltsövka Village, Iskitim District, Novosibirsk Province.

When Valerii Nevzorov entered the fifth form, he showed many signs of ill-adjustment and deviation from the norms of expected conduct and attitude. This was evident in his disobedience to teachers, noncompatibility with other children, his refusal, in many instances, to do homework, insolence, refusal to participate in activities, etc.

"The teachers of 5A decided that they would have to train Nevzorov to work properly, and that they would have to use a skillful, pedagogical approach and to be stubborn, persistent, and at the same time gentle, if they were to be successful."

Descriptions of specific behavioral patterns are included in the discussion, for example: Nevzorov's balkiness in class, his nonparticipation in a young fisherman's circle which he was induced to join, his friendship with a younger boy, and an example of his personal truthfulness.

The problem was brought to a head at a general meeting of the school body, during which he was criticized by his peers. When it was decided to ". . . regard him as a member of the school only when we see that he behaves as a pupil should, when he begins to respect the pupil's committee, the school organizations and our meetings." His performance improved and he soon moved up to the sixth form.

95. Mace, D. R., "The Employed Mother in the USSR," *Marriage and Family Living,* XXIII (November, 1961), 330-334.

The Soviet Union has done everything it could to put women on the labor market and has eliminated the guilt and anxiety by making it socially acceptable and providing for motherhood and child care in these circumstances. Having women employed is good for the country, but the author raises the question: "Does the woman herself, however, share in the view that by being employed she is achieving gains that do not conflict with family obligations?"

To investigate this question, the author used a letter printed in the *Soviet Woman* and through conversations established its typicality. He supplemented with personal observations. He cites material assembled in 1931, which shows how 841 Soviet men and women, 25-35 years of age, spend an average day. Another table shows how a group of Soviet men and women, all heads of families, shared the household tasks of an average working day.

Although men and women spend the same amount of time at paid work, women spend more time than men at domestic duties.

Child care is largely outside of the home, but that within the home is quite evenly divided between men and women.

The author's objective impression: "Women are still carrying the heavy end of the stick," but they are proud of their economic independence and enjoy their fuller life.

96. Mace, David, "Report on Soviet Marriage," *Marriage Guidance,* V (November, 1960), 347-349.

97. Marenko, I., "Parents and Extra-Curricular School Activities," *Semya i Shkola* (1952), 2, 20; in D. Meek, *Soviet Youth* (London: Routledge & Kegan Paul, 1957), 86-90.

A discussion of the participation of parents in organized extracurricular activities of a constructive and/or instructive nature.

Extracurricular activities play a great part in the education of the child. Some schools, however, have been unable to organize such activities because of a lack of trained experts in the fields to be included in the program. It is suggested, by the author, that schools facing this problem follow the example of other schools where parents have been induced to participate in the programs. By this method trained experts in the fields to be taught can be readily found and most of these parents willingly spend the few hours a week necessary with the children.

Schools where parents are participating in extracurricular activities report great success with their activities programs. Even parents with no educational experience but with knowledge of a field can help through individual aid, such as collecting libraries. In communities where parents are participating, they have established clubs specializing in everything from railroad maintenance to theatrical productions.

Parents having experiences of a valuable historical and nationalistic nature can instill in the children, through lectures and meetings, a greater patriotic spirit.

In one school, parental participation was found to have a beneficial effect on the children's school work and grades.

"The Soviet family and school share the same task—to rear and educate well-rounded, highly developed, active and conscientious builders of communism. It is therefore the teachers' duty not merely to maintain contact with the parents, but to attract them into extensive participation in the whole life of the school."

98. Marin, Yury, "Current Komsomol Poblems," *Bulletin,* IV (Munich: December, 1957), 38-42.

99. Marin, Yury, "The Seventh World Youth Festival" (Vienna, Austria. July 26-August 4, 1959); *Institute of Study, USSR Bulletin,* VI (September, 1959), 23-30.

100. Marin, Yury, "The Soviet Communist Party's Policy toward Soviet Youth," *Bulletin,* III (Munich: April, 1956), 35-40.

101. Marin, Yury, "Soviet Youth in Search of the Meaning of Life" (As revealed in correspondence and stories in various periodicals), *Institute for Study of USSR Bulletin* 7 (September, 1960), 41-44.

102. Markov, K., "Trust and High Standards," *The Soviet Review,* III, 4 (April, 1962), 3-7.

Reply to Alexandrov (*The Soviet Review,* III [March, 1962], also concerned with curricular programs).

103. Matthew, Eunice S., "What Is Expected of the Soviet Kindergarten," *Harvard Educational Review,* XXIX, 1 (Winter, 1959), 43-53.

104. Maurer, R., "Recent Trends in the Soviet Family," *American Sociological Review,* IX (1944), 242-249.

105. Mead, Margaret, *Soviet Attitudes Toward Authority* (New York: Rand Series, 1955).

106. Medvedvev, P., "The Outstanding Student is a Beacon for Others." *The Soviet Review,* III, 4 (April, 1962), 13-15.

Medvedyev, a fourth-year student of Soil Biology at Moscow State University and a recipient of the Lenin Scholarship, believes that satisfaction in work is dependent on proficiency and that ". . . nothing can be worse than to be a poor specialist." He disagrees with Alexandrov and believes that students should be well-rounded and that proficiency in one's specialty is still no excuse for receiving poor grades in other courses. He believes that the good student is well informed in all areas, ". . . almost invariably finds time for research along with classwork and who less than any others complains about being overloaded with assignments."

Medvedyev also believes that class attendance should be compulsory and that ". . . staying away from class demoralizes the student, disrupts his whole study program and makes him into an incompetent specialist." He believes that, far from being overworked, the student is usually underworked and that for many the school experience consists of having a good time with a minimum of work. He believes that "Profound absorption in scientific study and a light study schedule are mutually exclusive."

107. Medynsky, E., "Schools and Education in the USSR," *American Sociological Review,* IX, 3 (June, 1944), 287-298.

108. Meek, D., *Soviet Youth: Some Achievements and Problems; Excerpts from the Soviet Press* (International Library of Sociology and Social Reconstruction) (London: Routledge & Kegan Paul, Ltd., 1957).

109. Mehnert, Klaus, *Youth in Soviet Russia,* (translated by Michael Davidson) (New York: Harcourt, Brace and Company, 1933).

110. Moffitt, J. C., "Children, Parents and Schools in Soviet Russia," *PTA Magazine,* LIV, 9 (May, 1960), 10.

111. Mudd, Emily H., "The Family in the Soviet Union," *Marriage and Family Living,* X (Winter, 1948), 7.

112. Marinzani, S., "The Youngest," *Komsomolskaya Pravda* (January 31, 1950); in D. Meek, *Soviet Youth* (London: Routledge & Kegan Paul, Ltd., 1957), 187-188.

Youth who took over their parent's jobs during the "Patriotic War" are now well established in industry making good salaries, and attending schools for industrial advancement. Roads for advancement lie, however, not only in industry but in the political sphere as well and many agitators are former pupils of the industrial schools.

113. "Soviet Youth: the Bewildered Generation," *New York Times Magazine* (July 28, 1957), 9.

114. "Generation of Changes: Russia's Fences Begin to Come Down," *Newsweek* (May 7, 1962).

115. Novak-Deker, N.K. (ed.), *Soviet Youth: Twelve Komsomol Histories* (Munich: Institute for the Study of the USSR, 1959).

116. Novoplyansky, D., "Into the Fifth Form," *Komsomolskaya Pravda* (July 20, 1949); in D. Meek (ed.), *Soviet Youth* (London: Routledge & Kegan Paul, Ltd., 1957), 57-60.

117. Panteleyes, L., "Do Not Pass By, Comrade,"*Literaturnaya Gazeta* (January 26, 1954); in D. Meek, *Soviet Youth*, op. cit., 109-115.

118. Pares, Dir Bernard, A *Wandering Student: The Story of a Purpose* (Syracuse: University of Syracuse Press, 1948).

119. Parry, A., "Will Russia's Youth Go Anti-Red?" *Columbia*, XXXVII (March, 1957), 15-16.

120. Pavlov, S., "Sovetskaja molodez v bor'be za kommunizm" (Soviet Youth in the Struggle for Communism), *Kommunist*, XXXVI, 4 (Moskva: March, 1960).

121. Percernikova, I. A., V*ospitanie disciplinirovannosti u podrostka v sem'e* (Disciplinary Training of Adolescents in the Family) (Moskva: Izdatel' stvo Akademii Pedagogiceskih Nauk RSRSR, 1956).

122. Perkins, W. A., "Restless Soviet Youth," *Economist*, CLXXXII (1957), 37.

123. Permyak, Yevgeni, "Long Engagements," *The Soviet Review*, III, 4 (April, 1962), 33-38.

From *Izvestia* (December 24, 1961).

124. Petrushanskaya, P., "Youth Cafe," *Soviet Woman*, N. 3 (1962).

125. Phelan, F. J., "Iron Curtain Youth," *Ave Maria*, LXXXVII (January 4, 1958), 18.

126. Ploss, Sidney I., "Forty Years of the Komsomol from Youthful Zeal to Middle Age," *Problems of Communism*, VII (Washington: September/October, 1958), 8-17.

This article deals with the 40-year history of Komsomol, the All-Union Leninist Communist League of Youth, telling how it originated, how it was constrained for service to the Soviet state, and what its impact has been on the Soviet youth.

The Communist Party persistently "discouraged individualism, factionalism, initiative; bored the members of Komsomol with its emphasis on political studies; failed to keep promises. This has resulted in indifference on the part of a majority of the members.

Because of the potential threat of a liberal, genuine youth organization, the party controls, at the same time putting a damper on enthusiasm. What was started as an organization for youth, a means for them to take an active role in the Soviet Union, was slowly turned into a party instrument for the indoctrination and molding lives of young workers. The schools have now assumed this duty and are better able to do it. The author predicts that even so, Komsomol will continue on as an organization "not of youth, but of, by, and for the Communist Party."

The authors found that some Soviet youth see no point in the existence of Komsomol.

127. Ploss, Sidney I., "Political Education in Postwar Komsomol," *American Slavic Review*, XV (1956), 489-505.

128. Pospieszalski, Antoni, "Wayward Youth on the Vistula," *Soviet Survey* (London: Summit House, January/March, 1961).

129. Pustovachenko, V., "Only Plus," *The Soviet Review*, III, 4 (April, 1962), 9-12.

Pustovachenko, a student at the Kahabarovsk Medical Institute, wrote, in reply to Alexandrov, on the question of enthusiasm for one's profession. Using as examples a short description of two fellow students, he declares that enthusiasm strictly on the plane of one's science is not really enthusiasm for science but rather enthusiasm for personal advancement. He believes that one should, in addition to enthusiasm for a profession, have enthusiasm for, and a sense of conjunctivity with, one's group of comrades.

"Enthusiasm ought to be warm, generous, breathing love of life and people. To me an enthusiast is like a ball of lightning that electrifies everything in its path. . . . I do not see as either strong or talented the person who thinks only of himself."

130. Ragger, H., "Frustration and Boredom in Russia," *Reporter*, XVIII (February 20, 1958), 17-20.

131. Raymond, Ellsworth, "What Russians Told Me Off the Record," *Reader's Digest*, LXXIII, 440 (December, 1958), 46-52.

132. "Recent Social Measures in the USSR Concerning Young Persons," *International Labour Review*, L (December, 1944), 768-771.

This article discusses the educational reforms undertaken by the USSR following the German occupation. The author notes the restoration and expansion of the physical system with particular emphasis on the Ukraine. The war years also produced a great number of young technicians and students enrolled in industrial programs.

Among the educational reforms noted by the author were: a lowering of the age for compulsory education from 8 years old to 7 years old; introduction of I.D. cards; the separation of boys and girls in urban high schools; the regulation of student activities outside of the school; expansion and improvement of the school inspection system and pupil examination; and the abolition of the system of socialist competition among the students and teachers in the area of school work.

The war effort also led to the employment of both parents in government enterprises. To some extent the care of the children was intrusted to Pre-School Centers which took over a great part of early education and physical care such as clothing.

133. Report for the Peoples Commissar of Justice, N. V. Krylenko, to the 2nd Session of the All-Russian Central Executive Committee of the XVI Congress (translated from *Izvestia,* February 12, 1936).

134. "Restless Soviet Youth," *Economist,* CLXXXII (January 5, 1957), 37.

135. Rhine, Virginia (trans.), *Young Communists in the USSR* (Washington: Public Affairs Press, 1950).

136. Rogger, Hans, "Frustration and Boredom in Russian Youth," *Reporter,* XVIII (February 20, 1958), 17-20.

137. Rogger, Hans, "Government and Schools in the USSR; Growing Vocational Orientation of the Soviet School" [may lead to even greater cynicism and unwillingness to take an active part in the building of communism than now exists], *Current History,* XL (June, 1961), 333-339.

138. Rossi, Alice S., *Generational Differences in the Soviet Union* (Cambridge: Russian Research Center, Harvard University, 1954).

139. "Russia's Problem Children," *Economist,* CLXXXVII, 5985, 490.

140. Sase, H. and S. Iwamoto, "Labor Education in Russian Families," *Gendaishinri l (Modern Psychology)* (July, 1949), 80-87.

141. Schlesinger, Rudolf, *The Family in the USSR* (London: Routledge & Kegan Paul, Ltd., 1960).

142. Schuessler, R., "Rebellion in the New Soviet Generation," *Apostle,* XXXVIII (January, 1960), 4-5.

143. Shatunovsky, I., "The Evil Eye," *Komsomolskaya Pravda* (December 18, 1955); in D. Meek, *Soviet Union* (London: Routledge & Kegan Paul, Ltd., 1957), 181-186.

144. Shimkin, Dimitri Boris, "Soviet-U.S. Education," *Science Newsletter*, LXXV (April 11, 1959), 234-244.

145. Shklayeva, N., "I Disagree," *The Soviet Review*, III, 4 (April, 1962), 12-13.

Shklayeva, a second-year student of Philosophy at Leningrad State University, disagrees with V. Pustovachenko and believes that the student should be devoted to his field over and above being concerned with whether or not his fellow students should not concern themselves with students who are unable to pass courses which are "after all . . . designed for average students" and that the student's first duty is to become very good in his field.

146. Silhajoris, Rimvydas, "Stepchildren of Communism" (Unrest and Delinquency among the Youth of Russia), *Lituanus* (June, 1957), 3-8.

147. *Soviet Commitment to Education:* Report of the First Official US Education Mission to the USSR (*U.S. Department of Health, Education and Welfare Bulletin*) (Washington, D.C.: U.S. Government Printing Office, 1959).

148. "Soviet Heroes Are Tired," *Economist*, CXCVII (December 24, 1960), 1322.

149. "Soviet Youth and Religion " *Perspectives*, IV (November, 1959), 18-22.

150. "Soviet Youth Marches Forward," *Soviet News* (1945), 48.

151. Stalin, Iasif, *The Tasks of Youth* (New York: International Publishers, 1940).

151. Stern, B. J. and Smith (eds.), *Understanding the Russian, a Study of Soviet Life and Culture* (New York: Barnes and Noble, Inc., 1947).

153. "A Student's Meeting in Moscow: Shift in Communist Tactics" (International Union of Students), *Times*, CLXXV (1954).

154. "Study While You Work," Economist, CLXXXIX (October 11, 1958), 152. (Russian edition)

A discussion of the Soviet work-study program whereby students leave school at age fifteen for work in the factory, farm, or office while they continue their education on a part-time basis. The selection for higher education thus becomes a reward for orthodoxy as well as intellectual accomplishment. It is through this plan that Khrushchev hoped to eliminate political unrest among the students. Dissenters were sent to the factories.

151. Stern, B. J. and Smith (eds.), *Understanding the Russians, a Study* N. 6 (1955), 31; in D. Meek, *Soviet Youth*, op. cit., 175-176.

A discussion of the summer recreation of the young in Russia with emphasis on the role of the Komsomols in the organization of summer activity. Thus excursions, sports, summer work projects are all discussed with reference to the value of Komsomol organization and the participation of Komsomol activists.

156. Tanin, E., "My Youth in Soviet Russia," *American Mercury*, LXXXIX, 431 (December, 1959),

A look at Russia's regenerate intelligentsia.

157. Tatarinove, N., "Living and Working Conditions of Women in the USSR," *International Labour Review*, LXXXII (October, 1960), 341-357.

158. "Teddy Boyars" [Youthful Eccentrics of Moscow], *Economist*, CLXXXVIII (August 30, 1958), 659.

159. Teitelbaum, S. M., "Parental Authority in the Soviet Union," *American Slavic Review*, IV (December, 1945), 54-69.

A discussion of the various attitudes toward sex education which have been forwarded in the Soviet Union in the past few decades.

160. Teitelbaum, S. M., "Sex Education in the Soviet Union," *Harvard Educational Review*, XVI, 2 (Spring, 1946), 85-91.

161. "Longing for Truth," *Time Magazine*, LXXIX (April 13, 1962), 28-32 (Russian Youth), microfilm copy—film 1686.

162. Tkachenko, I. G., "It Concerns the Whole Community," *Semya i Shkola* (1954), 8, 15; in D. Meek, *Soviet Youth* (London: Routledge & Kegan Paul, Ltd., 1957), 81-85.

163. Tortora, V. R., "Communist Close-up: A Roving Reporter behind the Iron Curtain" (Exposition Press, 1954).

Account of the World Festival of Youth and Students for Peace. Berlin, August, 1951, by an American reporter who posed as a Communist.

164. Tracy, Arthur S., *What Ivan Knows That Johnny Doesn't* (New York: Random House, Inc., 1961).

165. Trow, William Clark, *Character Education in Soviet Russia* (Ann Arbor, Michigan: Ann Arbor Press, 1934).

166. "The Truth behind the Youth Festivals" (Political and Social Attitudes of the Youth of Eastern Europe), *Free Labour World,* VIII (July, 1957), 36-40.

167. Turgenev, Ivan S., *Fathers and Sons* (New translation by Barbara Makanowitzky) (New York: Bantam Books, Inc., 1959).

168. Turgenev, Ivan S., *Fathers and Sons* (Translated by Constance Garnett) (New York: Modern Library, Inc., 1950).

169. Tyvel, T. R., "Teddy Boys: Rebels without a Cause" (Recent restlessness among the youth of both the West and Russia), *Western World* (June, 1957), 25-28.

170. "The Upward Curve of Soviet Hooliganism," *Soviet Affairs Analysis Service,* 4 (1961-62), 1-4.

171. Utechin, S. V., "Educating the New Man," in Walter Laqueur and Leopold Labedz (eds.), *The Future of Communist Society* (New York: Frederick A. Praeger, Inc., 1962), 126-136.

Discusses the school reform law of 1958 which was to have been implemented by 1963. An evaluation at the half-way point. Comments only on the status of the law and application.

172. Vigdorova, F. V., "In One School Family Again," *Literaturnaya Gazeta* (October 21, 1954); in D. Meek, *Soviet Youth* (London: Routledge & Kegan Paul, Ltd., 1957), 65-72.

173. Viirsalu, Erika, *Women and Youth in Soviet Estonia* (Boreas Publishing Company, 1955). (East and West; Facts from behind the Iron Curtain No. 7), Published jointly with the Estonian Information Centre, Stockholm, Sweden.

174. Vtechin, S. V. and P., "Patterns of Nonconformity," *Problems of Communism,* VI (Washington: May/June, 1957), 23-29.

A discussion of the patterns of unrest among the Soviet youth following the death of Stalin. Both the content and the political importance of this nonconformity are discussed. Information for the discussion came from Soviet newspapers, visitors to Russia, and eyewitnesses to the activities of the youth.

The deviations discussed focus on the simplest form, absence from lectures, and progress to the asking of awkward questions following the 20th CPSU Congress which dealt with the "cult of personality" and the "crimes of Stalin." When the teachers refused to discuss the situation, open discussion groups were formed. The unrest was found among the professional, educated, and working youth. The authors note that, "for many students, of course, unrest remains an apolitical, passive, and sometimes even unarticulated discontent with 'things' as they are."

175. Williams, Frankwood, E., *Russia, Youth and the Present-Day World* (New York: Farrar & Rinehart, Inc., 1934).

176. Yachnik, E., "About Cinderella Again," *Komsomolskaya Pravda* (October 4, 1951); in D. Meek, *Soviet Youth* (London: Routledge & Kegan Paul, Ltd., 1957), 34-36.

177. Yakovlev, V. A., "Educational Value of Payment for Work Done By Students," *The Soviet Review,* III, 1 (January, 1962), 62-68.

A discussion of the value of paying senior level students for work done during training in production. The types of work camps and forms of payment are discussed. All the work camps are school associated. The method of investigation and substantiation of the conclusions are not discussed in any detail.

The first camps were established on collective farms with the students working for their room and board. This system failed to instill a value for labor on the economic level. The second type of camp paid in advance for the students' meals and he in turn paid the state farm as he earned his money. In this situation the participants tried hard not to make their stay a loss to the state farm. In the third type of farm the students were put into teams and the jobs done by the team were graded by difficulty and skill necessary to accomplish them. The students were then paid on the basis of the grading. This teaches that skilled labor is more rewarding than unskilled labor. The pay rate is a measure of the social significance of the particular job.

In conclusion the author notes, ". . . the basic approach to payment for work done by students should be a proper combination of the interests of the individual and the collective, teaching the students to give prime consideration to the collective interest, although personal interests should not be ignored."

178. Yakubov, F., "Let Us Not Nurture Egoists," *The Soviet Review,* III, 4 (April, 1962), 7-9.

YUGOSLAVIA

1. People's Youth of Yugoslavia, Central Committee, Fifth Congress of the People's Youth of Yugoslavia (Belgrade, March 6-9, 1953; Reports and resolutions) (Belgrade: 1953).

2. UNESCO and People's Youth of Yugoslavia under the System of Associated Youth Enterprises, "Cultural and Artistic Activities of the Yugoslav Youth" (Belgrade: Beogradski Graficki Zaved, 1960).

GENERAL

1. Bereday, George Z. F., "Education and Youth," *Annals of American Academics*, CCCXVII (May, 1958), 63-70.

   Successful and steady improvement in the pedagogical caliber of satellite schools since 1950; yet the same period witnessed a steady alienation of youth from Communism in Eastern Europe.

2. Bienenstok, Theodore, "Anti-authoritarian Attitudes in the Eastern European 'Shtetel' Community," *American Journal of Sociology*, LXVII, 2 (September, 1951), 150-158.

   Though generally applicable to adolescents as a part of the total social science, they are not discussed specifically. Deals rather with general patterns of socialization.

3. Chemadanoo, V., *Building a New World* (New York: Workers Library Publishers, 1936).

   Report delivered October 7, 1935 at 6th World Congress of Young Communist International.

4. "The Congress of the Latvian Komsomol," *Newsletter from behind the Iron Curtain*, VI (April 16, 1952), 69-71.

   Report of meetings, Riga, March, 1952: the present situation on the youth front.

5. "Crisis in the Youth Leagues" (Account of the meetings of the union of Polish youth, Warsaw, January 28–February 1, and the youth league of Czechoslovakia, Prague (February 3-6, 1955), *Newsletter from Behind the Iron Curtain*.

6. Keehn, J. D. and E. T. Prothro, "National Preferences of University Students from 23 Nations," *Journal of Psychology*, XLII (1956), 283-294.

7. National Committee for a Free Europe, Research and Public Service, "Communist Target: Baltic Youth," Edited by the Latvian, Lithuanian, and Estonian Sections (September, 1952).

   Study deals with the methods being used in cajoling and prodding the youth of the Baltic countries.

8. Pipes, Richard, "Muslims of Soviet Central Asia: Trends and Prospects," *The Middle East Journal*, IX (1955), 147-162, 295-308.

9. Prothro, E. Terry, "Cross-Cultural Patterns of National Stereotypes," *Journal of Social Psychology*, XL (1954), 53-59.

National stereotypes of 100 Armenian students.

The national stereotypes of 100 Armenian students were definite and resembled in many ways those held by other groups. The unique elements were related to identified social contact. The unusually definite and unfavorable stereotypes of Turks and English, for example, were related to severe persecution suffered by the Armenians at the end of the First World War. In general, it appears that stereotypes are useful devices for gauging social harmony and social tensions.

10. Wolfsy, Leon, "Toward Unity of the Working Youth for Peace, Jobs, and Democracy," *Political Affairs* (May, 1950), 155-167.

    Communist opinions on unemployment among the nation's youth; and certain aspects of the industrial concentration policy of Labor Youth League.

11. "The Youth Problem: Juvenile Delinquency in Eastern Europe," *East Europe*, IX (June, 1960), 3-13.

    This discussion of juvenile delinquency in Eastern Europe notes the increase of delinquency in both Communist and non-Communist youth since the end of the war. The teen-age culture of the West is seen by the Communists as an alien culture and is not tolerated. Nevertheless, the author notes that delinquency seems to involve similar factors everywhere.

    The main causes of delinquency are noted as mobility; urban congestion; the isolation of the individual; the erosion of traditional standards; and the lack of and source of security. Racial and ethnic friction are virtually absent. The author notes that these causes are generally characteristic of modern industrial society. The Communist approach to juvenile delinquency has little to do with the Church and the family. Rather, it seeks to instill new codes, respect for a new set and scale of institutions.

WESTERN EUROPEAN, MEDITERRANEAN, AND SCANDINAVIAN NATIONS

AUSTRIA

1. Ahendroth, Friederich, "Austria after the Invasion," *Christian Democratic Review*, IX (August/September, 1959), 3-7.

    Vienna Youth Festival (July 26-August 4, 1959).

2. Alfert, Elizabeth, "A Multiple Score Personality Test Administered to German and Austrian Students: Cross-Cultural versus Intra-

Cultural Differences," *Journal of Social Psychology*, L (1959), 37-46.

Comparisons of scores of Vassar College students with those of small samples of German and Austrian students indicate that intercultural differences were less significant than personality differences within each culture.

3. Axelrod, Joseph, "German and Austrian Reaction to the 'Blackboard Jungle,'" *School and Society*, LXXXV (February, 1957), 57-59.
4. Boynton, John, "Youth Festival in Vienna, Austria, July, 1959: What Lies behind the Lavish World Festivals of Youth, the Seventh of Which is Being Held," *Socialist Commentary* (May, 1959), 13-15.
5. European Assembly of Political Youth (Vienna, March 27-31, 1954: Texts of resolutions and motions), *Europe Today and Tomorrow* (May, 1954), 24-27.
6. "Eyewitness at Vienna: A View of the Communist Youth Festival" (Vienna, Austria, July 26–August 4, 1959), *East Europe*, VIII (November, 1959), 22-29.

Written by a Hungarian refugee who left his country after taking part in the 1956 revolt.

7. Roucek, Joseph S., "Primary and Secondary Education in Austria," *Harvard Educational Review*, XXIV, 3 (Summer, 1954), 188-201.

This article on primary and secondary education in Austria in 1954 begins with a short history of Austrian education, noting the significance of Nazi domination during World War II. After the war Austria was under quadripartite control. However, the educational process in the four zones was quite similar, with a few Russian exceptions. The plan was to revert to the educational program in effect just prior to the German control. During the war education in Austria came to a virtual halt.

At the present (1954) there are two school systems for the urban areas ages 6-10 and 10-14, while the rural areas combine the two into one that covers the ages 6-14. The single largest problem is overcrowding.

The author's general conclusion notes, "Today . . . the Austrian school system can be considered as not far removed from the school pattern in other modern democratic states."

8. Silvester, Anton, "The Thin Edge of the Wedge," *Christian Democratic Review*, IX (August/September, 1959), 3-7.

Vienna Youth Festival (July 26-August 4, 1959).

9. Steinem, Gloria, "The Festival That Wasn't" (Commentary on the World Youth Festival, Austria. July 26-August 4, 1959), *Institute of International Education News Bulletin.*

BELGIUM

1. Duyckaerts, F., "Psychology and the Religious Life of the Child and Adolescent," *Lumen Vitae,* XII (Brussels: March, 1957), 29-32.

2. Lunden, Walter A., *Juvenile Delinquency in Belgium, 1930-1956 and Holland, 1935-1951* (Iowa State, 1959).

Study of juveniles aged 16-18 convicted in the courts and rates per 100,000 for prewar, war, and postwar years.

DENMARK

1. Anderson, K. B., "The Folk High School in a Changing Society," *Fundamental and Adult Education,* XII (1960), 118-122.

2. Anderson, R. T. and G. Anderson, "Sexual Customs and Urbanization in a Danish Village," *Southewestern Journal of Anthropology,* XVI (Spring, 1960), 93-109.

The authors' attempt to approach the problem of the relationship between urbanization and the sexual practices of adolescents in a Danish community. The community selected was, in 1956-57, a suburb of Copenhagen. Previously it had been a fishing village, but the period between the two world wars transformed it to a suburb. The local residents had turned from the sea to become part of the urban labor market. Thus their orientations turned from the local community to the urban area. The authors discuss the change in sexual mores and norms from 1890 to the present. Data were collected through observation, interview, and secondary sources.

Among the findings the authors note that prior to the wars the youth met at organized functions. After the war the dating situation became freer. Today organized functions are no more and ". . . the peer group functions for youth as a primary reference unit. . .".

The traditional double-ring engagement, with its attendant sexual connotations and ritual, formal definition have been replaced by a more liberal attitude toward betrothal, sexual relations, and marriage. While the traditional taboos against promiscuity have changed and the situation has become more liberal, the youth today enforce their own type of social control in the form of ostracism within the age grade for promiscuous behavior.

The attitudes toward marriage, engagement, sexual relations, religion, divorce are traced and tied to the development of the urban orientation in the stream of local history and the "urbanization" of the village.

3. Bardis, Panos D., "Attitudes toward Dating among Foreign Students in America," *Marriage and Family Living,* XVIII (1956), 339-344.

4. Billgren, Poul, Borneforsorgsproblemer i Danmark" (Child Delinquency in Denmark), *Menneske og Miljo,* II (1947), 103-107.

5. Bjerstedt, Ake, "Reduction of 'Barrier Tendencies' during Experience of International Co-Living," *Nordisk Psykologi,* X (1958), 161-178. Also *Acta Psychologica,* XIV (1959), 329-346.

6. Campbell, Olive D., *The Danish Folk School: Its Influence in the Life of Denmark and the North* (New York: 1928).

7. "Cave City—A Danish Junk Playground," *The Times Educational Supplement* (1959), 542-543.

8. Christensen, Harold T., "Cultural Relativism and Premarital Sex Norms," *American Sociological Review,* XXV (February, 1960), 31-39.

The author attempts to illuminate the notion of cultural relativism by application to differing sets of sexual norms. Specifically, the author hypothesizes that the more permissive the culture regarding sexual matters the greater will be the incidence of premarital pregnancy, but the lesser will be the effects of such pregnancy as pressure for hasty marriage or for subsequent divorce. A further hypothesis relates to the cultural relevance of certain aspects of premarital pregnancy.

For the analysis he utilizes civil records of marriage from Utah, Indiana, and Copenhagen, Denmark. By comparison of these records with dates of recorded first births he arrives at an indicator of premarital relations and the length of time between conception and marriage. The divorce rates of these marriages are used as an index of the negative effects exerted by the particular culture upon the respective marriages. Of the three areas examined, Utah was felt to be the most conservative, with Indiana representing the United States as a whole and Copenhagen representing the liberal area with a not unfavorable attitude toward premarital intercourse.

Christensen's figures reveal that where cultural pressures against premarital sex are strong, less occurs and vice versa. The greatest pressure is put on couples in the more conservative culture once pregnancy is discovered. Denmark reveals less hasty marriages and a lower divorce rate.

9. Croog, Sydney H., "Aspects of the Cultural Background of Premarital Pregnancies in Denmark," *Social Forces,* XXX (December, 1951), 215-219.

The author attempts to examine the cultural bases for the present trends in premarital pregnancies in Denmark. Marriage and birth statistics and descriptive items of cultural background comprise the data utilized by the author.

It is noted that in 1948, 30 per cent of all legitimate first births arrived 6 months and less after marriage, 38 per cent of all legitimate first births occurred 8 months and less after marriage, 21 per cent of all marriages were followed by a birth within 6 months, and 27 per cent were followed by a birth within 8 months. The author feels that premarital sex relations are influenced by the traditional night visits. He notes a mixed reaction to premarital sex in Denmark and the availability of illegal abortions.

In conclusion he notes, "The premarital pregnancies in Denmark are a concomitant of broad cultural conditions. Traditions of courtship and adjustments in the institution serve to produce the pregnancies. Possible outlets are marriage after conception, abortion, and illegitimacy."

10. The Danish Government Youth Commission (ed.), *Danish Youth,* A Summary of a Statistical Inquiry into Problems of Danish Youth Undertaken by the Danish Government Youth Commission (Copenhagen: about 1951).
11. Danish Government Youth Commission, *Juvenile Employment and Education,* Report by the Danish Government Youth Commission (Copenhagen: about 1951).
12. Danish Government Youth Commission, *Summary Report on Youth and Leisure* (Copenhagen: about 1952).
13. Danish Government Youth Commission, *Summary Report on Maladjusted Youth* (Copenhagen: 1953).
14. Danish Youth Council, *Danish Youth* (Copenhagen: Denmark, 1962).

Discussion of the activities, organizations, and aims of the members of the Danish Youth Council.

15. Denmark, Ungdomskommissionen, *Den Danske Ungdom* (*Danish Youth*) (Copenhagen: J. H. Schulz A/S Universitets-Bogtrykkeri, 1951).
16. Denmark, Ungdomskommissionen, *Ungdommen Og Arbejdskivet* (*Juvenile Employment and Education*) (Copenhagen: J. H. Schultz A/S Universitets-Bogtrykkeri, 1952).

17. Hendin, H., "Suicide in Denmark," *American Scandinavian Review*, XLIX (December, 1961), 399-407.

18. Hjelholt, Gunnar, "The Neglected Parent," *Nordisk Psykologi*, X (1958), 179-184. Also *Acta Psychologia*, XIV (1958), 347-352.

An examination of the adaptation of young men forced to adjust to the environment of a military training school was attempted to illuminate the importance of mother-father roles in socialization.

The sample consisted of 272 young men, 16 to 20 years old (average was 17), who had enlisted as volunteers in the Royal Danish Army to take a one-year technical course.

A comparison of the trainees on the basis of adjustment and performance plus background of the family revealed that poor adjustment to the school was more common among the young men from broken homes than among those from intact families. More negative social characteristics were found among those who did not complete the training than among those who did. It was also found that misuse of leisure and loneliness were more frequent among those who had lost both parents, whereas truancy was frequent among those who had earlier lost a father.

19. Iisager, Holger, "An Evaluation of an Attempt to Form International Attitudes," *Journal of Social Psychology*, XXX (1949), 207-216.

A report of the effects of 3 or 5 months courses at an international folk high school in Denmark on 132 students from 13 nations during 1946-1948.

This article evaluates an attempt which was made in Denmark to form international attitudes (brotherhoods) in older students. The subjects were 73 men and 59 women between the ages of 18 and 35. These individuals represented 13 nations. In connection with their attendance at a Danish college (and their enrollment in a course concerning International Relations) they were asked to write on the question, "To what extent has your stay here at this college influenced your attitude toward internationalism?" In addition, 49 subjects were asked if they had changed their views on people from other nations during their stay at the college. Others (N of 107) were asked to rate the effects of the college experience on the students they knew best.

Analysis revealed that: (1) 49.2 per cent of the subjects were positively influenced toward internationalism, 37.9 per cent were negatively influenced away from internationalism and 6.1 per cent were unaffected. A great change toward was as rare as a great change away from internationalism; (2) The general life of the college seemed to have more effect than the course itself in changing attitudes; (3) Of the 49 asked to evaluate changes in their attitudes toward others, 13 had become less and three more prejudiced; (4) Less than 70 of the group of 107 were able or willing to rate the effect of the course on others. The author concludes, "It seems as if first and foremost an emotional attitude of friendship and common brotherhood is created by stay at college; more seldom, a well-integrated philosophy of life combining a human emotional internationalism with some religious or philosophic view is formed."

20. Iisager, Holger, "Factors Contributing to Happiness among Danish College Students," *Journal of Social Psychology*, XXVIII (1948), 237-246.

The sample consisted of 56 men and 57 women at the International Peoples' College, Helsingn, Denmark who were given questionnaires to approach the problem of the definition of factors critical to happiness in general and the role of the definition of happiness to the differences in the critical factors.

It was found that good health, joy of work, and love were rated as the most essential factors with clear conscience and freedom running a close second. Women tended to stress the cultural and conventional factors. The younger students (below 24) were not very different from the older students. They did show some slight preference for thrills, entertainments, and friends while the older subjects preferred art. While there were no significant differences between the happy and the unhappy, the happy subjects attached more importance to a clear conscience while the unhappy looked more to travel and economic independence.

The author concludes that a program of research incorporating questionnaire, essay writing, interview, and other sources might be more effective in approaching the problem among the more complex personalities.

21. Lund, Ragnar (ed.), *Scandinavian Adult Education*, 2nd ed. (Copenhagen: Det Danske Forlag, 1952).

22. Nordland, E., "Sammenheng mellom sosial atferd og oppdragelse" (Connection between social behavior and upbringing) (Oslo: Oslo Akademisk Forlag, 1955). C. R.: P. W. Perch, *Socialt Tiddskrift*, XXXI, 10 (Kopenhagen: October, 1955), 319-323.

23. Rosenau, Helen, "New Youth Centres in Sweden and Denmark," *Journal of Royal Institute of British Architects*, LXVIII (September, 1961), 443-445.

24. Skrubbeltrang, Fridlev, *The Danish Folk High Schools,* 2nd ed. Revised by Roar Skovmand (Copenhagen: 1952).

25. Svalastaga, K., et al., "Differential Class Behavior in Denmark," *American Sociological Review,* XXI (1956), 435-439.

The problem under investigation in this article is based on the hypothesis that vertical mobility in Denmark is not a simple change of wealth, power, knowledge, or social acceptability but also a transition to a new style of life.

The sample consisted of 2,505 males over 21. The author's analysis of the data on status sensitivity, class identification, life styles, and formal and informal participation leads him to the support of the original hypothesis.

26. Thrane, Eigil, *Education and Culture in Denmark: A Survey of the Educational and Cultural Conditions* (Copenhagen: G-E-C Gad Publishers, 1958).

FINLAND

1. Allardt, Erik, "Community Activity, Leisure Use and Social Structure," *Acta Sociologica,* VI (1962), 67-82.

2. Allardt, Erik, et al., "On the Cumulative Nature of Leisure Activities," *Acta Sociologica,* III (1958), 165-172.

3. Allardt, Erik, et al., "Nuorison harrastukset ja yhteison rakenne" (The Leisure-Time Activities of Youth and Social Structure) (Helsinki: WSOY, 1958), 136-141.

4. Croog, S. H., "Premarital Pregnancies in Scandinavia and Finland," *American Journal of Sociology,* Chicago, LVII (1958), 358-365.

5. Esselstrom, Josef and Ilmari ja Nieminen, "Vassan nuorisotutkimus 1954" (A Social Study on Youth in the City of Vassa in 1954), *Alkoholikysymys,* XXV (1957), 12-62. (English Summary.)

6. *Facts about the Finnish Students' Economic and Social Situation,* For the International Student Conference in Paris 29.9-3.10.52 collected by the National Union of Students of Finland, Helsinki (1952).

7. Fieandt, Kai von, "Soziale Lebensformen und Erscheinungen im finnischen Internat fur Ostkarelische Jugend" (Social Relations in the Finnish School for East-Carelians), *Schweizerische Zeitschrift fur Psychologie und ihre Anwendungen,* VII (1948), 64-70.

8. Finland, Ministry of Education, *Youth Services and Organizations in Finland* (Helsinki: 1954).

9. Heinila, Kalevi, "Leisure and Sports: A Sociological Study on Men's Use of Leisure and Sports Activities," *Publication No. 5 of the Institute of Sociology, University of Helsinki* (Helsinki: Finland, 1959), 205-212.

10. Heinila, Kalevi, "The Preferences of Physical Activities in Finnish High Schools," *Research in School Physical Education—Report of a Conference Held at Vierumaki, July, 1961*, Publication No. 14 of the Institute of Sociology, University of Helsinki (1961), 70-112.

11. Helanko, Rafael, Turun poikasakit, *Sosiologinen tutkimus 9-16 vuotiatten poikien spontaanisista rhymista vv. 1944-51* (*The Boys' Gangs of Turku, during the Years 1944-51. A sociological study of spontaneous groups formed by 9 to 16 year old boys*) (Turku: 1953). Annales Universitatis Turkuensis, Ser. B, Tom. 46.

12. Helanko, Rafael, "The Hang-Outs of Boys' Gangs," *Trans. Westermarck Soc.*, 3 (1956), 77-87.

13. Helanko, Rafael, "Sports and Socialization," *Acta Sociologica*, II (1957), 229-240.

14. Helanko, Rafael, "The Tard Group in the Socialization of Turku Girls," *Acta Sociologica*, IV, 4 (1959), 38-59.

15. Kallio, N., *The School System of Finland* (Helsinki: 1956).

16. Littunen, Yrjo, *Opintoympariston vaikutus korkeakouluopiskelussa* (*The Effects of the University Environment*) (Forssa: 1956).

17. Lund, Ragnar (ed.), *Scandinavian Adult Education*, 2nd ed. (Copenhagen: Det Danske Forlag, 1952).

18. Nieminen, Armas, *Effects of Social Change on the Relationships between Parents and Children and on the Development of Growing Children in Finland* (Gottingen: 1957). Untersuchungen ube die Familie 11. Schriftenreihe des UNESCO—instituts fur Sozialwissenschaften, 5.

19. Ristimaki, Toini, *Nuorukaisten ja taysi-ikaisten meisten arkaijan kaytto. Masseudun Tyovoiman tutkimuksia* (*Annual Round of Activity of Youths and Adult Men. Finnish Rural Labor Force Studies*) (Helsinki: 1955). (English Summary), Acta Forestalia Fennica 63.3.

20. Saari, Erkki, "Kasvatuslaitospoikiin kohdistunt tutkimus. Undersokningen rorande gossar, som varit pa uppfortringsanstalt," (Investigation into Reformatory Boys), *Sos. Aikakausk*, XLVI (1952), 3-12, 85. (English Summary)

21. Sewell, William H. and Oluf M. Davidsen, "The Adjustment of Scandinavian Students," *Journal of Social Issues,* XII, 1 (1956), 9-19.

22. Sipinen, Olli, *The Effectiveness of Punishments and the School Climate,* Research Bulletin, Institution of Education, University of Helsinki (1957) (1).

23. Takala, Annika. *Oppilaiden ja opettajien suorittamista persoonallisuudenpiirteiden arvioinnista* (*Judgments of Personality Traits in School*) (Helsinki: 1953).

24. Takala, Annika, et al., "Child-Rearing Practices and Attitudes as Measured by Different Techniques: I. Parental Attitudes and Child Rearing Practices. A Methodological Study," *Acta Academiae Paedogogical Jybaskylaensis,* No. 19 (1960), 1-75.

25. Takala, Annika, "Child-Rearing Practices and Attitudes as Measured by Different Techniques: II. Child-Rearing Practices and Attitudes in Different Social Environments," *Acta Academiae Paedagogical Jynaskylaensis,* No. 19 (1959), 76-152.

26. Waris, Heikki, "Oppikoulu sosiaalisen Kohoamisen vaylanaindustraialismin murtautumiskaudella. Tilastollisia tietoja oppikouln oppilaitten syntyperasta 1870-1906 (The High School as a Channel for Social Mobility During the Period of Industrialization)," *Valtio ja yhteiskunta. Valtiotieteellisen yjdistyksen vuosikirja* 1947 (Vammala: 1947), 235-246. (English Summary)

27. Westling, Achilles, "On the Correlation of the Consumption of Alcoholic Drinks with Some Sexual Phenomenon of Finnish Male Students," *The International Journal of Sexology,* VII (1954), 108-115.

28. Westling, Achilles, "Tutkimuksia vakijuomien kaytosta seka alkoholohumalan esiintymisesta suomalaisilla miesylioppilailla (A Study Concerning Finnish Male Students' Use of Alcohol and Accumulative Incidence of Alcohol Intoxication), *Alkoholikysymys,* XX (1952), 117-132. (English Summary)

29. Ylostalo Liisa, "Ylioppilaiden asunto-olot syyslukukaudella Studenternan bostadsforhallanden under hosten 1949 (High School Students Housing Conditions in the Autumn Term of 1949)," *Sos. Ailakausk,* LXIV (1959), 265-277, 335. (English Summary)

30. *Youth Services and Organizations in Finland* (Helsinki: 1954).

FRANCE

1. Amado, Georges, "Ethique et Psychologie d'un Groupe d'Adolescent Inadaptes" (Ethical Standards and Psychology of a Group of Maladjusted Adolescents), *Evolut. Psychiatry, Paris,* No. 1 (1951), 3-30.
2. Bastide, R., "Les Etudiants africains en France," *Bulletin International des sciences sociales,* VIII, 3 (Paris: 1956), 496-498.
3. Bastide, R., "Les etudiants d'Afrique noire en France," *Encyclopedie mensuelle D'outre-mer,* 80 (Paris: April, 1957), 151-154.
4. Benavides, L., "Juventud en rebeldia" (Youth in Rebellion), *Nuestro Tiempo,* LXX (April, 1960), 409-423.
5. Benedict, L. (translator), and H. Lauger, "Reconstruction in France and Educational Equality," *Free World,* VI (August, 1943), 161-165.
6. Bolshakoff, S., "Modern Education and its Social Implications: Report of the 45th French Social Week," *Social Justice Review,* LI (November, 1958), 231-233.
7. Borne, E., et al., *La France va-t-elle perdre sa jeunesse?* Paris, A. Fayard, Centre catholique des intellectuels francais (Recherches et debats, nouv. ser, No. 8, 1954).
8. Brown, John L. and Jerome S. Bruner, "Contemporary France and Educational Reform," *Harvard Educational Review,* XVI, 1 (January, 1946), 10-20.
9. Bursten, J., "Aspects de L'evolution Sociomorale de L'adolescent" (Aspects of the Socio-moral Development of the Adolescent), *Enfance,* VI (1953), 97-146.
10. Chaumont, M., "Jeunesse et classes ouvrieres," *Revue nouvelle,* 11 (Tournai: November, 1958), 389-401. (Belgique)
11. Chaumont, M., "Jeunesse et societe," *Revue nouvelle,* No. 3 (March, 1958), 225-232. (Belgique)
12. Chazal, J., "Unruly Gangs of Children and Their Readjustment to Society" (*UNESCO*) *Vagrant Children,* XXVI, 5741, 44-59.

The author, a judge in the Seine Childrens' Court (France), is concerned with what can be done to socially reintegrate gang members. He discusses the characteristics of gangs, the reasons for formation of gangs, and suggests that "Friendship Teams" may be a solution to readjusting gangs to society.

The author believes that it is best for the juvenile to have his liberty rather than to place him in detention. Since this doesn't alter the environment he suggests that the best way to deal with the gang is through the "Friendship Teams" that he proposes to accomplish this end.

13. Collar, J., "Una encuesta sobre la juventud francesca" (A research inquiry on French youth), *Nuestro Tiempo,* V, 44 (February, 1958), 184-194.

14. Deriviere, Raoul, "Les Difficultes D'apprentissage Scolaire des Ralentis Pubertaires" (The Trade-School-Training Difficulties Associated with Delayed Pubescence), *Enfance,* 3 (1960), 225-290.

15. Dintzer, Lucien, *Le Jeu D'Adolescence* (Adolescent Play) (Paris: Presses Universitaires de France, 1956).

16. Fontes, V., et al., "Influence de la guerre sur la jeunesse d'un pays qui n'a pas fait la guerre" (Influence of war on youth of a nonbelligerent country), *Enfance,* IV (1951), 175-182.

17. Fourastie, J., "La croissance des classes jeunes et le probleme de l'emploi," *Population,* II, 1 (Paris: January-March, 1956), 13-28.

18. France, Ministere de l'Education Nationale, *La Vie Scolaire en France.* No. 1 Collection Images de la Vie Scolaire (Paris: l'Institut Pedagogique National, 1956).

This picture story of school life in France covers types of schools, student life in and out of class, validation of studies, and teacher training. Organizational charts are included.

19. Francois-Unger, C., *L'adolescent inadapte; readaptation sociale et formation professionnelle,* Preface de H. Pieron et de W. D. Wall (Paris: Presses Universitaires de France, 1957).

20. Gallagher, O. R., "Looseness and Rigidity in Family Structure," *Social Forces,* XXXI (May, 1953), 332-339.

The object of this article is to describe the family in a rural central France commune. In the particular area under discussion there are two major types of family structures, the peasant family and the nonpeasant family.

Within the peasant family land distribution and inheritance patterns play a large role in the organization of the family. Care is usually exercised in these families to compensate the children who do not receive land. Parents usually decide the future of surplus children, but many get freedom of choice and eventually leave the commune to go to the city.

Among the nonpeasants (about two-thirds of the population of the commune) are, in effect, satellite to the peasant community. They are the merchants, etc. The turnover in the job structure is great and occupational mobility is high. Most nonpeasant sons leave the commune after their elementary education and rarely return. This family type is rigid and suffers great strain in the commune.

21. Gillespie, J. M. and G. W. Allport, *Youth's Outlook on the Future* (Garden City, New York: Doubleday and Company, Inc., 1955). (1,819 case studies from 10 countries.)

    This was a successful pilot study the object of which was to examine the attitudes of college students in ten countries toward their individual and collective futures; no hypotheses were tested. At least partial answers were sought to three questions: (1) How do youth in various countries view the future? (2) Do young people in different countries view their futures in essentially the same way? (3) Is international social research at the present time practicable and beneficial? A cross-cultural analysis of attitudes, aspirations, and moral values among students from the United States, New Zealand, Egypt, Mexico, France, Italy, Germany, Japan, Israel, and South Africa was attempted by administering a questionnaire—including both multiple-choice and open-ended questions—to 100 males and 100 females from each country. (This was the goal; the attempts occasionally fell short.) In addition an essay entitled "Autobiography: from Now to 2000 A.D.," was required from each respondent. Some of the similarities discovered were: "Familism is a universal foundation for individual and group life." "Basic moral values and ethical codes of conduct are everywhere prized." "Most students (Africaners excepted) . . . desire to see greater equality between white and colored races." "Most youth regard war as needless and preventable . . . [but are] . . . pessimistic as to the possibilities of avoiding a third world conflict." There were, of course, a great number of national differences, but the authors conclude that, ". . . it is a wholesome corrective to note that these differences may be dramatic figures etched upon a ground of basic resemblance."

22. Giroud, F., *La Nouvelle Vague; Portraits de la Jeunesse* (Paris: Gallimard, 1958).

23. Guth, P., "Youth Interrupted; the Broken Lives of French Youths," *Free World*, XII (December, 1946), 21-22.

24. Idoppenot, V. "French Youth and English Youth" (translated by P. Macpherson), *Life and Letters Today*, XXVI (July 1940), 12-61.

25. "Les Jeunes au Travail," *Information sociales*, Paris, XIII, 12 (December, 1959), 3-112; XIV, 1 (January, 1960), 3-53.

26. Keilhacker, M., "Le Cinema et les Reactions des Enfants et des Adolescents" (Movies and the Reactions of Children and Adolescents), *Cahiers de Pedagogie de l'Universite de Liege,* XIV (1955), 67-75.

27. Koskas, R., "L'adolescent et sa famille" (The Adolescent and His Family), *Enfance,* II (1949), 68-71.

28. Lanz-Stuparich, Maria, "Les Adolescents et le cinema" (Adolescents and the Cinema), in F. Baumgarten (ed.), *La Psychotechnique dans le Monde Moderne* (Psychotechnology in the Modern World) (Paris: Presses Universitaires de France, 1952), 557-561.

    A study of 200 boys and the same number of girls was made by means of interviews, examinations, and clinical analysis. Results indicate that much identification and projection on the part of the young spectators in the situations presented by the film, suggesting that serious consideration be given by those responsible for this influence on the lives of these future citizens.

29. Larteguy, J., *Les Jeunes du Monde Devant la Guerre; Documents* (Paris: Gallimard, 1955).

30. Laverys, J. A., "La Situation Mondiale, Source de Conflicts Chez la Jeunesse" (The World Situation, a Source of Conflict in Youth), *Annee Medicale Psychologique, Paris,* CIV (1946), 471.

31. Lebovici, S. and Y. Roumajon, "L'adolescent et les Bandes" (The Adolescent and Gangs), *Hygiene Mentale,* XLIX (1960), 259-277.

    Gang mores, structure, types of activities, characteristics of members, and the psychological and sociological factors behind them are discussed.

32. Leon, Anloene, "Quelque Aspects de l'apprentissage de Metier Chez l'adolescent" (Some Aspects of Learning a Trade by the Adolescent), *Annee Psychologie,* LIV (1954), 139-156.

33. Levy-Bruhl, Odette, "Les Adolescents et la Lecture" (Reading Interests of Adolescents), *Enfance,* V (1957), 561-567.

34. Levy-Valinsi, Amado, "Les Problemes Sexuels des Etudiants" (Sexual Problems of the Students), *Hygiene Mentale,* XLVIII (1959), 112-115.

35. Lopez, P., "La Jeunesse Catholique," *Esprit,* XXXIV, 9 (Paris: September, 1956), 294-299.

36. Mabit, C., "Emploi des Jeunes dans les Prochaines Annees," *Journal Official Avis et Rapports du Conseil Economique* (Paris: February 23, 1957), 65-78.

37. Mallinson, V., "The Voluntary Principle in French Education: a Dual System," *Dublin Review*, CCXXXI, 473 (1957), 121-128.

38. Naville, Pierre, "La Crise de 'l'Illusion Professionnelle' Chez L'enfant et L'adolescent" (The Crisis of "The Vocational Illusion" in the Child and Adolescent), *Enfance*, II (1949), 41-53.

39. Philippon, O., "L'influence du Cinema sur L'enfance et L'adolescence, L'enquete National Francaise" (The influence of moving pictures on the child and adolescent, National French Inquiry), *Nouvelle Revue Pedagogique*, VII (1952), 526-530.

40. Preaut, "Scolarite et Conflict" (School Work and Conflict), *Semaines des Hopittaux de Paris*, XXVI (1950), 2266-2271.

41. "Problemes Actuels de la Jeunesse," *Cahiers du Communisme*, XXXVI, 2 (Paris: 1960), 155-219.

42. *Realities* for February, 1960, is a special issue entitled "French Youth." (Articles cover social, economic, political, and aesthetic attitudes and opinions).

43. Regrina, P., "Adolescents Modernes" (Modern Adolescents), *Nouvelle Revue Pedagogique*, V (1950), 402-408.

44. Robbins, Jhan, "We're Sorry Our Son Is a Genius," *Redbook*, CXIX, 4 (August, 1962).

This article discusses the discovery of genius-level intelligence of a French youth. It reports his background conditions and the effects of the discovery on his family.

Jean's IQ was uncovered by the French Army's IQ test. Prior to this his life followed closely the lives of other youth from his area. By age 20 he had left school and was working full time on the family farm. Family ties and loyalty in his home area are very strong, with the family taking precedence over the individual. Obedience and loyalty are instilled in the children from an early age. Jean's schooling was average with little indication that he was gifted.

The reaction to the discovery of his intelligence level placed stress on their traditional family structure and patterns of behavior. The solidarity of the family was threatened with the potential loss of the gifted son.

45. "Structure par Ages de la Population Universitaire," *Avenirs*, 68 (April, 1955), 17-19.

46. Subes, J. et al., "Preferez-vous Etre une Fille ou un Garcon?" (Do You Prefer To Be a Boy or a Girl?), *Enfance*, VII (1954), 197-220.

47. Taillander, M. Saint-Rene, "French Youth Today," *National Review,* CXXVI (May, 1946), 411-414.

48. Trichaud, Lucien, "Cultural Youth Centres in France," *International Journal of Adult and Youth Education* XIV, 2 (UNESCO, 1962).

This article takes a general look at a youth center, offering a description of the organization, administration, and activities. As a result of large housing programs, the pressures of the Algerian war (the psychological pressures) and the personal stress occasioned by the international situation in general, the youth center is seen as filling a necessary gap in the cultural and social development of the youth.

49. Wagner, Charles, *Youth* (New York: Dodd, Mead and Company, 1893).

50. Wallon, Germaine H., *Les Notions Morales Chez L'enfant* (Moral Ideas in the Child) (Paris: Presses Universitaires de France, 1949).

51. Willoughby, G., "The Family: Two French Studies," *British Journal of Sociology,* VI (December, 1955), 364-369.

52. "Youth Movements and Popular Education in France," *International Labour Review,* LIII (March/April, 1946), 275-276.

53. Zazzo, Bianka, "Une Enquete Sur le Cinema et la Lecture Chez les Adolescents" (An Inquiry on Movies and Reading Among Adolescents), *Enfance* (1957), Supplement, 389-411.

54. Zazzo, Bianka, "L'Image de Soi Comparee a L'Image de Ses Semblables Chez L'Adolescent" (The Self-Concept Compared with the Conception of Peers among Adolescents), *Enfance,* No. 2, 9-141.

GREECE

1. Aspiote, A. A., *Ho Ephebos Kai He Koinonia* (*Adolescent and the Community*) (Athens: Institute of Medical Psychology and Mental Hygiene, 1952), Studies No. 6.

2. Aspiote, A. A., *Ho Ephebos Kai He Paideia* (*The Adolescent and Education*) (Athens: Institute of Medical Psychology and Mental Hygiene, 1952), Studies No. 8.

3. Aspiote, A. A., *Ho Ephebos Kai He Oikogenia* (*Adolescent and the Home*) (Athens: Institute of Medical Psychology and Mental Hygiene, 1952), Studies No. 4.

4. Aspiote, A. A. (ed.), *He Krisis Tes Hephebikes Elikias* (*The

Crisis of the Adolescent Age) (Athens: Institute of Medical Psychology and Mental Hygiene, 1952), Studies No. 2.

5. Aspiote, A. A., *Ta Aisthemata Leionektekote'tas* (*Feelings of Inferiority*) (Athens: Institute of Medical Psychology and Mental Hygiene, 1952), Studies No. 5.
6. Aspiote, A. A., *He Hygea Astheneia Kai He Psycho Tou Ephebou* (*Health, Weakness and Mind in the Adolescent*) (Athens: Institute of Medical Psychology and Mental Hygiene, 1952), Studies No. 7.
7. Aspiote, A. A., *Apo ta psuhologika problemata ton efebon. Epaggeli atikos prosanatolismos* (*Psychological problems of adolescents. Professional orientation*) (Athenai: Psuhologia kai Zoe, 1958).
8. Bardis, P. D., "Attitudes toward Dating among Foreign Students in America," *Marriage and Family Living*, XVIII (1956), 339-344.
9. Bardis, P. D., "The Changing Family in Modern Greece," *Sociology and Social Research*, XL (September, 1955), 19-23.

The author discusses the changes in the modern Greek family which have come about in connection with the modern industrial expansion.

The growth of industrialization in the country has been bringing changes in the rural, patriarchal, and authoritarian patterns of arranged marriage, religious marriage, and engagement ceremonies. In the area of education the rate of illiteracy for women is significantly lower than it was in the 1920's. In the urban areas the change has been most noticeable in the dating patterns and the drop in arranged marriages. This has not been true of the rural areas.

The feminist movement in 1952 was a boon to the urban woman and social and occupational opportunities have increased correspondingly. The period following World War II was one of disruption which also served to "liberate the adolescent." This period also saw a rise in interest in juvenile delinquency.

The author generally concludes that the modern family in Greece has been experiencing a decrease in authoritarianism and conservativism, due mainly to the influence of industrial expansion, urban growth, and technological improvement. The rate of change in the traditional areas has been very slow.

10. Bardis, P. D., "Social Distance among Gymnasium Students in Southern Greece," *Sociology and Social Research*, XLV (July, 1961), 430-434.

The goals of this study were to develop the cross-cultural

utilization of research techniques and to investigate the nature of social distance in a non-American culture. Utilizing the Bogardus Social Distance Scale, 140 males and 65 females in a rural Greek gymnasium were examined. The sample was stratified by sex and school class and the subjects were all white, Greek, Orthodox, single, and between the ages of 15 and 20 years. It was hypothesized that the mean for these subjects on the Bogardus scale would be higher than that found in a comparable study done in the United States. The interview data were collected in 1956.

It was found that the Social Distance Scale was of great applicability in a cross-cultural setting. The mean score was higher for the Greek subjects than it was for the Americans. The Greeks revealed much more racial and national ethnocentricity than did the Americans. While there was no significant difference between males and females it was found that, among Greek students in the United States, those who had been in this country the longest had lower social distance scores. Age differenecs also failed to reveal significant differences.

11. "Child Delinquency Juvenile Courts," *Hellenia,* VI (June/ August, 1949), 11-12.

12. Claros, Thomas Stavros, *The Curriculum of the Greek Gymnasium* (Storrs, Connecticut: University of Connecticut, 1958) (Doctoral dissertation)

Discusses subjects taught in the different grades, time aspect on the various subjects, and teaching personnel as well as general background of secondary education in Greece. See Part I, No. 52, 159-161.

13. "Delinquent Children's Week," *Hellenia,* XVIII, 24.

14. Drosow, Maya, "Paichnidia apo te Dyse," *Teleftaia Koritsia ste ge* (Athens: 1939).

15. Ermonikos, I., "Maties ste sughrone neoteta" (Glances at Modern Youth), *Aktines,* XXI (1958), 435-439.

16. Greece, Prime Minister's Office, Information Department, Research Bureau, "Greek Youth After War" (December 30, 1957), Factual information from modern Greece, Series B, No. 2 (Reference No. 5100/6), 3 Zalokosta Street, Athens, Greece.

17. Papadimitriou, M., "Greece and the University Woman," *Hellenia,* II, 6-8.

18. Polites, Kosmas, *E. Koromelia* (N. Estia, Athens, 1939).

19. Rouska, G., "Keinonike kai Ethike Exelixis tou Paidiou sto Horio"

(The social and moral development of the village child), *Sholeion kai Zoe*, 3 (Athens, 1955), 36-63.

20. Sakellariou, G., Psychologia Tou Ephevou (Psychology of the Adolescent) (Athens: Xenos & Co., 1939).

    Greece—2,000 boys and girls, 12 to 21 years old.

21. Sakellariou, G., A *New Method of Character Training Applied on 200,000 Students in Greece and Egypt* (Athens, Greece: Athens University Psychological Laboratory, 1955).

22. Salmon, Brainerd P. (ed.), *Glimpses of Greece* (Washington, D.C.: Helleniic Information Bureau, 1928).

23. "The Second 'Akritia' and the 'Children's Centres,'" *Hellenia,* XXIII (July/September, 1953), 15-16.

24. Smothers, Frank, et al., *Report on the Greeks* (New York: Twentieth Century Fund, 1948).

    Discussing education and communication, the author notes that the proportion of illiterates in Greece is one of the highest in Europe. Lack of facilities, antiquated teaching methods, and the failure of many students to finish their secondary schooling create pressure in the educational system. While school is theoretically compulsory from the ages of 6 to 12, the requirement is not strictly enforced. In the universities, the students are deeply involved in political activities and are split fairly evenly between the left and the right.

25. Theotokas, George, "Ola en Taxei," *Euripides Pentozales kai alles istories* (Athens: 1937).

26. Tsaldaris, Lina P., "Child Welfare and Children's Camps in Greece," *Hellenia,* VIII (October, 1949), 11-12.

27. "The Y.M.C.A. of Greece," *Hellenia,* VI (June/August, 1949), 7-10.

IRELAND

1. Calvert, P. A. R., "Ulster Youth," *Spectator,* CCII (May 8, 1959), 662.

   A discussion of aspects of educational and occupational opportunities open to Ulster youth which includes some comments on recreational opportunities. It is noted that the postwar government program of school building has offered education to a great many Ulster youth. The program has improved both the quality and quantity of education available.

   With the expansion of the Queen's University of Belfast the

region has gained a cosmopolitan air. Many of the area's youth are not at school, and the occupational structure of the area is driving many into different localities.

The main recreational interests of youth in this area are sports and the opposite sex.

2. *Christus Rex* (October/December 1960), dedicated to "Youth Problems in Ireland Today" (papers read at the Christus Rex Congress, Carregart, Ireland, Easter, 1960).

3. Conway, William, "Youth Problems: Principles," *Christus Rex*, XIV (December, 1960), 237-246.

   The author attempts to answer two questions: what objectives should be aimed at in the apostolate toward youth and, second, which of these objectives are the most important.

   In general he notes that youth should be presented with the great ideals for living, with the idea of the Christian life lived for love and should be made cognizant with a deeper and richer meaning to life. Those who do not choose a priestly or religious calling should be aware of the Catholic ideals of marriage and parenthood.

4. Crowley, Timothy, "Modern Psychology and Some Problems of Youth," *Christus Rex*, XIV (December, 1960), 247-256.

   The author discusses two prominent problems of youth: juvenile delinquency and mental handicap. He notes that the number of juvenile delinquents found guilty for indictable crimes in Ireland took a sharp rise from 1954 to 1957. Offenders were mainly boys and engaged in such crimes as larceny, housebreaking assault, malicious damage, and indecency (preferred in that order). Statistics also reveal that a high rate of mental disorder is found among delinquents more than among nondelinquents. He also notes that delinquency is an urban phenomenon with the age group 14-16 being the most prolific in crime in Ireland.

   It is concluded that handicapped and delinquent children need more facilities such as training institutions and hospitals to combat the problem.

5. Dum, P., "Mentalities and Attitudes of Educated Youth," *Christus Rex*, XII (December, 1960), 257-266.

   An examination of the attitudes of youth (mostly university youth) toward religion and life in Ireland in general.

   While some youth feel that Ireland is a small and narrow-minded nation, most want to settle there. Many feel that the church places too much stress on the vices of youth and too little on the virtues. In general the author objects to the liberalizing influence of a materialistic world on the youth of Ireland and desires a retention of the traditional values.

6. Finnegan, Thomas A., "The Religious Formation of Adolescents," *Christus Rex*, XIV (December, 1960), 275-285.

   The initial assumption is made that, by the period of adolescence, youth is very religiously oriented. It is noted that youth need more to occupy their time. The church must give attention to instilling the proper attitudes toward authority in the youth. Sex and chastity is seen as a rising problem and priests and school authorities as well as parents should be concerned with sex education.

7. Hegarty, E. J., "Statistics: Juvenile Delinquency," *Christus Rex*, XIII (October, 1959), 297-302.

   Utilizing the statistics from 1958 statistical abstracts of Ireland and the report of the commissioner of the Garda Siochana the author comments on the state of crime in Ireland. In this article he considers only the statistics on the indictable offenses against persons or property.

   From the data on criminal prison convictions it is shown that crime may be more prevalent among juveniles than among adults. Juveniles comprise 34-36 per cent of the total number of all persons charged with crimes in the past ten years (1949-1959). The author suggests that this is a high figure since juveniles are easier to obtain evidence against and will implicate comrades when questioned. Juvenile larceny charges usually involve minor crimes. With the average at ten the data reveal some young criminals of seven years. While boys seem to prefer burglary and housebreaking, the girls tend toward larceny.

8. Hegarty, E. J., "Statistics: The Young Delinquent," *Christus Rex*, XIV (January, 1960), 60-65.

   Utilizing the same source of data as the previous article, the author attempts a description of the typical young delinquent.

   The average delinquent is between 14 and 16 years and is involved in petty larceny in his own neighborhood and with the assistance of one or more comrades. Unemployed adolescents are particularly susceptible.

   The greatest contributing factor to delinquency is seen as lack of parental control, followed by money for amusements and influence of the youth gang.

The author holds that highly commercialized amusements are dangerous to the juvenile.

9. Kennedy, M., "Opportunity for Rural Youth," *Studies,* XLIX (Summer, 1960), 194-200.
10. O'Doherty, E. F., "The Adolescent," *Studies* (March, 1953), 83-89.
11. O'Doherty, E. F., "Spiritual Formation of the Adolescent," *Studies* (Spring, 1959), 67-77.
12. O'Neil, Dermot, "Urban Youth Problems," *Christus Rex,* XIV (December, 1960) 267-274.

This author holds that the training of youth should be educational, recreational, and moral. While there are many organized activities for the age groups over 11, those over 13 suffer from lack of leaders and lack of funds. He feels that the greatest good can be done in the 15-17 age group. With regard to the problem of juvenile delinquency he feels that there is no one and simple solution to the problem.

13. "Special Number on Education in a Changing World," (10 good articles written from the Roman Catholic point of view), *Dublin Review,* XCVII, 472 (January, 1957), 228.

ITALY

1. Bartolomeis, F. De, *La psicologia dell'adolescente e l'educazione* (*Adolescent psychology and education*) (Firenze: la Nuova Italia Editrice, 1955).
2. Baxter, Celena A., "Sicilian Family Life," *The Family* (May, 1933), 82-88.

The data for this discussion were gathered from visits and talks with over 100 Sicilian families. These families were scattered in the hills, the port towns, and towns with the major tourist attractions.

In the Sicilian family there is a distinct differentiation between the training and expectations for girls and that for boys. The girls are trained from early childhood in the subservient role. The boys are taught to be strong and to inspire fear in both their women and other men. Since the male must be superior the early and later education of the male over the female is stressed. The girls' place is seen to be in the home.

Most Sicilians are very severe with their children in the matter of morals and a great drive is present to have children who are well reared. Education is seen as one avenue of improvement.

3. Cavalli, L., *La gioventu del quartiere operaio* (*Youth of the Working Neighborhood*) (Genove: Pagano, 1959).

4. Chircev, A., "Atitudini Sociale la Studenti" (Social Attitudes among Students), *Rivista de Psicologia Experimentala*, III (1940), 345-371.

   (Abstract Review; original not seen). The distribution of student attitudes toward the Church, nationalism—internationalism and tradition—progress was obtained by administering the social tests developed by Margineance Draser and Chircev to 800 students of different departments. The principle findings were that social attitudes are preponderantly influenced by the cultural and social setting and that the distribution follows more the tendency of homogeneity and similarity than that of polar differentiation.

5. Cortese, A., "Youth Activities in Southern Italy," *Fundamental and Adult Education*, X, 2 (1958), 59-61.

   This short article notes the efforts of the National Youth Secretariat among the youth of Southern Italy. The intervention of this agency in activities of the agricultural districts is mainly an attempt to introduce the people, particularly the youth, to the outside culture. This is attempted by means of television, films, and trips to parts of Italy and Switzerland.

   The author notes that there are already signs that the youth of the area are developing a greater awareness of their surroundings and are becoming more sensitive to interpersonal relationships.

6. Fantl, Berta and Joseph Schiro, "Cultural Variables in the Behavior Patterns and Symptom Formation of Fifteen Irish and Fifteen Italian Female Schizophrenics," *International Journal of Social Psychiatry*, IV (1955), 245-253.

7. Finer, Herman, *Mussolini's Italy* (London: 1935), Chapter 15, "The Fascist Party: Youth Organizations."

8. Fonzi, A., "Una Recerca Sperimentale delle Reazoni alla Frustrazione in Gruppi Culturalmente Diversi" (Experimental Study of Reactions to Frustration in Culturally Different Groups), *Rivista de Psicologia Sociale e Archivio Italiano di Psicologia Generale e del Lavoro*, VII (1960), 3-33.

   Northern and southern Italian boys showed considerable differences in their overt reactions to frustration, while covert reactions appeared bound to individual characteristics.

9. Garner, A. S. and A. Williams, "Giovani conservatori e giovani laburisti" (Conservative and Labor Youth), *Civitas,* VIII, 6-7 (Rome: June/July, 1957), 66-71.

10. Gastaldil, E., "L'assistenza publica al servizio della gioventu italiana" (Public Assistance in the service of Italian youth), *Civitas,* V, 11 (November, 1954), 66-75.

11. Gemelli, A., *La Psicologia della eta Evolutiva* (*The psychology of adolescence*), 4th ed. (Milano: A. Giuffre, 1955).

12. Gillespie, J. M. and G. W. Allport, *Youth's Outlook on the Future* (Garden City, New York: Doubleday and Company, Inc., 1955). (1,819 case studies from 10 countries.)

This was a successful pilot study the object of which was to examine the attitudes of college students in ten countries toward their individual and collective futures; no hypotheses were tested. At least partial answers were sought to three questions: (1) How do youth in various countries view their future? (2) Do young people in different countries view their futures in essentially the same way? (3) Is international social research at the present time practicable and beneficial? A cross-cultural analysis of attitudes, aspirations, and moral values among students from the United States, New Zealand, Egypt, Mexico, France, Italy, Germany, Japan, Israel, and South Africa was attempted by administering a questionnaire—including both multiple-choice and open-ended questions—to 100 males and 100 females from each country. (This was the goal; the attempts occasionally fell short.) In addition an essay entitled "Autobiography: from Now to 2000 A.D.," was required from each respondent. Some of the similarities discovered were: Familism is a universal foundation for individual group life." "Basic moral values and ethical codes of conduct are everywhere prized." "Most students (Africaners excepted) . . . desire to see greater equality between white and colored races." "Most youth regarded war as needless and preventable . . . (but are) . . . pessimistic as to the possibility of avoiding a third world conflict." There were, of course, a great number of national differences, but the authors conclude that ". . . it is a wholesome corrective to note that these differences may be dramatic figures etched upon a ground of basic resemblance."

13. Granat, A., "Changing Pattern of Education in Italy," *Catholic Educational Review,* LV (February, 1957), 108-114.

14. Grasso, Pier Giovanni, *Gioventi de Meta Secolo* (*Mid-Century Youth*) (Rome, Italy: A.V.E., 1954).

15. Hilton-Young, W., "Initiation Festival: the Italian Festa delle Matricole," *Spectator*, CLXXX (March 26, 1948).

16. "Italian Teddy Boys: Diagnosis and Remedies at Two Conferences," *Tablet*, CCXIII (October 10, 1959).

17. Kurci, A., "Sud'by rabocej molodezi Italii" (Destinies of Italy's working youth), *Sovietskie profsojuzy*, VI, 6 (Moskva: June, 1958), 84-88.

18. Lombardi, P., "Aspects of Family Life Education in the Community in Italy," *Marriage and Family Living*, XXIII (May, 1961), 176-178.

19. Marzolo, Renato, *The Youth Movement in Italy* (Roma: Societa Editrice de "Novissma," 1939).

20. Nosengo, G., *L'educazione morale dei giovani* (*The Moral Training of Youth*) (Brescia: La Scuola Editrice, 1955).

21. Palisi, G., "Il problema dei giovani nella democrazia italiana" (The Youth Problem of Italian Democracy), *Vita sociale*, XIV, 2 (Florence: March/April, 1957), 96-106.

22. Palma, L., "L'orientamento professionale dei giovani" (Professional Orientation of Youth), *Rassegna del lavoro*, II, 9-10 (Rome: September/October, 1956), 1559-1574 (Italy).

23. Piccoli, Domenico S. *The Youth Movement in Italy* (Roma: Societa Editrice de "Novissma," 1936).

24. Pitkin, D. S., "Land Tenure and Family Organization in an Italian Village," *Human Organization*, XVIII (Winter, 1959-60), 169-173.

25. Psathas, George, "Ethnicity, Social Class, and Adolescent Independence From Parental Control," *American Sociological Review*, XXII (1957), 415-423.

An analysis of the psychological factors defining differences in patterns of independence from parental authority in similar, but not identical, ethnic groups (Southern Italian and Eastern European Jews). The results are obtained by devising a 25-item questionnaire and submitting the responses to factor analysis. The factors isolated were described and discussed with reference to the present as well as previous research.

26. Sandercock, G. A., "Culture Conflict and the Behavior Difficulties of Adolescent Italian Boys," *Smith College Studies on Social Work*, X (1939), 159-160.

27. Van Niele, Albert, "Adolescenza e linguaggio" (Adolescence and Language), *Salesiaonum,* XV (1953), 3-44.

"The analysis of the answers to the questionnaire show: (1) a discrepancy between what the subject experiences and the expressive means at his disposal; (2) a feeling of inadequacy, in terms of what was really felt; (3) a desire for self-expression; (4) attempts at solving the discrepancy are made but it could not be stated that there exists a conscious and universal effort to bridge the gap between the inner world and the expressive possibilities; (5) there is a certain awareness as to the variation in word meaning expressing affective experiences, but it seems to be rather vague."

28. Schachter, M., "Tristezza e 'fatiga di vivere' in una giovane adolescente: Studio clinico-psicologico dei giovani" (Melancholy and the "tired of living" feeling in an adolescent youth. A clinico-psychological study of youth), *Infanzia anormale,* XVII (Rome: March/April, 1956), 143-151.

29. Serio, A., "La situazione universitaria italiana e le elezioni studenti" (The Italian University Situation and Student Elections), *Civitas,* VII, 12 (Rome: December, 1956), 72-80.

30. Veneziani, G., "I liceali italiani e la politica" (Italian Secondary School Students and Politics), *Occidente,* XI, 6 (Turin: 1955), 449-460.

31. Vergani, Ottavio. *Ragazzi Antisociali; il Problema della Delinquenza Minorile* (Antisocial Boys: The Problem of Juvenile Delinquency, 2nd ed.) (Brescia, Italy: La Scuola, 1954) (Bibliography, 44 items).

32. West, M. L., *Children of the Shadows; the True Story of the Street Urchins of Naples* (New York: Doubleday, 1957).

33. Zunini, Giorgio, "Sulle Attitudini Religiose de Studenti Universitari" (Religious Attitudes of University Students), *Arch. Psicol. Neur. Psich.,* XV (1954), 204-249.

The results are comparable with those obtained by Allport, Gillespie, and Young at Harvard and Radcliffe especially with reference to the value of religion in the formation of a philosophy of life. Other values such as humanity or social justice are also recognized by 32 per cent of the sample.

NETHERLANDS

1. Banning, W., *Terugblik op leven en strijo van althans een deel der generatie die idealistisch jong was a n het begin van de twintigste eeuw* (*Retrospective View on the Life and Conflict Today of a Part of the Generation of Idealistic Young at the Beginning of the Twentieth Century*) (Amsterdam: Arbeiderspers, 1958).
2. Beets, N., *De grote jongen: de psychologie van de jongen in de vlegeljaren* (*Adolescents: the Psychology of Youth During the War Years*) (Utrecht: Erven J. Bijleveld, 1954).
3. Bernarda, M., "Wat denken jonge mansen over den dood?" (What do Young People Think Regarding Death?), *Vlaamsch Opvoedkundig Tijdschrift*, XXX (1949), 32-40.

   Examination of the diaries of 10 young girls (15-19). "Their idea of death depends upon their conception of life." (P.A.)
4. Braak, G. J. M. ter, "Jeugdzorg en maatschappelijk werk" (Youth Care and Social Work), *Social Contact*, IX (1960), 235-241.
5. Buytendijk, F., "Unruhe und Geborgenheit in der Welt des jungen Menschen" (Unrest and Security in the World of Youth), *Universitas*, XIII (1958), 721-730.
6. *Digest of the Netherlands, 4 Education and Cultural Aspects* (The Hague: 1959).
7. Ginsburg, H. H., "Netherlands University Life—a Reappraisal," *Higher Education and Research in the Netherlands*, II, 4 (1958), 12-15.
8. Heijboer-Barbas, M. E., *Een Nieuwe Visie op de Jeugd uit Vroeger Ewwen* (*A New View on Youth of Earlier Centuries*) (Nijkerk: G. F. Callenbach, 1956).
9. Heinemeyer, W. F., *Jeugd en vriie tijd in Amsterdam* (*Youth on free time in Amsterdam*) (Amsterdam: Gemeentelijk Bureau voor Jeugdzorg, 1959). CR; J. S. Rienks and L. Turksma, *Mens in Mij*, XXXIV, 6 (November/December, 1959), 381-389.
10. Herold, J. L. N., "De moderne jeugd in het moderne bedrijf" (Modern Youth in Modern Industry), *Mens en Onderneming*, XIV, 3 (May, 1960), 150-158.
11. Perquin, N. C. A., "Jeugd in de wereld van heden" (Youth in the World of Today), *Schalm*, XVII, 4 (1960), 144-157.
12. Van Der Putt, J., "Jeugd en socialisme; over het idealisme van twee generaties" (Youth and Socialism on the Idealism of Two

Generations), *Socialisme en Democratie,* XVII, I (Amsterdam: 1960), 54-63.

13. Van Hessen, J., "Het georganiseerd zijn van de Nederlandse Jeugd" (The Organized Life of the Netherlands Youth), *Mens en Mij,* XXXIII, 1 (January/February, 1958), 32-41.

14. Vervoort, C., "Positie en rol van de student in de universitaire samenleving" (Position and Role of the Student in the University Society) *Sociologische Gido,* VI, 6 (Meppel: December, 1959), 242-258.

15. Vries, P. H. de, "Jeugdzorg en maatschappelijkwerk" (Youth Care and Social Work), *Social Contact,* VIII, 9 (Rotterdam, 1960), 229-235.

16. Vries, Reilingh, H. D. de, "Sociaal onderzoek onzer jeugdige bevolking" (Social Inquiry into Our Youth), *Volksopvoeding,* IV, 1 (Groningen: 1955), 26-34, Netherlands.

17. Wilson, Norman H., "Dutch Schools and Religious Segmentation," *Comparative Education Review,* III (October, 1959), 19-24.

    The author's thesis is that Dutch society is divided into three major groups: Catholic, Protestant, and neutral. This influences the development of the schools along religious lines, three types of schools being maintained.

18. Windey, R., "De Godsdienstige Belangstelling Bij Onye Studerende Jeugd" (The Religious Interests of Our Students), *Vlaamsch Opvoedkundig Tijdschrift,* XXVIII (1948), 212-213.

NORWAY

1. Campbell, A. and H. Valen, "Party Identification in Norway and the U.S.," *Public Opinion Quarterly,* XXV (Winter, 1961), 505-525.

2. "Education Research in Norway: The Developments Since 1950," *International Review of Education,* III, 3 (1957), 373-377.

    Among other items, this article notes the attempt to construct and standardize a battery of maturity tests for children. It is hoped that these tests will replace the standard intelligence tests as indicators of future school performance.

    It is noted that a new source of funds has greatly aided the development of research in Norway. The author lists several projects which have been sponsored by the Research Council.

3. Helgheim, J., "Aspirasjonsnivaet hja born" (Level of Aspiration in

Children), *Norsk Pedagogisk Tidsskrift,* XXXVI (1952), 271-284.

4. Lovass, O. Ivar, "Social Desirability Ratings of Personality Variables by Norwegian and American College Students," *Journal of Abnormal and Social Psychology,* LVII (1958), 124-125.
5. Lund, Ragnar (ed.), *Scandinavian Adult Education,* 2nd ed. (Copenhagen: Det Danske Forlag, 1952).
6. Lynn, D. B. and W. L. Sawrey, "The Effects of Father-Absence on Norwegian Boys and Girls," *Journal of Abnormal and Social Psychology,* LIX (1959), 258-262.
7. Nordland, Eva, *Ungdoms—Psykologi* (*Psychology of Adolescence*) (Oslo: H. Aschehoug, 1949).
8. Norstebo, Sigurd, "Stereotype-Studiar," *Pedagogisk Forskning,* No. 3 (1959), 146-175.

   "The stereotypes of 800 Norwegian children (aged 11-14) toward Swedes, Germans, English, Russians, Americans, and Norwegians were assessed, using a modified form of the Katz-Braly technique together with an augmented trait list from the Buchanan-Cantril study. Nationality stereotypes differed with the age level of the child, presumably due to differing amounts of knowledge about foreign countries. One-third of the children were unable to specifiy the source of their stereotypes; the others drew from one or more of the following sources: personal contact, geography, history news, and common talk. Personal contact and geography seemed to the whole to create good will and respect, while history had a tendency to keep old aversions alive."

9. Park, G. K. and L. Soltow, "Politics and Social Structure in a Norwegian Village," *American Journal of Sociology,* LXVII (September, 1961), 152-164.
10. Pihlblad, C. T. and D. Aas, "Residential and Occupational Mobility in an Area of Rapid Industrialization in Norway," *American Sociological Review,* XXV (April, 1960), 369-375.
11. Rommetveit, Ragnar, *Social Norms and Roles* (Minneapolis: University of Minnesota Press, 1955).
12. Simenson, William and Gilbert Geis, "Courtship Patterns of Norwegian and American University Students," *Marriage and Family Living,* XVIII (1956), 334-338.

   The data for this article were taken from the study discussed above. The aim in this analysis was to provide comparative data on the alleged sexual promiscuity of the Scandinavian countries.

The analysis indicates that the Norwegians are more conservative in the initial stages of a relationship, but believe in greater sexual freedom in the later stages, particularly during the engagement; 81 per cent of Norwegian males and 39 per cent of Norwegian females approve of intercourse during engagement as compared to 33 per cent of American males and 14 per cent of the American females. It was also noted that the Norwegian male tends to form close relationships while in college in comparison to the relatively unattached status of the American male sample.

13. Simenson, William and Gilbert Geis, "A Cross Cultural Study of University Students," *Journal of Higher Education*, XXVI (1955), 21-24, 56-57.

The authors examine data on 145 students at the University of Oslo and 275 students at the University of Wisconsin in order to show the similarities and differences in various aspects of the university groups. It was hoped that the information from the questionnaires would prove more useful in comparison than the typical generalizations usually voiced in discussions of university students from different cultures.

Among other findings we note:

1. The Wisconsin women reported enjoying college life more than the American men or the Norwegians.

2. Both samples were very similar in their prestige ranking of occupations.

3. The American student is more likely to have a part-time job than the Norwegian student.

4. In terms of regional background, the Norwegian is more often rural, but in both groups the women tend to come from urban homes.

5. On the average, the Norwegian student is two years older than the American student.

6. While the Norwegian reports only 6 hours per week in lectures to the American's 16, the Norwegian spends 36.2 hours per week in study as compared to the American average of 19.6.

7. It was noted that the Norwegian student is not withdrawn from the community as is the American student, and therefore does not have to select activities almost wholly from the university community.

14. Skard, Oyvind, "Measurement of Students' Interests," *Acta Psychologia*, VIII (1952), 264-278.

This article is concerned with the development of a Norwegian interest schedule. It was noted by the author that the Thurstone Interest Schedule has been the best received by the students and is shorter and more convenient than the Kuder or the Strong interest schedules.

In the main the article deals with correlations between the tests to determine the reliability of the Thurstone schedule.

The study was part of a larger research program in the field of student guidance and selection conducted in Norway.

15. Skard, A. G., "Why Norwegian Teachers Fight Nazism," *American-Scandinavian Review,* XXX (December, 1942), 314-320.
16. Taylor, Denise E., "Oslo and After" (World Conference of Christian Youth), *Religion in Education,* XV, 1 (1947), 20-21.
17. Tiller, P. O., "Father Basence and Personality Development of Children in Sailor Families," *Nordisk Psykilogias Monograph Series,* IX (1958).
18. Vikvaering, B., "Revolt of the Children in Oslo against Hitlerism," *American-Scandinavian Review,* XXV (June, 1941), 159-160.

SPAIN AND PORTUGAL

1. Boleo, J. P., *Tendencias Psicologias da Mocidade Escolar* (*Psychological Trends of School Youth*) (Lisbon: 1945).

   One hundred and fifty-five high school bys, Spain. An adjustment inventory was given to 155 high school boys, who were motivated by the promise of interpretation of results to them. The home patterns were thoroughly explored, as were reading habits, study difficulties, and vocational uncertainties—H. D. Spoerl (American International College).

2. Collignon, Theo, "La Recherche des Causes Criminogenes chez les Enfants" (Investigation into the Causes of Criminal Tendencies in Children), *Crianca Portuguesa,* XI (1951/1952), 45-87.

   The movement of social defense, directed by Count F. Gramatica of Genoa, rests on principles of preventative educational and environmental measures, revision of ideas of what is antisocial, and improvement in legislative and judicial procedures. Heredity is important, and some children's constitutions predispose to delinquency, making social recovery difficult. Movies, night clubs, literature, have had bad effects on the young. Sociologists and governments should give priority to problems affecting children growing up in the present disturbed social atmosphere.

3. Farreras, F., "Perfil de las nuevas generaciones espanolas" (Profile of the New Spanish Generations), *Cuadernos,* XLI (March/April, 1960), 60-66.

4. Fontes, Vitor, "Notas a Margem de Dois Diarios Intimas de Adolescentes" (Notes on two Intimate Diaries of Adolescents), *Crianca Portuguesa,* V (1945-1946), 67-91.

5. Losada, A., "El ideal profesional en el muchacho obrero," (The Professional Ideal of the Young Worker), *Fomento Social,* Spain, XI, 41 (Spain: January/March, 1956), 38-48.

6. Nieva, J., *Algunas Consideracoes Sobre a Psicologia Dos Adolescentes* (*Some Considerations of the Psychology of Adolescents*) (Lisbon: Biblioteca Cosmos, No. 33, Sect. 7, 1943).

   The mental outlook of adolescents is considered in the light of formulations of Hull, Stern, Binet, etc.

7. Ridrueja, D., "Dei studierende Jugend unter dem spanischen Regime" (University students under the Spanish regime), *Frankfurter Hefte,* XII, 3 (March, 1957), 157-168.

8. "Students versus the Falange," *New Statesman,* LI (March 24, 1956), 262.

9. Valle, Rodrigo, "Spanish Youth and the (Roman Catholic) Church," *Iberica,* VIII (March 15, 1960), 6-7.

10. "The Youth of Spain and the (Francisco) Franco Regime: an Interview with Father (Enrique Maria De Laburu, S.J.)," *Iberica,* V (September 15, 1957), 3-4.

SWEDEN

1. Bailyn, L. and H. C. Kelman, "Effects of a Year's Experience in America on the Self-Image of Scandinavians," *Journal of Social Issues,* XVIII, 1 (1962), 30-40.

2. Clinard, M. B., "A Cross-Cultural Replication of the Relation of Urbanism to Criminal Behavior," *American Sociological Review,* XXV (April, 1960), 253-257.

   In this article the author attempts to show the necessity and feasibility of cross-cultural replications in the behavioral sciences. The original study was reported in 1942. Sweden was chosen for the replication because of its similarities and differences to the United States. It was felt to be a good testing ground for findings derived in the more heterogeneous atmosphere of the United States.

   In the Swedish sample the subjects were restricted to property offenders between the ages of 17 and 29 selected at random by penal institutions. Questionnaires were applied to 101 subjects. This duplicated the situation of the original Iowa sample and instrument.

   The original five hypotheses tested in the Iowa sample (and

the Iowa duplication) were supported in the Swedish replication. Briefly these hypotheses were: (254-256)

1. "The greater the degree of urbanism in a community, the greater the rate of property offenses . . ."

2. "The rural criminal is likely to be characterized by having considerable contacts of an impersonal nature . . . (contacts outside the community—high horizontal mobility—nonattachment to the community.)"

3. "Since urbanism is characterized by impersonal behavior, crimes are generally committed in the impersonal areas of the criminal offender's life. Therefore, in rural areas the place of occurrence of crimes is usually not the same as residence of the offender."

4. "As urbanism is characterized by cultural heterogeneity, criminal offenders tend to build up and pass on a cultural organization outside the traditional norms. As urbanism increases, networks of criminal relationships increase. Therefore, in rural areas there is a comparative absence of continuity in the criminal culture . . ."

5. "The criminal culture of the heterogenous urban community produces a criminal social type, characterized by criminal techniques, criminal argot, and a definite progressive criminal life history." (This will not be true of the rural criminal.)

3. Eysenck, H. J., "Primary Social Attitudes: a Comparison of Attitude Patterns in England, Germany, and Sweden," *Journal of Abnormal Psychology*, XLVIII (October, 1953), 563-568.

4. Husen, T., *Adolescensen* (*Adolescence*) (Uppsala: Almquist and Wiksells, 1944).

   Investigation of 1,000 Swedish adolescents.

5. Husen, T., *Svensk Ungdom: Psykologiska Undersokninger av Ynglingar: Aldern 17-20 År* (*Swedish Youth: Psychological Examinations of Youth of 17-20 Years*) (Stockholm: Geber, 1944).

   Attitudes, reading interests of 1,000 volunteers for military service.

   "This is the first psychological survey of the country's youth ever made in Sweden, the subjects being over 1,000 volunteers for military service of a 17 per cent sampling of the age class. The free essays, questionnaires, exploratory interviews were used to ascertain attitudes toward parents and upbringing, schools and teachers, social contacts, choice of and attitudes toward jobs, attitudes toward nature as represented by early home territory, and reading interests (books and periodicals).

Answers were correlated with intelligence ratings. Besides the statistical breakdowns, the reader is given a larger selection of the free-essay material submitted, and every social class is represented as well as every type of environment—city, large town, small town, and country. In each section the techniques and results of similar inquiries made in other countries are noted, and the probable sources of error in the author's procedures are pointed out. It is shown that the early natural surroundings are evaluated aesthetically by younger children more often than by older youths who tend to regard them in purely utilitarian or recreational terms. Reading is by the book far more than by the author, half the subjects failing to answer the question whether they had a favorite author."

6. Kalvesten, Anna-Lisa, *The Social Structure of Sweden* (Stockholm: The Swedish Institute, 1961).

7. Karlsson, Georg, "Political Attitudes among Male Swedish Youth," *Acta Sociologica*, III (January 4, 1958), 220-241.

   This article examines the political attitudes of a sample of Swedish youth and attempts to associate political attitudes with group membership and background and personality characteristics.

   Questionnaires were applied to a quota sample of Swedish men, ages 20-30. Laborers and agricultural workers are underrepresented in the sample.

   It is noted in the findings that personal influence is more effective than mass media in influencing personal opinions on political issues. The author notes, "The possibility of an individual following in his father's footsteps politically or of his having a deviant opinion and lacking definite political views here appears as a clearly visible function of his occupational group and the political views held by his best friends."

   The author utilizes norm theory in explanation and notes, "According to this theory our conception of reality and our valuations are greatly influenced by verbal pressures, norms that are directed toward us in the groups to which we belong."

8. Larson, Carl A., "The Frequency of First Cousin Marriages in a South Swedish Rural Community," *American Journal of Human Genetics*, VIII (September, 1956), 151-153.

9. Lund, Ragnar (ed.), *Scandinavian Adult Education*, 2nd ed. (Copenhagen: Det Danske Forlag, 1952).

10. Scott, Franklin D., *The American Experience of Swedish Students* (University of Minnesota Press, 1956).

11. Skard, Ase Gruda, "*Karakterdaning og oppeding*" (Character Training and Impairment), *Menneske og Miljo*, III (1948), 26-37.
12. Sturup, G. K., "Sex Offenses, the Scandinavian Experience," *Law and Contemporary Problems*, XXV (Spring, 1960), 361-375.
13. Thuren, Gunnar, "Ungdomsfangelseidnes Utformning i Swerige" (Youth Penal Training in Sweden), *Menneske og Miljo*, II (1947), 14-20.
14. "Ungdomsproblem pa RFSU-Konferens" (Youth Problems at the conference of the RFSU), *Sociala Meddelanden* 4 (Sweden: 1956), 249-252.
15. "Vocational Guidance for Young Persons in Sweden," *International Labour Review*, LI (April, 1945), 471-479.

SWITZERLAND

1. Abegg, Walter, *Aus Tagebuchern und Breifen junger Menchen; ein Beutrag zur Psychologie des Entwicklungsalters* (*From Diaries and Letters of Young People; A Contribution to the Psychology of Puberty*) (Basel, Switzerland: Ernst Reinhart, 1954).

   "It is chiefly with questions from diaries that the author explains the emotional stages through which human beings pass from puberty to adolescence. The writers of these, 10 girls and 2 boys, come from Swiss and German middle-class families. The general characteristics of puberty are discussed as to: 'Weltschmerz'; anxiety and loneliness; suicide; sexuality, erotics and love; development of the conscious self; the environment, including family and school, nature, art, literature, music, religion, philosophy, politics, social life, vocation."

2. Aeschbach, K., "Junge Generation und Sozialpolitik" (Young Generation and Social Policy), *Rote Ruvue*, XXXIX, 9 (Zurich: September, 1960), 253-258.
3. Clapp, H., "Some Lessons from Swiss Education," *Modern Age* II (Winter, 1958), 10-17.
4. Montalta, E., *Jugendverwahrlosung* (*Juvenile Delinquency*) (Zug, Switzerland: Kalt-Zehnder, 1939).
5. Mueller, G. O. W., "Resocialization of the Young Adult Offender in Switzerland," *Journal of Criminal Law*, XLIII (January, 1953), 578-591.

   Account of the correctional policies as applied at the work-education institution, Vitikon, A. Kanton, Zurich, Switzerland, and an interpretation of the methods in terms of theories of criminal causation.

6. Naf, Hans, "Ursachen der Jugendkriminalitat" (Causes of Juvenile Delinquency), *Psychol. Prax.*, No. 12 (1953), 104.

Adolescents in Basel, Switzerland.

7. Ramseyer, Pierre, "The Swiss School," *Harvard Educational Review*, XXII, 1 (Winter, 1952), 49-56.

UNITED KINGDOM

1. Abbott, E., "Juvenile Delinquency during the First World War; Notes on the British Experiences, 1914-1918," *Social Service Review*, XVII (1943), 192-212.

During World War I England experienced a grave increase in juvenile delinquency. This article includes the court statistics for the war years broken down by age, sex, and nature of offense; a comparison is made with the German experiences. Of the many causes for this increase, the author was able to distinguish several especially clear ones: changes in home life, disruption of elementary education, the increase in juvenile employment, and the changed conditions in the juvenile labor market. The increase was much greater in Germany, and the author concludes that this was largely because the children were left primarily in the care of women for whom the society had little respect.

2. Aberdare, Lord, "Boys' Club in Britain," *Fortnightly* (July, 1947), 56-60.
3. "The Adjustment of Youth; A Study of a Social Problem in the British, American, and Australian Communities," Melbourne University Press (1951), VIII. (Published for the Australian Council for Educational Research. Being a report of a team of Australian investigators who visited the United Kingdom, Canada, and the United States, Bibliography).
4. *Advances in Understanding the Adolescent* (London: Home and School Council of Great Britain, 1938). (See also Educational Abstracts 4: 803)
5. Allaway, A. M., "Social and Educational Change Since 1900," *Sociological Review*, XLIII (1951), 143-157.
6. Allcorn, Derek, "The Unnoticed Generation: Notes on the Social Life of Young Men in an Industrial Suburb," *Universal Left Review*, I (Summer, 1958), 51-58.
7. Allen, Eric A., "Attitudes to School and Teachers in a Secondary Modern School," *British Journal of Educational Psychology*, XXXI (February, 1961), 106-109.

To ascertain the attitudes of secondary-school students toward school, personal interviews were conducted with 68 secondary school students in their last year. There were 35 boys and 33 girls in the sample, and the school's total enrollment was 250. It was found that there were no great differences between the boys and girls in regard to their topics of concern. In general the students' attitudes were favorable toward school, although it was conjectured that the girls had become somewhat discontented with their present status within the school. The author concludes that students must feel that they are being taught interesting material that is relevant to them, and that they should be controlled in a manner befitting their present status or the status that they wish to have.

8. Arnon, Yosef, "Hanoar Haovaryon B'Anglia" (Delinquent Youth in England), *Ofakim*, X (1956), 23-30.

9. Arnon, Yosef, "Hanoar Bakefar Hoangli" (Youth in the English Village), *Ofakim*, XI (1957), 25-37.

10. Asquith, J., "Frustrated Youth," *Spectator*, CLXXXIII (December 30, 1949), 912.

11. Balough, P., "Student Suicides," *New Statesman*, XLVI (November 14, 1953), 591-592; Discussion XLVI (November 21-December 12, 1953), 637, 673-674, 716, and 761.

12. Bamford, W., "Public Schools and Social Class, 1801-1850," *British Journal of Sociology*, XII (September, 1961), 224-235. (Bibliography)

13. Banks, C., "Fighting Facts," *20th Century*, CLXX (Winter, 1962), 43-49.

14. Barker, T., "Twenties Vote," *Spectator*, CLXXIV (July 15, 1945), 545.

15. Barker, T., "Youth and the Churches," *Spectator*, CLXXV (November, 1945), 458. Discussion CLXXV (November 23, 1945—Jan. 4-11, 1946), 488, 513, 540, 568, 592, 620-621, CLXXVI, 12-13, 36-37.

16. Barker, R. G. and Louise S. Barker, "Behavior Units for the Comparative Study of Culture," in B. Kaplan (ed.), *Studying Personality Cross-Culturally* (New York: Harper & Row, Publishers, 1954).

This is primarily a study of units of behavior, "behavior settings" in a town in Kansas and Yoredale, Yorkshire. The focus is on the behavior system of children. The sample consisted of a town in Kansas with a population of 715 (128 children under twelve) and Yoredale with a population of 1,300 (245 children under twelve). Both of these towns are approximately midway between seacoasts, are separated from the surrounding farming areas by areas of a higher population density and both are characterized by behavior patterns which are different from the farming areas. Both are connected by communication networks to the larger regional and national cultures and both are typical of the regions. Both are centers of government and are nonindustrial. The study is concerned with the ". . . functional relations between settings and the behavior of individuals."

Directly applicable to our concerns are the conclusions noted for childhood and adolescent behavior. The Midwest, it was noted, demands greater participation by its children and adolescents in a greater number of behavior settings and considers participation necessary for full personality development. Children and adolescents are functionally more important in the Midwest than in Yoredale. Yoredale does not demand a great deal of participation by its children and adolescents in social interaction and it places greater emphasis on the qualitative aspects of participation than on the quantitative. A great deal of interaction by children and adolescents is not considered necessary for full social development in Yoredale and the emphasis is on development for future participation.

17. Barschak, Erna, "A Study of Happiness and Unhappiness in the Childhood and Adolescence of Girls in Different Cultures," *Journal of Psychology*, XXXII (1951), 173-215. (England, America, Switzerland, and Germany)

Purpose of study to make a comparison of attitudes of adolescent girls of four different societies.

Four groups of women between the ages of 17 plus and 27 in teacher training departments or teacher training colleges in England, America, Germany, and Switzerland were asked to complete a schedule on the causes of happiness and unhappiness in childhood and adolescence. The numbers were approximately alike in the three countries, about 130, and the Swiss figure was 65. The experience of happiness and unhappiness as the girls see it is related to the closeness or remoteness from the war scene.

Of the American group 84.4 per cent rated themselves as happy both in childhood and adolescence. Of the Swiss group, 91.6 per cent rated themselves as happy both in childhood and adolescence (Bale) 91.4 per cent (Zurich). . . . Of the English group, 81.6 per cent rated themselves as happy both in childhood and adolescence.

Of the German group 74 per cent rated themselves as happy

both in childhood and adolescence (Goettingen), 47.9 per cent (Berlin)

Whereas most of the relations of childhood are happy ones, fewer from those of the teens' are happy. This definitely points to an increased emotional stress in the teens.

There is evidence that for all the girls home and family decline in its importance in the teens and wider social environments become more significant. In the references to the family, there is a qualitative change. There are more mentions in the teens of conflict difficulty and criticism.

Social relationships are of greater importance in the teens. There is a marked difference, however, due to the different societies in which the girls grew up, as to the importance of organized group life. The German group stresses the "former youth movement" and its impact.

Games, sports, and hobbies and intellectual interests, while offering a refuge, were often an escape from stress and strain of life for all the groups. They differ very much according to the cultural pattern in which the girl is growing up.

The event of war in Europe was the frame in which the adolescence of these girls occurred. Its impact can be detected with various emphasis in all the groups.

The cultural pattern that a given society imposes on adolescents can be better detected in areas other than the family. The author feels that the attitude of all the girls toward school and university matches the type of school the particular society provides for them. The English girls stress the importance of subject matter, examination, and discipline in their questionnaires. The English educational system emphasizes just that. The German girls' questionnaires point to the personality of the teacher. This seems to them the most important experience in their school life. The Swiss educational system, entirely untouched by the war, seemed to be the most stable of the four systems. The Swiss girls, in the author's opinion in accordance with traditional European adolescents' attitude or pre-1939 experiences, severely criticize their teachers and the high demands of the Swiss educational system. The American educational system emphasizes educational aims different from European counterparts. Education for citizenship and good personal relationships are stressed more than scholarship. The American girls in the questionnaire seem to agree with those aims.

All four groups stress the importance of social relations; one can see the emphasis of the adult society on adolescents.

18. Barschak, Erna, "Happiness and Unhappiness in the Childhood and Adolescence of a Group of Women Students: a Comparative

Study of English and American girls," *British Journal of Psychology,* XLIII (1952), 129-140.

19. Bathurst, M. E., "Juvenile Delinquency in Britain during the War," *Journal of Criminal Law,* XXXIV (January, 1944), 291-302. (Bibliography)

    A discussion of juvenile delinquency, its causes and preventive measures in Britain in World War II. Among the contributing factors to the delinquent behavior during the war were the periods of blackout, the family and home disruption which led to looting, the abnormal conditions of the bomb shelters, the disruption of school life and freedom from its regulations, the release of inmates from institutions, and the lack of parole officers. These are among the factors discussed. Included in the steps to prevent the rise of delinquency were the establishment of the Youth Service, the raising of the school-leaving age, the organization of school activities to generate a feeling of contribution to the war effort, and the establishment of hostels for displaced and homeless youth. Other steps, both official and organizational, are noted.

20. Baxter, A. B., "Britain's Wild Kids: The Teddy Boys," *Maclean's Magazine,* LXVIII (July 23, 1955), 68.

21. Baxter, A. B., "What Has Led British Youth Astray," *Maclean's Magazine,* LXXI (April 12, 1958), 10, 64-65.

22. Baxter, A. B., "Crime and Punishment among the Teddy Boys," *Maclean's Magazine,* LXXI (June 7, 1958), 8, 54-55.

23. Beattie, J. H. M., "Culture Contact and Social Change," *British Journal of Sociology,* XII (June, 1961), 165-175. (Bibliography)

24. Beavan, J., "Home Notes," *20th Century,* CLXIV (1958), 375-378.

    Two articles, the first discussing the racial conflict in Notting Hill and the second discussing the problem of violent youth.

    The comments on Notting Hill are based on the reported events and comments in the British press. It is noted that the racial conflict centered around colored immigrants from the Commonwealth. The influx provided a setting for the expression of antisocial and deviant behavior on the part of the youth. The author notes that the violence which ". . . began as another horrid chapter of juvenile crime could too easily become the first act in a real and beastly race conflict."

    The second discussion notes that the problem of youth gangs and violence is not as bad today (1958) as it was in the past and is, generally, not due to instances of personal antisocial behavior, but to a reaction by youth to societal trends. Background factors both in the home and in the society in general produce a disturbing effect on youth above that produced by individual, recent occurrences and events.

Beavan believes that youth movements and clubs, which are seeking new methods of dealing with the problem of delinquency could effectively utilize American social workers. These people, coming from outside the system, would provide the British youth with a significant other with whom they could identify.

25. Bednarek, Karl, *The Young Worker of Today: A New Type.* Edited by J. P. Mayer; trans. by Renee Tupholme (London: Faber & Faber, Ltd., 1955).

Impact of improved standard of living and prosperity on young workers. Attitudes toward work, social values, religion, politics and society.

26. Bell, Colin, "A Protest. Don't Care Was Made to Care," *20th Century* (November, 1960), 388-392.

27. Berger, B. M., "How Long Is a Generation?" *British Journal of Sociology,* XI, 1 (March, 1960), 10-23.

28. Berger, B. M., "Rosy Youth," *Economist,* CXCIV (1960), 392.

A Young Socialists movement is being formed in Great Britain partly to answer the Young Conservative movement which serves as both a political movement and as a social club. The Young Socialists movement, to be established at the national level, will also offer many events of a social nature. There are, however, many obstacles to be overcome before the movement can be adequately established.

The article is a short journalistic sketch of events on the social scene and is not based on research or reference.

Some of the obstacles which must be overcome before the movement can be established at the planned level are: the indifference of many Labour leaders to the youth movement; too serious political goals, due to the larger share of funds and to the greater freedom of discussion given it by the Labour Party, and the neglect of social aspects which would frighten a large segment of the less politically minded youth away from membership. One other serious danger to the movement is that it will lean further to the left than was anticipated by its founders.

"Some enthusiasts are now saying confidently that the movement is to concentrate on producing majority resolutions in favor of public ownership and nuclear disarmament. It will fail both as a social group and a political force if it does."

29. Berger, B. M., "Teen-agers Re-visited," *Economist,* CXCV (1960), 1084.

Problem: To discuss the trend in adolescent behavior in Great Britain from role behavior correspondent to that of an older child to that expected of a young adult and the evidence of such a change in expected behavior. Also to discuss the resulting behavior patterns.

The basis of the argument is two studies done of Ilford schoolchildren, one by Mary Stewart, "Leisure Activities of Schoolchildren" and one done three school generations later. The instrument was a questionnaire.

The change in adolescent behavior is evident by the material aspects of the subculture, for example, ". . . enthusiasm for coffee-bar-and-juke-box sociabilities," and the avid reading of "love comics" by the teen-age girls.

Conclusion: In addition to the influence of the adult world the power system of the adolescent subculture must be considered when evaluating adolescent behavior and its causal factors. Also important is the ". . . rapid turnover of power and influence as (on the miniature time-scale of the republic's history) generation succeeds generation."

Decisions as to the nature of the real causes of adolescent misbehavior cannot be made by "snap judgments" but must be made through careful study.

30. Bernstein, B., "Some Sociological Determinants of Perception: An Enquiry into Sub-cultural Differences" [relations between social class and education], *British Journal of Sociology,* IX (June, 1958), 159-174. (Bibliography)

An examination of 309 male students between the ages of 15 and 18 years old. All the subjects were from unskilled and semiskilled backgrounds. 295 were in scondary schools, 5 in technical schools, 3 in central schools, and 6 in grammar schools. The purpose of the study was ". . . to indicate a relationship between the mode of cognitive expression and certain social classes." It was suggested that the lower social classes would reflect more resistance to education and formal learning. This resistance will be a function of the social strata of the individual. "It is suggested that resistance is a function of a mode of perceiving and feeling which is characterized by a sensitivity to the content rather than to the structure of objects."

The data were gathered through the use of the Mill Hill

Vocabulary Test. Some of the findings and conclusions are noted as follows.

". . . [T]he middle class child is capable of responding to, manipulating and understanding a public language, expressive symbolism and a formal language which is structured to immediate personal qualifications as a result of his class environment."

"Because of the different structuring of the working-class environment the working class child does not learn a language which is structured to immediate personal qualifications but is limited to expressive symbolism and a public language." This affects his school and learning capabilities in many ways, including lack of communication with and conflict with the teacher, lack of interest in matters not giving immediate gratification, restriction of vocabulary leading to restriction of learning capabilities, etc.

The middle-class child, on the other hand, ". . . is predisposed towards the ordering of symbolic relationships and more importantly, imposing order and seeing new relationships. His level of curiosity is high. There is a conformity to authority and an acceptance of the role of the teacher, unrespective of psychological relationships to his personality." The middle-class child is capable of using two languages, the public one used with his peers and the formal language ". . . which permits sensitivity to role and status."

31. Beverstock, A. G., "The Education of the Young Worker," *Adult Education*, XXIII (June, 1950), 30-34.

32. "Birmingham's Adolescents" (Review of Eighty Thousand Adolescents, Investigation by Students and Staff of Westhill Training College), *Times Educational Supplement* (April 28, 1950), 325.

Out of concern for the lack of purpose of the youth service, this study was done to find out how often young people attend youth organizations.

One quarter of the 1,400 youth units were visited in the survey. Age range of the youth: 14-19.

This review of the book, *Eighty Thousand Adolescents*, concerned itself mostly with the evaluative suggestions of the survey report rather than the empirical findings.

Basic findings mentioned: 35 per cent of boys and 45 per cent of girls are not in school and belong to no youth organization; one-half the members of the clubs remain in membership less than a year.

The report suggests that the increasing maturity of the

members is not recognized, that programs are too stereotyped, etc.

It recommends that the number of trained voluntary workers be increased.

It suggests that a faith in democracy must be created by helping youth to experience democratic living, discover significance in daily work, enrich home life, engage in community service.

It found that youth are not convinced the Church has something important to say. The authors say that religious issues cannot be evaded.

33. Bodsworth, C. F., "Why Half Our High School Students Quit," *Maclean's Magazine,* LXIII (August 1, 1950), 6-7, 31-32.

34. Borthwick, Alastair, "Scotland's Young Farmers," *Scotland's Magazine* (May, 1954), 21-23.

35. Boyne, A. W. and J. R. Clark (Powett Research Institute, Bucksburn, Scotland), "Secular Change in the Intelligence of Eleven Year Old Aberdeen School Children," *Human Biology,* XXXI (1959), 325-333.

36. Breco, Josephine M., *Youth and Youth Groups* (London: Faber & Faber, Ltd., 1957).

37. Bermner, Marjorie, "The Three R's in England and in America," *Future,* IV, 1 (1949), 67-75.

38. Brennah, T., E. W. Cooney and H. Pollins, *Social Change in South West Wales* (Watts and Company, 1954).

39. Brew, Macalister, "What Are Teddy Boys Made Of?" [The wider social implications of adolescent dress and behavior], *Family Doctor* (July, 1955), 516-519.

40. Brew, Macalister, "If in Doubt Look in Their Eyes: Girls Have to Face Problems," *Family Doctor* (April, 1956), 324-326.

41. Brew, Macalister, "There's Nothing Wrong with Rock 'n Roll (Adolescent Psychology)," *Family Doctor* (February, 1957), 95-99.

42. Brew, Macalister, "The Darling Young," *Social Service Quarterly,* XXII (December, 1948), 101-108.

43. Brewer, R., "Vocational Guidance for Juveniles in Britain," *Occupations,* XXV (1946), 105-107.

44. Bridgewater, J., *A Descriptive Study of a Group of Adolescents at a Youth Club,* Unpublished M. A. Thesis, University of London, 1950.

45. "British Report on Juvenile Offenses in War Time," *Social Service Review,* XVI (September, 1942), 537-541.

46. Brown, F. K., "Fathers of the Victorians: The Age of Wilburforce," *Review Spectator* (1956), 207.

47. Bryant, A., "Citizens of Tomorrow: A Study of the Influences Affecting British Youth Today," *Illustrated London News,* CCXXVII (November 5, 1955), 768.

48. Bryden, R., "Generation in Exodus," *Political Quarterly,* XXVI (June, 1955), 286-296.

49. Buchanan, R. A., "University Cynicism," *New Statesman,* XLVII (May 8, 1954), 600; Discussion—XLVII (May 15-June 12, 1954), 633, 662, 700, 732, 759.

50. Burt, Sir Cyril, *The Young Delinquent* (London: University of London Press, 1925).

51. Butchart, P., "These Teenage Gangs," *Saturday Night,* LXIV (May 10, 1949), 31.

52. Butler, R. A. et al., "Accent on Youth: Six Oxford Lectures" (February, 1961) (C.P.C. #216), Conservative Political Centre.

53. Calvert, P. A. R., "Teddy Boyars," *Economist,* CLXXXIX (1958), 659.

54. Cameron, Mary Y., "An Enquiry into the Factors Governing Membership of Youth Clubs and Juvenile Organizations," *British Journal of Educational Psychology,* XVIII (1948), 48.

55. Campbell, F., "Groping in the Dark," *New Statesman,* LXII (August 25, 1961), 236.

56. Carr-Saunders, A. M., H. Mannheim and E. C. Rhodes, *Young Offenders: an Inquiry into Juvenile Delinquency* (London: Cambridge University Press, 1942).

57. "Challenge for British Youth: the YMCA National Camp and Training Center," Lake Windermere, *Illustrated London News,* CCXL (January 27, 1962), 139-142.

58. Chisnall, B., "The Interests and Personality Traits of Delinquent Boys," *British Journal of Educational Psychology,* XII (1942), 76.

59. "Citizens of Tomorrow: A Study of the Influences Affecting the Upbringing of Young People," *King George's Jubilee Trust* (Odhams, 1955).

60. Cole, G. D. H., "General Education and Vocational Training in Great Britain," *International Labour Review,* LXXII (August/September, 1955), 164-186.

61. Colville, Lady Cynthia, *Social Progress and the Individual* (London: Clark Hall Lecture, N. 14, 1954).

62. Comfort, Alex, "Growing Up Faster," *Listener* (July 7, 1960), 15-16.

A discussion of the physical maturity of youth. The author utilizes the findings of J. M. Tanner in this survey discussion. He notes that the average age of menarche has dropped from 17 to 13 years old over the period between 1850 and 1950. Absolut height and weight has also increased. He notes that the children of the poor remain smaller and mature later than the children of those who are economically better off. The author proposes that the earlier maturity of the adolescent considerably shortens the childhood plateau.

63. "Conference Compels a Dictionary for Youth" (Offers 12 definitions from the publication entitled "Report on Terminology in the Youth Service" issued by the Standing Conference of National Voluntary Youth Organizations, London), *Municipal Journal,* LX (November 21, 1952), 2259.

64. Connor, C. V., "Behavior in Class Groups of 'Contrasting Climate,'" *British Journal of Educational Psychology,* XXX (November, 1960), 244-249.

65. *Conservative and Unionist Central Office,* "The Young Britons Organization," Organization Serial No. 11 (May, 1949).

66. Conway, Edward, *Post War Employment* (London: J. Cape, 1943).

67. Crichton, R. M., "Study of the Occupational Histories of Juveniles in Edinburgh, 1943-1945," *Sociological Review,* XXXVII (January, 1945), 10-27.

68. Crosland, A., "Patterns of Revolt," *New Statesman,* LXII (October 6, 1961), 477-487.

69. Delany, Lloyd T., "Establishing Relations with Anti-Social Groups and an Analysis of their Structure," *British Journal of Delinquency,* V (1954), 34-45.

70. Diath, W., "Debs Delight" (London Debutante World), *New Statesman,* LXII (August 4, 1961), 152-155.

71. Dudley, Kenneth, "Tackling the Teenager," *Family Doctor* (N. 9 of 10 articles) (September, 1957), 593-606.

72. Dyer, Peter John, "Youth and the Cinema, 1. The Teenage Rave," *Sight and Sound,* XXIX, 2 (1960), 61-65.

73. Dyer, Peter John, "Youth and the Cinema. 2. Candid Camera," *Sight and Sound*, XXIX, 2 (1960), 61-65.

74. East, Norwood, "Delinquency and Crime," in G. W. T. H. Fleming, *Recent Progress in Psychiatry*, XI (2nd ed.) (London: Churchill, 1950), 551-586. (Bibliography)

75. East, Norwood, et al., *The Adolescent Criminal* (London: Churchill, 1942).

76. "Education of the Adolescent," *Nature*, No. 177 (1956), 149-151.

77. Elkin, W. A., *English Juvenile Courts* (London: Kegan Paul, Trench, Trubner, and Co., Ltd., 1948).

78. Ellis, F. H., "Some Social Consequences of Environment," Leeds Institute of Education, Research and Study, No. 3 (1951), 57-69.

This is a study of a small group of children in a poor district. Locality and home conditions were studied in each case; IQ's were secured. The article gives the facts but without any statistical elaboration, since the group is too small. A striking feature is the wide variation of mental ability in children living on the same street. The children are not frustrated; nor are they, with two exceptions, antisocial.

79. Ellis, Sarah, *The Daughters of England, Their Position in Society, Character and Responsibilities* (New York: D. Appleton; Philadelphia: G. S. Appleton, 1843).

80. Eppel, E. M. and M., "A Pioneer Investigation of the Needs, Interests and Attitudes of 380 Young Workers Attending a County College," *British Journal of Educational Psychology* (June, 1953), 29-44, 87-96.

81. Erskine, Sir George W. E. J., "Youth Today and Tomorrow," *Journal of the Royal United Service Institution* (August, 1957), 322-333.

82. Evans, J. T., "Student Underworld," *Spectator*, CLXXXII (February 25, 1949), 251.

83. Everett, Samuel P., *Growing Up in English Secondary Schools—Significance for American Practice* (Pittsburgh: University of Pittsburgh Press, 1959).

The author outlines purposes in undertaking research on English secondary schools; he discusses the programs for superior students and for nonscholars, including secondary modern schools and technical schools, and gives an evaluation of the schools from the point of view of what we can learn from them.

84. Eysenck, H. J., "Primary Social Attitudes: A Comparison of Attitudes Patterns in England, Germany, and Sweden," *Journal of Abnormal Psychology,* XLVIII (October, 1953), 563-568. (Bibliography)

Attitudes of a group of middle- and working-class Germans proved similar to parallel groups of English and Swedish.

Social attitudes form definite patterns. The study was first done in England, then in the United States, in Sweden, and finally in Germany. It was expected that the results in the United States and England would be similar. Sweden was chosen because its past history and political aspiration are less similar. The writer wanted to show that two main principles of organization are radicalism-conservatism and tough-mindedness-tender-mindedness.

The 40-item attitude inventory was given to 750 middle-class English subjects, 263 midlde- and working-class Germans. Factor analysis was used to investigate the underlying principles of patterning.

The factors were shown to be similar in the four populations. The structure of attitudes in the four countries is similar—if not identical.

85. Faithfull, Davies B., "The British Youth Movement," *Britain Today* (May, 1953), 15-19.

86. Falls, C., "British Youth under the Lords," *Illustrated London News,* CCXX (January 19, 1952), 88.

87. Faludy, S., "Dancing Youth," *New Statesman,* LIII (1957), 87.

88. Faludy, S., "Guilded Youth," *Economist,* CLXXXVI (1958), 94-96.

89. Farber, Maurice L., "English and Americans: Values in the Socialization Process," *Journal of Psychology,* XXXVI (1953), 243-250.

90. Ferguson, T. and J. Cunnison, *The Young Wage-Earner: A Study of Glasgow Boys* (London: Oxford University Press, 1951).

Published for Nuffield Foundation, England. Records the circumstances of district, home, and family in which the boys grew up; their physical, scholastic, and personal qualities as assessed at the time they left school; their health, industrial progress, and leisure interests over a period of three years, January, 1947 to January, 1950.

91. Ferguson, T. and J. Cunnison, "In Their Early Twenties: A Study of Glasgow Youth," VI (London: Oxford University, 1956). Published for the Nuffield Foundation, Continuing study of a group of youth who left school in January, 1947.

The study dealt with two groups: those who had been called up for National Service (including 346 men) and those who had been rejected on medical grounds as unfit for National Service (222 men). All had been in the earlier study and extensive information was available on all of them. For the most part the boys came from the lower social strata. The rejected group came from the poorer districts, a higher proportion were the sons of unskilled laborers, and they had shown a much lower standard of performance at work from 14-17 than those who were called up. National figures showed a lower proportion of rejection on medical grounds than among Glasgow lads.

Of those who completed 2 years National Service, 58 per cent reported that they had enjoyed their experience, 18 per cent reported they had disliked it, 24 per cent were neutral, 7 per cent expressed a preference for Service life over civilian life. "There was a tendency for those who expressed dislike for Service to include more than a fair share of lads of low scholastic ability and a relatively high proportion living in 'new' local authority housing schemes."

Two-thirds of those in Service went back to work within one month of their return to civil life; 62 per cent went back to their pre-Service job; 21 per cent experienced some difficulty in settling back to civilian life. Difficulties were: dislike of job or wages and adaptation to civilian values. The proportion reporting difficulty in settling was lower among those who returned to pre-Service jobs.

"The difference in unemployment experience between men fortunately placed at the good end of the social scale and those more poorly circumstanced tended to be wider among those who had been called up for Service than among those rejected as unfit, which suggests that absence on Service may have had a particularly unfortunate influence on the amount of subsequent unemployment among men of poorer social and environmental background."

Only a small proportion of the men who had said they wanted skilled manual work when they left school at 14 were actually in that work at 22—25 per cent of those rejected as unfit and 27 per cent of those called up for Service. "When groups of similar scholastic ability were compared, there was little difference between those called up for Service and those rejected as unfit in the proportion of men who had expressed a desire for skilled manual work who were in fact engaged in such work at the age of 22."

There was very little difference between the leisure interests of those who had been on Service and those rejected.

The proportion of men convicted between the ages of 20

and 22 was almost the same among both groups. In both groups the amount of crime was found to be very much influenced by earlier social and environmental background. The rate of crime increased as the occupational status declined, and also greatly with an increase in unemployment.

93. Fleming, C. M., "New Light on Adolescence," *Health and Education Journal* (January, 1950), 2-5.

94. Fleming, C. M., D. F. Digaria, and H. G. R. Rewth (University of London), "Preference and Values Among Adolescent Boys and Girls," *Educational Research,* II (1960), 221-224.

95. Ford, B., "Assessing the Modern Child" (Secondary), *New Statesman,* LXII (July 27, 1961), 78-79.

96. Franks, H., "A Regular Boys Service Corps," *Army Quarterly,* LIX (July, 1950), 251-256.

97. Fraser, Elizabeth, *Home Environment and the School* (Scottish Council for Research in Education, University of London Press, 1959).

98. Fraser, G. S., "Youth Speaks From England," *Woman's Press* (October, 1947), 22-23.

99. Freeston, P. M., "The Influence of the War on Juvenile and Adolescent Vocational Interests," *Occupational Psychology,* London, XX (1946), 139-149.

100. Gallagher, M. A., "The Prospect of Marriage: a Study of the Attitudes toward Further Education of a Sample Group of Secondary Technical and Secondary Grammar School Leavers," *British Journal of Educational Psychology,* XXVII (1957), 24-28.

101. "Gangs and the Police," *Economist,* CXCV (June 18, 1960), 1185-1186.

102. Garrity, Frank D., "A Study of Some Secondary Modern School Pupils' Attitudes toward Religious Education," *Religious Education,* LVI (1961), 141-143.

103. Gibbens, T. C. N., "Car Thieves," *British Journal of Delinquency,* VIII (1958), 257-265.

104. Glatt, M. M., "Alcoholism, Crime and Juvenile Delinquency," *British Journal of Delinquency,* IX (1958), 84-93.

105. Glover, J., "Wealthiest Children in Town," *Saturday Night,* LXXIV (July 4, 1959), 44.

106. Godfrey, J. L., "The Problem of Guiding Youth in English Schools," *South Atlantic Quarterly,* CLV (October, 1956), 449-462.

107. Godson, R., "The Regional Distribution of Juvenile Labour," *Bulletin of the Oxford University Institute of Statistics,* XI (September, 1949), 269-278.

108. Gosling, Ray, "Dream Boy" (Sociology of the British teenage popular singer), *New Left Review,* LI (May/June, 1960), 30-34.

109. *Great Britain Ministry of Canteens in Youth Clubs,* H. M. Stationery Office, 1945.

110. Great Britain Ministry of Education, *Out of School* (London: Her Majesty's Stationery Office, 1948).

111. Grunbaum, Werner F., "Academic Freedom in Great Britain, 1948-1956," *Harvard Educational Review,* XXVII, 1 (Winter, 1957), 28-37.

112. Grygier, Tadeusy, "Leisure Pursuits of Juvenile Delinquents: A Study in Methodology," *British Journal of Delinquency,* V (1955), 210-228.

113. Haig-Brown, R. L. H., "Problems of Modern Life and Young Offenders," *Saturday Night,* LXX (May 28, 1955), 9-11.

114. Hall, Wendy, "Education in the Commonwealth," *United Asia,* XIII, 1 (1961), 39-41.

115. Halliday, C., "Why High School Students Smoke," *Saturday Night,* LXXV (January 23, 1960), 35.

116. Halsey, A. H. and L. Gardner, "Social Mobility and Achievement in Four Grammar Schools," *British Journal of Sociology,* IV (1953), 60-75.

117. Hammond, W. H., "An Analysis of Youth Centre Interests," *British Journal of Educational Psychology,* XV (1945), 122-126.

An inquiry into the recreational interests of a group of adolescents at the Holystone Youth Centre, Hebburn-on-Tyne. 140 members were considered in the study. The sex breakdown was 74 males and 66 girls. The mean age of 16.2 years. The recreational interests were expressed in a checklist of activities. The members of the Centre revealed a wide range of interests with the active participation activities prevailing over the intellectual and individual activities. Thus sports and social activities were more of a general interest than were hobbies, art, reading, etc. Sex differences in the number and types of interests were evident. The girls preferred the more intellectual and social activities, while the boys preferred the more active participation interests. It was also noted that the initial expressed interests were a poor indicator of the individual's remaining in the Centre. The evidence did suggest that class differences were occasionally active in the attrition of the members. Members from the better class homes revealed a significantly greater tendency to leave the Youth Centre.

118. "Hard Heads in the High," *New Statesman,* LV (March 22, 1958), 361.

119. Healy, W., *The Individual Delinquent* (London: William Heinemann, Ltd., 1915).

120. Henriques, B. L. Q., "Childrens Courts in England," *Journal of Criminal Law,* XXXVII (November, 1946), 295-299.

121. Henriques, B. L. Q., "The Detection and Prevention of Anti-Social Behaviour in Young Persons," *Journal of the Royal Society of Arts* (May 27, 1955), 452-465.

122. Henriques, B. L. Q., "Training Centres," *Spectator,* CCVI (May 12, 1961) 675-676.

123. Herburg, W., "Religious Stirring on the Campus: a Student Generation Accessible to Good," *Commentary,* XIII (March, 1952), 242-248.

124. Heron, Alastair, "Adolescents and Preparation for Parenthood," *British Journal of Educational Psychology,* XXII (1952), 173-179.

125. Hesketh, Alan, "Youth in Agriculture," *Communist Review* (September, 1953), 274-279.

126. Hiles, M., "The Young Farmer's Club Movements," *World Crops* (April, 1950), 169-172.

A discussion of the history, growth, organization, and functions of Young Farmers Clubs in England. The goals of the clubs are noted as: providing rural youth with a gathering place with the notion of community service, the promotion among young people of the importance of country life and agriculture, and the encouragement of the continuation of education among rural youth. Two types of clubs are discussed: the school club which derives its membership from the population of a particular school, and the open club which recruits its members from all classes of the community, both rural and urban.

127. Hill, G. C. N., "An Evaluation of the Development of Pupils in Secondary Modern Schools," *British Journal of Educational Psychology* (June, 1958), 177-178.

128. Himmelweit, H. T., "A Study of the Attitudes, Value Systems, and Behavior of Young Adolescents Belonging to Different Social Status Groups," *Bulletin of the British Psychological Society,* XX (1953), 7.

129. Himmelweit, H. T., A. H. Halsey, and A. N. Oppenheim, "The Views of Adolescents on Some Aspects of the Social Class Structure," *British Journal of Sociology*, III (1952), 148-172.

This study examines the adolescent's views on the social class structure and asks to what extent adolescents view society in terms of adult frames of reference and also what are the relative influences of home and school in determining the adolescents' outlook? A sample of 13-14 year olds was investigated. These boys belonged to different status groups.

The findings indicated that 60 per cent of the boys did not know what the term "social class" meant. In spite of this the authors are convinced that all of the boys had a thorough understanding of the social class system. This knowledge is very effectively transmitted between generations. They note that the adolescent is influenced by his class position when they attempt to explain their social position. It was noted that the way in which the stratification system was viewed was related to the individual's aspirations for improved status. The middle-class boys tended to stress those status symbol which were primarily dependent on training in the home such as dress, manners, and speech patterns. These symbols tend to differentiate them from the other boys at school.

130. Hodgkin, R. A., "Nice To Be Stretched" (Review of *Outward Bound*, edited by D. James), *New Statesman*, LV (January 11, 1958), 36; Discussion—LV (January 18-25, 1958), 71, 105.

131. Holbrook, D., "Down the C Stream," *Spectator*, CCXCVII (September 22, 1961) 381.

132. Hollis, S., "Public Schools for Whom?" *Spectator*, CCVII (September 22, 1961) 378.

133. Hunt, Sir John, "Youth Today and Tomorrow," *Royal United Service Institution Journal*, CII (August, 1957), 322-333.

134. Husng, Lucy Jen, "Marriage Counseling and Family Life Education in England," *Marriage and Family Living*, XXIII (May, 1961), 146-154.

135. Hutchin, Kenneth C., "Age of Transition," *Family Doctor* (February, 1960), 83-86.

136. "Hysteria, Inc.: In America Young People Spend Millions on Products Identified with Popular Entertainers; Now Fan Exploitation on a Large Scale is Coming to Britain," *Scope* (March, 1957), 38-41.

137. Ianni, Frances J., "Youth Shows the Way: Labour Policy," *Economist*, CXCII (1959), 906.

138. Iga, M., "Daring Young Men," *Economist*, CCI (1961), 116.

139. "Importance of Not Being Earnest" [question of student awards], *Economist*, CLXXXVII (April 19, 1958), 200.

140. Ince, Sir Godfrey, "The Development of the Youth Employment Service," *Education* (May 6, 1949), 851-852, 855-856.

141. "International Youth Rally in London," *Nature*, CXLVIII (October 18, 1941), 464.

142. Jackson, B., "Moronic Mass," *New Statesman*, LXII (November 3, 1961), 644.

143. Jackson, B. and C. Marsden, "Education and the Working Class," *New Statesman, The Weekend Review, 50's* (10 Great Turnstile, London WCL).

144. Jackson, L., "Emotional Attitudes Toward the Family of Normal, Neurotic and Delinquent Children," *British Journal of Psychology*, XLI (1951).

145. Jahoda, Gustav, "Adolescent Attitudes to Starting Work," *Occupational Psychology*, London, XXIII (1949), 184-188.

In this study 200 boys and girls 13 and 14 years of age who were attending a secondary school near London were asked to imagine that they had started to work the day before and were requested to write an essay entitled "My First Day at Work." The analysis was pointed toward an evaluation of the vocational guidance program which is designed to match the child's personality to job requirements and to prepare the child for the transition from school to job situation. While the essays revealed enthusiasm at the prospect of working and the choices revealed a fairly realistic approach, few of the students had an accurate picture of the physical and social conditions of the jobs they described. There was a great deal of importance attached to the establishment of good social relations with fellow workers. The attitudes toward authority were ambivalent.

The author concluded that the occupational preparation in the schools was inadequate. Vocational guidance is needed in all the years of schooling rather than in the final year only. It is also noted that successful adjustment of the adolescent to the job situation may depend greatly on the employers' understanding of the psychological needs of the adolescent.

146. James, H. E. O. and C. Tenen, "How Adolescents Think of Peoples (of other countries)," *British Journal of Psychology* (December, 1950), 145-172.

Purpose was to find out what children know about other countries and people (sponsored by UNESCO).

120 Secondary Modern school girls, 11-15 (England) were interviewed. The interviews were informal; the child was allowed to talk as long as she wanted. The interviews ran from 1 hour to 1¾ hours.

In looking at favorable and unfavorable attitudes toward the Germans, it was found that personal contact can change attitude and that they outweigh other considerations.

Those things mentioned as likable about the Germans reflect personal relations, those disliked items reflect war attitudes.

The Italian pattern was similar to the German.

A strong hostile attitude toward the Japanese had been built up through second-hand evidence by many. These hostile attitudes persisted even after three or four years had passed since the war.

The Chinese pattern was like the Japanese in respect to dislike of the physical characteristics, however they had benign entries as well as bad in regard to other traits.

The American pattern was the opposite of the Japanese. It was based on second- and first-hand evidence, and emphasized social virtues.

There is a strong case for the hypothesis that personal contacts can change attitudes and do so better than observation. Favorable contact led to mention of sociable items rather than disturbing items.

147. James, H. E. O. and E. T. Moore, "Adolescent Leisure in a Working Class District. Part II," *Occupational Psychology, London,* XVIII (1944), 24-34.

148. James, H. E. O. and E. T. Moore, "Adolescent Leisure in a Working Class District," *Occupational Psychology, London,* XIV (1940), 132-145.

The purpose is to study adolescent leisure activities and to trace their changes with age.

Five hundred and thirty-five adolescents kept diaries for one week each. Surveys of street population and activities were taken. All elementary school adolescents filled out a questionnaire. Ages ran from 12 to 21.

Activities were classified in nine categories: cinema, reading and radio, clubs, play, talk, dancing, duties, personal, meals and travel.

After leaving school there is a steady decline in play and duties and increase in talk and dancing.

Secondary-school boys show more similarity to elementary-school boys than to working boys of their own ages. The working boy tends to put aside things that would be considered childish quickly as he is now in an adult world.

Girls do not show such a marked and fast change after they start working for they have to continue with duties for a longer time.

Club activities are confined to week nights as they are one-sex organizations.

149. Jenkinson, A. J., *What Do Boys and Girls Read?* (London: Methuen & Co., Ltd., 1940).

150. Jephcott, Agnes Pearl, *Some Young People* (London: George Allen and Unwin, Ltd., 1954).

The problem:

A. "To consider the membership of the youth organizations and to ascertain how this membership is distributed over the adolescent period; to analyze the duration in individual membership; to ascertain the causes of unsatisfactory leakage; and to recommend methods by which this might be reduced."

B. "To ascertain what proportion of the adolescent population is not attached to any youth organization; to analyze the composition of this proportion; to discover the reasons for its not being attracted to youth organizations; and to make recommendations as to how young people who might benefit might be attracted either to existing organizations, or to new types of organizations."

The two-year Enquiry covered seven small areas, selected as being representative of a variety of social conditions in England. No form of sampling was attempted. The conclusions were based not on statistical material but on the opinions of the adolescents and adults who knew the adolescents. As a supplement, a factual schedule was filled in for all the boys and girls living in the areas between the ages of 14-17.

A Pilot Enquiry was undertaken in London, Nottingshire, and Oxfordshire. The Main Enquiry included the same areas of the Pilot plus four new areas. The study then included: two London Boroughs, a district in Nottingham, and four small rural communities.

The conclusions of the Enquiry fell into two categories:

1. "Why a large proportion of the nine hundred and thirty-nine boys and girls did not think it worth their while to join any of the organizations set up specifically for the enjoyment and welfare of the adolescents of their neighborhood.

2. "This category 'concerned the general well-being of the

boys and girls, particularly in so far as this was affected by the way in which they spent their free time.' "

One in three belonged to youth organizations (232 out of 643 in London, 44 out of 129 in Nottingham, and 59 out of 167 in the villages). In London about three boys belonged for every girl and in Nottingham about two for every girl. About twice as many belonged to un-uniformed organizations as to uniformed organizations.

In all areas, the boys' and girls' comments tended toward regarding the local organizations as juvenile. To the working sixteen- and seventeen-year old, the program seemed geared to younger school children.

In London, the fact that certain Church units made Church attendance compulsory kept boys and girls from joining. Most had gone to Sunday School as children, but when they started working, they reflected the adult attitude toward religion—indifference. The Enquirers concluded that "today spiritual issues might be more readily brought to the notice of adolescents in general through secular rather than religious societies."

The boys and girls criticized the youth organizations for their out-of-dateness—in programs and equipment.

The Enquirers concluded that one of the major points affecting joining was the parent's relationship with the local youth organizations. They found that parents often did not recognize them as useful to the upbringing of their offspring. Also seen was the need for fitting the boy or girl into the right organization.

151. Jephcott, A. P., "Going Out to Work: a Note on the Adolescent Girl in Britain," *Indian Journal of Social Work*, XVIII, 1 (Bombay: June, 1957), 12-16.

152. Jones, R. H., "An Inquiry into Juvenile Delinquency in an English Town: a Comparison between the Effects of Peacetime and Wartime Conditions," *Social Service Review*, XIX (1945), 525-531.

153. Joseph, Joyce, "Research Note on Attitudes to Work and Marriage of Six Hundred Adolescent Girls," *British Journal of Sociology*, XII (June, 1961), 176-183.

The sample for this investigation consisted of 600 girls between the ages of 14 and 17 from 15 different schools. All of the schools were located in agricultural areas. The majority of the subjects were due to graduate from their technical, modern, or grammar schools within the following year. These subjects were administered a questionnaire on occupational choice and expectations and were, in addition, asked to write an essay assuming they were at the end of their lives and looking back to review their lives since school.

The analysis of the data revealed that the majority of the subjects were not thinking in terms of a vocation, but rather in terms of being a housewife and having a full or part-time job as a secondary interest. Their primary role is seen as homemaker and mother. It was felt to be highly significant that such a high proportion were planning some form of employment after marriage.

154. Jupp, Arthur E. and Bernard D. Rhodes, "Teenage Trade" (Great Britain: Significance for the cooperative movement), *Cooperative Review*, XXXV (May, 1961), 114-118.

155. Katz, S. M., "It's a Tough Time to Be a Kid," *Maclean's Magazine*, LXIII (December 15, 1950), 7-9, 33; LXIV (January 1, 1951), 10-11, 40; (January 15, 1951), 14-15, 44-45.

156. Katz, S. M., "Truth about Teenage Drinking," *Maclean's Magazine*, LXXI (June 21, 1958), 13-15, 51-54.

157. Katz, S. M., "Is Our Youth Equipped to Face the Future?" *Maclean's Magazine*, LXXII (October 10, 1959), 13-15, 83-91.

158. Kegel, C. H., "Lord John Manners and the Young England Movement: Romanticism in Politics," *Western Political Quarterly*, XIV (Summer, 1961), 691-697.

159. Kellham, E. J., "British Youth: Submerged Generation?" *Spectator*, CLXXI (September 3, 1943), 216; Discussion—V. CLXXI (September 10-17, 1943), 244, 266.

160. Kerridge, R., "Voice of the Yob," *New Statesman*, LIX (April 30, 1960), 618.

161. Kerridge, R., "Teenage Who's Who," *New Statesman*, LX (September 24, 1960), 422.

162. Kirkpatrick, Milton E., "The Mental Hygiene of Adolescence in the Anglo-American Culture," *Mental Hygiene*, New York, XXXVI (1952), 394-403.

163. Klingender, F. D., "Students in a Changing World," *Yorkshire Bulletin of Economic and Social Research*, VI, 2 (September, 1954), 91-127.

164. Kok, Winifred de, "Difficulties of Adolescence in Girls," *Family Doctor* (June, 1957), 498.

165. Kuenstler, P. H. K., *Youth Work in England* (London: University of London Press, 1954) University of Bristol, Institute of Education, Publication #6.

166. Kuenstler, P. H. K., *Spontaneous Youth Groups* (London: University of London Press, 1955). University of Bristol, Institute of Education, Publication #8.

167. L., M. W., "The Service of Youth," *Police Journal, London*, XV (1942), 153-158.

168. Labour Party, "Youth Community. The Younger Generation: Report" (1959). (Problems of British youth; contribution which the government and other agencies can make to their solution.)

169. Lancaster, Lorraine, "Some Conceptual Problems in the Study of Family and Kin Ties in the British Isles," *British Journal of Sociology*, XII (December, 1961), 317-333.

170. "Leaving School: The Next Step," *The Economist*, CXLVIII (March 11, 1961) 938.

171. Lees, J. P. and L. J. Newson, "Family or Kinship Position and Some Aspects of Juvenile Delinquency," *British Journal of Delinquency*, V, 1 (1954), 46-65.

172. Lewis, Arthur, "Health Interests of Children," *Health and Education Journal*, London, VII (1949), 66-73.

173. Lindsay, M., "Beware of Sympathy," *Spectator*, CCIV (March 11, 1960), 350.

174. Lindsay, K., "Undirected Youth," *Spectator*, CLXVI (February 21, 1941), 196.

175. "Little Fling on Youth" (Recommendation of Albemarle Committee), *Economist*, CXCIV (February 6, 1960), 508.

176. Liversidge, W., "Life Chances," *Sociological Review*, X (March, 1962), 17-34.

177. Lochhead, Marion, *Young Victorians* (London: Murray, 1959).

178. Logan, R. F. L. and E. M. Goldberg, "Rising Eighteen in a London Suburb: Some Aspects of the Life and Health of Young Men," *British Journal of Sociology*, IV (December, 1953), 323-345. (Bibliography)

An investigation of the health of, environmental aspects of, and community preparation for adult roles of 85 eighteen-year-old men. Data were gathered from tests of arithmetic and spelling ability, physical examinations, official documents, and a questionnaire of background factors.

It was noted that the physical health of the subjects was, on the whole, good. However, a great deal of emotional disturbance, apparently tied to family background, was found. The youth who were employed in semiskilled and unskilled jobs revealed the most bad health as well as a lack of maturity. These subjects also were relatively uninterested in their jobs and derived little satisfaction from them. Little concern was seen concerning the labor turnover rates for youth. In the area of leisure activity, there was a high degree of similarity with the exception of reading habits. The reading habits were the only factors associated with class differences. No evidence of interest in participation in community activities could be found.

The authors conclude, "When seen against this background of contradictions and uncertainties which offers so little guidance and no goals to the young, these youths show more resilience and fewer problems than one might expect."

179. Louden, J. B., "Kinship and Crisis in South Wales," *British Journal of Sociology*, XII (December, 1961), 333-350.

180. Lovell, K. and G. E. White, "Some Influences Affecting Choice of Subjects in School and Training College," *British Journal of Educational Psychology* (February, 1958), 15-24.

181. Lunden, W. A., "War and Juvenile Delinquency in England and Wales," *American Journal of Scientific Research*, X, 3 (June, 1945), 390-393.

182. Mace, David R., "What Britain is Doing," *Marriage and Family Living*, X (Winter, 1948), 6.

183. MacInnes, Colin, "See You at Mabel's" [drinking clubs], *Encounter* (March, 1957), 21-26.

184. MacInnes, Colin, "Pop Songs and Teenagers," *20th Century*, CLXIII (February, 1958), 122-132.

185. MacInnes, Colin, "Sharp Schmutter; Pop Dress Styles in the Fifties," *20th Century*, CLXVI (August, 1959), 46-53.

186. MacInnes, Colin, "English Queerdom," *Partisan Review*, XXVIII (January, 1961), 146-153.

187. MacKenzie, N., "Strains and Stresses," *New Statesman*, LXI (April 14, 1961), 571.

188. Maclure, S., "Fifteen to Eighteen," *Spectator*, CCIII (December 11, 1959), 871.

189. Madden, Tom, "The British Youth Movement" [Development and present problems of youth organizations and the role of the Communist Party in meeting the needs of the youth] *Communist Review* (November, 1953) 329-335.

190. Mallalieu, J. P. W., "Jobs for School Leavers," *New Statesman*, LVIII (September 26, 1959), 38, 3-4.

191. Mannheim, Hermann, *Juvenile Delinquency in an English Mid-*

dletown (London: Kegan Paul, Trench, Trubner & Co., Ltd., 1948). (Bibliography)

192. Mannheim, Karl, "The Problem of Youth in Modern Society," in *Diagnosis of Our Time* (London: 1943), 31-53.

193. "Marchioness of Lothian" (Youth and the New Order), *Spectator,* CLXXII (March 3, 1944), 193; Reply, R. Rumbald, CLXXII (March 17, 1944), 245.

194. Mays, John B., "A Study of a Delinquent Community," *British Journal of Delinquency,* III (1952), 5-19.

195. Mays, John B., *Growing Up in the City* (London: University Press of Liverpool, 1954).

196. Mays, John B., "Why Are Today's Teenagers Living for Kicks? Crime Is on the Increase among Young People," *Family Doctor* (July, 1960), 425-427.

197. Mays, John B., "Teen-age Culture in Contemporary Britain and Europe," *The Annals of the Academy of Political and Social Science,* CCCXXXVIII (1961), 22-32.

    The author notes a marked similarity between the youth cultures of Western Europe and the United States. He feels that this similarity is a product of similar social and economic influences operating in the two areas. Both areas have an emphasis on security and affluence. It is also noted that uncertainty of role and status may lead to acute alienation between the adult and the youth generation.

198. McGhee, Margaret, "School Girls' Attitudes to Films, Youth Clubs, Homework Discipline and Sport," *British Journal of Educational Psychology,* XX (1950), 144-145. (abstract of B. E. thesis)

199. McGregor, O. R., "Some Research Possibilities and Historical Materials for Family and Kinship Study in Britain," *British Journal of Sociology,* XII (December, 1961), 310-317.

200. McKellar, Peter and Ralph Harris, "Radio Preferences of Adolescents and Children," *British Journal of Educational Psychology,* XXII (1952), 101-113.

201. Mercer, E. O., "Some Occupational Attitudes of Girls," *Occupational Psychology,* London, XIV (1940), 14-25.

202. Merseyside, R., "Jobs for Boys: Scottish Breathing-Space," *Economist,* CXCVII (December 3, 1960), 1000-1001.

203. Mitchison, N., "Young Laird," *New Statesman,* LI (March 17, 1956), 238.

204. Moir, Guthrie, "Leaders or Rebels?" (Coordination of British

youth movements with those on the Commonwealth), *New Commonwealth* (January 12, 1957), 55-56.

205. Monkhouse, G., "Youth in Industry," *Industrial Welfare*, XXIII (January, 1950), 7-10.

206. Montague, Joel B., Jr., "A Study of Anxiety among English and American Boys," *American Sociological Review*, XX (1955), 685-689.

207. Montague, Joel B., Jr., "Anxiety among English and American Boys—an Emendation," *American Sociological Review*, XXI (1956), 226-227.

208. Moreton, F. E., "Attitudes to Religion among Adolescents and Adults," *British Journal of Educational Psychology*, XIV (1944), 69-79.

209. Morgan, E. A., *The Needs of Youth* (New York: Oxford University Press, 1939).

210. Morgan, J. G., "What the Students Want," *New Statesman*, LXI (March 3, 1961), 344-345.

211. Morgan, W. J., "Getting Shot of Phoniness," *New Statesman*, LVIII (September 9, 1959), 344.

212. Morris, May, "Young People and Their Opportunities," *Universities Quarterly* (August, 1950), 343-350.

    How adolescents spend their leisure time with references to 80,000 adolescents.

213. Morton, G. F., "Living with (and Educating) Adolescents," *New English Review* (August, 1949), 95-100.

214. Ness, M. E., "School Dating is Expensive—But Heck!" *Saturday Night*, LXV (November 8, 1949), 38-39.

215. Ness, M. E., "Who's Afraid of Teenage Problems?" *Saturday Night*, LXVI (March 13, 1951), 28-29.

216. Newsome, D., "Godliness and Good Learning: Four Studies in a Victorian Ideal," *Review Spec.*, CCVII (December 15, 1961), 905.

217. "Next Social Revolution," *New Statesman*, LXI (March 3, 1961), 332.

218. "No Kicks in Politics" [Labor and youth], *Economist*, CXCI (May 9, 1959), 507.

219. Oppenheim, A. N., "Social Class Differences in Adolescent Values and Attitudes," *Bulletin of the British Psychological Society*, XX (1953), 8.

220. Oppenheim, A. N., "Social Status and Clique Formation among Grammar School Boys," *British Journal of Sociology,* VI (September, 1955), 228-245.

221. "Other Haleys," *Economist,* CLXXX (September 15, 1956), 873.
Young people excited by the rhythms of rock and roll.

222. Packer, E. L., "Conflict in the Schools," *Spectator,* CLXXV (July 6, 1945), 9.

223. Pedley, R., "Comprehensive Education: A New Approach" (Review), *Spectator,* CXCVII (October 5, 1956), 443-445; E. James, Discussion—CXCVII, 571, 608, 717, 932; CXCVIII (October 26-November 2), 23; (December 28, 1956-January 4, 1957), 19.

224. Peel, E. A., "Delinquency and the Education of Society" [review article], *British Journal of Educational Studies* (November, 1957), 76-80.

225. "Pegs for Holes," *Economist,* CLXXXI (December 29, 1956), 1121.

Youth and its problems, particularly in regard to National Service.

226. Percival, A. C., *Youth Will Be Led: the Story of the Voluntary Youth Organizations* (Collins, 1951). (Bibliography)

227. Pirrie, G. D., et al., Symposium on Youth and Work: The problems of young people during the transition from school child to adult worker (with emphasis on health) with discussion, *Royal Sanitary Institute Journal,* LXXIV (August, 1954), 740-755.

228. Raven, Ronald M., "Smoking Habits of Schoolboys," *Lancet* (June 1, 1957), 1139-1141.

229. Raven, S., "What Teenagers Do: Careers," *Economist,* CXCI (1959), 827.

230. Raven S., "Home from Home," *Spectator,* CCVII (1961), 736-738.

231. "Recruitment and Training of Young Persons for Industry," *Great Britain Ministry of Labour,* LVII (October, 1949), 343.

232. "Red Strokes and Black Circles," *New Statesman,* XLIV (August 23, 1952), 205.

Index of the educational activities of thirty eleven-year-old Londoners.

233. Reed, Bryan H., *Eighty Thousand Adolescents* (London: George Allen and Unwin, Ltd., 1950).

234. Richardson, I. M., "Adolescents Mental Health. 1, Adolescent and Maturity," *Nursing Mirror* (January 11, 1957), 1033-1034; "Attitude toward Work, Leisure, Sex" (January 18, 1957), 111-112.

235. Richardson, J. E., et al. (ed. by C. M. Fleming), *Studies in the Social Psychology of Adolescence* (London: Routledge & Kegan Paul, Ltd., 1951).

236. Richardson, W. C., "Trends in Public School Education in England," *Journal of Educational Sociology*, XXVII (September, 1953), 4-15.

This article surveys the British educational system, dealing particularly with the integration of the public schools (the independent schools) and the state-controlled system of schools.

An historical approach is used to evaluate the educational system. Figures and policies were taken from *The Public School Year Book Report* of the Fleming Committee in 1943 and from legislative actions.

The public school values little concerned with the practical business of making a living. It stresses the broad, liberal background, although most try to combine the liberal with the practical to meet the current national need for trained personnel.

To give working-class children a better chance, a setup whereby the public schools admit a minimum per cent of underprivileged boys and girls has been instigated since 1944. It has proven beneficial to the public schools and to the country as it makes possible education on a wider base—to more youth.

237. Rippon, G., "Youth and the Future," *Spectator*, CLXXII (January 14, 1944), 27. Discussion—CLXII (January 21-28, February 11-18, 1944), 56, 81-82.

238. Ross, M., "Decline of the Parent Image," *Saturday Night*, LXXVI (July 22, 1961), 24.

239. "Rosy Youth" [Young Socialists, Labour's new youth movement], *Economist*, CXCIV (January, 1960), 392.

240. Rumbald, R., "Defeated Generation," *Spectator*, CLXXI (August 20, 1943), 168.

241. Schuller, E., "British Youth Organization and Rehabilitation of Liberated Europe," *National Conference of Social Work* (1944), 160-169.

242. Scotland Education Department, Youth Advisory Committee, *The Recruitment and Training of Youth Leaders and Organizers: A Report* (H. M. Stationery Office, [Edinburgh], 1946).

243. Scott, P. D., "The Natural History of the Spiv," *Biology and Human Affairs,* XX (1955), 3.

244. Scott, Peter, "Gangs and Delinquent Groups in London," *British Journal of Delinquency,* VII (1956), 4-26. (Bibliography)

A discussion of individual and group juvenile crimes in London in 1956. The author examined boys between the ages of 8 and 17 years. One group was under investigation for proved offenses conducted in groups. A second comparison group was comprised of boys who were under investigation for present offenses but who had never operated in groups. The first group was studied for age, type of association, composition of the group, and damage done.

The author notes an increase in group participation in delinquent activities for all age groups since 1920. He goes on to note the types of groups in London. The *Adolescent Street Group* has no particular delinquent character. The aim of proving one's self is prevalent. *Gangs* reveal antisocial character and very disturbed home backgrounds. The author notes a decrease in these groups as slum areas are eliminated. *Loose Antisocial Groups* are loose, fluid groups which combine delinquency and promiscuity.

245. "The Service of Youth Today," *Planning,* XIV (April 9, 1948), 285-308.

246. Shears, L. W., "The Dynamics of Leadership in Adolescent School Groups," *Bulletin of the British Psychological Society,* XIX (1953), 20-22.

247. Spender, Stephen, "The English Adolescent," *Harvard Education Review,* XVIII (Fall, 1948), 228-239.

This is one in a series of addresses at a Seminar in preparation for a book on education in many societies. The writer is the English representative who describes the "English adolescent as he is affected through his education by the English social background and cultural tradition."

English education deeply ingrains class feelings as it is on a class basis. The poor are conscious of their place through education. The only way they can continue into higher education is by winning scholarships. If he goes on to the University he may enter a profession and be absorbed into the middle class.

The educational experiences of the working class and middle class and up are quite different. The physical development of the classes is different also. The boys in boarding schools are fed a simple diet and exercise is stressed while the working class youth is subject to home conditions and sometimes poverty.

Another class difference is in the development of attitudes toward courtship, marriage, and sex. The working-class adolescent adopts many of his parents' attitudes and begins dating at a time when the other children are separated from the opposite sex in boarding schools. Here a problem exists. Complete denial of sexual impulse is expected which results often in killing or perverting it.

The public school is a type of small city state. It builds a strong civic sense of responsibility as it teaches the students to "take themselves seriously as functions of an institution before they take themselves seriously as persons or as individuals."

The weakness of the system is that it produces men and women who are spiritually deprived and immature; teaches them to treat physical instincts as irrelevant; neglects the relationship of a growing child to his parents. Also the energy of the boys is directed to the school itself.

The schools produce toughness and integrity. The teachers are responsible for physical and moral development as well as learning.

248. Spinley, B. M., *The Deprived and the Privileged* (London: Routledge & Kegan Paul, Ltd., 1953).

249. Sprott, W. J. H., "Delinquescent Worlds" (With reference to growing up in the city, by J. B. Mays), *Listener* (June 9, 1955), 1013-1014.

The author utilizes a "social background" explanation of delinquency. He insists that the physical background and social environment of the delinquent must be known. He notes that the delinquent culture is a phase coming between 7 and 18 years old. The emphasis in the article falls on the subcultural aspects of delinquent youth in particular and adolescents in general. He notes the influence of middle-class standards in the interpretation of the attitudes and activities of adolescents in general.

250. Stephenson, R. M., "Stratification, Education and Occupational Orientation: A Parallel Study and Review," *British Journal of Sociology*, IX (March, 1958), 42-52.

A study which uncovers and discusses striking parallels between the United States and Great Britain in the areas of stratification, education, and occupational orientation. The study was conducted on 700 London adolescents and 1,000 New Jersey adolescents. The analysis focuses on class and orientation factors. The British youth were found to be quite similar to the United States youth when matched by class level.

251. Stern, H. H., "A Follow-up Study of Adolescents' Views of their Personal and Vocational Future," *British Journal of Educational Psychology*, XXXI (June, 1961), 170-182.

252. Stewart, Mary, "The Leisure Activities of Grammar School Children," *British Journal of Educational Psychology*, XX (1950), 11-34.

253. Stott, D. H. (Glasgow University, Scotland), "Delinquency, Maladjustment and Unfavorable Ecology," *British Journal of Psychology*, LI (1960), 157-170.

254. Struthers, A. M., "Juvenile Delinquency in Scotland," *American Sociological Review*, X, 5 (October, 1945), 658-662.

245. "Students' Expenses," *The Times Educational Supplement* (May 6, 1955), 447.

255. "Students' Expenses," *The Times Educational Supplement* (May 665-666.

256. "Students in the 60's," *New Statesman*, LXI (April 28, 1961), 39.

257. "Teddy Boy Jungle," *New Statesman*, LXI (January 13, 1961), (1960), 341-343.

258. "Teenage Education in England" [Editorial], *Nature*, CLXXXV 1959), 1046.

259. "Teenaged Girl in Employment," *Labour Gazette*, LIX (October,

260. "Teenagers Revisited," *Economist*, CXCV (June 11, 1960), 1084. *Educational Psychology* (June, 1947), 72-82.

261. Tenen, Cora, "The Adolescent in the Factory," *British Journal of* Factories," *Occupational Psychology*, XXI, 2 (1947), 75-81.

262. Tenner, C., "Some Problems of Discipline Among Adolescents in

263. *Times Educational Supplement*, September 14, 1962. 1958), 21.

264. "To School Until Sixteen," *Economist*, CLXXXVI (January 4, (March 3, 1962), 806.

265. "Tory Hopefuls" [Young Conservatives], *Economist*, CCII

266. Trenaman, J., *Out of Step* (London: Methuen & Co., Ltd., 1952). in P. H. Kuenstler (ed.), *Spontaneous Youth Groups and Gangs*, Chap. 4, 56-59.

267. Turner, M. L. and J. C. Spencer, "Spontaneous Youth Groups" in P. H. Kuenstler (ed.), *Spontaneous Youth Groups and Gangs* (London: Allen I. Unwin, Ltd., 1959), Chap. 4, 56-59.

268. Turner R. H., "Preoccupation with Competitiveness and Social Acceptance Among American and English Students," *Sociometry*, XXIII (1960), 307-325.

In general, the results suggest that the scales are useful, and that English and American students are similar with respect to these preoccupations in spite of surface cultural differences.

269. Tyler, Leona E., "A Comparison of the Interests of English and American School Children," *Journal of Genetic Psychology*, LXXXVIII (1956), 175-181.

This study is an attempt to provide comparative data in interests of English and American school children, because "if we wish to go beyond empirical predictions and use the information we have as a part of an inclusive theory of human motivation, it will be necessary to make such comparative studies."

Forty-six boys and 49 girls, about 10-11 years of age, in a primary school at Hendon, England, a northern suburb of London, were subjects. Data from several American groups of the same age were available for comparison.

The Dreese and Mooney Interest Inventory for Elementary Grades was used.

"The questions around which the principal investigation was centered are these: Is there a greater degree of similarity between children in different parts of the United States than between one of these groups and English children? If there is, how large and important is the difference and how can we account for it?"

Findings are based on an item analysis.

1. ". . . [H]igh degree of similarity between the interest patterns of English and American children." It seems that differences in child-rearing and education practices are not affecting the children's interests very much. Of some importance is that sex differences in the two countries are similar.

2. There is more difference between American and English children than between American groups. In accounting for this, the greater tendency for English to register dislikes stands out.

3. Sex groups are less like one another than nationality groups.

4. Sex differences follow the same pattern in both countries.

5. There is a consistent tendency for English children to like fewer things and dislike more things than American children do.

270. Tyvel, T. R., "The Insecure Offenders: Rebellious Youth in the

Welfare State," Bulletin of the Public Affairs Information Service (1961).

271. Valentine, C. W., "Adolescents and Some Problems of Youth Training," *Nature,* CLII (July 31, 1943), 122-124. (Bibliography)

272. Valentine, C. W., "Adolescence and Some Problems of Youth Training," *British Journal of Educational Psychology,* XIII (1943), 57-68.

273. Venables, P. F. R., "Education and the Challenge of Change," *Memoirs and Proceedings, Manchester Literary and Philosophical Society,* XCVII (1957), 31-42.

274. Vernon, M. D., "A Study of Some Effects of Evacuation on Adolescent Girls," *British Journal of Educational Psychology,* X (1940), 114-134.

275. "Very Heaven? Is an Affluent Teenage Group an Insoluble for an Affluent Society? Or is the Trouble a Failure in the Older People to Use a Sense of Proportion and Then Find a Sensible Approach?" *Economist,* CXCIV (March 5, 1960), 878-879.

276. Wall, W. D., "The Educational Interests of a Group of Young Industrial Workers," *British Journal of Educational Psychology,* XV (1945), 127-134.

277. Wall, W. D., "The Newspaper Reading Interests of Adolescents and Adults, Part I," *British Journal of Educational Psychology,* XVIII (1948), 26-40.

278. Wall, W. D., "Happiness and Unhappiness in the Childhood and Adolescence of a Group of Women Students," *British Journal of Psychology,* XXXVIII (1948), 191-208.

279. Wall, W. D. and W. A. Simson, "The Effects of Cinema Attendance on the Behavior of Adolescents as Seen by Their Contemporaries," (2) "The Film Choices of Adolescents," *British Journal of Educational Psychology* (February, 1949), 53-61; (June, 1949), 121-136.

280. Wall, W. D. and W. A. Simson, "The Emotional Responses of Adolescent Groups to Certain Films," *British Journal of Educational Psychology* (November, 1950), 153-163.

281. Warner, Alan (ed.), *Days of Youth: Selections From Autobiography* (London: Oxford University Press, 1960).

282. Welch, Louise T., "Recent Studies in Adolescence," *Bulletin of the Maritime Psychological Association* (April, 1953), 34-38.

283. "What Kind of Secondary Schools?" *Tablet,* CCXII (December 6, 1958), 501-502.

284. "What Teenagers Do," *Economist*, CXCI (May 30, 1959), 827.

285. Whitehorn, K., "Addle Essence," *Spectator*, CCIV (April 29, 1960), 641.

286. "Who Leaves School?" *Economist*, CXCVI (July 16, 1960), 257.

A discussion of the Crowther Report, a survey of education, work, and leisure of young people in England. The present discussion stresses the statistics on school leavers. It is noted that 40 per cent of the parents of Grammar and Technical school children who left school at 15 said that they would have preferred the child to stay in school longer; 19 per cent of the males and 14 per cent of the females (15 years old) also said they wished they had stayed in school longer. For the 16-17 year group the percentages climb to 28 per cent and 24 per cent, respectively. Among those who wished they had remained in school the most frequent reason for leaving was desire to earn money. It was also noted that children from large families were more likely to leave school than those from smaller families.

287. Wilding, R., "Regimentation of Youth," *Labour Monthly*, XXIII (May, 1941), 228-233.

288. Williams, H., "Sex Offenses, The British Experience," *Law and Contemporary Problems*, XXV (Spring, 1960), 334-360.

289. Willmott, P. and M. Young, *Family and Class in a London Suburb* (London: 1960).

290. Wilson, B. R., "Teenagers: Frustration and Aggression," *20th Century*, CLXVI (August, 1959), 34-45. Reply—G. Gorer, CLXVI (October, 1959), 302.

A discussion of teen-age frustration and aggression in England. The author notes the role of adolescents in society and comments that their activity is largely unpurposive tension reducing rather than directed toward social ends. The frustration of the youth stems from their lack of goals and their inability to adjust in the changing social world. He notes several dimensions of social change and their relevance for the problem of teen-age frustration and aggression. Among those noted are the following:

(1) The technological development of industry; (2) the economic conditions; (3) a confusion of norms, values, standards, etc., due to the leveling of the class structure; (4) alienation from work and the emphasis on leisure; (5) failure of the youth to internalize the war values and attendant religious values of the previous generation; (6) the increase of the youth to mass media and the increase of upward mobility.

291. Wilson, Mary D., "The Vocational Preferences of Secondary Modern School Children: Part I," *British Journal of Educational Psychology*, XXIII (1953), 97-113.

292. Wilson, Mary D., "The Vocational Preferences of Secondary Modern School Children: Part II," *British Journal of Educational Psychology*, XXIII (1953), 163-179.

293. Wolfenden, J. F., "Educational and Moral Values," *Spectator*, CXL (January 2, 1953), 5.

A discussion of education and moral values with special emphasis on the influence of the family regarding the proper bringing up of children. The maladjustment of children is attributed to the rejection of moral values inside the family, selfishness, and intolerance in the relationship between children and parents. The mental and physical health of each generation is strongly influenced by the parental generation. Juvenile delinquency is treated as a moral and a social problem.

294. Wolfenden, J. F., "Citizens of Tomorrow," *Listener* (October 27, 1955), 704-709.

295. Wray, J. V. C., "Trade Unions and Young Workers in Great Britain," *International Labour Review*, LXXV (April, 1957), 304-318.

296. Wynne-Evans, L., "Ironworks Schools in South Wales, 1784-1860; Early Leaving Age and Irregular Attendance," *Sociological Review*, XLIII (1951), 203-228.

297. "Young Conservative and Unionist Organization. The Young Idea: A Report on Youth in the 1960's," *Conservative Political Centre*, CPC #228 (February, 1961).

298. "Young Fag," *Spectator*, CCVIII (January 26, 1962).

299. "Young Fags: The Psychology of Juvenile Crime" (Institute for the Scientific Treatment of Delinquency Conference), *Times Educational Supplement* (May 12, 1950), 369.

300. "Young People at Work: Some Statistics," *Occupational Psychology* (July, 1958), 133-152.

301. "The Youth Movement" (From a report to the Youth Advisory Committee of the Communist Party concerning the activities of the young Communist League, Great Britain), *Communist Review* (December, 1952), 371-378.

302. "Youth Movements," *London Quarterly Review*," CLXVII (April, 1942), 202-204.

303. "Youth Registration in Great Britain in 1942; Results of Enquiry

into Conditions of Work and Leisure Activities," *International Labour Review,* XLVIII (September, 1943), 383-386.

A description of the leisure activities and working conditions of British youth in 1942 (age 14-17). About 610,600 youths were interviewed at the time of their registration. The purpose was to help them find a way to support the national effort. Among the findings noted by the report were the following: (a) 75 per cent of those interviewed intended to join a youth organization. Criticism of such organizations centered around their leadership, equipment, and programs. The interviews stimulated the youths' interest in their society and in its organized activities but also pointed out the need for a publicity campaign for these activities. (b) 25 per cent to 30 per cent of the youth interviewed were working hours too long or irregular to enable them to participate in other organized activities. Many were fatigued, resulting in ". . . mental staleness and lack of interest in public affairs. . . ." Industrial work made greater demands on youth than did other forms of employment. Some cases of illegal working hours were found. These were reported to the authorities. (c) Many youth lacked intellectual interests and initiative. In many cases the only leisure activities mentioned were light reading, films, and dance halls. There was little interest in national or world affairs and leisure activity seemed, on the whole, aimless. Few youth were interested in reading and many considered their education complete after leaving school. It was suggested, by the interviewers, that the public libraries could make more of an effort to contact and interest youth.

WEST GERMANY

1. Balzano, V., "Dove vanno i giovani della Germania di Bonn?" ("Whither Is Bonn Germany Youth Heading?") *Mondo operaio,* XIII, 2 (February, 1960), 18-23.

2. Barschak, Erna, "A Study of Happiness and Unhappiness in the Childhood and Adolescence of Girls in Different Cultures," *Journal of Psychology,* XXIII (1951), 173-215. (See United Kingdom, Abstract # 17.)

3. Becker, Howard, "Changes in the Social Stratification of Contemporary Germany," *American Journal of Scientific Research,* XV (June, 1950), 333-342.

4. Becker, Howard, *German Youth: Bound or Free* (London: K. Paul, Trench, Trubner and Co., Ltd., 1946).

A discussion of the history of German youth movements,

their activities, their effects on German life, and their participation in the German political scene.

Information was obtained from secondary reference sources, from the accounts of individuals involved in the activities discussed, and from field work and travel in Germany.

German youth has played a significant and vital part in German life and history. Starting with the Roamers, youth movements, aside from organizations organized for youth by the adult world, have had, as their motivational force, reaction against the adult world. It was this reactionary tendency which, essentially, lent itself to the ready adoption, by totalitarian and militaristic regimes, of the youth movements, or movement if such activity is considered as continuous. Hitler, particularly, was dependent on the youth of Germany for the support of his policies. Devotion to das Vaterland, anti-intellectualism, and reactionary philosophy are characteristics running through the whole of the movement from the conception of the Roamers by Karl Fischer in 1896 to the end of, and even after, World War II.

5. Becker, Howard, "What the Hitler Youth Inherited: A Methodological Note," *Phylon*, XII, 1 (1951), 39-54. (Bibliography)

"What are the connections, if any, between the older German youth movements and the Hitler Youth?"

Conceived during the period of German unification, the youth movements were a reaction against adult society. Based on the following of charismatic leaders, the movements became more patriotic as they grew. Though youth-oriented, nationalism became an increasing part of the movement. The rapid turnover of charismatic leadership, which depended on its youth and its emotional appeal for power, lead to the establishment of bureaucratic administrative structures which became organizationally powerful.

The influence of the youth-controlled Roamers and the adult-organized youth organizations eventually merged and increasingly stressed nationalism. By 1920 these movements had some influence in the lives of all German youth, and by 1927 or 1928 the movements' goals had shifted from "youth for youth's sake" to "youth for the sake of almost anything else but youth." At this time there was an absence of available charismatic youth leaders. Hitler, challenging the social system, though not from the same angle as the youth movements, assumed leadership of the movements. His leadership was facilitated since he eliminated all organized youth movements other than those which he controlled.

6. Becker, W. and H. Claussen, *Sozialreform und Jugend* (Social Reform and Youth) (Berlin: H. Luchterland, 1959).

7. Biesanz, J., "Nazi Influence on German Youth Hostels," *Social Forces,* XIX (May, 1941), 554-559.

8. Boeker, Alexander, "German Youth Today," *Liberal Monthly,* LVII (April, 1949), 182-185.

9. Bondy, Curt, "Pubertat als Sozialkulturelles Phanomen" (Puberty as a Socio-Cultural Phenomenon), *Praxis der Kinderpsychologie and Kinderpsychiatrie,* V (1956), 198-201.

10. Bondy, Curt, "Versagung und Aggressionals Kulturelles Problem" (Frustration and Aggression as a Cultural Problem), *Psychologische Rundschau,* IX (1958), 249-255.

11. Bosc, R., "Youth in Europe," *America,* CIII (June 18, 1960), 372-374.

A discussion of youth camps, meetings, and organizations in Europe. From an informal beginning in Germany in 1945, the movement spread to such countries as Spain and Switzerland by 1950. Today the organizations reach as far as North Africa and Arabia. One goal of the movement is the preparation of a generation in Europe which is better prepared to enter the international scene than were their parents.

12. Bornemann, Ernst, "Jugendprobleme Unserer Zeit" (Problems of Youth in Our Times), *Psychologische Rundschau,* IX (1958), 77-104.

A discussion of the problems of youth in Germany. Emphasis is placed on the effect of industrialization on the social structure and the resulting effects on the youth. The author notes the changing attitudes toward the family, work and leisure time, sexual relations and the law. A 98-item bibliography is included.

13. Brady, Robert A., *The Spirit and Structure of German Fascism* (New York, 1937), esp. Chap. 5, "Training the Youth to Become Soldiers of Labor."

14. Brailsford, H. N., "Psychological Disarmament in Germany After the War," *New Statesman and Nation,* XXV (January 16, 1943), 35-36. Discussion—XXV (Jan. 23, 1943), 58.

15. Brennecki, Fritz, *The Nazi Primer* (New York: Harper & Brothers, 1938), with Preface by H. L. Childs.

Problem: To describe, in part, the system used by the Nazi Party and Government in Germany, after the installation of the Hitler Government, to select and train its leadership. Also, to describe the basis of personnel selection used in the system and the individual requirements necessary for mobility in the system. A short description of some of the physical plant used for the education of German youth is also included.

Conclusions: A system of training and indoctrination, starting with the child, based on the Nazi philosophy of race, nationalism, and goals was designed by the Nazi party and government to produce, on a highly selective basis, its future leadership. The system was designed to admit only the cream of Nazi youth to the positions of high leadership after the completion of the program. Admission to the various levels of the program was dependent on character development, physical perfectability, and achievements in areas associated with the national cause plus the ascribed membership in the Aryan race.

The framework within which the education of German youth and the selection of eventual leaders took place was the Hitler Youh organization, which was organized on a hierarchical basis similar to the army and the Nazi party. The requirements for admission to and retention in the program increased with advances in the various levels of the program. Admitted to the program at the age of six, when the child normally started school, the selective process began in reality at the age of ten when membership in the Hitler Youth organization became possible for those youth selected. From this point the control over formal education rested with the organization and as each level of the program was reached the process of selection and retention became stricter until, for those reaching this point, admission to the National Socialist Order of Leaders, for party members between the ages of twenty-three and thirty who were physically perfct, Aryan and who had actively served the party, became possible.

The Nazi Primer is the work of many men and contains the basic material on Nazi goals and philosophy taught to German youth at the time.

16. Buller, E. A., *Darkness over Germany* (London, New York: Longmans, Green & Co., Inc., 1943).

17. Bundesvereinigung der Deutschen Arbeitgeberverbande, *Die junge Generation in unserer sozialan Ordnung* (The Young Generation in our Social Order) (Bonn; B. D. A., 1955).

18. Busemann, A., *Krisenjahre im Ablauf der menschlichen Jugend* (Critical Years in the Emergence of the Young Man), 2nd enlarged and revised edition (Ratingen, A. Henn, 1959).

19. Butler, Eliza M., *The Saint Simonian Religion in Germany: a*

Study of the Young German Movement (Cambridge: Cambridge University Press, 1926).

20. Cardinal, Clive H., "The New Generation in West Germany," *Canadian Forum*, XXXIX (June, 1959), 57-59.
21. Crespi, Leo P., "Germans View the U. S. Reorientation Program; II Reactions to American Democratization Efforts," *International Journal of Opinion Attitude Research*, V (1951), 333-346.
22. Garrit, Grahm, "Bundische Jugend," *New Statesman and Nation*, XIV (July 3, 1937), 9.
23. "Die Demokratic und ihr politscher Nachwuchs" (Democracy and the political formation of the rising generation) *Politische Studien*, VIII, 83 (Munchen: March, 1957), 22-28.
24. Dethleffsen, E., "Staat, Jugend, und Verteidigung" (State, Youth and Defense), *Aussenpolitik*, VII, 9 (September, 1956), 548-558.
25. Deutschland (Bundesrepublik), Statistisches Bundesamt, *Die Jugend im wirtschaftlichen und socialen Leben der Bundesrepublik Deutschland* (Youth in the Economic and Social Life of the German Federal Republic) (Stuttgart: W. Kohlhammer, 1959).
26. "Disciplina y libertad. Una encuesta sobre la actitud de la juventud alemana" (Discipline and Freedom. An Investigation on the Attitude of German Youth), *Arbor*, XLII, 155 (November, 1958), 271-276.
27. Eagle, Lilian, "Moral Revolt of Germany's Youth: The 'Wandervoegel' Movement and its Significance for the Regeneration of the Country," *Current History*, XVI (June, 1922), 447-491.
28. Ebeling, H., *The German Youth Movement: Its Past and Future* (New Europe Publication, 1945).
29. Ebeling, H., "German Youth Movements: What Part Can They Play Now?" *Free Europe*, XIII (December, 1946), 373-377.
30. Eisenhuth, H. D. and P. Kempe, *Die Jugend in der Geschleschtsreife* (Sexually mature youth) (Jena: Wartburg Verlag M. Kessler, 1954).
31. Eysenck, H. J., "Primary Social Attitudes: a Comparison of Attitudes Patterns in England, Germany, and Sweden," *Journal of Abnormal Psychology*, XLVIII (October, 1953), 563-568. (Bibliography)
32. "Failure of America to Train German Youth," *World Report* (October 21, 1947), 19.
33. Fried, Edrita G. and Marjorie F. Lissance, "The Dilemmas of German Youth," *Journal of Abnormal and Social Psychology*, XLIV (1949), 50-60.

Problem: To appraise the extent to which the hopes of reeducating German youth for democracy were justified and to discover the nature of the possible impediments to a democratic Germany.

Two hundred and twenty-five men and women between 18 and 25 were interviewed. The sample represented one-half professional, one-half nonprofessional. Also material was collected from 15 group discussions and 6 detailed case histories.

Despite bad economic conditions, 86 per cent want to get married and raise a family in the near future. Men want a wife who is thrifty, clean, cooks well, whom they can share worries with, and who are intellectually inferior. Women want a husband who is understanding and a good provider. Looks and social accomplishments were hardly mentioned by either sex. A tendency to limit relationships to those who are very much like oneself was noticed. The idea of adjustment is absent. All wanted children, 51 per cent three or more. They believe in semiauthoritarian principles of upbringing—corporal punishment, humiliation, and shaming were considered the best ways to handle disobedience. The majority believe self-expression of young children should be kept at a minimum.

Political concepts: One-half believe that democratic government would be best for Germany. Almost half want to emigrate. 50 per cent are for a strong-hand rule, dictatorship, or monarchy. The conception of democracy is not that of a free functioning system. There is a definite tendency to put nation first and home town last. Switzerland received the most choices (35 per cent) for the country that has the best forms of government, with England placing second (28.4 per cent).

Forty-four and six-tenths per cent of the professional group and 48.8 per cent of the nonprofessional group said they would leave Germany if they could.

In case of another war 65.6 per cent say Germany should stay out of it, while 25 per cent (most frequently front-line veterans) say Germany should take sides.

When asked questions about the war and its causes, their answers employed explanations that had been worked out by the former Propaganda Ministry—Nazi slogans.

They listed as the main obstacles to Germany's reconstruction, the occupation policy and German administration.

They saw as weaknesses of the German national character too great a willingness to defer to authority and an inability to compromise and stick together.

34. Friedlaenden, E., "West German Youth," *Spectator*, CLXXXVII (September 21, 1951) 353.

Many people underestimate the power that the Communists have over East German youth through mass psychology. The "Sovietization" of the youth is a greater threat than terror. But a democracy cannot use such means to train its youth as it believes in the individual. It would be useless for West Germany to imitate the Communists in their totalitarian method even if Communism was an acute threat in West Germany.

One ideal appeals to the youth of Europe and West Germany—the ideal of a United Europe.

Love of liberty can only come from the experience of liberty. Money must be put into a bigger youth program in Germany to give the young people greater opportunity and taste of liberty.

35. Frietag, Gunter, "Die Literarischen Interessen von Schulern und Schulerinnen Einer Hoheren Lehranstalt" (The Literary Interests of High School Students), *Psychol. Beitr.*, I (1953), 264-311.

An investigation of the reading interests of 201 male and 43 female German adolescents. Interviews and questionnaires supplied the data. The analysis indicated that boys in the 10-13 age group preferred adventure stories written for their age group. In following years they became more interested in well-known writers. In the early ages the girls also prefer stories written especially for them. They shift then to sentimental love stories during puberty and read the works of the great poets during adolescence. All of the students reported reading a daily newspaper when one was available to them.

36. Germany (territory under U. S. occupation) Educational and Cultural Relations Division. "Group Activities Branch, German Youth Between Yesterday and Tomorrow: April 1, 1947-April 30, 1948" (Washington, D. C.: Civil Affairs Division, U. S. War Department, 1948.

37. Gilen, Leonhard, *Das Gewissen bei Jugendlichen; Psychologische Untersukhung* (The Conscience of Adolescents; Psychological Studies) (Gottingen: Hogrefe, Verlag fur Psychologie, 1956).

38. Gilen, Leonhard, "Phanomene des Gewissens bei Siebzehnjoehrigen" (The Conscience of the Seventeen-Year-Old), *Zeitschrift fur Experimentelle und Angewandte Psychologie,* II (1954), 383-411. (English summary)

39. Gillespie, J. M. and G. W. Allport, *Youth's Outlook on the Future* (Garden City, New York: Doubleday and Company, Inc., 1955). (1,819 case studies from 10 countries.)

40. Glockel, Hans, "Eine Vergleichsuntersuchung zur Frage jugendlichen Idealerlebens" (A Comparative Investigation on the Ques-

tion of Teenage Experience of Ideals), *Psychologische Rundschau,* XI (1960), 1-20.

The results of this replication of a 1935 study indicate little change among subjects. The majority of the adolescents investigated selected their ideal personalities from among persons in their immediate environment. Closely following this group are the familiar personalities living or dead. The most important determiners of significant differences in ideals are educational level and sex of the respondent.

41. Graham, R. A., "Germans Probe the Youth Problem," *America,* CIII (April 9, 1960), 46-47.

42. Graupner, H., *Sohne und Tochter; ein Schlussel zur Welt der Jugendlichen* (Sons and Daughters; a Key to the World of Youth) (Munchen: R. Piper, 1957).

43. Haiker, Friederich, "Ausehen und Belieftheitsgrad in der Volkschule" (Appearance and Degree of Popularity in Public School), *Psychologische Rundschau,* No. 1 (1950), 285-290.

44. Hartmann, K., "Spielaspekti des Jugendkrawalls" (Aspects of Play in Juvenile Rioting), *Zeitschrift fur Psychotherapie und Medizinsehe Psychologie,* VIII (1958), 159-170.

45. Hartmann, K., "Spielaspekte des Jugendkrawalls: Objektive Spielmerkmale," (Aspects of Play in Juvenile Rioting: Objective Characteristics of Play), *Zeitschrift fur Psychotherapie und Medizinsehe Psychologie,* IX (May, 1959), 108-121.

46. Hartshorne, Edward Y., *German Youth and the Nazi Dream of Victory* (New York: Farrar and Rinehart, Inc., 1941).

47. Hemm, L., "Die Untern Fuhrer in der Hj. Versuch Ihrer Psychologischen Typengliederung," (The Minor Leaders of the Hitler Youth, Investigation of Their Psychological Types), *Beihefte der Zeitschrift fur Angewandte Psychologie und Charakterkunde,* No. 87 (1940).

48. "Herr Ulbricht's Students Revolt," *Economist,* CLXXXIV (July 6, 1957), 43-44.

49. Herrfahrdt, Ilsemarie, "Beitrag zur Entwicklung des Interesses an Theater bei 13-bis 19-johrigen Schulerinneg" (Development of Theatrical Interest in 13 to 19-year-old School Girls), *Psychologische Beitrage,* II (1956), 390-408. (English summary)

50. Hirt, E., "Jugend, Sport und Politik," (Youth, Sport, and Politics), *Politische Rundschau,* XXXIV, 7 (Bern: July, 1955), 201-207.

51. Hitler, Adolf, Speech given on May 1, 1937 in *Frankfurter Zei-*

tung, May 3, 1937, in *The Speeches of Adolf Hitler, April, 1922-August, 1939.* Norman H. Baynes (ed.) (London, 1942), 549.

52. Hormann, Hans and Ernst Timaeus, "Altersabhangigkeit einiger Gruppenstrukturen bei Obserschulerenner," *Psychologische Rundschau,* XII (1961), 93-99.

    A study of the variation of social relationships with increasing age. Twenty German secondary school classes were given a sociometric test. The classes ranged from the fifth to the twelfth grades. The following hypotheses were tested: (1) (general) group coherency or integration increases with age; (2) the frequency of sociometric stars decreases with age; (3) the number of isolates decreases with increasing age; (4) the number of mutual choices decreases with increasing age. All of the hypotheses were supported at statistically significant levels.

53. "Idle Youth in Germany" (excerpt), *Social Service Review,* CXXIV (March, 1950), 102.
54. Jewitt, Moya, "Youth and Peace," *Arbitrator* (London: April, 1924), 27.
55. Jouhy, Ernest, "German Youth and German History" (Background Causes, Reflections of Some of Their Attitudes and Beliefs Regarding Outcome of the War, The Hitler Regime, and Anti-Semitism), *Commentary,* XXIX (April, 1960), 308-314.
56. Juta, Rene, "Young Germany and the New Youth Movement," *English Review,* LXVI (April, 1928), 445-449.
57. "Juvenile Delinquency in Germany," *Social Service Review,* XX (December, 1946), 269-273.
58. Kaiser, G., *Randalierende Jugend* (Rowdyism of Youth), (Heidelberg: Quelle, 1959).
59. Kath, G., *Das soziale Bild der Studentenschaft in Westdeutschland und Berlin. Sommersemester 1953* (The Social Tableau of the Student Body in Western Germany and Berlin. Summer semester 1953) (Berlin, Colloquium-Verlag, 1954).
60. Keilhacker, Martin, "Kinder und Jugend Psychologische Fragen des Felms" (Child and Adolescent Psychological Problems of the Film), *J. Psychol. Psychotherapy,* II (1953), 9-20.
61. Kellermann, H. J., "The Present Status of German Youth," *U. S. Department of State Bulletin,* XV (July 14-28, 1946), 49-55, 83-88, 139-149.
62. Kemmler, Lilly, "Erziehungshaltungen von Muttern Vierzehnjahriger Jungen" (Educational Attitudes of Mothers of 14-Year-Old Boys), *Psychologische Rundschau,* XI (1960), 197-218.

While this study deals with the attitudes of mothers, it is extremely applicable to our topic since it is concerned with mothers' attitudes toward their 14-year-old sons and the "proper" ages for them (the sons) to be allowed to undertake certain types of behavior. The sample consisted of 180 nonworking urban mothers. The families were all intact. 90 of the adolescents in these families were students in secondary schools while 90 were apprentices in the trades. All of the boys were 14 years old.

It was generally found that the mothers of the secondary school students were less authoritarian, more liberal, and more concerned with self-control than were the mothers of the apprentices. The data were compared with data reported by Gesell in the United States and Schelsky in Germany.

The following examples of the results are listed for illustrative purposes.

Behavior Questioned	*Mean Age*	*Per Cent Saying "Never"*
1. Activity in politics	19.75	
2. Join youth organizations	12.00	
3. Choose own books	18.00	
4. Receive letters without control	18.50	35
5. Criticize his parents	17.50	24
6. Obtain sex education on intercourse	15.00	
7. Marry	24.90	
8. Bring a girl friend home	19.00	
9. Decide on church attendance	13.75	
10. Know how much father earns	16.25	18

63. Kirkpatrick, C., "Recent Changes in the Status of Women and the Family in Germany," *American Sociological Review,* II (1937), 650-658.

64. Kluth, H., U. Lohmar, and R. Tartler, *Arbeiterjugend gestern und heute. Socialwissenschaftliche Untersuchungen* (The Young Worker Yesterday and Today. Sociological Investigations), Published and with an introduction by H. Schelsky (Heidelberg: Quelly und Meyer, 1955).

65. Knirck, E., *Die junge Gesellschaft* (The Young Society) (Dusseldorf: W. Rau, 1957).

66. "'Konformistische' Jugend (Die)" (The "Conformist" Youth), *Offene Welt* (Frankfurt an Main), LIV (March, April, 1958), 187-195.

67. Kruger, Fritz K., "Spirit of the German Youth Movement and Its

Effect on Education in Modern Germany," *School and Society,* XXX (October 12, 1929), 489-493.

68. Kunzer, Edward J., "The Youth of Nazi-Germany," *Journal of Educational Sociology,* XI (February, 1938), 342-350.

69. Kuzmenko, V., "German Youth against War, *New Times* (June 14, 1950), 21-24. (Concerning the All German Youth Rally, Berlin, May 27-29, 1950.)

70. Lahy, Bernard, "German Youth and Understanding Between Nations," *International Journal of Opinion Attitude Research,* IV (1950), 297-299. (Abstract)

71. Laqueur, Walter Z., "Tusk (Eberhard Koebel) and German Youth" [The man who played a major role in the Youth Movements of pre-Hitler Germany but whose influence continues to be felt], *New Leader,* XLIII (October 31, 1960), 18-20.

72. Lehmensick, E., "Die Jugendlichen Berufwunsche" (Adolescent Vocational Desires), *Zeitschrift fur Angewandte Psychologie und Charakterkunde,* LVIII (1940), 343-357.

73. Lewin, Herbert S., "Hitler Youth and the Boy Scouts of America: A Comparison of Aims," *Human Relations,* I (1947), 206-227. (Bibliography)

Problem: ". . . [T]o reveal in a comparative fashion the major aims and goals of the two youth groups by means of a content analysis of their published literature."

Material was taken from literature designed for members of the organizations and for leaders in the organizations. *Boy's Life* and *Jungen—Eure Welt,* Baden-Powell's *Scoutmastership* and Schnach's *Die Hitler Jugend, Idee und Gestalt.*

Findings:

1. The Hitler Youth derive their goals from their National Socialist membership and these goals conform to those of the National Socialist society as a whole. The goals of the Boy Scouts, stress "personal achievement and self-development."

2. Both organizations stress practical experience for learning "rather than mere verbal recommendations." The Hitler Youth had more control over the activities of the individual member than did the Boy Scouts. There was a great emphasis on indoctrination (political) in the Hitler Youth, though it provided more "real try-out experiences," than did the Boy Scouts.

3. The ends of the Hitler Youth were strongly emotional in motivation. Though the Boy Scouts did not reject emotional appeal, particularly in the area of patriotism, their goal acceptances were motivated in a less emotional manner.

4. The ends of the Hitler Youth were accepted by the

member as an obligation to the nation. The ends of the Boy Scouts were oriented to the individual and toward his satisfaction.

74. Liddell, H., "Education in Occupied Germany: A Field Study," *International Affairs,* XXIV (January, 1948), 30-62.
75. Limbert, P. M., "Youth Activities in Germany," *Educational Record,* XXVIII (January, 1947), 33-44.
76. Lohbauer, H., "Die soziale Herkunft der Studierenden an den bayerischen Hochschulen" (The Social Origin of the Students in Bavarian Institutions of Higher Education), *Bayern in Zahlen,* IX, 2 (Munchen: February, 1955), 49-51.
77. Luchsinger, F., "German Youth Today," *Swiss Review of World Affairs,* V, 6 (September, 1955), 7-10.
78. McClelland, David C., J. F. Sturr, R. H. Knapp, and H. W. Wendt, "Obligations to Self and Society in the United States and Germany," *Journal of Abnormal and Social Psychology,* LVI (1958), 245-255.
79. McGranahan, D. V., "A Comparison of Social Attitudes Among American and German Youth," *Journal of Abnormal and Social Psychology,* XLI (July, 1946), 245-256.

A report on an attitude questionnaire applied to German and American samples. The German youth contained elements of Nazi and non-Nazi youth. Both boys and girls were included. The German youth were higher in values of obedience toward authority, honor, and loyalty to the state than were the American youth. The Germans also revealed less tolerance for individuals and had more faith in national superiority than the Americans. When the anti-Nazi group and the Nazi group are compared, it is seen that the anti group was more like the American group than the Nazi group with the exception of the items on parental authority. The author notes that the Nazi youth apparently substitute state authority for parental authority. It was also noted that the girls in both countries tended to reflect the national pattern of attitudes more extremely than did the boys.

80. McGranahan, D. V. and M. Janowitz, "Studies of German Youth," *Journal of Abnormal and Social Psychology,* XLI (January, 1946), 3-14.

A report on the application of attitude questionnaires to four samples of German youth between the ages of 14 and 18. It was found that the boys, in general expressed pro-American and pro-democratic attitudes, but revealed inconsistencies when asked about race and power. The authors note that the acceptance of pro-American views reflects more the uncritical acceptance of power figures than it does a conversion to democratic principles. A sample of girls from an anti-Nazi school revealed less pro-American feeling, but were, in effect, more democratic and better balanced in their views.

81. Mallinson, Vernon, "British and German Education: A Comparison of Aims and Ideals," *Journal of Education* (February, 1955), 45-47.

82. Mann, Thomas, "Tonio Kroger," in *Stories of Three Decades* (New York: Alfred A. Knopf, Inc., 1936). Translated by H. T. Lowe-Porter.

83. "Manpower Policy in Germany; Employment of Children and Young Persons," *International Labour Review*, XLIX (February, 1944), 229-233.

84. Meister, Charles W., "A Year in Berlin Education," *Harvard Educational Review*, XVI, 4 (Fall, 1946), 255-272.

Here is a highly specific report concerning the problems which arouse during the first year of inter-Allied administration of primary, secondary, and higher education in Berlin. The author brings out with particular clarity the frequent clashes which occurred between the ideologies and ethics of the Western democracies and those of Soviet Russia. He shows the good as well as the bad policies of Russia and particularly America. There were unity barriers (language and culture), authoritarian problems, what type of educational philosophy to be taught, Allied inconsistencies of goals, the problems of private and religious schools, school administration, control of Berlin education, need for teachers and expansion of school systems.

The findings indicate that the United States is going to remain in Berlin and that the only alternative is to revise the basic agreement under which the United States, Great Britain, and France entered the city. The new proposal is that the school governing board should be run on democratic ideals and not by men who represent 10 per cent of the Berlin population. The Berlin public would be free to elect men who represent their viewpoints of school control. There is much Russian obstinacy towards the Allies. In fact, they are opposed to more issues than agreed to. There is hope for Germany, for the people who have worked in Berlin education feel that if the desirable elements of the German tradition are stressed sufficiently, the Germans may someday develop into a peace-loving and altruistic nation. Germany must be convinced for the need of "One

World" for she could be an important bridge between the East and West.

85. Miller, James W., "Youth in the Dictatorships," *American Political Science Review*, XXXII (October, 1938), 965-970.

86. Muhlen, N., "German Youth in a Vacuum; The Threat of a New Lost Generation," *Commentary*, IX (May, 1950), 426-434.

87. Muhlen, N., "New Nazis of Germany; the Totalitarians of the Eastern Zone," *Commentary*, XI (January, 1951), 1-10.

88. Muhlen, N., "The Young Germans Today," *Freeman*, IV (June 28, 1954), 705-707.

    It is not the ghosts of Nazism that haunt Germany's youth, but rather the fear of being rejected in their fervent hope to participate in and even fight for an European community of free nations.

89. Nasarski, P. E., *Deutsche Jugendbewegung und Jugendarbeit in Polen 1919-1939) German Youth Movement and Youth Work in Poland, 1919-1939*) (Wurzburg: Holzner, Verlag, 1957).

90. Nasarski, P. E., "Jugend zwischen Ost und West" (Youth Between East and West), *Politik und Zeitgeschichte* (Bonn: November, 1958), 634-640.

91. Nielsen, A. K., "Youth Groups in Germany," *Recreation*, IV (November, 1947), 396-397.

92. Office of Military Government, Education and Cultural Relations Division. *German Youth between Yesterday and Tomorrow*, April 1947 to April 1948 (Berlin: Office of Military Government, 1948).

93. Paetel, K. O., "Die deutsche Jugendbewegung als Politisches Phanomen" (The German Youth Movement as a Political Phenomenon), *Politische Studien*, VIII, 86 (Munchen: June, 1957), 1-14.

94. Paz Otero, Gerardo, "La Nueva Generacion en Alemania, Abandono y Delincuencia Infantil" (The New Generation in Germany, Immorality and Delinquency of Children), *Revista de Medicina Legal Colombia*, IX (1947), 34-44.

    A moralistic discussion of the material and spiritual ruin of German youth. The author feels that German youth have all the makings of degeneracy. A plea is made for action to halt the premature delinquency of the youth in occupied Germany.

95. Pipping, K., R. Abshagen, and A. E. Brauneck, *Gesprache mit der deutschen Jugend. Ein Beitrag zum Autoritatsproblem* (*Talks with*

German Youth. A Study on the Authority Problem) (Helsingfors, Societas scientiarum fennica. 1954).

96. "Post-Hitler Youth," *Social Justice Review*, L (December, 1957), 272.

97. Potter, G. R., "Educational Framework of an Industrial Society: Germany Since 1945," *Research* (May, 1958), 173-177.

98. Radosavljevich, Paul R., "Ideals and Methods of the Proletariat Youth Movement in Germany," *School and Society*, XXXI (May 3, 1930), 601-603.

99. Rauch, K., *Junge Menschen Heute* (*Young People Today*) (Munchen: List, 1956).

100. Reimann, G., *Verderbt, verdammt, verraten? Jugend in Licht und Schatten* (Disgraced, Damned, Betrayed? Youth in Light and Shade) (Stuttgart, F. Decker, Verlag Nachf. 1955).

101. Reynolds, Quentin, "Children Behind Barbed Wire," *Collier's*, CXVI-CXVII (October 27, 1945), 18-19, 32.

102. Roessler, W., *Jugend im Erziehungsfeld; Halting und Verhalten der deutschen Jugend in der ersten Halfte des 20. Fahrhunderts unter besonderer Berucksichtigung der westdeutschen Jugend der Gegenwart* (*Youth in the Educational Field; the Attitude and Behavior of German Young People in the First Half of the Twentieth Century, with Special Emphasis on the West German Youth of Today*) (Dusseldorf: Padagogischer Verlag Schwann, 1957).

103. Ross, Albion, "Report From Berlin," *The New York Times* (February 2, 1955).

104. Schelsky, H., *Die skeptische Generation: eine Soziologie der deutschen Jugend* (The skeptical generation; a sociology of German youth), 2nd ed. (Dusseldorf: E. Diederich, 1958).

105. Schepses, E., "Juvenile Vagrancy in Germany," *Social Service Review*, XXII (March, 1948), 40-45.

106. Scheuch, Erwin K., "Inquiries into the Present State of German Youth," *Kolner Zeitschrift fur Soziologie und Sozialpsychologie*, VIII (1956), 124-142.

107. Schmidt, R. C., "German Youth Movement: A Typological Study," *Summary of Doctoral Dissertations, University of Wisconsin*, VII (1942), 167-169.

108. Siebert, J. G., *The Remaking of German Youth* (I. N. G. Publications, Ltd.).

109. Seiffert, W., "Zur Entwicklung der Rechte der Jugend in der

D. D. R." (On the Development of the Rights of Youth in the D. D. R.), *Staat und Recht*, VIII, 2 (Berlin: Gebl, 1959), 215-231.

110. Soddai, A., "German Youth Group," *Spectator*, CLXXXII (June, 1949), 855.

111. "Some Characteristics of the Younger Generation in Western Germany," *World Today*, X (September, 1954), 406-412.

112. Stackelberg, K. G. (ed.), *Jugend zwischen 15 und 24. Eine Untersuchung zur Situation der deutschen Jugend im Bundesgebiet* (*Young people between the age of 15 and 24. A study on the situation of German youth in the federal territory*) (Hamburg: Jugend werk dir Deutschen Shell, 1954).

113. Storring, G. E. and H. N. Lownau, "Zur Problematik der Jugend in der Gegenwort" (Concerning the Problem of Youth in the Present), *Praxis der Kinderpsychologie und Kinderpsychiatrie*, VII (1958), 1-8.

114. Strasser, O., "German Youth as a Postwar Problem," *Catholic World*, CLVI (February, 1943), 530-532.

115. Sullwold, Fritz, "Empirische Untersuchungen Iber Die Sorgen und Probleme von Jugendlichen in Deutschland und den U. S. A." (Empirical Investigations of Youth Troubles and Problems in Germany and the U.S.A.), *Psychologische Rundschau*, X (1959), 49-66.

117. Taylor, John W., *Youth Welfare in Germany* (Nashville, Tennessee: The Baird-Ward Co., 1936).

118. Thomas, H., "Beziehungen Zwischen Freizectverbolten, Sozialen Faktoren und Personlichkeitsstruktur" (Relationships Between Spare Time Activities, Social Factors and Personality Structure), *Psychologische Rundschau*, XI (1960), 151-159.

119. Thomas, H., "Gegenwartsjugend und Gegenwartsgesellschaft" (Modern Youth and Present-Day Society), *Zeitschrift fur Politik* (Berlin), III, 2 (Berlin: October, 1956), 166-175.

120. Thompson, J. A., "No Duels, No Beer," *Spectator*, CLXXXV (August 11, 1950), 175.

121. Ulbricht, Walter, "Our Youth in the German Democratic Republic," *North Central European Observer*, III (June 10, 1950), 132-133.

122. Ulich, Eberhard, "Uber die Beshaftigunsgen Jugendlicher Schuler in der Freizeit" (Spare Time Activities of Teen-Age Pupils), *Psychologische Rundschau* (July, 1959), 180-190.

Four hundred and fifty-six mothers of teen-age high school pupils in Munich were interviewed about the activities of their sons during spare time constructively. Sports, model building, and stamp collecting topped the list of activities for pupils up to 15 years old. Sport still ranks first, while music, drawing, and similar occupations take second place for the age group over 16. Stamp collecting sinks to sixth place for the older boys.

123. Ulich, Robert, "The German Youth Movement and Its Social Effect," *Institute of Public Affairs, Athens, Georgia Proceedings* (1930), 43-56.

124. Undeutsch, Udi, "Die Sexualitat im Jugendalter" (Adolescent Sex Behavior), *Stadium Generale*, III (1950), 433-454.

125. Valentiner, T., "Die Arbeit des Instituts fur Jugendkunde in Bremen" (The Work of the Bremen Institute for Youth Study), *Zeitschrift fur Pedagogische Psychologie und Experimentelle Pedagogik*, XLI (1940) 186-192.

126. Walter, H., "German Students Seek Peace with the Jews: Behind the Fight against Nazi Movie Makers" *Commentary*, XIV (August, 1952), 124-130.

127. "Wartime Civilian Service and the Hitler Youth Organization," *International Labour Review*, XXIV (August, 1940), 147-148.

128. Wilson, J. S., A. E. Morgan and J. Nowell, "What Way for Youth?" (by a visitor to Berlin), *Spectator*, CLXXXVII (August 24–September 14, 1951), 234-245, 261, 289-290, 325; Discussion—CLXXXVII (August 31-September 7, 21, 1951), 271-298, 384.

129. Wiskemann, Elizabeth, "A Short History of the German Student Corporation," *History Today* (December, 1954), 835-843.

130. Wolf, H. E., "Shellengnahmen von Schulern zu Konfessionell-religiosen und Regiovalen Gruppen" (Attitudes of Students toward Confessional-Religious and Regional Groups), *Kolner Zeitschrift fur Soziologie und Sozialpsychologie*, XII (1960), 473-490.

131. Wolber, H. O., *Religion Ohne Entscheidung* (Gottingen: 1959).

132. Young, Erle F., "German Youth Movement," *Sociology and Social Research*, XVI (March, 1932), 367-379. (Bibliography)

133. "Youth in Berlin," *Spectator*, CLXXXVII (August 17, 1951), 203; Discussion CLXXXVII (August 24, 1951), 242.

134. Zaugg, E., "German Youth is Disillusioned," *The Christian Science Monitor Magazine* (June 24, 1949), 3.

135. Ziemer, G., "Rehabilitating Fascist Youth," *Public Opinion Quarterly*, VII (1943), 583-591.

136. Zillig, Maria, *Psychologie des Jungmadchens* (Psychology of the Adolescent Girl) (Heidelberg: Quelle and Meyer, 1949). (Bibliography)

137. Ziman, N. J., "Life in the Studentenbunker," *Spectator*, CLXXXVII (October 26, 1951), 534.

GENERAL

1. Abel, Theodore M. and Natalie F. Joffe, "Cultural Backgrounds of Female Puberty," *American Journal of Psychotherapy*, IV (1950), 90-113.

In this article an attempt is made to describe dominant and contrasting themes in the attitudes which different European cultures, important in the culture of the United States, display toward female puberty, and to show how these various themes relate to the developing attitudes in the United States. Rather than a statistical enumeration of attitudes, the author is interested in the description of attitude themes.

Interviews were held with several informants from Italy, Germany, Poland, Ireland, and the United States. Orthodox Jews were also included in the sample. Part of the information was gleaned from the literature on the subject.

Among the findings for the various cultures we note the following examples.

ITALY: The attitudes toward the onset of puberty regard the girl as an object to be protected and pitied. The menstruating girl is both vulnerable and dangerous. The flow is a sign of fertility and the period is surrounded with an assortment of tabus and cautions.

GERMANY: In Germany the issue is more open than in either Italy or France but less open than in Poland or Ireland. The liberals and intellectuals are moving toward a more modern viewpoint. In the middle classes the mothers are the informants, while among the Catholics the sisters are prime sources of information.

POLAND: In Poland the process is considered disgusting and is tabu. Mothers do not discuss it with their daughters, the daughter is supposed to "know" about the process without instruction. In this area liberals are also attempting to change the tradition.

IRELAND: While the mother is the informant the subject is generally tabu. There is isolation of the girls from boys.

UNITED STATES: The situation is changing rapidly. With the changing ideas on sports, boyfriends, wearing apparel, etc., the subject is losing some of its characteristic concealment.

2. Aranguren, J. L., "La juventud Europa de hoy" (European Youth of Today), *Europa,* IX, 33 (1960), 113-141.

3. Council of Europe, "Juvenile Delinquency in Postwar Europe," European Commission on Crime Problems (Some aspects of postwar juvenile delinquency in twelve of the member countries of the Council of Europe) (1960).

4. Cressey, P. F., "Chinese Traits in European Civilization," *American Sociological Review,* X, 4 (October, 1945), 595-604.

    On level of material, philosophical, and art—deals with integration of some Chinese traits into European life.

5. Greenfield, S. M., "Industrialization and the Family in Sociological Theory," *American Journal of Sociology,* LXVII (November, 1961), 312-322.

6. Gross, F., "Educational Reconstruction in Europe," *American Sociological Review,* VIII, 5 (October, 1943), 543-550.

7. Holland, Kenneth, *Youth in European Labor Camps* (Washington, D. C.: American Council of Education, 1939).

8. "Influx of Young People into the Employment Market in Western and Northern Europe," *International Labour Review,* LXXV (April, 1957), 335-353.

9. Keehn, J. D. and E. T. Prothro, "National Preferences of University Students from 23 Nations," *Journal of Psychology,* XLII (1956), 283-294.

    ". . . To demonstrate the feasibility of cross-national research on international attitudes," questionnaires were given to college or university students aged from 16 to 25 from 30 countries. The 30 national groups were listed on the questionnaire, and questions involving a preference among the countries were asked. In general, and in agreement with other research, the British, Swiss, and Americans were most preferred. The Swiss seemed to enjoy the most general popularity. English-speaking countries tended to prefer Britain, Canada, New Zealand, Australia, and America; the Japanese, Egyptians, Israelis, and Turks were rejected. Students from the Arab-Mediterranean area preferred the Egyptians, Syrians, Germans, and Swiss; they rejected the Turks and Israelis. Western Europeans preferred the Dutch, Finns, Swiss, and Germans, rejecting Middle-Easterners.

10. *Look,* XXV, 1, "How Americans are Young Europeans" (January 3, 1961) 62. All of issue is on youth—"The Explosive Generation of the 60's."

This article in the popular press poses the question, "Have young Europeans reacted to the postwar world in the same way as American teen-agers?"

In spite of adoption of American material traits, the youth of many countries maintain significant cultural differences. For example in Sweden, France, and Hungary, the youth enter the labor market earlier than in the U. S. and many fewer attend college. While few French youth go to college they prepare extensively for the baccalaurate exams necessary for graduation from high school.

Even in Hungary one sees a more permissive atmosphere in the acceptance of Western dress and other phenomena which reflect a loosening of controls following the Hungarian revolt.

The article notes that the youth of the world today seem to have much in common. It states, "No one can say what such uniformity portends for an otherwise divided humanity. But there seems to be little doubt that, in its young people, the world today is more united than ever."

11. Mays, John Barron, "Teen-age Culture in Contemporary Britain and Europe," *The Annals of the Academy of Political and Social Science,* CCCXXXVIII (1961), 22-32.

    The author notes a marked similarity between the youth cultures of Western Europe and the United States. He feels that this similarity is a product of similar social and economic influences operating in the two areas. Both areas have an emphasis on security and affluence. It is also noted that uncertainty of role and status may lead to acute alienation between the adult and the youth generation.

12. Neumann, Sigmund, "Conflict of Generations in Contemporary Europe," *Vital Speeches of the Day,* V (August 1, 1939), 623-628. (Account of the youth movement.)

13. Saunders, Richard, "Children in Europe in an Age of Anxiety," *Journal of Educational Sociology,* XXVIII (March, 1955), 295-298.

    The author, 1955 president of the Save the Children Federation, states, ". . . the children of Europe, in this age of anxiety, need our continued concern and enlightened assistance." He cites four needs among European children; improved morale, intercultural understanding, education, and community, and notes that a better milieu for children can become a community objective.

14. Steel, William H., et al., "Scandinavian Students' Images of the

United States: a Study in Cross-Cultural Education," *Annals of the American Academy of Political and Social Science,* CCXCV (1954), 126-135.

The problem posed here is the study of the processes involved in cross-cultural exchange. The effects of the foreign educational experience are also discussed. Attitudes toward the United States take central concern.

Interviews were taken from 38 students at the University of Wisconsin. These students were from Norway, Sweden, and Denmark.

The authors note, "One of the striking impressions resulting from interviewing Scandinavian students is that they all consider Americans rather immature in one respect or another, whether their general attitude toward America is favorable and tolerant or impatient and antagonistic."

Among the positive attitudes noted were; warm friendliness, informality, constant activity and motion. Negative attitudes were seen toward installment buying and lack of artistic tradition.

The constant conforming of Americans to group norms was generally seen by the subjects as a form of superficiality of values.

In contrast to other groups of students from foreign lands the Scandinavian students, on the whole, adjust very well to the host culture.

15. Titmuss, R. M., "Industrialization and the Family," *Social Service Review,* XXXI (March, 1957), 54-62.

A discussion of the impact of industrialization for those countries which have been industrialized for considerable periods of time, namely Western Europe and the United States.

Discussing the impact of industrialization on the family and particularly the wage earner, the author notes that today the wage earner, the husband, is the earning agent for the whole family; thus the condition of the father determines the context of the family as a social unit. In the West, the laborer is faced with irregularity, impermanence, unemployment, short time working, technological change, and uncertainty of the future. While the older middle-class worker has some job security in middle age, this is not true of the laborer.

The author concludes that today's family is facing conflicting values and must choose between kinship and economic progress. The family also faces instability and conflicts or roles, two factors which in themselves, are changing the values and structure of the family.

16. Wise, James W., "Youth and the Old World," *Century*, CXV (January/April 1928), 257-267; 601-609; 704-712.

17. Yard, J., "New Liberation of Western Europe; Youth Movements to Stimulate Democracy," *Free World*, XII (November, 1946), 41-44.

18. *Youth in the Western European Union Countries* (London: 1957).

GENERAL

1. Adler, J. H., *The Under-developed Areas and their Industrialization*, VI (New Haven: Yale Institute of International Studies, 1949).

2. Al-Khatabi, L., "Les problemes de notre jeunesse vus a la lumiere de la realite," *Confluent*, IV (December, 1959-January, 1960), 417-423.

3. Althoff, Becky, "Observations on the Psychology of Children (And Adolescents) in a D.P. Camp," *Journal of Social Casework*, XXIX (1948), 17-22.

   The author discusses the psychological effects of experiences of adolescent displaced persons. She finds that the "characteristic" adolescent D.P. reflects a similarity of background, of traumatic experiences, of defense mechanisms for survival, and of general behavior patterns. She describes both the typical adolescent boy and girl and notes that group therapy on these children had positive results. Tensions and anxiety were reduced and strength and emotional stability increased.

4. Anderson, C. A., "The Social Status of University Students in Relation to Type of Economy: an International Comparison," *Transactions of the Third World Congress of Sociology*, V (London: International Sociological Association, 1956), 51-63.

5. Anshen, Ruth N., *The Family: Its Function and Destiny* (New York: Harper & Brothers, 1949).

   Includes family patterns and structure in different countries.

6. Bardis, Panos, "Social Distance among Foreign Students," *Sociology and Social Research*, XLI (1956), 112-114.

7. Barry, Herbert III, I. L. Child and M. K. Bacon, "Relation of Child Training to Subsistence Economy," *American Anthropologist*, LXI (February, 1959), 51-63.

8. Beals, Ralph L., "Urbanism, Urbanization and Acculturation," *American Anthropologist*, LIII (1951), 1-10.

While this article does not bear directly on the phenomena of adolescence it is of tangential interest in its discussion of the interdisciplinary research possibilities in the areas of acculturation, urbanism, and urbanization. Specific areas of interest for the investigation of adolescence are found in topics such as industrialization, family size, transformation of village life to city life, and the influence of the city on rural areas.

9. Benedict, Ruth, "Continuities and Discontinuities in Cultural Conditioning," in Kluckhohn, Murray, and Schneider, *Personality in Nature, Society and Culture* (New York: Alfred A. Knopf, Inc., 1954).

10. Benedict, Ruth, *Patterns of Culture* (New York: New American Library, 1959).

11. Bettelheim, Bruno, "Feral Children and Autistic Children," *American Journal of Sociology*, LXIV, 5 (March, 1959), 455-467.

While marginal to the direct study of adolescents, this article on feral children points up the importance of the cultural factor in childrearing procedures. Comparisons are made between Amala and Kamala (two feral children) and other autistic children. Bettelheim concludes that there is no such thing as a feral child. He attributes their behavior to a combination of extremely threatening situations and extreme emotional isolation.

12. Bienenstock, Theodore, "Social Life and Authority in the East European Jewish Shtetle Community," *Southwestern Journal of Anthropology*, VI (1950), 238-254.

In this study Bienenstock discusses the relationship between the religious and the secular influences on the life of the Shtetle community. The interviews were gathered by the Columbia University Project in Contemporary Cultures. Analysis of the interviews provides information on the stratification system, power and authority structure, informal social life, and reactions to authority. The author comes to the conclusion that there has been a fusion of the religious and the secular aspects of everyday life in the Shtetle community of Eastern Europe.

13. Bloch, Herbert A. and Arthur Niederhoffer, *The Gang: A Study in Adolescent Behavior* (New York: Philosophical Library, 1958).

14. Bossard, J. H. S. and E. S. Boll (eds.), "Adolescents in Wartime," *Annals of the American Academy of Political and Social Science*, CCXXXVI (1944), 1-168.

15. Bott, Elizabeth, "Urban Families: The Norms of Conjugal Roles (A Psychological Study)," *Human Review*, IX (1957), 325-342.

16. Brown, J. S., "A Comparative Study of Deviations from Sexual Mores," *American Sociological Review*, XVII (April, 1952), 135-146.

The author has gathered information on more than 100 primitive societies in Africa, North and South America, Eurasia, and Oceania. Her interest lies in the investigation of the direction and strength of sexual tabus. She discusses similarity of tabus, severity of punishments, and the nature of the sanctions which support the mores in various societies. She found a high correlation between the severity of the punishment and the frequency with which a given behavior is tabued, a general tendency to punish certain types of deviant sexual behavior more severely than others, and general support for sexual mores through intervention of human agents rather than supernatural agents which tend to be supplementary rather than substitutive.

17. Brown, Oril, *Youth under Dictators: A Study of the Fascist and Communist Youth* (Evanston, Ill.: Row, Peterson and Co., 1941).

18. Brynner, Yul, *Bring Forth the Children: Journey of the Forgotten People of Europe and the Middle East* (New York: McGraw-Hill Book Company, Inc., 1960).

19. Cabot, P. S. de Q. (comp.), *Juvenile Delinquency: A Critical Annotated Bibliography* (New York: H. W. Wilson, 1946). (972 references from 1914-1944)

20. Calverton, V. F., *The New Generation* (New York: The Macaulay Company, 1930).

A 700-page book consisting of articles about: Parents versus Children, The Child versus Civilization, The Family Romance, Potentialities of the Child, Education and Enlightenment.

21. Cater, Douglass, "Collapse of Youth's One World: the Second War Generation in Its Turn Has Had to Learn the Sad Lesson of Disillusionment from the Implacable 'Our Way or None' Dialecticians," *Reporter* (August 30, 1949), 15-16. (At the World Student Congress, Prague, 1946 and 1947)

22. Cheesman, Evelyn, "Child Nations: The People of Papua," *Journal of the Royal Central Asian Society*, XXXII (January, 1945), Part 1, 91-97.

23. Coelho, George V., "Impacts of Studying Abroad," *Journal of Social Issues*, XVIII, 1 (1962), 7-87. (Bibliography)

24. Cohen, Eli E. and Louise Kapp, "Youth and Work: The Second Challenge," *Children*, IX (March/April, 1962), 79.

25. Curle, Adam, "Some Aspects of Educational Planning in Under-

developed Areas," *Harvard Educational Review*, XXXII, 3 (Summer, 1962), 292-300.

26. Davis, A., "Socialization and Adolescent Personality," in E. Harltley and T. Newcomb (eds.), *Readings in Social Psychology*, rev. ed. (New York: Henry Holt and Company, Inc., 1952), 520-531.

Utilizing descriptive data from both sociological and psychological investigations, the author explores the notion that successful socialization of the adolescent depends upon the degree of adaptive or socialized anxiety which has been instilled in him by his society. It is felt that a certain degree of such anxiety acts as a push toward the internalization of culturally required behavior, which, in turn leads to approval, prestige, and security in the adolescent's group.

Among the significant points discussed by the author are: the importance of the individual's maintenance of a certain level of anxiety with regard to status-appropriate behavior, the importance of separating and understanding the culturally typed and the individual aspects of personality as they relate to the socially adaptive functions of anxiety.

With regard to adolescent socialization and normal anxiety the author notes, "It is derived from a long and complex series of training situations in which punishment is invoked. Increased striving for prestige is maintained partly by the anxiety to avoid social punishment and partly by the drive to attain the rewards of social prestige. Anxiety of this type, therefore, is an effective motivation toward social learning because it leads to reward." He goes on to say that if we would make low-status children *anxious* to work hard, study hard, save their money, and abide by strict sexual codes we will be obliged to convince them that at the end of their efforts there are *real* rewards waiting. While this presents little problem for the child of high status, it is more critical for the lower-status child. "Our society cannot hope, therefore, to educate the great masses of lower-class people in any really effective manner until it has REAL rewards to offer them for learning the necessary anxiety.

The applicability of these comments to the study of adolescence on a cross-cultural level can only be determined by comparison of the phenomena in different settings. One would speculate however that similar processes are at work in other societies, regardless of the cultural content.

27. Dean, Vera Micheles, et al., *The Nature of the Non-Western World* (New York: New American Library, Inc., 1957).

28. Dodson, Dan W. (ed.), "Educational Sociology Through Twenty-

Five Years," *Journal of Educational Sociology*, XXVI (September, 1952), 7-9.

29. Duvall, Evelyn, "International Conference on The Family," *Marriage and Family Living*, XXIII (February, 1961), 12-15.

30. Ellapola, D. B. and T. L. Green, "The Education of Backward Peoples," *Journal of Educational Sociology*, XXVI (April, 1953), 374-379.

    The author maintains that the underdeveloped countries have little programming of education. Even where it does exist it often appears to be the wrong kind of education. He notes several criteria for educational systems in underdeveloped countries: social organization should not be disturbed, education must be centered in local conditions, education must be concerned with the problem of living, and education must be practical. Among the questions raised in the article we note a question on the time periods for review of teaching procedures, a question on the amount of change desirable in an educational system, and a question on whether or not we should take education to the masses whom we think are ignorant.

31. Eliott, M. A., "Delinquent Behavior of People," *Phylon*, X, 3 (1949), 242-251.

    The author discusses differential patterns of delinquency in various culture groups. She presents five postulates of criminal theory and discusses each. (1) "A given society by its peculiar norms of behavior in itself is a stimulus to antisocial conduct." (2) "The crime rate is related to the type of social organization and to the degree of social consensus." (3) "Crime is an index to social disorganization and to confusion in our social values." (4) "There is a differential patterning of crime and delinquency in the various cultural groups." (5) "Delinquent behavior is relatively common in all classes of society although delinquents in the upper middle and upper classes are seldom brought into court."

32. Fallding, H., "Family and the Idea of a Cardinal Role: A Sociological Study," *Human Relations*, XIV, 4 (1961), 329-350.

33. Fleege, U., "Education of Girls Across the World," *Catholic Educational Review*, LV (September, 1957), 378-388.

34. Foster, George M., "Interpersonal Relations in a Peasant Society," *Human Organization*, XIX (Winter, 1960-61), 174-184.

    This author examines peasant behavior in an attempt to answer the question of why peasants will not cooperate with one another in economic enterprises which would raise the standard of the entire community. His data consist of existing literature and information from informants and personal obsevations. The results are summed up in the following four comments:

1. The division of labor does not require them to cooperate other than in exchanges of services between individuals.

2. An individual gain in prosperity is seen by the group as having been won at the expense of the entire group and is resented.

3. Any attempt at cooperation is dangerous and is presumed to be undertaken by the organizer for his own ends and at the expense of the rest.

4. With this attitude it follows that there is no room for population increase without a reduction in the share of the economic pie which goes to each member.

The implications of the discussion for work in developmental programs are seen in the initial approach to the village and educational programs. It is suggested that villages be approached with the assumption that most of its people are naturally uncooperative. It is also noted that a major educational effort will be needed to break the traditional image of a static economy in the minds of the villagers.

35. Foster, George M., *Traditional Cultures: The Impact of Technological Change* (New York: Harper & Row, Publishers, 1962).

36. Francois, P., "Action by Youth Organizations to Promote Mutual Appreciation of Eastern and Western Cultural Values," *Orient Occident*, II, 5 (October, 1959), 3-7.

37. Frankel, S. Herbert, *The Economic Impact on Underdeveloped Societies; Essays on International Investment and Social Change* (Cambridge, Mass.: Harvard Univerity Press, 1953).

38. French, John R. P., Jr. and Robert B. Zajonc, "An Experimental Study of Cross Cultural Norm Conflict," *Journal of Abnormal and Social Psychology*, LIV (1957), 218-224.

The authors conducted an experimental study in which they examined normative conflict of foreign students. By treating norms as force fields they were able to make predictions concerning the resolution of intergroup norm conflict. These predictions were made under varying conditions of saliency of group membership.

39. Frenkel-Brunswik, E., "Differential Patterns of Social Outlook and Personality in Family and Children," in M. Mead and Martha

Wolfenstein (eds.) *Childhood in Contemporary Cultures* (Chicago: University of Chicago Press, 1955).

40. "Further Reading on Student Movement: a Selected Bibliography," *New South,* XV (October, 1960), 13-14.

41. Gennep, Arnold van, *Rites de Passage* (Paris: E. Nourry, 1909; also published as *The Rites of Passage,* Chicago: University of Chicago Press, 1960).

42. Gillin, J., "Personality in Preliterate Societies," *American Sociological Review,* IV, 5 (October, 1939), 681-702.

43. Goust, Francois, *L'adolescent Dans le Monde Contemporair* (*The Adolescent in the Contemporary World*) (Paris: Bloud and Gay, 1946).

44. Grabinska, W., "Backgrounds of Delinquency in War Torn Countries," *National Probation Association Yearbook* (1948), 227-238.

45. Hambly, W. D., *Origins of Education Among Primitive Peoples* (New York: Harcourt, Brace & World, 1926).

46. Hassum, H. C., "Social Rights of Muslim Women," *Asiatic Review,* LII, 190 (April, 1956), 158-160.

47. Haugland, Age, "Education Research in Countries Other Than the U.S.A.," *Review of Educational Research,* XXVII (1957), 119-125.

48. Havighurst, R. J., *Intelligence and Cultural Differences* (Chicago: University of Chicago Press, 1951) Chap. 3.

49. Henry, Jules, "A Cross-Cultural Outline of Education," *Current Anthropology,* I, 4 (July, 1960), 267-305. (See also "More on Cross-Cultural Education," *Current Anthropology,* II, 3 [June, 1961], 255-263.)

50. Hsu, F. L. K., B. G. Watrous, and E. M. Lord, "Culture Pattern and Adolescent Behavior," *International Journal of Social Psychiatry,* VII (1961), 33-54.

51. Inkeles, A., "Some Sociological Observations on Culture and Personality Studies," in C. Kluckhohn, H. A. Murray and D. M. Schneider (eds.), *Personality in Nature, Society and Culture,* 2nd ed. (New York: Alfred A. Knopf, Inc., 1953), 577-592.

52. Inkeles, A. and D. J. Levinson, "National Character: The Study of Modal Personality and Sociocultural Systems," in G. Lindzey (ed.), *Handbook of Social Psychology* (Reading, Mass.: Addison-Wesley Publishing Company, Inc., 1954), 977-1020.

53. International Council of Religious Education, Committee on Re-

ligious Education of Youth, *United Christian Youth Movement*, 1948.

A classified bibliography of youth publications that can be used by youth groups and their leaders in the church and the field of informal education in other social and fellowship groups.

54. "The International Girl Guides Congress," *Hellenia*, XXIII (July/September, 1953), 14-15.

55. Joesten, Joachim, *Youth Abroad* (New York: Alfred A. Knopf, Inc., 1958).

56. Jousselin, J., "The Problem of Youth-Adult Relations," *Fundamental and Adult Education*, XII, 3 (1960), 153-164.

57. Kalsey, A. H., et al. (eds.), "Education, Economy, and Society; A Reader in the Sociology of Education," *Bulletin of the Public Affairs Information Service*, (1961).

58. Katscher, Freidreich, "Counterblast at the Vienna Festival: Democratic Youth Stymie Communist Impact" (World Youth Festival, Vienna, Austria, July 26–August 4, 1959), *New Leader*, XLII (August 17-24, 1959), 16-17.

59. Keohane, Robert E., "Toward Understanding International Realities," *School Review*, LXIV (November, 1956), 337-345.

The author points out the trend toward more and better education around the world and emphasizes the benefits to be derived from an objective study of comparative education. A brief description of certain educational practices in Mexico, Russia, and Sweden is included.

60. Leebrick, K. C., "Youth Movements as a Factor in the International Situation," *Institute of World Affairs Proclamation*, XIX (1941), 147-151.

61. Leebrick, K. C., et al., "Youth of the World," *Institute of World Affairs Proclamation*, XIX (1941), 145-181.

Symposium with summary of round table discussion.

62. Levin, M. L., "Social Climates and Political Socialization," *Public Opinion Quarterly*, XXV (Winter, 1961), 596-606.

This study examines the political party preferences of adolescents from ten selected high schools in 1957 and 1958. Both the parents and the students were polled in the attempt to assess the influence of the climate of political opinion in the school, the family, and the larger social system on the adolescents' preferences.

Specific conclusions arising from the analysis include: (1) the boys were less influenced than the girls by the family and the national political climate and more influenced by the high school community; (2) Adolescents who are very interested in politics are (a) less likely to go along with their family's party choice, (b) less likely to be influenced by the national climate of opinion, and (c) more likely to be influenced by peers.

It was noted that the nuclear family, the high school society, and the larger society as a whole each pressures the adolescent to choose the political party which represents its particular consensus.

The author also discusses the effectiveness of the various subsystems with regard to socializing the adolescent. Political interest was utilized as an intervening variable. The observation is made that, depending on their political interests, the adolescent is differentially affected by the subsystems. The author concludes with the observation that the strength of attachment of the adolescent to the subsystem should be considered as another intervening variable in the investigation of lines of influence in political socialization.

63. Levy, M. J. and L. A. Fallers, "The Family: Some Comparative Considerations," *American Anthropologist,* LXI (August, 1959), 647-651.

Discussion of concepts necessary for comparative analysis of family structure and interaction at the cross-cultural level.

64. Linton, R., "Age and Sex Categories," *American Sociological Review,* VII (October, 1942), 589-603.

In this article the author supports the classification of the members of a society in terms of age and sex rather than other available devices. Age and sex, being common to all social systems, are of primary importance in the study of social structure. In connection with such a classificatory scheme Linton offers a series of propositions as follows:

1. "Members of subadult categories . . . have their distinctive culture patterns which are not learned from adults."

2. "No age-sex grouping is likely to be terminologically differentiated for any long period after it has ceased to be functionally differentiated."

3. "There is a tendency to distinguish more male than female age groups and the female transition to the adult category tends to occur at a somewhat earlier age than the male transition."

4. "There is a minimum of seven groupings which appear to be basic to all systems of age-sex classification."

5. While ritualization accompanying the entry into a new group varies culturally, ". . . the one transition which is well-nigh universally ritualized is that of entrance into the adult group."

6. "Age alone does not increase the individual's prestige."

65. Lower, A. R. M., "Our Elderly Adolescents," *Saturday Night*, LXX (May 28, 1955), 31-32.

66. Mara, Gilda, "Prejudice among Youth," *International Social Science Journal* (UNESCO), XIII, 4 (1961), 653-658.

This article, which is based on a series of UNESCO meetings on the prevention of prejudice, deals in a general way with the trend of prejudice in youth organizations throughout the world.

A number of points were generally agreed upon by the participants at the conference. These points appeared to be little more than statements of general social principles to be applied to the general problem of prejudice. They include such observations as the individuals' behavior changes at all age levels, the formation of prejudices in early life, the effectiveness of social norms in proportion to the sanctions attached to them, and the importance to people of the social norms to be found in their communities.

Conference participants from the United States reviewed the assumptions which guide educators who work with the problem of prejudice.

The general conclusion is noted in the feeling that the conference provided a "map of the world" with regard to the world wide approach to the problem of prejudice among youth.

67. McCandless, Boyd R., *Children and Adolescents; Behavior and Deveopment* (New York: Holt, Rinehart and Winston, Inc., 1961).

68. McClelland, Dalton F., *World Revolution, The College Student and the Y.M.C.A.* (New York: The International Committee of the Y.M.C.A.s of the United States and Canada).

This YMCA pamphlet approaches young college men with the opportunity to express their concern for the world in a tested significant world service. It offers them a chance to be of service to God and mankind through the World Service Program, a program of the YMCA.

69. McConnell, J., "Abstract Behavior among the Tepehuan," *Journal of Abnormal and Social Psychology*, XLIX (1954), 109-110.

70. Mead, Margaret, "Adolescence in Primitive and Modern Society,"

in V. F. Calverton and S. Schmalhausen (eds.), *The New Generation* (New York: 1930).

The ceremonial and role expectations of adolescents in primitive and modern society. Mostly primitive, while the modern is about the United States.

71. Mead, Margaret, "Changing Patterns of Parent-Child Relations in an Urban Culture," *International Journal of Psychoanalysis,* XXXVIII (1957), 369-378.

    This article discusses patterns of child-rearing and parent-child relationships in both industrialized and primitive cultures. The emphasis is on comparison. Some of the areas of discussion involve, the expanding role of the father in modern societies, the kind of child-training most recommended in our society, and the inconsistencies between different social attitudes and the current child-development practices.

72. Mead, Margaret, "Cultural Patterning of Maturation in Selected Primitive Societies," *Archives of Neurology and Psychiatry,* LVII (Chicago: 1947), 119-125.

73. Mead, Margaret (ed.). *Cultural Patterns and Technological Change* (New York: UNESCO, 1955).

    Another Edition: Mead, Margaret (ed.), *Cultural Patterns and Technical Change* (New York: New American Library, Inc., 1955).

74. Mead, Margaret, "The Cultural Picture," *American Journal of Orthopsychiatry,* XIII (1943), 596-600.

    Cultural implications of wartime conditions on adolescents.

75. Mead, Margaret, "Culture and Personality: Social Research in Adolescence," *American Journal of Sociology,* XLII (1936), 84-87.

    This article attempts a definition and examination of the adolescent personality and cultural conditioning. It is mainly an exploratory type article utilizing critical analysis of existing literature.

    In the discussion of adolescent personality the authors note that the first four or five years of the child's development are very important and imply several later strains. In our culture a great strain is placed upon the adolescent when he is expected to adjust to both the adult institutional life and his own physiological maturation.

    The authors recommend that studies be conducted in small

communities where contrasting cultural features represent various segments of the society as a whole. They also support the utilization of ethnological field work, case work, and life-history materials. A principle suggestion is a national study of the adolescent and the mass media.

In conclusion they note, "Unless the role of culture in standardizing personality is first accurately known, any discussion of personality in adolescence is meaningless, for the social theorist will be unconscious that he is using cultural standards for adolescence and he will be unable to isolate the problems involved."

76. Mead, Margaret, *From the South Seas* (New York: William Morrow and Company, Inc., 1939).

77. Mead, Margaret and Martha Wolfenstein *Childhood in Contemporary Cultures* (Chicago: University of Chicago Press, 1955).

Additional references on preadolescents.

78. Mesnil, Adelee G. du, "The Role of Sport in Education," *UNESCO Chronicle*, V, 6 (June, 1959), 200-202.

Discussion on the conference "Sport and Education" which was held in Helsinki, August 10-16, 1959. Report on: Sport and Work; Sport and Culture; Sport and International Understanding.

79. Metrovic, M., "Its Great Failure—Communism," *Commonweal*, V, LXVIII (April 18, 1958), 75-77.

80. Miller, Nathan, *The Child in Primitive Society* (Brentano's, 1928).

81. Morgan, A. E., *The Needs of Youth* (New York: Oxford University Press, 1939).

Youth organizations in England, Scotland, and Wales.

82. Morris, Richard T., "National Status and Attitudes of Foreign Students," *Journal of Social Issues*, XII, (1956), 20-25.

In this article the author investigates the attitudes of foreign students in the United States with respect to the perceived status of their home country. He notes that when these students compare their estimation of the home country with American students' estimates of that country some gain and some lose. That is, some estimate their country lower than the American students and some estimate it higher than American students. He notes that those foreign students who estimate their country higher than the American students tend to hold unfavorable attitudes toward this country. On the other hand, those who evaluate their country lower than the American students tend to have favorable attitudes toward the United States. The degree of involvement of the individual student with his home country is a critical factor in the formation of his attitudes toward the United States. The fact of a self-assigned low national status alone does not, in itself, make for any significant differences in attitudes.

83. Morris, Richard T. and Olaf M. Davidson, *The Two-Way Mirror* (Minneapolis: University of Minnesota Press, 1960).

Material for this book, and for the preceding article, was gathered as part of an extensive study on cross-cultural education. The investigating committee was established in 1952 by the Social Science Research Council for the purpose of examining the difficulties which foreign students encounter in adjusting to a new culture.

The primary focus of investigation was the status shock suffered by foreign students upon their arrival in a host country. It was noted by the author that "Status variables will be more important than other variables in determining the adjustment of foreign students to their environment."

The data were gathered by means of interviews conducted with 318 foreign students at UCLA in the spring of 1955. This sample comprised 87 per cent of the foreign student population at UCLA. Information was gathered on the following topics: subjective national status; perceived accorded national status; national status gain and loss; actual accorded national status; involvement with own country; perception and favorableness toward the United States academic satisfaction; and background factors.

It was found that the three main measures of national status —subjective, accorded, and objective—were all positively related to one another at a high level. It was also noted that favorableness to the United States was positively related to the student's satisfaction with his stay in this country and his academic satisfaction.

Among the foreign students it was found that males made fewer close friends among the American students. The number of friends also depended on the length of time in the United States and the foreign student's field of study. Those who had been here the longest had the most friends. Foreign students working in the humanities and the social sciences were found to have more friends than those in the natural sciences.

The general conclusion was reached that the foreign student, in general, was a fairly well-adjusted person.

84. Murdock, George P., "The Cross-Cultural Survey," *American Sociological Review*, V, 3 (June, 1940), 361-370.

85. Murdock, George P., "Family Stability in Non-European Cultures," *Annals of the American Academy of Political and Social Science*, CCLXXII (November, 1950), 195-201.

This article reports on a study of the stability of marriage in 40 non-European societies. The purpose was to place the contemporary American situation in cross-cultural perspective.

Data were collected from 40 randomly selected societies in Asia, Africa, Oceania, North America, and South America which could be found in the Human Relations Area Files. Areas of focus included the relative rights of the two sexes in divorce and the degree of family stability relative to the United States.

Among the findings we see that almost every society makes some provision for the termination of marriage through divorce. Twenty-four of the forty societies examined had divorce rates in excess of that found in the United States.

With regard to the initiation of divorce it was found that in thirty of the forty societies it was impossible to find a difference in the rights of men and women in initiating divorce. Four societies gave women superior rights and six gave the male superior rights in initiating divorce.

86. Murdock, George P., "Feasibility and Implementation of Comparative Community Research: With Special Reference to the Human Relations Area Files," *American Sociological Review*, XV, 6 (December, 1950), 713-720.

87. Neill, Stephen, "YMCA: A World Wide Movement," *Church Quarterly Review*, CLVII, 323 (1956), 175-184.

88. Neumeyer, M. H., "International Trends in Juvenile Delinquency," *Sociology and Social Research*, XLI (November, 1956), 93-99.

General discussion of research, prevention, legislation, and definition of juvenile delinquency on the international plane.

89. Newberger, Howard, "Bibliography on Juvenile Delinquency," *Psychological Newsletter*, 48 (1953), 25-37.

A bibliography of 201 items.

90. Newman, R. E., "Personality Development in a Primitive 'Adolescent' Group," Z. *Diagnost. Psychol.*, VI (1958), 241-253.

Rorschach protocols were gathered from 18 subjects in two randomly selected adolescent groups of Otomi Indians. Comparison was made between these subjects and European and

North American adolescents. Analysis of the protocols revealed statistically insignificant differences with respect to twenty-five Rorschach scoring variables. The inference from the data is that the storm-and-stress and aggression assumed to be characteristic of European and North American adolescents may be absent in the adolescent period of another, more primitive culture. In general the findings support anthropological observations on adolescence in various environments.

91. Nomvete, B. D., "Labor in Underdeveloped Countries," *Science and Society*, XX (Summer, 1956), 227-240.

Discussion of economic (mainly) and educational provisions necessary for the creation of an efficient labor force in underdeveloped countries—no youth.

92. Parsons, T., *Family, Socialization and Interactional Process* (New York: The Free Press, 1955).

93. "Partial Revision of the Convention Concerning the Night Work of Young Persons Employed in Industry: Discussion at the International Labor Conference, 1948," *International Labour Review*, LVIII (October, 1948), 468-471.

94. Pingrey, Jennie L., "Teen-Age World History," *Social Education*, XXI (May, 1957), 209-210.

This article tells how the Hastings High School (Hastings-on-the-Hudson, New York) History Club collected national histories written by teen-agers in 33 UNESCO member countries.

95. Plotnicoo, L., "Fixed Membership Groups: The Locus of Culture Processes," *American Anthropologist*, LXIV (February, 1962), 97-103. (Bibliography)

96. "Post-War Youth," *Royal Bank of Canada Bulletin* (1945), 1-40.

97. "Prejudice vs. the World We Want," *Senior Scholastic*, LXX (March 15, 1957), 6-8.

Reported are the views of high school students from 12 foreign countries who participated in the *New York Herald Tribune* forum discussion on "how prejudice affects world affairs."

98. Queen, Stuart A. and John B. Adams, *The Family In Various Cultures* (Philadelphia: J. B. Lippincott Company, 1952).

99. Rickover, H. G., "A Comparison: European Versus American Secondary Schools," *Phi Delta Kappan* (November, 1958), 60-64.

100. Roosevelt, Eleanor, *Partners: The United Nations And Youth* (Garden City: Doubleday, 1950).

101. Rose, Edward and Gary Willoughby, "Culture Profiles and Emphases," *American Journal of Sociology,* LXIII (1958), 476-491.

This is a comparative study of primitive and modern cultures. Data were obtained from the Human Relations Area Files on the types of cultural emphases found in various cultures. It was found that, among modern cultures there is a correlation between type and extent of emphasis on modern culture categories. No analogous correlation was found, however, when primitive cultures were compared for similarity of emphasis on primitive culture categories.

102. Roucek, Joseph S., "Age as a Prestige Factor," *Sociology and Social Research,* XLII (1958), 349-352.

This study investigates and compares attitudes toward tradition and age as determinants of prestige in various cultures. Special attention is given age and tradition in the American culture.

103. *Youth Movements Here And Abroad* (New York: Russell Sage Foundation, 1936).

104. Sapir, E., *Culture, Language and Personality* (Berkeley, Calif.: University of California Press, 1956).

105. Saunders, I. T., J. R. Schwendeman, and R. B. Woodbury, *Societies Around The World* (New York: The Dryden Press, 1953) (2 vols.).

Selected references: p. 132, p. 412, p. 92 (vol. 2).

106. Schild, E. D., "Foreign Student as Stranger, Learning the Norms of the Host Culture," *Journal of Social Issues,* XVIII (1962), 41-54. (Bibliography)

107. Schmidt, F., "A Mai Leang" (The Girl of Today), *Gyermak,* 1 & 2 (1939).

Orientations of girls between the ages of 13 and 20.

108. Schnapper, Morris B. *Youth Betrayed* (New York: International Relief Association, 1937).

109. Schnull, Dorothy M., *Characteristics of Adolescence* (Minneapolis: Burgess Publishing Company, 1946, 1958).

References in above pp. 58-68.

110. Schuessler, K. F. and H. Driver, "A Factor Analysis of Sixteen Primitive Societies," *American Sociological Review,* XXI, 4 (August, 1956), 493-499.

111. Schwartz, Morton, "Moscow's Experimental Venture: the Vienna World Youth Festival" (Vienna, Austria: July 26-August 4, 1959), *Problems of Communism,* VIII (September/October, 1959), 53-56.

112. Scotti, Rezia, et al., "European Youth Looks at America; Radio Discussion," *Town Meeting* (September 1, 1953), 1-15.

113. Sears, R. R., E. Maccoby, and H. Levin, *Patterns of Child Rearing* (Evanston, Ill.: Row, Peterson & Company, 1957).

114. Seidman, Jerome M. (ed.), *The Adolescent; A Book of Readings* (New York: The Dryden Press, 1953).

A bibliography of 363 items.

115. Selltiz, C. and N. S. W. Cook, "Factors Influencing Attitudes of Foreign Students toward the Host Country," *Journal of Social Issues,* XVIII, 1 (1962), 7-23. (Bibliography)

116. Shuttleworth, Frank K., *The Adolescent Period: A Graphic Atlas* (Evanston, Illinois: Child Development Publications, 1951).

117. Simpson, G. E. and M. J. Yinger, *Racial And Cultural Minorities* (New York: Harper & Brothers, 1958), 282-287.

118. Sjoberg, Gideon, "Familial Organization in the Preindustrial City," *Marriage and Family Living,* XVIII (1956), 30-36.

Sjoberg draws upon data from *The Preindustrial City* for this discussion of familial organization. It is assumed by many that the urban family is less organized than the rural family and places more emphasis on the conjugal family. The author notes that family structure in the preindustrial city is distinct from that of the industrial city. It is more highly organized than the rural family.

In the preindustrial city, the family is the main security and the basis of social power. Relatives of the family are active in the selection of mates for the young while the parents provide the dowry. The family group is the center of recreation and leisure activities. The family is a strict hierarchy based on age and sex. Children are economically and socially desirable.

119. Skransky, M. A. and S. O. Lichter, "Some Observations on the Character of the Adolescent Ego," *Social Service Review,* XXXI (September, 1957), 271-276.

120. Smith, R. J., C. E. Ramsey, and G. Castillo, "Parental Authority and Job Choice: Sex Differences in Three Cultures."

Still in process of editorial review.

121. Smythe, H. H., "Israel and Africa, Some Common Problems," *Jewish Social Studies,* XXIV (April, 1962), 97-107.

122. Solomon, D., "Adolescents Decisions: A Comparison of Influence from Parents with That from Other Sources," *Marriage and Family Living,* XXIII (November, 1961), 393-395.

123. Sorenson, Ray, "Youth's Need for Challenge and Place in Society," *Children,* IX, 4 (July/August, 1962), 131.

124. Spindler, George, *Education And Anthropology* (Stanford, Calif.: Stanford University Press, 1955).

125. Spiro, Melford E., "Is the Family Universal," *American Anthropologist,* LVI (1954), 839-208.

126. Stern, B. J., "The Family and Cultural Change," *American Sociological Review,* IV (April, 1939), 199-208.

This is primarily a historical discussion of the place of women in the family situation. He covers the period from roughly A.D. 900 to the present and attempts to support the argument that while women have gradually improved their position from that held in the patriarchal family, the rise of Fascist states threatens to put the woman back in the patriarchal situation. Using governmental reports, contemporary commentaries and sociological reports and surveys he documents this rise and imminent fall. (The article was written in 1939.)

127. Stewart, W. A. C., Book Review of *Adolescence: Its Social Psychology,* in *Higher Education Journal,* VII (1949), 13-14.

128. Stoddard, Theodore L., *The Story of Youth* (New York: Cosmopolitan Book Corporation, 1928).

129. Theodorson, G. A., "Acceptance of Industrialization and Its Attendant Consequences for the Social Patterns of Non-Western Societies," *American Sociological Review,* XVIII (October, 1953), 477-484.

Of tangential but significant importance to the study of adolescence is the topic of the development of adolescent phenomenon in conjunction with the development of industrialization and urbanization in the West. In this paper Theodorson discusses the development of new social patterns in non-Western countries—social patterns which arise in conjunction with the introduction of the industrial complex. He notes that emerging patterns in time will resemble Western patterns of industrialized society. He maintains that these patterns may not be rejected by the people who accept the machinery of the West.

The disorganizing effects of the new patterns are the principal foci of discussion in the article.

Among the disrupting factors we note the following; (1) a new pattern of role behavior arising from the introduction of new roles, mainly economic; (2) the resistance to the decline of older, traditional roles by those in the role positions; (3) the production of a great deal of relatively cheap goods has implications for the masses, if the distribution is not widespread, an explosive situation can be created; (4) another disrupting factor is the emotional dependence of the workers on the community. This dependence slows down the change and is disrupted by the introduction of the factory. The reorganization of the given social system is discussed with reference to Talcott Parson's pattern variables.

130. Tumin, M., "Culture, Genuine and Spurious: A Re-evaluation," *American Sociological Review*, X, 2 (April, 1945), 199-207.

131. Tyvel, T. R., "Delinquents, International," *New Leader*, XLI September 29, 1958), 14-16.

The world-wide rebellion of youth in the leading industrial countries points up the problems of mass culture and the loss of traditional values.

132. UNESCO, "Action by Youth Organizations," *Orient Occident*, V, 1 (February, 1961), 4-5.

This article discusses a proposed research on the values and attitudes of youth in various countries. The project arose from a meeting in 1959 in which representatives from fourteen countries met in France. The questionnaire was constructed by Dr. Andre Berge and will be used in a six-country study. The countries to be included are Austria, Canada, Cuba, India, Japan, and Malaya. Various youth organizations in these countries are responsible for the testing.

The questionnaire will give an indication of the values of the youth in various countries and will, it is hoped, offer comparative data to establish similarities and differences between the youth of the various countries.

133. "UNESCO and Youth," *UNESCO Chronicle*, VII, 1 (1961), 7-11.

A short statement of the work of UNESCO with relation to the youth of the world. They see their main task as the distribution of new information, ideas, and techniques to the leaders of youth organizations. They also encourage research on the youth of the world and assist in programming the travels of youth groups. Conferences, seminars, and meetings are held regularly for the interchange of opinions. Technical assistance to youth organizations is offered by the UNESCO Youth Institute at Gauting.

One of the most effective means of developing youth activities perfecting techniques has been found in the experimental projects carried out in various countries. As of 1961, 88 projects concerning youth have been initiated by UNESCO.

134. UNESCO, *Basic Facts And Figures: International Statistics Relating to Education, Culture and Mass Communications, 1952-1960,* Paris.

135. UNESCO, "Bibliography on Vocational Guidance" (*Bibliographical Contributions* No. 21), Limited, 1961.

Bilingual text—English and French.

136. UNESCO, "Children in National Development," Notes and recommendations by the Executive Director, April 7, 1962.

137. UNESCO, "Conference of Representatives of International Youth Organizations and Youth Serving Agencies" (Paris: UNESCO House, November 21-27, 1951) (Final Report, Paris, February 18, 1952).

138. UNESCO, "Draft Resolution Submitted by the Delegation of Cuba" (Concerning the effects of television programs on youth) (November 14, 1960).

139. UNESCO, "Draft Resolution Submitted by the Delegation of France" [concerning the prevention of juvenile delinquency and social unadaptation of young people] November 14, 1960).

140. UNESCO, "Draft Resolution Submitted by the Delegation of the Socialist Republic of Czechoslovakia" (concerning films for youth).

141. UNESCO, "The Education of Rural Youth: Some Out of School Activities," *Educational Abstracts,* VIII, 3 (March, 1956), UNESCO Publications Centre.

A combination essay and annotated bibliography on the out-of-school activities of rural youth in general. The author discusses the techniques in the organization of rural youth organizations. One noted recent trend is the attempt to associate youth organizations with fundamental education programs in the underdeveloped areas of the world. The review of the literature and annotations cover over forty publications in the area of youth work in rural areas.

An important source of information for those interested in rural youth programs.

142. UNESCO, "Forming the Future: *The Crowther Report*," Tablet, CCXIV (April 30, 1960), 403-404.

143. UNESCO, "The Gauting Institute," *UNESCO Chronicle*, VII, 1 (January, 1961), 11-14. (Gauting-bei-Miichen: UNESCO Youth Institute, 1952).

A general statement on the work aims and organization of The Gauting Institute, the UNESCO institute for youth.

144. UNESCO, "The influence of the Cinema on Children and Adolescents" (Reports and papers on mass communication, 31), 1961.

An extensive annotated international bibliography on the effect of cinema on children and adolescents. Presents listings and annotations on nearly 500 studies. Includes sections on The Attitude of Youth toward the Cinema; Analysis of Film Content; The Process of Seeing a Film; Influence and After Effects of Films; Educational Aspects and Practical Measures; and Miscellaneous.

While no bibliography is ever exhaustive and definitive, this publication offers a valuable source of information for those interested in the international implications and involvement of youth and adolescents in the mass media.

145. UNESCO, "Mass Media in the Developing Countries; A UNESCO Report to the United Nations" (Paris: 1961).

146. UNESCO, "Meeting of Consultants on Problems of Young Workers" (Geneva, October 30-November 4, 1961), *Official Bulletin*, XLV, 1 (January, 1962), 54-57.

147. UNESCO, "New Trends in Youth Organizations: A Comparative Survey" (*Educational Studies and Documents* No. 35), 1960.

A valuable study, published in 1960 and written in 1958-1959, concerning the development, activities, and trends of youth organizations throughout the world. It includes information on the whole spectrum of youth and youth activities. An extensive list of references is cited.

Topics discussed include: Contemporary Youth; Youth Movements and Associations; The Members of Youth Movements and Their Numbers; Evolution of Programmes and Methods; Administrators and Leaders of Youth Associations; Changes in Structure; Relations between Youth Associations and the Public Authorities; Plans and Prospects.

While the emphasis seems to lie in the structure of youth organizations, a great deal of information can be found here on the activities of youth throughout the world.

148. UNESCO, "The Participation of Youth in Technical Assistance," statement submitted by the World Assembly of Youth, a nongovernmental organization granted consultative status in Category B (January 19, 1951).

149. UNESCO, "School and Social Maladjustment of Youth," prepared by UNESCO, Note by the Secretariat (June, 1960).

150. UNESCO, "A Survey of Post-Primary Education in Non-Self-Governing Territories, 1958-60," Report prepared by UNESCO (March 29, 1962).

151. UNESCO, "Survey of Traditional Youth Values" (June, 1961).

152. UNESCO, "Survey on the Needs of Children," Report by ILO (March 14, 1961).

153. UNESCO, *Vagrant Children* (Paris, 1951).

154. UNESCO, *World Illiteracy at Mid-Century* (Paris, France: The Organization, 1957).

This "first systematic survey of illiteracy on a world-wide scale" by an international organization discusses its magnitude (44 per cent of those 15 years old and older), methods of countering it, its extent by countries, major and lesser areas of illiteracy, illiteracy and school enrollment, illiteracy and national income, and illiteracy and urban industrialization.

155. UNESCO, "Youth and Fundamental Education," International Documents Service (December, 1954) (*Monographs on Fundamental Education* 9).

Sets forth some of the world's needs and proposes a number of activities which youth organizations might undertake to help meet them.

156. UNESCO, "Youth Centres and the Social Maladjustment of Youth," prepared by UNESCO, Note by the Secretariat (June 10, 1960).

157. UNESCO, Education Clearing House, collaborator, "Cross-Cultural Factors in Education of Underdeveloped Regions," *The Journal of Educational Sociology*, XXIX (March, 1956), 273-320.

Five articles plus a note excerpted from a UNESCO publication from this special issue. The role of education in closing the gap between technologically advanced and less-developed cultures is examined. Interaction of ideas and systematic marshalling of knowledge about man is presented as leading to a positive, constructive program.

158. UNESCO, International Bureau of Education, *International Yearbook of Education:* 1958 (Publication No. 202, French ed., No. 201) (Paris/Geneva: The Organization/The Bureau).

This yearbook, the twentieth, presents a country-by-country account of educational progress prepared by 64 countries for the 21st International Conference on Public Education held in July, 1958.

159. UNESCO, United Nations, Commission on Human Rights, Sub-Commission on Prevention of Discrimination and Protection of Minorities. *Study of Discrimination in Education* (New York: United Nations, November 7, 1954).

This second draft of the first in a series of studies on discrimination authorized by the Council, was prepared for consideration by the expects on the Sub-Commission and by representatives of Governments on the Commission and the Council at sessions in 1957. The rapporteur was instructed to use data supplied by Governments, the Secretary General of the United Nations, the specialized agencies, and nongovernmental organizations, and "writings of recognized scholars and scientists." The study deals with education in terms of Article 2 of the Universal Declaration of Human Rights which condemns "distinction of any kind, such as race, color, sex, language, religion, political or other opinion, national or social origin, property, birth, or other status" and "on the basis of the political, jurisdictional, or international status of the country or territory to which a person belongs. . . ." Information is supplied in relation to more than 80 countries which are members of the United Nations and/or the specialized agencies.

160. U.S. Office of Education, *Education in* . . . (Washington: Government Printing Office, 1943).

Planned and executed to provide all basic data on educational systems at all levels, these publications are authoritative to their date of publication. The Office of Education in the Department of Health, Education, and Welfare issues other useful and valuable items from time to time on Latin American education, and occasionally can provide special bibliography. Country studies to date are:

a. *Bolivia,* by Raymond H. Nelson, 1949.
b. *Chile,* by Cameron D. Ebaugh, 1945, o.p.
c. *Colombia,* by John A. Furbay, 1946.
d. *Costa Rica,* by John A. Furbay, 1946.
e. *Cuba,* by Severin Turosienski., 1943.

f. *Dominican Republic,* by Gladys Potter and Cameron D. Ebaugh, 1947, o.p.
g. *Ecuador,* by Cameron D. Ebaugh, 1947.
h. *El Salvador,* by Cameron D. Ebaugh, 1947, o.p.
i. *Guatemala,* by Cameron D. Ebaugh, 1947, o.p.
j. *Haiti,* by Mercer Cook, 1948.
k. *Haiti, Education in the Republic of,* by George A. Dale, 1959.
l. *Honduras,* by M. Weldon Thompson, 1955.
m. *Mexico,* by Marjorie C. Johnston, 1956.
n. *Nicaragua,* by Cameron D. Ebaugh, 1947.
o. *Panama,* by Delia Goetz, 1948, o.p.
p. *Peru,* by Cameron D. Ebaugh, 1946, o.p.
q. *Venezuela,* by Delia Goetz, 1948, o.p.

161. Watson, Goodwin. *Youth after Conflict* (New York: Association Press, 1947).

    European and American youth.

162. Weller, George, *The Crack in the Column* (New York: Random House, 1949).
163. Westley, William A. and Frederick Elkin, "The Protective Environment and Adolescent Socialization," *Social Forces,* XXXV (1957), 243-249.
164. Wile, I. S., *The Challenge of Adolescence* (New York: Greenberg, 1939).

    Contains some information on youth movements.

165. Winslow, W. Thacher, *Youth: A World Problem.* National Youth Administration (Washington, D.C.: U.S. Government Printing Office, 1937).
166. "World Youth Forum," *World Affairs,* XV (February, 1950), 18-19.
167. Worsley, T. C., "Youth Movements and the Board of Education," *New Statesman and Nation,* XX (September 21, 1940), 279-280. Reply—Clarke, F., XX (September 28, 1940), 308.
168. "Yearbook of Youth Organizations," *Annuaire des Organisations de Jeunesse* (Munich: UNESCO Youth Institute, November, 1954).
169. Young, Frank W., "The Function of Male Initiation Ceremonies; A Cross-Cultural Test of an Alternative Hypotheses," *American Journal of Sociology,* LXVII, 4 (January, 1962), 379-396.

170. "Youth Leagues in Central Europe," *World Today*, XI, 9 (London: September, 1955), 380-390.

171. *Youth Movement Bibliography*, Carnegie Endowment for International Peace, Library.

The Youth Movement in its reading list, No. 19, February 15, 1940 (revised), May 24, 1934.

172. "Y.W.C.A.s of the World: Partners in a Common Task; 27 Countries Describe Their Work," *Woman's Preview*, (October, 1948), 10-11.

173. Zajonc, R. B. and N. K. Wahi, "Conformity and Need-Achievement under Cross-Cultural Norm Conflict," *Human Relations*, XIV, 3 (1961), 241-250. (Bibliography)